Dictionary of Philosophy

About the Author

Peter A. Angeles received his B.A., M.A., and Ph.D. degrees from Columbia University. He has taught philosophy at the University of Western Ontario, Albert Schweitzer College, and the University of California at Santa Barbara. Currently, he is Professor of Philosophy at Santa Barbara City College. He is the author of *An Introduction to Sentential Logic; The Possible Dream: Toward Understanding the Black Experience; The Problem of God;* and *Critiques of God* (Ed.); as well as numerous articles in scholarly journals.

Dictionary of
PHILOSOPHY

Peter A. Angeles

BARNES & NOBLE BOOKS
A DIVISION OF HARPER & ROW, PUBLISHERS
New York, Cambridge, Hagerstown, Philadelphia,
San Francisco, London, Mexico City, São Paulo, Sydney

FIRST EDITION

Designer: Ruth Markiewicz

Library of Congress Cataloging in Publication Data

Angeles, Peter Adam, 1931–
  Dictionary of philosophy.
  (Everyday handbook)
  Includes index.
  1. Philosophy—Dictionaries. I. Title.
B41.A53   1981   103′.21   80–8419
ISBN 0–06–463461–2

85 10 9 8 7 6 5

Acknowledgments

Countless persons are to be acknowledged in the preparation of this dictionary. Because of space, I can name but a few. The others will know and understand.

Nancy Cone, Editor, Barnes & Noble Books, who unhesitatingly accepted the concept of a dictionary of philosophy and nursed it through to its publication with patience and gentleness.

Dr. Gladys Walterhouse, who as a philosopher and editor worked through every sentence making valuable suggestions, corrections, comments, additions, deletions, and stylistic changes.

Mrs. Simone Woodcock, who typed the many drafts of the dictionary with excellent skill, unfailing dedication, open eagerness, and interest. Her loving attention to the details of grammar, style, and word use eased much of my labor.

Dallas Pottinger, my friend, assistant, typist, and colleague, who began this project with me and saw it through to the final manuscript. His typing, clerical work, and research, and our daily intellectual exchanges, added a sparkling excitement and energy to the project.

Professor Adam Sebestyen, my friend, whose library talents and general knowledge were extremely useful.

Mrs. Anne Munoz, whose helpful cooperation with Simone was a beautiful sight.

The Teachers' Aides Mrs. Doris Sofas, Mrs. Dora Braden, and Mrs. Sharon Pifer, who assisted me in my administrative and teaching responsibilities while I was busy writing.

Miss Mary Nagelmann, my reader, who unflinchingly accepted more than her share of my philosophy papers to grade and whose uncomplaining presence gave support.

Santa Barbara City College Faculty, Staff, and Administrators, who were helpful directly and indirectly in providing the atmosphere and means conducive to writing and teaching.

My children, Beth, Jane, and Adam, who in their unselfish, loving way were patient, kind, gentle, and helpful in giving their father the time, care, and privacy to work. And most of all my wife Elizabeth—I owe all this to you. . . .

Preface

This dictionary presents informal and understandable definitions for important philosophic terms. Emphasis is on terms most commonly covered in beginning philosophy courses: epistemology, metaphysics, ethics, aesthetics, logic, and the philosophies of religion and politics.

The book is intended as an at-hand reference for students, laypersons, and teachers. It can be used as a supplement to texts and philosophy readings; it can also be consulted for philosophy's own enjoyment and enlightenment. Small capitals are used for cross-references.

A

absolute (L., *absolutus, ab,* "from," "away," and *solvere,* "to loosen," "to free"). **1.** Free from limitations, qualification, or restrictions. ("Absolute Being." "Absolute Beauty." "Absolute Good." "Absolute authority.") **2.** Independent and not relative. ("Absolute space." "Absolute time.") **3.** Free from variability, change, error. ("That is the absolute truth.") **4.** Certain and true without reservation. (" 'Matter is physical' is a statement of an absolute.") **5.** Not arbitrary or relative but **(a)** as in aesthetics, objectively real and applicable (Proportionality, symmetry, harmony, consistency, suggestibility, economy of attention, unity in variety, and richness of imagination are a few of the absolute standards by which a work of art is judged.) or **(b)** as in ethics, completely and universally binding ("It is an absolute duty."). **6.** In metaphysics, *absolute* is used with concepts such as completeness, totality, all-inclusiveness, perfection, independence, objective reality; that which is underived, unconditioned, uncaused, unchanging, unwavering, pure, positive, simple, universal.

absolute, the. 1. The ultimate, underlying Reality, World Ground, or Cosmic Principle that is the origin of existence and all its activity, unity, and variety (see entries under LOGOS). **2.** That Being which depends on nothing else for its existence and activity, but **(a)** upon which all other things depend for their existence and activity and **(b)** to which they can ultimately be reduced. See NECESSARY BEING (THEOLOGY) **3.** The all-inclusive, perfectly interrelated organic and thinking Whole (Reality, Being) that is in the process of actualizing and fulfilling all finite, transient existence. See entries under IDEALISM, ABSOLUTE. **4.** Reality (Being, Substance) as it is in itself in contrast to its appearance to us. See entries under NOUMENON.

The Absolute in all the above senses is regarded as ONE, perfect, eternal, uncaused, complete, all-embracing, infinite. Actualized Thought (Spirit, Ego) engaging in the multifarious activities of a finite and imperfect universe. The concept of The Absolute is found in varieties of IDEALISM. The Absolute is not directly given to us in the world of phenomena or appearances and is often believed to be unknowable in any complete sense.

absolutism. 1. The view that truth (value, reality) is objectively real, final, and eternal. **2.** The belief that there is only one unchanging and correct objective explanation of reality. Contrast with entries under RELATIVISM and SUBJECTIVISM. **3.** In political theory, the demand for unquestionable allegiance to a ruler or ruling class.

abstraction (L., *ab(s),* "from," "away," and *trahere,* "to draw," hence "to draw away from"). **1.** That which is regarded apart from reference to any particular object or event and which represents symbolically, conceptually, or imaginatively something not directly or concretely perceivable in experience. Examples: the abstraction (abstract concept) of redness, justice, humanity. **2.** The end product of a process (of abstracting) by which a quality, or a relation, or some feature of a whole (class) is separated as an idea from that whole. **3.** In traditional logic, the universal derived from an examination of what is common to a number of particular things. Abstraction is also the *process* of deriving a universal. Example: Deriving the universal "human" from an examination of particular instances of women and men.

abstractionism. See HYPOSTATIZATION; REIFICATION/REISM.

absurd (L., *absurdus,* "harsh-sounding"). **1.** Contrary to reason, to the rules of logic, to what is obvious to common sense and to the truth. **2.** In existentialist philosophies, absurd refers to life's meaninglessness, inconsistency, and lack of structure.

accident (L., *accidere,* "to happen," from *ad,* "down," "to," and *cadere,* "to fall"). **1.** An event that occurs without intention, foresight, necessity, or expectation, and which need not have occurred at all. **2.** That which interferes with (or assists in) a process without itself being necessary or integral to that process.

accidental attribute. Sometimes also referred to as *accidental property, characteristic, quality,* or *predicate.* **1.** An attribute not definitely excluded by the essence of a thing that may or may not be possessed by that thing during its existence. Example: Having measles is an accidental attribute which may or may not be possessed by an individual. **2.** A quality (characteristic, feature, property) of a thing which (**a**) is not essential to the thing's true nature, (**b**) is not needed by the thing in order to be what it is, and (**c**) cannot be inferred from the essential nature of that thing.

Example: the redness of an apple. **3.** An incidental quality of a thing that is not essential or necessary for its inclusion as a member of a particular class. Example: Having black skin is an accidental attribute that cannot be used to include or exclude a person from membership in the class *homo sapiens.* **4.** The characteristic of a thing which can be removed or abstracted away without altering the essential and necessary defining characteristics of that thing. Example: Hearing is an important but accidental attribute to humanness. Compare with entries under ATTRIBUTE; QUALITY; PREDICATE; PROPERTY.

accidentalism. 1. The theory that some or all events do not have to happen as they do. **2.** The theory that all events are caused, but **(a)** that some cannot be predicted, and **(b)** some are inherently unpredictable. Compare with CASUALISM; TYCHISM. Occasionally used incorrectly as a synonym for INDETERMINISM. Opposite to NECESSITARIANISM.

Achilles and the tortoise argument. See ZENO'S PARADOXES.

act/action (L., *actum,* "a thing done," from *agere,* "drive," "do"). **1.** That operation, function, or activity which has been done, or is being done. Examples: counting, jumping, thinking, willing, bribing. **2.** The exertion of energy resulting in a deed, performance, behavior, or event. Examples: slapping someone, hiding, painting, making a face. **3.** The effect produced upon something. Example: blinding a person. See VOLUNTARY ACTION.

act, pure. See PURE ACT.

activism (L., *actum,* "a thing done"). **1.** The belief that action, as opposed to intellectual theorizing, is the way to truth and constructive social change. **2.** In metaphysics, the theory that activity (process, change, action) is the essential and necessary feature of reality.

acts, speech. See SPEECH ACTS.

actuality. 1. The domain of factual events. **2.** Existence; reality. **3.** The achievement of a thing's full potential. See ACTUALIZATION. Opposite to POTENCY. Compare with *ENERGEIA.*

actualization. 1. The *process* of manifesting in reality the potential inherent in a thing. **2.** The *state* of completed realization in time of all the latent potential inherent in the nature of a thing. **3.** In metaphysics and theology, the Absolute or God are thought to be Completed, Perfect, Pure Actualizations (Pure Actuality) since they manifest themselves completely, perfectly, and eternally in pure form thus containing no potential that has to be realized. See entries under ENTELECHY.

ad hominem **argument.** See FALLACY, TYPES OF INFORMAL **(3).**

adiaphora (Gk., *a,* "not," and *diaphora,* "different," "unlike," meaning "something that does not make a difference to something else"). **1.** Indifference. **2.** Moral indifference. Used in Greek philosophy, especially Stoicism (see STOICS, THE) to refer to those morally indifferent things that in themselves are not and do not cause good or bad, right or wrong, virtue or vice (but are things in which these qualities may be found or by which they may be attained), such as knowledge, health, life, pleasure, money, art, social position, career.

aesthetic detachment. Sometimes *psychic* or *psychical distance.* The state of being empathetically or contemplatively absorbed in an aesthetic situation, but not being involved in or responsive to the situation's own reality or to the reality it is depicting. Aesthetic detachment from a drama, for example, includes (**a**) detachment from concern about what is happening in the minds of the actors as they are acting; (**b**) detachment from what is happening behind the scenes to keep the drama going; (**c**) detachment from the desire to participate in the activity of the drama as it is unfolding; (**d**) detachment from the belief that what is happening on the stage is continuous with the reality occurring outside the theater. Compare with AESTHETIC DISINTERESTEDNESS.

aesthetic disinterestedness. That perception of an object or event in and for itself without any practical or cognitive purpose. To be distinguished from AESTHETIC DETACHMENT.

aestheticism. 1. The belief that the aesthetic experience is the highest form of human experience. All other experiences are only means toward aesthetic experience. Nothing should interfere in this pursuit. **2.** The view that morality is the servant of art. (This is opposite to artistic moralism, which holds that art is the servant of a moral code.) The aesthetic experience, not moral behavior, is the SUMMUM BONUM of life.

aesthetics. Sometimes *esthetics* (Gk., *aisthētikos,* "one who is perceptive of things through his sensations, feelings, and intuitions." The word *aisthēsis* means "primary, rudimentary sensation"). **1.** The study of beauty, and of related concepts such as the sublime, the tragic, the ugly, the humorous, the drab, the pretty. **2.** The analysis of the values, tastes, attitudes, and standards involved in our experience of and judgments about things made by humans or found in nature which we call beautiful.

Some typical questions in aesthetics: What does the word *beauty* (and other words that refer to aesthetic responses) mean? What is it about us and what is it about an object that makes us call something *beautiful?* Is there a kind of experience that can be said to be uniquely *aesthetic?* What is the relationship between the aesthetic response to art and the aesthetic response to nature? What are the common and differing characteristics that exist among values such as beauty, good, truth, perfection, the pleasurable, the useful? How do aesthetic perception and feeling differ from other types of perceptions and feelings? Are there conscious or unconscious criteria influencing us in evaluating an object or event as *beautiful?* What role do such things as psychic distance, emotional detachment, impartiality, disinterestedness play in the aesthetic experience? Why is there a prevalent tendency in humans to respond aesthetically and to express themselves aesthetically in art and other forms of behavior?

aesthetic values. See entries under OBJECTIVISM; RELATIVISM; SUBJECTIVISM.

aetiology. Sometimes *etiology, aitiology* (Gk., *aitia,* "cause" or "the reason why a thing is what it is," and *logos,* "an account of," "a description of," "inquiry into," or "the study of"). **1.** The study of the types of causes of phenomena. **2.** The inquiry into the cause(s) of a thing. **3.** The actual assigning or finding of a cause for something. See *AITIA.*

aeviternity (L., *aevum,* "eternity," "uninterrupted and neverending time"). **1.** The name for eternity as an infinite, past and future totality. Used in the context of transcending time and change. **2.** Eternity imagined as that timeless or endless structure in which processes occur or in which they are predetermined. Compare with ETERNAL; ETERNAL, *A PARTE ANTE;* ETERNAL, *A PARTE POST;* SEMPITERNAL.

affective·The general name for the emotional or feeling quality of experience as found in pleasure, pain, and a variety of emotions, such as love, hate, fear, anger. See FACULTY.

a fortiori (L., "with greater force," "all the more"). **1.** Refers to having to accept something on the basis of even stronger and better evidence. **2.** Refers to the necessity of having to accept a further truth or argument as clearly more obvious on the basis of a truth one has already accepted. Example: "If you cannot get ready to go with me by this afternoon then *a fortiori* you surely cannot be ready before breakfast, which is when I am leaving."

agapē (Gk., "love," "moral, spiritual love," "brotherly love," "compassion," "charity." The plural *agapai* means "love feast"). **1.** In general, *agapē* was used to designate the highest form of human love in contrast to ERŌS, "sexual love," and PHILIA, "friendship." **2.** In PLATONISM, *agapē* is the love of the eternal, perfect Ideas such as the Good, Beauty, Truth. **3.** In Christianity, *agapē* is the love of man for God and of God for man. (*Agapē* was also used to refer to the love feast of early Christians that revolved around Holy Communion.)

agathon (Gk., "good"). **1.** In PLATONISM, the name given to the highest Good—the supreme Idea. **2.** The *ARETĒ*—the functioning excellence of a thing—is its *agathon,* its good, and its good is related to what it can fulfill or actualize out of its unique potential. See GOOD (PLATO AND PYTHAGOREANS.)

agathos (Gk., "good," "noble," "gentle," "brave"). Often found together with the Greek word *KALOS,* which means "good" in the sense of beautiful. The Greek saying *kalos kai agathos* meant "He is good (in the sense of a beautiful appearance), and he is good (in the sense of his moral, spiritual actions)."

agent (L., *agere,* "to act," *agens,* "that which is acting"). **1.** One who, or that which, exerts power upon something and produces an effect. (A cause is often personified as an agent "intending" to bring about, "to produce" its effect, or to "make something happen.") **2.** In ethics, a self (person, EGO) (**a**) who is capable of deliberate action or (**b**) who is in the process of an action.

agnosticism (Gk., *a*, "not," "no," and *gnōstikos*, "one who knows or has knowledge of"). **1.** The belief (**a**) that we cannot have knowledge of God and (**b**) that it is impossible to prove that God exists or does not exist. **2.** Sometimes used to refer to the suspension of judgment (see EPOCHĒ) about some types of knowledge such as about the soul, immortality, spirits, heaven, hell, extraterrestrial life.

agreement, method of. See METHODS, MILL'S INDUCTIVE.

aitia (Gk., "cause" or "the reason why a thing is what it is or acts as it does," "the conditions responsible for the occurrence of something"). *Aitia* has three principal levels of meaning: **1.** "Cause" in the sense of a mechanical or scientific description of the interacting events which produce the effect being studied. See CAUSE. **2.** "Cause" in the sense of presenting all the possible ways we can *talk about* (describe) how things come to be the way they are—how things develop in a process from a beginning point to their completed state. These *aitiai* (causes) are then seen to be the reasons for becoming—for the temporal development of all change from a state of potentiality to actuality. See CAUSES, ARISTOTLE'S FOUR. **3.** "Cause" in the sense of giving reasons for something being (becoming) the way it is rather than its being (becoming) something else. See AETIOLOGY; REASON, PRINCIPLE OF SUFFICIENT.

akrasia (Gk., "bad mixture," "ill-tempered," "lacking in self-control," "incontinent," "immoderate"). That condition of character where one knows what should (must) be done but is unable to do it. Lack or weakness of willpower (self-determination, self-discipline, self-direction). See INCONTINENCE.

alēthic (Gk., *alētheia*, "truth," "real as opposed to unreal," "real as opposed to appearance"). Used as an adjective to mean "relating to truth." See MODES, ALĒTHIC.

alienation (L., *alienus*, "alien," related to Latin *alius*, "another"). That state of awareness in which things become foreign, or strange to consciousness. Feelings range from indifference and unconcern to aversion and disgust, whereas before there may have been love, attraction, friendship, and excitement about these very objects. Alienation is characterized by qualities such as lack of the desire to identify and participate with the object of consciousness; lack of commitment to the goals within social groupings; detached viewpoint which has no inclination for involvement. See ENNUI; ESTRANGEMENT; SELF-ALIENATION. Contrast with DEALIENATION.

als ob (Ger., "as if," referring to something hypothetical, postulated, pragmatically acceptable but not [necessarily] true or real). Associated with Hans Vaihinger's philosophy especially as expressed in his book *The Philosophy of "As If,"* in which knowledge is based not on objective truth but on assuming as true certain unverifiable fictional constructions which are useful as conceptual tools for the formation of intellectual systems. Sometimes this philosophy is called *fictionism*.

alteration. Qualitative change. See CHANGE (ARISTOTLE).

altruism (L., *alter,* "another" or "other"). **1.** The promotion of the good of others. (To be distinguished from (**a**) the promotion of the good *for* others as in benevolent tyranny, and (**b**) the promotion of the good *with* others as in the cult activities of a fraternity.) **2.** A selfless and benevolent love for humankind and dedication toward achieving the well-being of people and society.

Altruism may be motivated by (**a**) a disinterested sense of duty to humans and society, or (**b**) the disciplined attempt to overcome one's self-centeredness and selfish desires in love of others, which involves such qualities as compassion, sympathy, and selflessness. Altruism may involve (**a**) self-abnegation or self-denial in which one's own good is thought less of, or not considered at all, or (**b**) a self-interest in which one's own good is taken into account and is a requisite for promoting or achieving the good of others. (The former is related to the concept of martyrdom and the latter to the concept of enlightened self-interest.) Contrast with EGOISM.

ambiguity, process-product. The ambiguity committed when a statement can refer either to a process or to its product and it is unclear from the context which of the two is intended. Example: "Adam went to see the construction." The word *construction* can refer to a process or to a product. If it refers to a process, Adam went to see the builders in the act of constructing. If it refers to the end product of the act of constructing, Adam went to see that which was constructed.

ambiguity, semantical. Refers to a word(s) in a sentence in which the word(s) can have more than one meaning, sense, or reference and there is doubt as to which is intended. Example: "Adam rented two apartments." One possible meaning is that Adam rented two apartments for his own use. Another possible meaning is that Adam rented out two apartments to others (or kept one for himself and rented out the other). See EQUIVOCATION.

ambiguity, syntactical. See AMPHIBOLY.

ambiguity, type-token. The ambiguity committed when an expression can refer either to a type or to a token and it is unclear from the context which is meant. Example: I write the sentence "Jane is a student" on the board ten times. I then ask, "How many sentences have I written?" If the question intends to refer to "type," then the answer is that I have written only one (type of) sentence. If the question intends to refer to "token," then the answer is that I have written ten sentences. See TYPE/TOKEN DISTINCTION.

ambiguity of accent. See FALLACY, TYPES OF INFORMAL (**9**).

amoral. Literally "not moral." (The prefix *a* represents the Greek negation.) **1.** *Amoral* may be contrasted with *nonmoral* (that area where moral categories cannot be applied), and with IMMORAL (evil, sinful, wrong). Choosing a necktie is a nonmoral act: that is, one which does not involve moral values. Killing a person in violation of moral and social standards is immoral. Killing a person without any concern or commitment to moral or social concepts of good or bad is amoral. An amoral person in this sense is one who is indifferent to and does not care to abide by the standard moral codes of society. **2.** *Amoral* has also been defined with reference to action or behavior that is morally value-free: that is, neither moral nor immoral, neither right nor wrong. (This definition makes *amoral* synonymous with *nonmoral* or *nonethical*.) Science has been called amoral in this sense of the term. Contrast with MORAL.

amphiboly (syntactical ambiguity) (Gk., *amphibolos,* "not regular speech," or "a sentence whose meaning is doubtful or confusing"). An amphiboly is committed when it is unclear due to the grammatical structure (syntactics) of a sentence which of several possible meanings the sentence has. Example: "He rode a horse with a muzzle on his mouth." The *semantics* (meaning) of each of these words may be clear, but the *grammatical* relationship among the words produces a confusion of possible meanings. Grammatical constructions that produce amphibolous expressions include misplaced modifiers, loosely applied adverbs, elliptical constructions, and omitted punctuation.

analogical reasoning. Sometimes *arguing from analogy* or *analogical inference.* Arguing by comparing the similarities between things: If two things are alike in many respects, it is probable that they will be alike in other respects. The specific argument form is: Since *X* and *Y* are observed to be alike in respects *a, b, c* . . . , they therefore are probably alike in further respects *m, n, o* . . . , which characteristics have been observed in one of the two things being compared but not yet in the other. Such specific arguments from analogy are never conclusive and do not serve as proof.

analogy (Gk., *analogia, analogos,* "proportionality," "proportion." From *ana,* "up," "upwards," "upon," "throughout," "continuous," and *logos,* "ratio," "reasoned") Originally a mathematical term. In such a context *analogy* signified a common or reciprocal relationship between two things or a similarity of two proportions. The Greek term came later to mean the (usually linguistic) comparison of similarities in concepts or things. **1.** The pointing out of similarities or resemblances between things. **2.** A form of (usually inductive) inference in which from the assertion of similarities between two things it is then reasoned that the things will probably also be similar in yet other respects.

The value ("correctness," "fruitfulness") of an analogy is often judged by criteria such as (**a**) the quantity of resemblances (similarities) that exist between the things compared; (**b**) the quantity of further resemblances suggested which on testing are verified as correct; and (**c**) the quantity of suggestions about resemblances implied in the analogy for further follow-up.

Analogies are pictorial, metaphorical, or model methods of thinking which may be highly suggestive of what to look for. But whether that which is suggested is the case can be determined only by empirical means such as observation and/or experimentation.

analogy, refutation by logical. See COUNTEREXAMPLE, METHOD OF.

analysis (Gk., *analysis*, from *analyein*, "to resolve," "to unloose," from *ana*, "up" and *lyein*, "to loosen," "to untie"). **1.** The mental (or actual) separation of something (a whole, an entity, a problem) into its component parts in order (**a**) to study the parts separately, or (**b**) to study their interrelationships, or (**c**) to study how they relate to the whole. **2.** The process of attempting to uncover the implicit meanings and presuppositions of a system of beliefs or of a statement.

analysis, linguistic. Also *linguistic philosophy.* The view that by analyzing ordinary language, we can better understand the nature of philosophical problems. Philosophical problems can be seen to be: (**a**) verbal problems without any basis in reality but based only on verbal confusions (see VERBAL DISPUTE) or (**b**) problems which dissolve of themselves once the linguistic confusions are seen. The aim of linguistic analysis is to make philosophical questions disappear. For example, the traditional problem of induction (see INDUCTION, PROBLEM OF) is a pseudo-problem. Once one is clear about the linguistic uses and meanings of words such as "evidence," "reason," "past," "future," "prediction," "recurrence," there is no reason to see induction as a real problem. Some of the views found in linguistic analysis: **1.** Language is not pictorially related to the external world, nor is it related isomorphically (in a one-to-one correspondence). Language does not resemble the things to which it is applied. **2.** Language is not a system of meanings obtained in the act of naming independently existing entities or facts. **3.** Language is a very diversified tool (for usage). **4.** The meanings of words and sentences are derived from their use within a context. They do not refer to or name anything independent of their usage. **5.** Words, sentences, meanings perform a variety of functions such as naming, classifying, cataloguing, commanding, prescribing, describing, referring, expressing, evoking. See LANGUAGE, FUNCTIONS OF. **6.** The meanings of words and sentences must be considered in the context of the rules, habits, and conventions that control the uses of words and sentences. Meaning has little to do with the actual relationship between words and the objects that they represent.

Some of the antimetaphysical claims of linguistic analysis: (**a**) Language (propositions, statements) cannot present us with a picture of reality as a whole. (b) Language cannot represent (correspond to) reality (the facts that are being talked about). (c) Language is an attempt to say what can only be *seen* (had as experience; shown). By the very nature of all languages, it is impossible to go beyond (behind) their symbols. We would have to use their symbols, or other symbols, to talk about what is beyond those symbols and we thus would still be involved in symbols. The attempt to go beyond language with the use of language is in effect to construct a metaphysical structure that reveals only its own content and system. (d) Philosophy clarifies concepts but does not give us scientific or metaphysical knowledge about the world.

Some linguistic analysts or linguistic philosophers: Ludwig Wittgenstein; John Wisdom; Gilbert Ryle. In most cases it is difficult to draw a sharp line between linguistic analysis and ANALYTIC PHILOSOPHY. Compare with ORDINARY LANGUAGE PHILOSOPHY; POSITIVISM, LOGICAL. See LANGUAGE, PHILOSOPHY OF.

analytic, transcendental. See TRANSCENDENTAL ANALYTIC (KANT).

analytic judgment. See JUDGMENT, ANALYTIC (KANT).

analytic philosophy. A twentieth-century philosophic movement particularly strong in England and the United States that concentrates on language and the attempt to analyze statements (or concepts, or linguistic expressions or logical forms) in order to find those with the best and most concise logical form which fits the facts or meanings to be presented. Central to analytic philosophy is the forming of definitions—linguistic or nonlinguistic, real or contextual. (Contextual definitions primarily refer here to those that define the specific use of symbols whereby one set of symbols may be substituted for another.) The following are four of the many views that can be found in analytic philosophy: **1.** Bertrand Russell: The aim of analytic philosophy is to translate grammatically misleading statements into logically correct forms. **2.** G. E. Moore: Analytic philosophy does not discover facts about the world but rather defines and clarifies concepts. The *analysandum* is the concept to be analyzed and the *analysans* is the logically equivalent concept which is substituted for it. They thus become synonymous, and this synonymity gives greater clarity. **3.** Ludwig Wittgenstein: The purpose of analytic philosophy is to translate all complex and descriptive statements (propositions, linguistic expressions) into elementary propositions. These are then put into ultimate, unanalyzable units which represent the simple irreducible units of the real world. A basic tenet is that philosophy cannot transgress the limits of language. Philosophy cannot describe or explain how language is related to the world. This relationship can only be shown. The proper task of philosophy is to make clear what can and what cannot be legitimately said. **4.** Rudolph Carnap: Analytic philosophy is the systematic uncovering of the logical syntax (the grammatical structure and its rules) of concepts and language, especially of the language of science, which is purely formal. The main concern here is not with the meanings (semantics) of words and not with the meaning relation between our language and the real world but rather with the structural interrelationships of languages themselves. In some cases it is difficult to distinguish sharply between analytic philosophy and linguistic philosophy. See ANALYSIS, LINGUISTIC. Compare with ATOMISM, LOGICAL; EMPIRICISM, LOGICAL; ORDINARY LANGUAGE PHILOSOPHY.

analytic statement. See STATEMENT, ANALYTIC.

anamnēsis (Gk., "remembrance," "recollection," "mental recovery," "recalling to mind"). **1.** The bringing back to mind of a previous experience. **2.** The activity of recollecting knowledge attained in a previous existence. (In Plato and Platonism, *anamnēsis* is the knowledge gained from a remembrance of the Perfect Forms which the soul has innately as *a priori* knowledge or has experienced in an existence prior to its embodiment. Often referred to as Plato's Doctrine of Reminiscence (Recollection or Remembrance, [see RECOLLECTION].)

anangkē (Gk., "necessity," "that inner force which impels certain things to be done or prevents them from being done"). *Anangkē* was used in three main senses in Greek philosophy: **1.** Physical necessity understood as the constantly present, irrational, nonpurposeful, undirected, and uncontrolled element in the universe. **2.** The intrinsic resistance or recalcitrance of matter to be completely shaped by a rational force toward a good. (In Plato's *Timaeus* these qualities are the principal characteristics of matter which cannot be eliminated from the universe. Not even the DEMIURGE, who rationally manipulates all matter, can overcome those inherent and limiting qualities.) **3.** The logical necessity by which the conclusion of a valid categorical syllogism (necessarily) follows from its premises.

anarchism (Gk., privative prefix *a,* "not," "the want of," "the absence of," "the lack of," and *archos,* "a ruler, director, chief, person in charge, commander." The Greek words *anarchos, anarchia* meant having no government—being without a government). *The positive connotation:* Anarchism is the social ideology that refuses to accept an authoritarian ruling government. It holds that individuals should organize themselves in any way they wish in order to fulfill their needs and ideals. In this sense anarchism is not to be identified with NIHILISM but can be seen to have similarities to political libertarianism and antinomianism (see ANTINOMIAN). *The negative connotation:* Anarchism is the belief which denies any respect for law or order and actively engages in the promotion of chaos through the destruction of society. It advocates the use of individual terrorism as a means toward advancing the cause of social and political disorganization.

angoisse. Sometimes *anomie* (Fr., "anguish," "anxiety," "distress," "agony"). Used to refer to: **1.** a feeling of "free-floating" dread or despair, **2.** a state of disorientation, and **3.** a sense of isolation. **4.** Also used in the sense of ANGST.

angst (Ger., "dread," "despair," "anxiety," "anguish"). The dread of nothingness, annihilation, meaninglessness, unconcern. See EXISTENTIALISM.

animism (Gk., *anemos,* "that which blows," or "that which breathes," "wind," whence Latin *animus,* "breath," "soul," "life principle"). **1.** The belief that all things are alive. **2.** The belief in the reality of soul immanent in and pervading all things—humans, animals, rocks, rivers, trees, the earth, the moon, the stars—as their guiding force. **3.** The belief that there is an invisible, intangible, nonmaterial soul that is the underlying ground for life distinct from the material body it inhabits and acts upon to cause the body to behave. **4.** In ancient cosmology, the belief that the universe—our world as well as all the heavenly bodies—possesses eternal souls that are the source of all motion and change. There was thought to be a hierarchy of souls attached to the various levels of existence. **5.** In metaphysics, the view that Existence (Being, the universe) as a whole is alive, or that there is a pulsating life-force or will intimately connected with and propelling its processes and direction. The universe itself is either a living, organic whole, or is infused with an inner living principle. Compare with HYLOMORPHISM; HYLOZOISM; PANPSYCHISM; PANTHEISM; PERSONALISM; VITALISM. **6.** Epistemologically, the belief in the tendency of human nature to project its own inner life qualities upon external inanimate (and animate) reality. In early thought, for example, trees, rivers, the moon were believed to have a will, feelings, thoughts, and intentions. Compare with ANTHROPOMORPHISM. All forms of animism are not anthropomorphic since in animism the objects may possess life qualities without possessing human form. Such animism occurs in many areas of language: for example, in common talk: "The door pushed me out of the room." Compare with EMPATHY; PERSONIFICATION; SYMPATHY. It is found in the language of metaphor and of poetry: "He is a wily old fox." See ANALOGY; METAPHOR. It is found in scientific language: "The pressure in the container burst open the lid." Contrasted with MECHANISM.

animism, teleological. The theory that **(a)** parts are adapted (coordinated, adjusted) to other parts within a whole in order to achieve the purpose of the whole, and **(b)** the whole itself sets the purpose and causes the adaptation. See entries under TELEOLOGICAL and TELEOLOGY.

anoetic (Gk., *a,* "not," and *noētikos,* from *noein,* "to perceive," or *nous,* "mind"). **1.** Referring to the states of SENTIENCE, such as pure emotions or sensations that have not yet come to full cognitive awareness. In this sense the anoetic is a precognitive state. Contrast with NOETIC. Compare with PRECONSCIOUS. **2.** Referring to the states of sentience that do not come into full cognitive awareness except with the application of deliberate means such as hypnosis. In this sense the anoetic is an acognitive (or noncognitive) state. The terms *anoetic, subnoetic,* and SUBLIMINAL are sometimes used interchangeably.

anomie. See ANGOISSE.

anschauung (Ger., "intuition"). See INTUITION (KANT).

ante res (L., "before [prior to] reality" or "before [prior to] things"). Used by medieval philosophers (a) in the context of REALISM whereby universals were regarded as existing prior to the existence of material objects in which they could be found, and (b) in the context of natural law (see entries under LAW, NATURAL) whereby God's laws are prior to and the cause of natural phenomena. Compare with *IN RES; POST RES.*

anthropocentric (Gk., *anthrōpos,* "man" or "mankind," and *kentron,* "center"). **1.** Referring to any view which maintains that man is the center and ultimate goal of the universe. **2.** Referring to the view that man's values are central to the functioning of the universe and the universe sustains and progressively supports those values. **3.** Occasionally, the term is used to refer in a negative way to the belief that reality can be correctly explained only on the basis of the forms of subjective human experience.

anthropomorphism (Gk., *anthrōpos,* "man" or "mankind," and *morphē,* "form," "shape," "figure"). **1.** The representation of God, the gods, or natural forces as having human form and attributes. **2.** The belief that God, or the gods, have characteristics similar to man's such as consciousness, intention, will, emotions, sensations. An extreme form of anthropomorphism maintains that God or the gods exist in the shape of man but are more perfect and powerful. **3.** Often refers to the belief that animals possess human abilities and qualities such as thought, communication, feelings, motivation.

antientropic factor. See ENTROPIC, ANTI-.

antilogism (Gk., *antilogia,* "contradictory," from *anti,* "against," and *legein,* "to speak," "to reason"). **1.** Any inconsistent triad of statements whereby if any two are true the third can be seen to be inconsistent, false, or contradictory (see EVIL, THEOLOGICAL PROBLEM OF). **2.** An argument whose conclusion is stated as a contradiction to its valid conclusion. Example: Socrates is a human. All humans are mortal. Therefore, Socrates is not mortal.

antinomian (Gk., *anti,* "against" and *nomos,* "law"). **1.** One who desires to be free from the regulations and laws of a society. One who wants to live either outside society in a state of nature (like the CYNICS) or within society but adhering to as few social norms as possible. (Antinomians, as opposed to activists or anarchists, do not directly engage in overthrowing the laws and political structure of a society.) See ANARCHISM. **2.** In theology, (a) one who believes that faith alone, not moral law, is necessary for salvation. (b) In a stronger theological sense, one who despises and holds himself above all laws and social restrictions because of some special faith, grace, or knowledge that makes for salvation.

antinomies, the four (Kant). Also *the four theses of rationalistic metaphysics,* each contradicted by an antithesis. Kant believed that solid arguments could be given for both the thesis and its antithesis (see ANTI-

NOMY) for the following: (**a**) The universe has a beginning in time and is finite in space. The universe has no beginning in time and is not finite in space. (**b**) All things are made up of simple constituents. Nothing is made up of simple constituents. (**c**) All things have a cause. Not all things have a cause. (**d**) A Necessary Being exists that explains the universe. No Necessary Being exists. See DIALECTIC, TRANSCENDENTAL (KANT).

antinomy (Gk., *anti,* "against," and *nomos,* "law"). A contradiction between two principles each of which appears to be true but which cannot both be true. Often regarded as an extreme kind of PARADOX.

antithesis (Gk., *antithesis,* from *anti,* "against," and *tithenai,* "to set"). **1.** The opposition and contrast of words or concepts. **2.** That statement or ideology presented in opposition to a declared position (thesis). **3.** In dialectical materialism, the antithesis is the second member of a process of change and advance which counters the first member (thesis). Out of this opposition emerges a third member, called the SYNTHESIS, which incorporates the positive qualities or truths of both the thesis and antithesis and which transcends them both to become itself a thesis to be met by an antithesis, and so on. See DIALECTIC (HEGEL); LOGIC, DIALECTICAL; MATERIALISM, DIALECTICAL.

apatheia (Gk., from *a,* "not," and *pathos,* "suffering," "pain"). Used especially by the Stoics to mean "indifference to pleasure and pain," "the state of tranquility or peace of mind and body resulting from the emotional detachment from the everyday world." See STOICS, THE.

apeiron (Gk., "limitless," "boundless," "without limit," "INFINITE," "endless," "the indeterminate"). **1.** The concept of the *apeiron* as "infinite" spatial extension of substance is found in many Greek philosophers (Anaximander, Anaximenes, Xenophanes, Melissus, the Atomists, etc.), but philosophers such as Plato, Aristotle, and the STOICS believed the universe to be finite. **2.** The concept of the *apeiron* as "infinite divisibility" or as an INFINITESIMAL continuum with reference to the analysis of motion, time, and magnitudes in space was accepted by Zeno. Aristotle accepted the *apeiron* with respect to counting numbers. **3.** Anaximander was the first to use the word *apeiron* to refer to the universe as spatially unbounded and "from which" opposite substances, attributes such as hot/cold, dry/wet, came into being, and "in which" they opposed each other. The *apeiron* was eternal, imperishable, primal, indeterminate, and the inexhaustible material source for the existence of all things. There was a trend in Greek philosophy toward hypostatizing this word (see HYPOSTATIZATION; REIFICATION/REISM). **4.** The Pythagoreans (**a**) put the *apeiron* and the *peron* (or PERAS) in their list of irreducible opposites which form the basic underlying structure and principles of all becoming and of all reality. The *apeiron* is classified in a dualism with such opposites as: the even number; the unintelligible; the many; the moving; the ugly; the bad. The *peron* is classified with: the odd number; the intelligible; unity; nonmotion; beauty; the good. The Pythagoreans also used the word *apeiron* to refer to (b) the formless (that which must be put into an order), or (c) the inchoate flux of opposites or contraries (such as hot, cold, even, odd, wet, dry) that are put into an ordered and intelligible arrangement by the principle of *peras* (limit), or (d) the principle of disorder or disharmony causing things to lose their order.

aperçu (Fr., "intuitive insight," "immediate recognition or awareness," as opposed to insight stemming from cognitive processes).

apodeictic. Sometimes spelled *apodictic* (Gk., *apodeiktikos,* derived from *apo,* "from," and *deiknynai,* "to show," meaning "showing that which one must prove"). **1.** Clearly provable or demonstrable. (Or clearly impossible, or undemonstrable.) **2.** Necessarily true. **3.** Absolutely certain. Aristotle contrasted apodeictic, which meant "certain beyond dispute," with eristic dialectic, which meant "subject to dispute." See DIALECTIC.

Apollonian spirit. The impulse toward order, proportion, rationality, harmony, pattern, measure, and intellectual explanation. Its opposite is the DIONYSIAN SPIRIT. Both concepts are found in Friedrich Nietzsche's *The Birth of Tragedy* (1872). Compare with CLASSICISM.

apologetics (Gk., *apologētikos,* "speaking in defense of"). **1.** Methods which attempt to defend and vindicate a doctrinal position against its critics. **2.** In theology, the endeavor to rationally justify the divine origin of a faith.

a posteriori (L., "that which follows after," from *a, ab,* "from," "out of," and *posteriori,* "latter"). After or coming from sense experience. Opposite to A PRIORI. Used in the context of concepts such as CONTINGENT, PROBABLE, EMPIRICAL, INDUCTION, scientific, verifiable, SYNTHETIC, factual, EXPERIENCE, OBSERVATION. See KNOWLEDGE, A POSTERIORI.

appearance (L., *a, ad,* "to," "toward," and *parere,* "to come forth," "to become visible"). **1.** That which is seen, or the sense content immediately present to consciousness. **2.** The sense content that is believed to have some vague or illusory semblance to that from which it originates. **3.** The way a thing seems to be (as opposed to the way it is in itself, or to an objective way of viewing it). **4.** The sense content that has no resemblance to that from which it originates or to which it is said to refer.

appearance/reality. Contrasting terms that refer to the distinction between what things are like (APPEARANCE) to the perceiver (knower, observer) and what they are like in themselves (REALITY). The distinction accepts the notion that there are things (or there is a reality) existing independently of our knowledge of their appearances (or its appearance) but emphasizes (a) (the strong view) that we can never know these things as they are in themselves (or as that reality is in itself), or (b) (the weak view) that only a few things can be truly known about things as they are in themselves (or about that reality as it is in itself). See NOUMENON; PHENOMENON.

Arguments used in support of the RELATIVITY OF SENSE PERCEPTION are also used to support the distinction between appearance and reality. See RELATIVISM, PROTAGOREAN.

apperception (L., *ad,* "to," "toward," and *percipere,* "to perceive," or "to mentally apprehend"). **1.** The perception of one's own consciousness, in contrast to PERCEPTION, which is the mental state that refers to external things. Used in the context of concepts such as reflective consciousness, self-awareness, introspection, self-perception (perception of one's mental functioning), self-reflection. See SELF-CONSCIOUSNESS. Used with reference to such acts as selecting, concentrating, attending, deciding, choosing, assimilating, intending, avoiding, willing. **2.** The deliberate assimilating and reorganizing of ideas by an act of intellectual will. In this sense apperception requires qualities of willing and attending (the recognizing, interpreting, identifying, explaining, subsuming, rejecting of ideas). **3.** The mental activity which (**a**) brings faint items of knowledge (indistinct impressions, vague notions or feelings) out of the subconscious to the level of conscious attention and which (**b**) puts them into intellectual patterns, thereby making sense of them.

apperception, empirical (Kant). The ego's awareness of actual, concrete, changing states of consciousness. This function was performed by the empirical ego in contrast to the pure ego, which produced a transcendental apperception. Contrast with APPERCEPTION, TRANSCENDENTAL. See EGO, EMPIRICAL (KANT).

apperception, transcendental. Sometimes referred to as: the *transcendental* (or *pure) ego of apperception;* the *transcendental unity of apperception.* **1.** The inner, fundamental, and unchanging sense of a unity of our consciousness. That aspect of a person's consciousness that endures as a unity throughout the immediate and momentary changes. **2.** For Kant, transcendental apperception is the structured unity (pure ego, self) of consciousness which precedes (is transcendent to) the content of our perceptions and makes possible their experienced order and meaning. This structured transcendent unity consists of (**a**) the intuitions of space and time which are modes *by which* we perceive and are not objects *of* our perception, and (**b**) the categories of understanding such as quantity, quality, relation, and modality. See CATEGORIES OF THE UNDERSTANDING (KANT). Transcendental apperception was thus thought to be the necessary condition for having an experience and for synthesizing experience into a unity. Contrast with APPERCEPTION, EMPIRICAL. See EGO, TRANSCENDENTAL (KANT); IDEALISM, TRANSCENDENTAL (KANT).

appetitive (L., *appetere,* "to strive after," "long for"). Pertaining to the basic wants or desires, such as those for food and water, exercise, sex. See FACULTY.

apprehension (L., *apprehendere,* "to seize," "to grasp"). **1.** The process of conceiving, perceiving, or understanding an idea or concept. **2.** The act of becoming consciously aware of the bare presence of an object or idea. Contrasted with the act of naming, judging, and intellectually grasping an object. See COMPREHENSION.

a priori (L., "that which precedes," from *a, ab,* "from, "out of," and *prior,* "former," "before," "prior"). Prior to and independent of sense experience. Opposite to *A POSTERIORI.* Used in the context of concepts such as necessary, certain, definitional, deductive, universally true, innate, intuitive. See KNOWLEDGE, *A PRIORI.*

a priori judgment. See JUDGMENT, *A PRIORI* (KANT); KNOWLEDGE, *A PRIORI.*

archē (Gk., "the beginning," "the starting point," "the origin of a thing," "first"). **1.** The basic, underlying substance or principle out of which all things come to be. Its first use as a philosophic concept in this sense is found in Anaximander, who conceived the *archē* as (**a**) eternal, with no beginning and no end, and (**b**) the source of all things that are, have been, and will be. **2.** That first and originating point from which a thing comes to be what it is.

archetypes (Gk., *archē,* "first," and *typos,* "pattern," "stamp," "mold"). **1.** The original models from which things are formed, or of which things are copies. For example, Plato's ideal forms (Beauty, Truth, Good, Justice) are regarded as archetypes. See FORMS, PLATO'S THEORY OF IDEAL. In some interpretations of Plato, the Good is the one and only archetype, from which all other forms receive their being. **2.** In the psychology of Carl Jung, the patterns of thought and the imagery that emerge from the collective unconscious of humankind. In literature they are referred to as *primordial images* or *archetypal symbols* and are found, for example, in recurring myths.

aretē (Gk., "the goodness of a thing," "that at which a thing excels"). In Greek literature, when applied to persons it signified qualities such as valor, prowess, courage, strength. In a moral sense it meant virtuousness, meritoriousness, goodness of service. It is often translated as virtue. See entries under VIRTUE.

The philosophic meaning of *aretē* has to do with the "functioning excellence" of a thing. When something performs the function it is designed to perform and it does this excellently then it has *aretē;* it is "virtuous" in that respect. Example: The *aretē* of a pruning scissors is to cut branches. It was intended for this purpose. It does this better than anything else. In so far as it performs its function well is has *aretē.*

To determine human *aretē,* the Greeks asked "What is unique to the human? What functions does a human perform which no other thing performs as well?" It is not locomotion, not growth, not sensating, not procreating; these and many other functions are shared in common with other beings such as animals. The *aretē* of humans will be found in that which they can do uniquely: reason. The use of the rational faculty is that which distinguishes a human from all other beings. A human's *aretē* consists of the development and use of his reason to the utmost level of functioning excellence. (And for Aristotle, in this consists also an individual's ultimate happiness.) See AGATHON; entries under ESSENCE; *EUDAEMONIA*.

argument (L., *arguere,* "to make clear"). **1.** The reasons (proof, evidence) offered in support or denial of something. **2.** In logic, a series of statements called *premises* logically related to a further statement called the *conclusion.* Arguments are divided into two general categories: deductive and inductive. See DEDUCTION; INDUCTION.

argument, invalid. See INVALID.

argument, open-question. See OPEN-QUESTION ARGUMENT (G.E. MOORE).

argument, sound. See SOUND (LOGIC).

aristocracy (Gk., *aristos,* "best," and *kratein,* "to be strong," "to govern or rule over"). **1.** A government ruled by the best (aristocrats) who are chosen by such criteria as intellect, virtue, rank, status, power, achievement, fortune, noble birth—or combinations of these. **2.** Rule by a small class regarded as privileged and superior to the rest of the community and which thereby has a natural right to lead.

art (L., *ars, artis,* "skill"). **1.** Creations (works, productions) of humans that have aesthetic qualities or values. **2.** Skills acquired in experience that make **1** possible: the ability to contrive, to systematically and intentionally use physical means to achieve desired results according to aesthetic principles, whether intuitively or cognitively understood. See FINE ARTS; *TECHNĒ.*

art, philosophy of. The philosophy of art is concerned with the conceptual problems arising from our understanding of art. Questions such as these are asked in the philosophy of art: How is art defined? What makes a work of art beautiful, appealing, ugly? How do we respond to a work of art? Does art symbolize? What kind of meaning or knowledge does art communicate? Is artistic expression a unique form of expression? Does art reveal a truth about anything? Why do humans create works of art? See AESTHETICS.

asceticism (Gk., *askētikos,* "one who exercises"). In general, the view that man should deny his desires. **1.** The strong version: man ought to deny all desires without exception. **2.** The weak version: man ought to deny only the base desires of the body (lust, lasciviousness, sensuousness) and of the world (desire for material possessions, fame, achievement). The desires of the flesh must be repressed. Only in this way can one free the soul to attain virtue and salvation.

Both senses of asceticism have been associated with celibacy, austerity, simplicity, obedience, poverty, fasting, discipline, penance, mutilation of the body, the solitary and contemplative life, self-denial.

a se (L., "from itself," "by itself"). Refers to an eternal self-sustaining, self-sufficient, and self-subsisting substance or ultimate existence that exists of itself by its own power and is underived from any other source whatever. Its essence is to exist and its existence is its essence. In medieval philosophy, applied only to God. See ASEITY; *IN SE; PER SE.*

aseity (L., *aseitas,* "being by, for, and of itself"). The state of being of a thing (**a**) which is utterly, completely, absolutely independent of other things, (**b**) upon which all other things depend for their total existence, and (**c**) which manifests its nature (essence) in a perfectly pure way without manifesting nonessential (see *PER ACCIDENS*) characteristics. Traditionally the word *aseity* has been applied to God. See PERSEITY.

assent (L., *assentire,* "to feel, think"). To intellectually accept the truth of a statement.

assent (Hume). 1. Acceptance of an immediate feature of our consciousness about which we can do little (except accept it). Things that have the quality of assent: our desires, wants, wishes, drives, likes and dislikes, impressions. **2.** An emotional attachment to or preference for something that is, at the moment had, beyond rational judgment as to its truth/falsity, goodness/badness.

association, laws of. 1. The patterns or forms by which ideas are connected, such as similarity (resemblance), contrast, contiguity in space and time, causality, propinquity. **2.** The forces or principles causing the patterning in **1.** See CONTIGUITY, LAW OF; CONTRAST, LAW OF.

associationism. Sometimes referred to as *associationistic psychology.* The theory (**a**) that all mental states are made up of unique, simple, discrete, irreducible elements (such as impressions, sense data, sensations) and (**b**) that these elements combine and recombine by laws of association (see ASSOCIATION, LAWS OF) to form our complex mental states. (Associationism is identified with philosophers John Locke, David Hume, and John Stuart Mill.) Compare with ATOMISTIC PSYCHOLOGY.

assumption associationism (L., *assumere,* "to take," "to adopt," "to accept"). **1.** A statement (idea, belief) that is accepted as true (**a**) without clear proof or (**b**) without presenting an argument to support it. **2.** A statement that is accepted in order to develop the ideas it can lead to. Example: "On the basis of acting *as if* x is true, what conclusion can then be drawn?" See POSTULATE.

ataraxia (Gk., "imperturbability," "lack of disturbance," "equilibrium," from *a,* "not," and *tarazein,* "to stir up," "to trouble," "to confound," "to agitate"). *Ataraxia* is translated as "tranquility or imperturbability of mind and body" and was used especially by the Epicureans much as the Stoics used the word *APATHEIA,* to signify the goal of human life and the highest form of happiness. See HEDONISM (EPICURUS).

athanatism (Gk., *athanatos,* "immortal," from *a,* "not," and *thanatos,* "death"). **1.** The belief in the survival of the soul (consciousness, mind, self, ego, personality) in some form or other, and in some place or other after death. **2.** The belief in immortality. Opposite to THANATISM.

atheism (Gk., *atheos,* "without God," from *a,* "not," and *theos,* "God"). **1.** The belief that gods do not, or God does not, exist. **2.** The disbelief in any kind of supernatural existence that is supposed to affect the universe. **3.** The lack of belief in a particular God. (The Greeks called the Christians atheists for not believing in their gods and the Christians called the Greeks atheists for not believing in their God.)

atomic fact. The simplest, most rudimentary, elementary, and irreducible kind of fact consisting of a quality in some particular thing or a relation between particular things. There is a one-to-one (see ISOMORPHISM) relationship between an atomic proposition (atomic language) and an atomic fact. For example, subjects (proper names) correspond to terms (particulars); adjectives correspond to qualities; verbs correspond to relations. See ATOMISM, LOGICAL.

atomism, Greek. The philosophy developed by the early Greek philosophers Leucippus, Democritus, and Epicurus (and the Roman, Lucretius), which maintained that reality is composed of atoms. The Greek word *atomos* from which our word *atom* is taken means "indivisible," "having no parts," "uncuttable," and is made up of the privative letter *a,* "not" and *topos,* "able to be cut." The atoms as minute material particles are the ultimate constituents of all things and have properties such as size, shape, position, arrangement, movement. Atoms are eternally present, simple, separate, irreducible to anything further, impenetrable, unchangeable (their essential nature remains eternally the same), and invisible to the naked eye. There are infinitely many atoms in existence. Atoms in themselves do not possess qualities such as color, taste, heat, smell. These qualities are produced by the activity of the atoms upon sense organs. The atoms are eternally in motion in empty space, colliding with each other and forming objects. Their sizes and geometric shapes interlock into configurations producing the variety of existing things. The existence of any individual thing can be explained in terms of the arrangements of the positions and figures of the atoms of which it is composed.

In general, atomism is the materialistic view that the universe consists of ultimately simple, independent, and irreducible entities that are only contingently interrelated (as opposed to necessarily interrelated) to form objects. See entries under MATERIALISM. See VOID (ATOMISTS).

atomism, logical. The name given to the philosophic outlook primarily identified with Bertrand Russell and Ludwig Wittgenstein, characterized by such theories as: **(a)** Language and thought can be analyzed in terms of indivisible and discrete components called atomic propositions that correspond to ATOMIC FACTS. **(b)** Logic organizes atomic propositions into systems of knowledge. **(c)** A fundamental identity of structure exists between a symbol and the fact it represents. **(d)** The complexity of the symbol corresponds to the complexity of the facts symbolized by it. (**e**) There is a close similarity (possibly an ISOMORPHISM) between the structure of a formal (ideal) language and the real structure of the world. (**f**) Relations are externally real.

The major discussions of logical atomism center around concepts such as "fact," "atomic and molecular propositions," "simples," "properties," "relations," "thing," "object versus sense data," "the construction of logical and linguistic meanings." See ANALYTIC PHILOSOPHY.

atomistic psychology. The attempt to explain mental phenomena and all experiences by reference to the combining and recombining of minute, indivisible, irreducible, successive occurrences of unchangeable items variously called: psychological atoms, logical atoms, impressions, sensations, sense data, atomic facts. Whatever they are called, they are viewed as distinct and unique mental entities, separable and existing independently, needing nothing else to explain or support their presence. Compare with ASSOCIATIONISM.

attribute (L., *attribuere,* from *ad,* "upon," and *tribuere,* "to assign," "to bestow," "to bestow upon"). **1.** A characteristic or PROPERTY of a thing. Attributes are linguistically expressed as adjectives or as an adjectival clause or phrase. (Substances, or things which are said to have attributes, are expressed as nouns.) Examples: sweetness is an attribute of honey; goodness is an attribute of God; thinking is an attribute of a human. **2.** In logic, attribute is used synonymously with PREDICATE—that which is asserted or denied about the subject of a categorical proposition. Example: "The chair is brown." "Brown" is an attribute of "chair"—the predicate of the sentence with "chair" as its subject. **3.** In metaphysics, attributes may be classified as essential, necessary, accidental, or contingent. See ACCIDENTAL ATTRIBUTE; QUALITY.

autarkeia. Sometimes *autarkia.* Greek "self-sufficiency," "individualism," or "autonomy," which was thought to be the principal characteristic of happiness and the virtuous man in Greek ethical systems. In Aristotle, *autarkeia* is essential to EUDAIMONIA, self-realization, and the contemplative life. In stoicism, *autarkeia* refers to the state of nondependence upon another for the satisfaction of physical and emotional needs. See STOICS, THE.

authoritarianism. The view that advocates unwavering obedience to some authority as the true source of knowledge (or political belief) that is beyond questioning, as opposed to the individual pursuit of knowledge or the free spirit of inquiry.

authority (L., *auctor,* "originator," "leader," "head"). An individual or group considered to have valid knowledge and/or legitimate power. **1.** In its positive sense, authority is accepted for the benefits derived that could not be derived, or as easily derived, from any other source, especially under the social and personal limitations under which people must necessarily exist. **2.** In its negative sense, authority is regarded as oppressive and an illegitimate exercise of knowledge and power.

autocracy (Gk., *autos,* "same," "self," and *kratos,* "strength"). A form of rule in which one individual has absolute, supreme control of a people.

automatism (Gk., *automatos,* "self-moving"). The view that all living things are machines (automata) explainable by the mechanistic descriptions given by sciences such as physics, chemistry, and physiology.

autonomy (Gk., *autos,* "self," and *nemein,* "to hold away," "to assign"). **1.** The power of self-regulation. **2.** The act of self-governing, self-determining, self-directing. **3.** Independence from the will of others. **4.** The right to follow one's own volitions. An "autonomous self" is one that functions in an integrated way (as opposed to responding randomly and inconsistently to stimuli as they arrive), choosing and directing activities relevant to its own needs. "Moral autonomy" is the freedom to reach one's own moral values about right and wrong.

awareness. The conscious act of attention to what is being experienced. Awareness may refer (**a**) to the attention given to the content of a sensation or experienced object, or (**b**) to the attention given to the act of attending itself. The former is synonymous with CONSCIOUSNESS and the latter with one of the meanings of SELF-CONSCIOUSNESS (SELF-AWARENESS).

axiology (Gk., *axios,* "worthy," and *logos,* "the study of"). The analysis of values to determine their meaning, characteristics, origins, types, criteria, and epistemological status.

axiom (Gk., *axioma,* "that which is thought to be worthy"). **1.** The most basic and necessary self-evident (or assumed) truth upon which a logical or mathematical system is built and which cannot be denied without destroying the consistency of the system. **2.** A fundamental statement that cannot be deduced from other statements and is the primitive beginning point from which other statements can be inferred. Axioms are not regarded as "provable" in the same sense as those statements deduced from them are provable. Their "proof" is related to the extent to which they can be used to construct a coherent and inclusive system. See ASSUMPTION.

B

Baconian method. A method proposed by Francis Bacon of obtaining knowledge of natural phenomena by induction that stressed (**a**) the importance of drawing inferences from an examination of particular, concrete facts to generalizations about these facts, and (**b**) the necessity of testing hypotheses by means of observations and experiments. The goal of Bacon's scientific, inductive methodology was to control, manipulate, and use natural phenomena for the benefit of man. The purpose of knowledge for Bacon may be summed up in the phrase "Knowledge is power." See IDOLS (BACON); TABLES OF INVESTIGATION, THE THREE (BACON).

bad faith (Sartre). 1. Self-deception, especially the act of not admitting that one has freedom of choice (authentic choices) or not allowing oneself to see possible choices, and thereby avoiding responsibilities and the anxieties of decision-making. See EN SOI (SARTRE); POUR SOI (SARTRE). **2.** Lack of self-acceptance, especially the act of not admitting—or deceiving oneself about—what is true about oneself. **3.** Lack of self-assurance or self-esteem that prevents one from acting *upon* existence and provides the conditions for acting as a thing *in* existence.

beauty (L., *bellus,* "pretty"). **1.** That which is pleasing. **2.** That quality or group of qualities which pleases a sense organ such as the eye or the ear, and/or pleases the intellect by proportion, unity, variety, symmetry, simplicity, grace, fitness, suggestiveness, intricacy, perfection, or excellence. **3.** The quality or property of a thing that produces aesthetic pleasure or satisfaction. Comprises one of the triad of ideals—Truth, Goodness,

Beauty—with which classical philosophy has been especially concerned. Beauty has been viewed (**a**) as a formal property or quality inherent in the object itself that exists independently whether or not it is perceived (OBJECTIVISM [VALUE THEORY]), (**b**) as a name for the subjective emotional response the viewer has to the object viewed (SUBJECTIVISM [VALUE THEORY]), (**c**) as a simple, indefinable, unanalyzable quality (such as "good," "yellow") whose presence is intuited or directly apprehended and which cannot be empirically verified by scientific tests.

In the view of Plato and the Neo-Platonists such as Plotinus, (1) the soul strives toward possession and understanding of beauty. Beauty was regarded (as were truth, love, goodness, justice, and so on) as one of the active forces in the universe, an aspect of the ideal and spiritual powers propelling all reality. (2) The degree to which the property of beauty is present in an object determines the degree to which that object is beautiful. (3) To the degree to which an object imitates (partakes of) the ideal perfect unchanging form of Beauty, to that degree it is beautiful.

Beauty arouses joy, cheerfulness, happiness, affinity, attraction, and is contrasted with the SUBLIME, which arouses feelings of amazement, awe, and with the ugly (see UGLY, PARADOY OF THE), which arouses disgust, antipathy. In some philosophies the three are mutually exclusive, in others they can exist together and/or all can be pleasurable.

becoming. 1. The act of changing from one form of existence to another. (Mere change of position or of motion is not considered becoming.) **2.** That kind of change actualizing the potentiality of something toward being something other than it once was, in a process of realizing its goal, purpose, or end. **3.** In Plato and the Platonists, becoming refers to ordinary sensuous experience and the mundane world in which things come and go, in contrast to the true BEING of the unchanging, eternal Ideas or Forms. Contrast with IDEAS (PLATO).

begging the question. See FALLACY, TYPES OF INFORMAL (**13**); *PETITIO PRINCIPII.*

behaviorism. A type of reductive materialism that attempts to explain all consciousness in terms of overt behavior responses and/or covert dispositional states and excludes any reference to mental states. Opposed to the subjectivism of introspection (and introspective psychology) as a source of knowledge about something called consciousness. Radical or metaphysical behaviorists believe that there are no inner private mental states distinct from behavior of some sort. (Some *radical behaviorists* enlarge the meaning of behavior to include neurological processes.) Mental-concept words such as "choosing," "deciding," "intending," "willing" do not stand for mental events or states. They are explainable in terms of either (**a**) the occurrence of publicly observable behavior, or (**b**) dispositional behavior (tendencies) for publicly observable events to occur. For example, thinking is explained in terms of subvocal speech, laryngeal movements, muscular contractions, skin and eye responses, etc. Emotions are explained in terms of visceral reactions. Language and speech are complex stimuli-response systems, and provide no ground for inferring unobservable mental states. *Methodological behaviorists* believe that mental states do (or might possibly) exist, but they cannot be of any scientific interest—they cannot be objectively examined, predicted, verified, confirmed, or quantified. *Epiphenomenalistic behaviorists* believe that nonbehavioral mental states do exist but have no causal influence upon human behavior. See MIND, TYPES OF THEORIES OF (8); and entries under PSYCHOLOGY.

being. Contrasted with NONBEING, VOID, and with BECOMING. **1.** Existing. **2.** Whatever exists as the subject of distinctions or the object of a language. **3.** All that is. The totality of existence. Being in this all-inclusive sense is not a GENUS. We can generalize about any and all particular beings (bodies, objects, actions) but not about the "everything-that-is." **4.** That which is regarded as the most fundamental reality. Being was thought by the early Greek philosopher Parmenides to be that which is eternal, one, all-inclusive, and unchanging. Parmenides' famous passage from which this was inferred: "That which is, is; and that which is not, is not and can never be." The things we perceive are many, transient, varied, changing, and therefore cannot be called true Being. This Parmenidian use of the word implies the distinction between a true realm (reality) and one of illusion (appearance). Being came to refer to that existence behind or above phenomena as their cause, or as that in which they inhere. In this sense Being is used synonymously with ultimate reality, substance, prime matter, God, the infinite reality, the Absolute, the One, etc. When used in this way, the reference is not to any particular being (existing thing) but to Pure Being, Being-in-itself, Being-*qua*-Being (Being-as-Being). The essence of such a Being is to exist necessarily; its essence is existence and its existence is its essence (expressed by the Latin phrase *esse ipsum subsistens*). **5.** In Plato and the Platonists, Being (the world of Being) refers to the heavenly realm of the perfect, unchanging, and eternal Ideas (Forms), in contrast to BECOMING (the illusory world of becoming or of sensations) in which things are in constant flux and change. Contrast with NONBEING (PLATO).

being, hierarchy of. The view that there are gradations of reality, or a scale of beings. Example: nonliving things, plants, living things, rational beings, angels, God. Some frequent assumptions: **(a)** There is a division between the visible (tangible, material) world and the invisible (intangible, immaterial) world. **(b)** The latter is more spiritual and hence superior. **(c)** The more self-sufficiency and reason a thing possesses, the higher it is on the scale. **(d)** The most self-sufficient, rational, and superior being is the infinite immaterial substance called God. **(e)** All things emanate in hierarchical succession from this God of which all things are a part. **(f)** The further away from this source of being a thing is the more it is composed of matter and the more evil it contains. See EMANATION.

being-as-such. Sometimes *being-qua-being, being-as-being, pure being, being-in-itself.* **1.** What existence would be like in itself, apart from human consciousness. **2.** That which possesses universal characteristics that belong to everything in existence and not only to a finite number of individual objects. See EXISTENCE. **3.** That which is the ground for the existence and the explanation of all things.

belief. 1. A state of mind in which confidence, trust, faith is placed in a person, idea, or thing. **2.** A conviction or feeling that something is real or true. **3.** Intellectual assent to an idea. **4.** That which is asserted or contained in an idea.

Belief may stem from an immediate, nonreasoned acceptance of an idea (a feeling, a hunch, a want) or from a deliberately thought-out argument. Compare with CERTAINTY, PSYCHOLOGICAL OR INTUITIVE; DOGMA; FAITH; OPINION.

best, principle of the. A common Platonic notion that (**a**) all things have an inner tendency to strive for their good—for the best that is possible for them, (**b**) no human who knows his good (or the good) would choose an evil, and/or (**c**) everything in the universe is rationally arranged for the best. Related to Socrates' belief that **1.** humans always choose what they regard to be the best or good (and do not ever choose what they regard to be bad or evil) and **2.** evil is due to ignorance of what is good. See SOCRATIC PARADOXES.

best of all possible worlds, the (Leibniz). The world as it exists could not possibly be better than it is since God's perfect wisdom, goodness, and omnipotence necessitate Him to create the best of all the worlds possible to create. See COMPOSSIBLES (LEIBNIZ); REASON, PRINCIPLE OF SUFFICIENT (LEIBNIZ).

best of all possible worlds, the (Stoics). Since the universe is rationally necessitated (fated) by the *LOGOS* then it is good and hence the best possible. See STOICS, THE.

bioethics. The study of the ethical problems that arise from the interrelationship between medical/biological research and technological advances on the one hand and the rights and the future of humans on the other. Examples of specific problems: euthanasia, abortion, eugenics, genetic manipulation, cloning, genetic screening, genetic therapy, fetal research, exogenesis (developing an embryo outside the mother's womb), brain control.

black-and-white thinking. 1. Thinking that is expressed in rigid extremes (polarities, contrasts) without qualifications and without sensitivity to the subtleties of the issues. **2.** Thinking that infers that because something is true it is extreme or something contrary to it must be false (or vice versa). Compare with FALLACY, TYPES OF INFORMAL (**1**).

body. Sometimes *material body*. **1.** Used synonymously with MATERIAL OB-
JECT, or MATTER. Example: A body in motion will remain in motion. **2.**
Often designates the material composition of the human (or animal) in
contrast with the mind, spirit, or soul. See entries under MIND.

bracketing (Husserl). The suspension ("bracketing off") of the presuppositions and abstractions implicit in the sciences, such as "matter-of-fact,"
"physical cause/effect relationship," "material object." By purifying
one's perspective in this way, one is able to see things as they actually appear to consciousness. The aim of philosophy is to describe, classify, and
intuitively grasp the variety of kinds of experience and consciousnesses in
their purest subjective state and in their concrete operations. See PHE-
NOMENOLOGY (HUSSERL).

bundle theory of the mind or self. See MIND, BUNDLE THEORY OF THE
(HUME).

C

calculus (L., *calculi,* "piles or rows of stones, pebbles," that stood for numbers and were manipulated to produce arithmetical results). **1.** Any formal system for solving logical problems. Inferences are drawn with the use of symbols, rules of inference, and methods of logical procedure. Used as a synonym for logic (as in sentential [propositional] calculus, predicate [functional] calculus). **2.** The principles regulating **(a)** the quantification of something (as in HEDONISTIC CALCULUS [BENTHAM]) or **(b)** the procedures and definitions to be followed in determining the application of concepts (as in the calculus of classes, the calculus of probability).

canon (Gk., *kanōn,* a rule such as used by carpenters to set a straight line or to measure by; a rod [shuttle] such as used in weaving.) A basic and important rule (principle, standard, criterion) to which logical and scientific methods must adhere. Example: John Stuart Mill's Five Canons of Induction. See METHODS, MILL'S INDUCTIVE.

capacity. The potential for a thing to do something, to act or react. In humans, capacities may be innate or acquired through conditioning. In ethics, what a person is able (has the capacity) to do in relation to what he ought to do. For example, the moral command not to steal has meaning only for one who is not a kleptomaniac and thus has the ability (capacity) not to steal. See DISPOSITION.

cardinal virtues. See VIRTUES, CARDINAL.

carnal (L., *carnalis,* from *caro, carnis,* "flesh"). **1.** Animalistic. **2.** That which has to do with the body as the source of cravings, appetites, desires, sensuality, sexuality, lust, indulgence. **3.** Material, worldly, hence temporal, transitory, and valueless. Contrast with SPIRITUAL.

Cartesianism. Those philosophies that existed for about a century after Descartes' death which used his major philosophic assumptions and methodology to develop their own systems. (They did not necessarily adhere to every detail of Descartes' philosophy but did retain his rationalistic and mathematical/geometric method.) Descartes' main aim was to reconstruct the whole of human knowledge by means of a rational, deductive (basically geometric) system. See *COGITO ERGO SUM.* The Cartesians also attempted to construct one all-inclusive science, which would explain all natural phenomena (biological, chemical, physical, psychological) in terms of common quantitative and mathematical laws. See VORTEX THEORY (DESCARTES).

casualism. The belief that all things happen by chance. Compare with ACCIDENTALISM; TYCHISM.

casuistry. 1. In the positive sense, (a) the art (science, ideology, doctrine) that deals with questions of right or wrong conduct, or (b) the actual application of moral principles to particular conduct. 2. In the negative sense, sophistical, equivocal, false, or misleading reasoning or teaching about one's moral conduct, duties, and principles. See ETHICS, CASUISTIC.

categorical. 1. Not hypothetical. 2. Unconditional. 3. Without qualification or exception. 4. Definite. 5. Obligatory; not conditional-on-a-wish. 6. Refers to the *names* of the categories of classification and/or the categories themselves that are being classified. See entries under CATEGORIES; CATEGORY.

categorical imperative, the (Kant). The necessary and absolute moral law believed to be the ultimate rational foundation for all moral conduct: "So act that you can will the maxim [principle] of your action to be a universal law binding upon the will of every other rational person." The categorical imperative is not conditional (hypothetical) based on a wish or consequences, as in "If you wish to have healthy gums, take vitamin C." It is absolutely binding. Compare with HYPOTHETICAL IMPERATIVE (KANT). See DUTY; ETHICS (KANT).

categories (Aristotle). 1. All things that can be conceived and named are subsumed under one or more of the following ten classes or genera: *substance (ousia),* e.g., man, animal, plant; *quantity (poson),* e.g., 175 lbs.; *quality (poion),* e.g., good, hot, brown; *relation (prosti),* e.g., dependent upon farming; *place (pou),* e.g., in the country; *time (pote),* e.g., 1978; *position, condition,* or *state (keisthai),* e.g., standing, being drunk; *possession (echein),* e.g., having hair; *action, activity (poiein),* e.g., plowing; *passion, passivity,* or *being affected (paschein),* e.g., becoming thirsty. The categories and their number vary slightly in Aristotle's writings. Substance (see SUBSTANCE [ARISTOTLE]) is the most important of them and Aristotle has much to say about how the other categories are related to it. Nothing is intelligible unless put into the framework of these categories. Our understanding of things is formed by the categories. And things themselves are formed by the forces acting in nature which operate according to these categories. **2.** In Aristotle's *Metaphysics,* there is a presentation of what might be called "metacategories," or the concepts which pervade and are common to all the categories as such. These are: "being" (existence), "oneness" (unity), "sameness" (identity), and "otherness" (variety). See TRANSCENDENTALIA.

categories (Plato). A number of categories are scattered throughout Plato's works, but five basic ones are listed in his *Sophist:* Being, rest, motion, identity, and difference. Plato laid the foundation for philosophizing in terms of categories.

categories of logic, the (Kant). The categories of logic, also called The Logical Table of Judgments, are grouped in the following way:

I.	II.
QUANTITY	QUALITY
1. Universal	1. Affirmative
2. Particular	2. Negative
3. Singular	3. Infinite

III.	IV.
RELATION	MODALITY
1. Categorical	1. Problematical
2. Hypothetical	2. Assertorical
3. Disjunctive	3. Apodeictical

The study of these twelve categories was the subject matter of what Kant called Transcendental Logic from which he deduced the categories of the understanding. See CATEGORIES OF THE UNDERSTANDING, THE (KANT); DIALECTIC, TRANSCENDENTAL (KANT).

categories of the understanding, the (Kant). The categories of the understanding are pure *a priori* concepts or principles that provide the necessary structure for the understanding to perceive and conceive what is given to it in experience. The Table of Categories, also called The Transcendental Table of the Pure Concepts of the Understanding, is grouped in the following way:

I.	II.
QUANTITY	QUALITY
1. Unity (the Measure)	1. Reality
2. Plurality (the Quantity)	2. Negation
3. Totality (the Whole)	3. Limitation

III.	IV.
RELATION	MODALITY

1. Substance/Subsistence
   (Inherence)

2. Causality/Dependence

3. Community/Interaction
   (Reciprocity)

1. Possibility/Impossibility

2. Existence/Nonexistence
   (Being/Nonbeing)

3. Necessity/Contingency

Some of the basic tenets in Kant's philosophy of the twelve categories:
(a) They are necessary conditions for any experience—without them
there can be no experience, no knowledge. All experience and knowledge
presuppose them. (b) They are a complete list of the forms of our understanding. (They are the only ways by which things can be experienced
and made meaningful.) (c) They do not describe or classify reality as it is
in itself. (We can never know the noumenal realm/world and thus (1)
can never know its intrinsic structure, and (2) can never apply these categories to it. These categories refer only to the phenomenal realm/world.)
(d) They are *applied* to (projected upon, imposed upon) the raw material
provided in experience but are not and cannot be obtained from experience. They transcend experience. See APPERCEPTION, TRANSCENDENTAL
(2); DEDUCTION, TRANSCENDENTAL; SUBSTANCE (KANT).

category (Gk., *kata,* "down," and *aporeuein,* "to assert"). **1.** A class, division, genus, family, or type with which distinctions are made among
things for conceptual analysis and classification. **2.** A class of things
which has a predicate or to which some term can be applied. **3.** Any basic
idea, concept, notion, or principle fundamental to a system of philosophy.
4. One of the ultimate conceptual forms by which knowledge is made
possible and which is a unique class in the following senses: (a) It may be
found in conjunction with other categories (classes, forms) but cannot be
described by them or reduced to them since it has nothing in common
with any other category (except metalinguistically). (b) It cannot be regarded as a member of any other higher class (except as a member of the
all-inclusive class of ultimate being or substance). (c) It gives form to the
content of our knowledge but does not itself provide that content. (d) It
serves as the foundation for all meaningful communication in subject-
predicate languages.

category mistake. The improper semantical grouping of .nrelatable classes
of meaning which results in some form of ABSURD (meaningless, ridicu-
lous, nonsensical "sound without sense") statement; no literal or meaningful translation of the resulting statement is possible which can avoid
the absurdity. Example: "The redness of time hits until it sleeps." This
sentence is syntactically (grammatically) but not semantically legitimate
due to category mistakes.

catharsis. See *KATHARSIS*.

causal chain. Sometimes *causal sequence, causal series*. The view that the cause-effect relationship is a time sequence where the effect produced becomes the cause of an effect, which in turn becomes a cause of an effect, and so on; also a reverse sequence in which a cause is an effect of a previous cause which in turn was an effect of a previous cause, and so on.

causal principle. Also *principle of universal causation* or *principle of causation*. The theory that every event has a cause. (Causes may not be known for specific events, but nevertheless if it is an event, it has a cause.)

causal regress, infinite. The view that the causal series of events leading into the past has no absolute Beginning Point; a cause can always be found for an event and these events extend backwards infinitely. There is no First Cause. The principal concepts involved in this view: (a) Any two causes, regardless of how far apart they are, are only a finite distance apart. (b) No two causal events are an infinite distance apart, but the series itself is infinite. (c) For any distance that can be designated between two causes, there will be an even greater distance that can be designated in the infinite series of causes. (d) No matter how far away that cause is which is pointed out in the regress, there will be an infinite number of other causes before it.

causal uniformity, the principle of. 1. The theory that similar causes produce similar effects and similar effects have similar causes. Commonly phrased: "same cause, same effect; same effect, same cause." Contrasted with CAUSES, PRINCIPLE OF THE PLURALITY OF. **2.** The theory that cause and effect relations can be stated in the form of general laws which assume that to some extent what happens in the future will be similar to what happened in the past. See UNIFORMITY OF NATURE, PRINCIPLE OF THE. Contrast with CAUSES, PRINCIPLE OF THE PLURALITY OF.

causa sui (L., "cause of itself," "self-caused"). **1.** The term has been applied to God to refer to His ability to cause Himself, to bring Himself into existence. The question "Where did God come from?" has been answered by saying that He is *causa sui,* his own cause. Aquinas argues against self-causation in the following way: God cannot cause Himself. If He existed to cause Himself, He did not need to cause Himself (since He already exists). And if He did not exist He could not be anything to be able to cause Himself. *Causa sui* is a contradiction in terms. **2.** *Causa sui* has erroneously been used to refer to concepts such as "self-activating," "self-existence," "necessary being," "absolute nondependence," "that which proceeds independently on its own and out of its own essence." It has also been confused with "eternal," "timeless," and "uncaused."

cause. 1. Anything capable of changing something else. **2.** That which "produces" something ("makes" something happen; "brings about" the occurrence of something) without which that thing would not have resulted. That which is produced (or changed) is called the effect and the effect is explained by its cause. **3.** Those conditions each of which is necessary for the occurrence of an event, and all of which are sufficient for its occurrence, and which precede the event in time. (A cause of an event may be thought of as the name for a multitude of relevant conditions none of which, exclusive of the others, can be called *the* cause.) **4.** When X occurs and Y invariably follows, then X is said to be the cause of Y (and Y the effect of X). **5.** The sufficient condition(s) for the occurrence of an event. See REASONS.

cause, efficient. See CAUSES, ARISTOTLE'S FOUR.

cause, final. See CAUSES, ARISTOTLE'S FOUR.

cause, formal. See CAUSES, ARISTOTLE'S FOUR.

cause, immanent. The internal conditions in a thing that produce change, as opposed to external conditions affecting it. Example: the act of willing to move one's hand and thereby "causing" it to move. Contrasted with CAUSE, TRANSCENDENT.

cause, material. See CAUSES, ARISTOTLE'S FOUR.

cause, transcendent. The external conditions that produce change upon, or in, a thing, as opposed to internal conditions affecting it. Example: water causing a seed to open. In this sense used interchangeably with efficient cause. Contrasted with CAUSE, IMMANENT.

cause and effect relationship. Three fundamental concepts are inherent in the definition of the cause and effect relationship: **(a)** Temporal precedence. The cause always occurs prior in time to its effect. Cause and effect cannot occur simultaneously. A cause cannot follow its effect. **(b)** The word "cause" is meaningful only when related to the word "effect" (and vice versa); that is, "to be a cause" or "to have a cause" can only be understood in the context of a related or relatable effect (and vice versa). **(c)** Cause and effect are related in an invariable sequence (succession, regularity, conjunction) in which whenever one occurs and the other always follows, then the former is labeled a "cause" and the latter its "effect."

cause and effect relationship (Hume). Prior to Hume the following notions were generally assumed about the concept of causality: **(a)** *Regularity of succession:* To say that C is the cause of E is to say that whenever C happens then E happens, or that any instance of C is always followed by an instance of E. (Hume's term for this invariable sequence of cause and effect was "constant conjunction.") **(b)** *Temporal precedence:* The cause precedes the effect. And **(c)** *Necessary connection* (which is the notion Hume rejected): there is a power, or force in C which *must make E* occur. A bond or tie was thought to exist that cemented a cause to its effect. The regularity of succession of C and E is due to a physical and logical necessity compelling the cause to produce the effect. Some of Hume's criticisms of necessary connection: (1) Necessity cannot be observed to exist between a cause and its effect. No power, force can be shown "making," "producing," "influencing" the effect. All that is observed is the constant conjunction (regular succession) of *C* followed by *E*. We can observe the fact of one thing being followed by another, but not any necessary connection purportedly existing between these facts. (2) No sensation (impression) exists from which our idea of such a power in the cause necessitating the effect can be derived. There is no sensation of any bond or tie necessarily connecting the cause with its effect. Events are conjoined but not connected. (3) One cannot infer an effect simply from observing or analyzing that event which is considered a cause. One cannot infer a cause simply from observing or analyzing another event which is considered an effect. Only our experience of what constant conjunction does take place gives us this notion of what causes are related to what effects. Necessary connection is a product of habits of the mind and has no external reality. People become familiar with constantly conjoined events and formulate a belief based on past experience. (4) Statements about causal connections cannot be logically necessary statements or truths. The idea of a cause can be clearly distinguished from the idea of its effect without contradiction. If they were necessarily connected this could not be done—the thought of one would automatically entail (necessitate) the other. It is possible to imagine a cause not being followed by the expected effect. It is as well possible to imagine some effect that in our experience did not follow a particular cause. (There is no logical contradiction in saying that when I let go of this pencil it will float in midair rather than fall to the floor; no amount of experience will ever be amassed to prove that its floating in midair cannot happen.) No real, objective, inductive grounds can be given for inferences from causes to effects. (Kant attempted a resolution of what he saw as problems in Hume's account of causality by making causality one of his CATEGORIES OF THE UNDERSTANDING.) See KNOWLEDGE (HUME); SKEPTICISM (HUME).

causes, Aristotle's four. 1. *Material cause:* the substrate, substance *out of which* a thing comes to be and which persists; that *in which* a change takes place. 2. *Formal cause:* that shape (pattern, configuration) *into which* something is changed. The essence (the essential characteristic) being manifested in the process of becoming. 3. *Efficient cause:* that *by which* some change is brought about; that which initiates activity. (The efficient cause is often referred to as the *propelling cause.*) 4. *Final cause:* that *for the sake of which* an activity takes place; that end (purpose, goal, state of completion) *for which* the change is produced, or for which the change aims (strives, seeks). Its *telos* or *raison dêtre.* (The final cause is often referred to as the *telic cause.*) These four causes answer the question of *why* and *how* a thing becomes what it becomes rather than becoming something else. Taken together they may be called *teleological causation.* For Aristotle, we understand a thing if we know four things about it: **(a)** what it is *made of* (material cause), **(b)** its *form* (formal cause which is taking shape or being expressed), (c) what (or who) *produced* (made) it (efficient cause), and (d) its *final state* (end, goal, purpose, state of completion) toward which the activity is progressing, toward which the change is striving. These four causes operate both in art (*TECHNĒ:* all those things created by humans) and in nature (*PHYSIS:* all things not created by humans). An artist makes the head of Zeus out of marble. The material cause is marble. The formal cause is the form of Zeus taking shape in the marble; this is in the artist's mind as an idea which he is impressing upon the marble. The efficient cause is the force of the hammer and chisel applied over a period of time by the artist. The final cause is that end product, the completed art work, for the accomplishment of which the whole process is taking place. In artistic creation, Aristotle's four causes have a transcendent teleological character. The artist is separate from (transcends) his medium. He gives a thought objective reality in a physical medium. In natural creation, Aristotle's four causes have an immanent teleological character. The form being developed is inseparably linked with its matter. The reason for an object's developing the way it does is an integral part of the thing itself. Examples are an acorn developing into an oak tree or a fetus developing into a child. The material cause is the material stuff of which the acorn or fetus is made. The efficient cause in the case of the acorn is the rain, sun, soil, temperature, wind; in the case of the fetus, the complex biochemical changes in the mother's womb affecting the fetus. The formal cause for the acorn is the seed's own character to become an oak tree rather than a maple tree, or a piglet; and for the fetus the formal cause is the pattern by which the fetus is developing toward maturing into a child. The final cause is the point of actualization of the process where what was striven for is reached. Aristotle's four causes assumed (1) a continuity and interdependence among all phenomena and (2) a hierarchical gradation in nature from inert matter receiving qualitative and quantitative change; to plants, which have the functions of nourishment and reproduction; to animals, which in addition possess sensation, mobility, and many types of mental functions; to the human being, who in addition possesses the supreme function of reason. Aristotle's word for cause (*AITIA*) meant "the reason for something happening." It denoted all the ways to describe in a language (the Greek language) how things come to be the way they are; how they develop from a beginning process to a completed state, potentiality to actuality. But for Aristotle, these four causes were not merely linguistic tools for talking about phenomena; they were actual operating principles in the universe to produce what is in existence. See CHANGE (ARISTOTLE); EXPLANATION, TELEOLOGICAL.

causes, principle of the plurality of. The view that the same effect can be produced by different causes. Examples: Death may be caused by drowning, a heart attack, a hit on the head. A sneeze may be caused by pollen,

by an itch, by a cold. Contrasted with CAUSAL UNIFORMITY, THE PRINCI-
PLE OF.

Sometimes includes the view that the same cause can at different times
produce different effects.

certain (L., *cernere,* "to perceive, decide, determine, resolve"). **1.** INDUBITA-
BLE. **2.** Thoroughly established as unquestionably true. There are no degrees of certainty as there are for notions such as clarity, CONFIRMATION,
reliability. A thing may be certain but not necessarily self-evident or tau-
tologically true. That which is certain is known, but that which is known
need not be certain. Contrast with DOUBT.

certainty, psychological or intuitive. The feeling of assurance (certitude)
that something is true and undeniable. Related to mental states or attitudes such as: acceptance, belief, trust, certitude, dependability, reliability, unquestionability, indisputable, fixed, settled. Example: The certainty that is associated with our belief that the sun will rise tomorrow
morning, or that we exist. Opposite to SKEPTICISM; DOUBT. Compare with
BELIEF.

chance (L., *cadere,* "to fall," as in the falling of the dice). In general, to
come to pass, to happen without design, intention, or purposiveness and
without expectation or prediction. The word *chance* has been understood
in a variety of contexts: **1.** Ignorance of the causes producing an event; a
chance event is an event whose cause is unknown. **2.** Not directed by intelligent foresight. **3.** The coming together of unexpected, unpredictable,
unintentional, and independent series (coincidences) of causes. Such
events are not physically necessitated nor are they determinable by the
mind. (Chance precludes necessity [and design]; what occurs by chance
cannot occur by necessity [or by design].) **4.** Lawless: no law can explain
it. (Although chance can be understood by laws of PROBABILITY.) **5.** Uncaused events. (This is an erroneous use.) See *TYCHĒ.* Compare with AC-
CIDENTALISM; RANDOM; TYCHISM.

change (L., *cambiare,* "to exchange or barter"). Involves—in lessening degrees of essentiality—the concepts of (**a**) succession (time); (**b**) an identity
which is involved in a change, or something that can be identified which
remains relatively the same within a changing state; (**c**) some degree of
variation or alteration of this identity (becoming different in some respects from what it once was); (**d**) often a direction or growth.

change (Aristotle). Aristotle used the word *KINĒSIS* to include any kind of
change or movement (motion). Aristotle discusses change in a rich variety of ways: **1.** Change (motion) is eternal (a tenet which all Greek philosophers except the Eleatics, who denied change, accepted as necessary
and indubitable). The essence of time is such that it excludes the possibility of a time—a state—without change. There could never have been a
time at which there was no time; hence there could never have been a
time without change (motion). **2.** All physical change requires these es-

sential elements: (**a**) *matter* (a substrate, substance): that which continues throughout the change, or that which is changing; (**b**) *privation:* the absence or lack of a particular form; (**c**) the *form* which appears during (or throughout) the change. All physical change consists of matter developing (or acquiring) a form which it did not previously possess. (An alternate way of putting it: All physical change consists of a form developing in matter, where form was not previously present in the same way.) **3.** Change may be divided into types such as: (**a**) *Qualitative change:* (sometimes referred to as *alteration*). Changes of the characteristics (qualities, properties, attributes) of an object. Examples: a green leaf turning brown; iron rusting; a liquid changing color. (Sometimes referred to as *accidental change.*) In qualitative change, the substance (the identity, or the substantial nature) of the thing does not change. (**b**) *Spatial-temporal change* (sometimes referred to as *change of place,* or *locomotion*): Change of the positions of objects. (**c**) *Quantitative change:* Change of number of a thing. This includes (1) change of size and shape (alteration of a thing's boundaries), (2) increase or decrease of size, shape, or number (augmentation or diminution), and (3) increase or decrease of motion or movement. Example: the multiplication or growth of living cells. Usually quantitative change involves both spatial and qualitative change. (**d**) *Substantial change:* The development of a thing's form or identity. The activity of a potential (a nature, or form, or essence, or potency) becoming actualized, becoming an existent. Two general kinds of substantial change: (1) *Generation:* The coming-to-be of something; a thing's becoming what it is intended to be; and (2) *Degeneration:* The passing-away from its developed, actualized state; the process of losing or destroying that which the thing was intended to be. See GENESIS (ARISTOTLE); CAUSES, ARISTOTLE'S FOUR; MATTER/FORM (ARISTOTLE); and entries under SUBSTANCE that refer to Aristotle.

change (Cratylus). The Greek philosopher Cratylus (a younger contemporary of Socrates) took Heracleitus' view of change to the extreme. Heracleitus observed that everything is in constant change and no one can step into the same river twice. Cratylus extended this to say that no one can even step into the same river once because not only is the river changing to prevent us from stepping into the same river a second time but we are changing also during the time it takes us to attempt to step into the river that first time. See SKEPTICISM (CRATYLUS).

change (Heracleitus). The Greek philosopher Heracleitus of Ephesus was one of the first philosophers to use the concept of change as the foundation of his philosophy: Unending FLUX is the most fundamental characteristic of the universe. He is famous for sayings: "All things change (flow, separate, dissolve)." "Nothing remains the same." "You cannot step into the same river twice." Compare with *LOGOS* (HERACLEITUS).

chaos (Gk., *chaos,* "gap," "chasm," from *chainein,* "to gape"). **1.** The disorganized, confused, formless, and undifferentiated state of primal matter before the presence of order in the universe. **2.** That condition of the universe in which chance is the principal ruler. **3.** An uncontrolled state of affairs. **4.** In Greek philosophy, the universe as it was before rational principles (laws) manifested themselves throughout the universe and brought about the world order as it is now. Sometimes regarded as a principle itself which prevents order or demolishes order. Compare with COSMOS. See DEMIURGE.

character (Gk., *charaktēr,* from *charassein,* "to make sharp," "to engrave"; often the sign or token imprinted on something to indicate such things as ownership, origin, name, or brand). **1.** The name for the sum total of a person's traits, which includes such things as behavior, habits, likes, dislikes, capacities, dispositions, potential, values, and thought patterns. **2.** That relatively fixed structure or feature of a personality that causes such traits. **3.** That relatively fixed framework of a personality in accordance to which such traits manifest themselves.

characteristic, defining. That quality a thing must have in order to be defined (classified, named) as that thing. Example: The defining characteristic of *bachelor* is to be unmarried. See CLASS.

characteristic, distinguishing. Sometimes *differentiating characteristic.* The distinctive quality that marks off (differentiates, distinguishes) a thing from other things.

choice. The decision reached between (or among) alternative possibilities. Some characteristics of choices: **(a)** They cannot be classified as true or false, but are classified as good or bad, right or wrong, preferable or not preferable. **(b)** The choices one continues to make are said to habituate one's character toward them. **(c)** Choices reveal the essential traits of a personality. **(d)** Choices require awareness of alternatives, deliberation, and intentional activity. **(e)** Choices may be related to, but can be distinguished from: motives, intentions, wishes, desires, consequences, and principles of conduct.

choosing. The traditional meaning: A voluntary act preceded by deliberation. Conscious selection. The mental act that causes an action to take place, which action is (usually) the one preferred from among alternative courses of action. Choosing rationally or voluntarily, as opposed to choosing irrationally or involuntarily in a forced manner, involves characteristics such as: **(a)** An *inclination* (or necessity) to act (usually in the face of a problem). **(b)** *Deliberation* about the problem. **(c)** A *decision* to act. **(d)** The perception of *alternatives*—of more than one possibility of action. **(e)** The evaluation of the *consequences*—the weighing of the relative merits of the results which may follow each alternative. **(f)** A CHOICE as to how to act or procede. **(g)** The *action* engaged in. (Usually the one preferred among the alternatives.) **(h)** *Volition*—the deliberate concerted effort in and commitment to making the choice and the action a reality. **(i)** Sometimes: *Appraisal* of what has occurred. See VOLUNTARY ACTION; WILL.

circularity. Also *circular reasoning* or *arguing in a circle.* **1.** Applied to ideas (arguments, reasoning, definitions) that repeat themselves. **2.** Applied to arguments which assume the conclusion that is to be proven. See DEFINITIONS, TYPES OF (**1**); FALLACY, TYPES OF INFORMAL (**13**).

clairvoyance (Fr., *clair,* "clear," and *voyant,* "seeing"). **1.** The ability to obtain information about objects or people by means other than our five senses. This includes reading thoughts (see TELEPATHY). **2.** The ability to perceive or discern objects not perceptible by our ordinary sensory means of perceiving. Clairvoyance is considered a direct and immediate transfer of information by "nonsensory" and noninferential means. See PARAPSYCHOLOGY.

class. Any group (collection) of things possessing common characteristics (properties, qualities, attributes). The common characteristics of the class define the class; they are called the class-defining characteristics. These may be multiple and complex characteristics, or a singular and simple characteristic. *Students* names a class. It is the name given to a group of characteristics that we believe a "student" has: engaged in study, registered at school, going to classes, being tested, etc. The Latin *GENUS* is often used as a synonym. See SET.

class, complementary. That collection of all things that do not belong to a given class. Example: the complement of the class "students" is the class of all those things that are *not* students: trees, clouds, planets, houses, cars, roads, satellites, etc. It is customary to form a complementary class by prefixing its name with "non." The complement of the class "students" would be the class "nonstudents." "Nonstudents" may be called a complementary term, or the complement of "students."

class, singular. Sometimes *unit class* or *unique class.* A class with only one member.

classicism. An expression of a temperament, or the product of that temperament, that is based on a desire for order, harmony, proportion, moderation, and perfection derived from the application of reason and intelligence directing emotion and feeling. Contrasted with ROMANTICISM.

clear and distinct ideas. See IDEAS, CLEAR AND DISTINCT (DESCARTES).

cogito ergo sum (L., "I think, therefore I am" or "I am thinking, therefore I exist"). Descartes' phrase for an immediate, necessary, and indubitable intuition, in which he recognizes himself clearly and distinctly as a *RES COGITANS* (a thinking thing or self). He cannot doubt that he thinks (doubts), for in the very act of doubting he proves the act of thinking (doubting) to be true. *Cogito ergo sum* serves as the self-evident truth or axiom from which Descartes develops his rationalistic system of explanation. See SKEPTICISM (DESCARTES).

cognition (L., *cognitio,* from *cognoscere,* "to become acquainted with," "to know"). **1.** Intellectual knowledge. **2.** The act of knowing.

coherence (L., *cohaerere,* "to adhere together," "to stick together," "to be united"). **1.** Connection by some common idea (principle, relationship, order, concept). **2.** Following logically without any inconsistency or gaps. Logical congruity. Opposite to INCOHERENCE. Contrasted with INCOMPATIBLE. Compare with COMPATIBLE; CONSISTENT. See TRUTH, COHERENCE THEORY OF.

collectively. Considering the members of a CLASS (group, SET) as one unit. What can be said about a class collectively may not be true of all, or any, of the members of the class. Opposite to DISTRIBUTIVELY.

comedy (Aristotle). A play in which the actions of the main characters are worse than the actions of ordinary men in daily life. Compare with TRAGEDY (ARISTOTLE).

commitment (Sartre). The free choice of principles of conduct and a way of life, in spite of the lack of any good reasons for accepting them. Their only defense is allegiance to them, and action on their behalf. See EXISTENTIALISM.

common consent argument for God's existence. Also known as the *consensus gentium* argument. The attempt to prove the existence of God by appeal to the universally held belief in all cultures in all ages that there is a God (of some kind or other). The argument which holds that God exists on the grounds that there is universal consent (belief, assent, assurance) that He exists. See FALLACY, TYPES OF INFORMAL (**16**); GOD, ARGUMENTS FOR THE EXISTENCE OF.

common sense. 1. That which seems sensible (rational, correct) to men "of good perception and abilities." **2.** That power or faculty used to come to conclusions which others in "their right minds" would also come to. **3.** Everyday, ordinary, common understanding. **4.** The "natural" beliefs shared by "normal" individuals, "plain" individuals, or the general judgment of individuals. **5.** Those ideas necessarily employed in practical activity. **6.** A general trust in the senses and common knowledge which puts them beyond argumentation. Truths of common sense are directly perceived, and no proof is needed for their support.

commonsense beliefs, fundamental. The commonsense outlook upon the world is characterized by assumptions about reality such as: (**a**) An external world exists distinct from consciousness and would remain in existence even if there were no consciousness. (**b**) Minds similar to our own exist externally in bodies similar to our own. (**c**) We all have a personal identity or unity about us which endures through time. (**d**) Individuals can act in a self-determining way. (**e**) Order exists independently of consciousness. (**f**) Cause and effect exist as relationships in nature. (**g**) Things exist in time and space.

commonsense realism. See REALISM, COMMONSENSE.

compatible (L., *compati,* "to have compassion," from *com,* "with," and *pati,* "to bear," "to suffer"). **1.** Capable of coexisting in harmony. **2.**

Statements (meanings, ideas) that are capable of being related logically
and/or conceptually (a) without being inconsistent and/or (b) without
leading to an inconsistency. Opposite to INCOMPATIBLE. Compare with
COHERENCE.

complement (L., *complementum,* "that which fills up or completes," from
com, "with" and *plere,* "to fill"). See CLASS, COMPLEMENTARY.

composition, fallacy of. See FALLACY, TYPES OF INFORMAL (**15**).

compossibles (Leibniz). Things that (a) are not contradictory, (b) belong to a
possible world, and (c) can therefore at some time exist together. Physical
laws (and ultimately God) determine the actualized existence in time of
all such possible worlds. In Leibniz' theory of compossibles there is an infinity of possible combinations that will never exist, and has never existed; that is, an infinite number of possibilities or noncontradictions, that
will never be realized and yet are known by God's omniscience. See REA-
SON, PRINCIPLE OF SUFFICIENT (LEIBNIZ); BEST OF ALL POSSIBLE WORLDS,
THE (LEIBNIZ).

comprehension (L., *comprehendere,* "to grasp"). The act of UNDERSTAND-
ING (imagining, conceiving, apprehending) the meaning or intent of
something. Some of the ways in which this is achieved: (a) subsuming
particular items under general and abstract explanations or classes; (b)
applying general and abstract principles to particular cases; (c) inferring
possibilities and anticipating future events based upon past occurrences;
(d) deducing implications or conclusions from a series of statements; (e)
relating or ordering seemingly disparate experiences; (f) comparing the
unfamiliar (the relatively unknown) with the familiar (the known). Compare with APPREHENSION; PREHENSION.

compresence (L., prefix *com,* "with, together," and *presentare,* "to be present before one"). The presence of two or more things together in consciousness, a coexistence that is fundamental to the act of knowing.

compulsion (L., *compellere,* "to drive together," "to compel," from *com,*
"with," "together," and *pellere,* "to drive"). The act of being forced (co-
erced, necessitated, driven, influenced, irresistibly forced, constrained,
etc.) to do or to respond to something. An extreme form of compulsion is
not being able to do other than what one is doing—a situation without
choice. A less extreme form of compulsion is being *able* to do otherwise
but not possessing the freedom or opportunity to do so. Compulsions are
divided into *internal* compulsions: those originating within one's own psyche (examples: obsessions, desires to do or say something); and *external*
compulsions: those originating from outside forces (examples: political
coercion, being knocked down). See entries under FREEDOM; FREE WILL.
Compare with VOLUNTARY-INVOLUNTARY ACTIONS.

conation (L., *conari,* "to attempt," "to strive," "to struggle"). The Latin
conatus is often used for conation. The volitional (willing) aspect of consciousness. The tendencies, urges, or powers impelling effort toward ac-

tion, and specifically toward self-preservation. Sometimes used with reference to deliberate VOLUNTARY ACTION directed toward something desired. See WILL.

conceive (L., *concipere,* "to conceive," "to take," "to seize"). **1.** To grasp by the mind. **2.** To form a conception of. To imagine. **3.** To comprehend. To understand. **4.** To suppose. **5.** To plan out.

Sometimes contrasted with "imagine," which is included in the class of "conceive." "Imagine" suggests a pictorial understanding, whereas "conceive" also includes nonpictorial understanding of abstractions (for example, of infinity). See IMAGE, MENTAL; IMAGINATION.

concept (L., *concipere,* "to conceive"). **1.** A mental impression, a thought, a notion, an idea of any degree of concreteness or abstraction, used in abstract thinking. **2.** That which enables the mind to distinguish one thing from another. **3.** What is meant (or imaged) by the term used to designate it. **4.** Sometimes refers to the universals abstracted from particulars.

concepts, polar. See POLARITIES.

conceptualism. 1. The theory that universals (general abstract concepts or ideas) exist in particular things as their essence, and never exist separately from them, but the mind abstracts (conceptualizes) them out of particular things and creates symbols or names for them which are retained and related to each other in understanding as abstractions. (In this sense, conceptualism is a compromise between REALISM and NOMINALISM. **2.** The theory that universals are concepts (abstract entities) that exist only as products of the mind, but are more than mere names; that is, they are mind-dependent but common to minds regardless of the names or language used. See UNIVERSALS (CONCEPTUALISM).

conceptualization. Involves a combination of the following: (**a**) Knowing the meanings of what is to be understood (conceived) indicated by such things as using a symbol, or referring to the things correctly without ambiguity, ambivalence, imprecision, or vagueness; (**b**) having an image of the thing to be understood; (**c**) recognizing (identifying) the thing to be understood when confronted by it; (**d**) being able to bring the thing to be understood to consciousness as an abstraction and/or as an image; (**e**) being able to communicate some of its essential characteristics to others. Compare with COMPREHENSION.

conclusion (L., *concludere,* "to conclude," from *con,* "with," and *claudere,* "to shut"). **1.** A statement that has been inferred from other statements. **2.** That statement that is the logical consequence (implication) of the premises of an ARGUMENT. Often conclusions are indicated by words or symbols such as: ∴, "therefore," "thus," "it follows that," "for," "consequently," "implies," "this proves that," "this indicates that," "hence."

concomitant (L., *con,* "with," and *comitari,* "to accompany"). **1.** Accompanying or attending each other. **2.** Associated or conjoined with each other, usually indicating a temporal, spatial, or causal interrelationship of things. Used in phrases such as concomitant circumstances, concomitant variations, concomitant effects. See METHODS, MILL'S INDUCTIVE.

concrete (L., *concrescere,* "to grow together"). That which is real, vivid, known by direct experience, belonging to actual existence, and specific. The individual, the practical, the particular, as opposed to the general, the abstract, the IDEAL, the VAGUE.

concreteness, fallacy of misplaced. The phrase was coined by Alfred North Whitehead and referred to what he considered the fallacy of taking an abstract characteristic and dealing with it as if it were what reality was like in its concrete form. See PROCESS PHILOSOPHY; REIFICATION/ REISM.

concretion (L., *concrescere,* "to grow together," from *con,* "with," and *crescere,* "to grow," in the sense of "to unite into one being"). The bringing together or the developing together of a variety of elements or processes and thereby creating unities.

concretion, principle of (Whitehead). Alfred North Whitehead's phrase for *God:* that drive given to things, or which things possess, impelling them toward actualization of their form. The creative urge by which new unities grow together, emerge, and advance, producing greater interrelatedness. See PROCESS PHILOSOPHY.

concretism. See REIFICATION/REISM.

condition, necessary. 1. A condition X is necessary for condition Y, if whenever X does not occur then Y does not occur. Example: Oxygen is a necessary condition for the occurrence of fire; if oxygen is not present then there can be no fire. **2.** The condition in the absence of which a specific event cannot take place. **3.** That condition in the absence of which a thing could not have events happening to it. Example: That I exist may be considered a necessary condition for the occurrence of events happening to me such as feeling pain caused by a pin. Compare with CONDITION, SUFFICIENT; NECESSARY EXISTENCE.

condition, necessary and sufficient. The condition whereby E will occur if-and-only-if C occurs, and C will occur if-and-only-if E occurs.

condition, sufficient. 1. That condition in the presence of which an event occurs. Example: Rain is a sufficient condition (but not a necessary condition) for the street being wet. **2.** That condition in the presence of which a thing exists (or subsists). Example: The presence of a combustible material, heat, and oxygen in proper combinations is the sufficient condition for the existence of fire. Compare with CONDITION, NECESSARY.

conditional (L., *conditio,* "agreement, condition"). **1.** Dependent on a state of affairs (condition) without which it will not take place. Found in phrases such as "a conditional wish," "conditional promise." **2.** Implying or expressing a supposition. **3.** A compound sentence of the form "If . . . then."

conditional, counterfactual. Sometimes *contrafactual,* or *contrary-to-fact conditional.* Conditional statements that have the form: "If event p had occurred, then event *q* would have occurred." Example: "If the train had come by two minutes earlier, I would have been killed." The antecedents of counterfactuals (**a**) are meant to be false (and cannot help but be false), (**b**) refer to a state of affairs that would have been true, if certain conditions had been obtained, and (**c**) in some way or other are intended as true statements even though they are not in *fact* true. Most counterfactuals are expressed in the subjunctive mood and are used for expressing disposition-type statements (tendencies, abilities, potencies, capacities). Counterfactuals are often used in a historical context. Example: "If Alexander the Great had not died so young he would have conquered China."

conduct (L., *conducere*, "to bring together"). **1.** In general, synonymous with behavior. **2.** One's manner of action. **3.** In philosophical psychology, any type of human activity or response in which the personality is involved. **4.** In ethics, any voluntary behavior, or intentional disposition to act, for which a person may be held responsible relative to standards of right and wrong.

configuration (L., *configurare*, "to form together, out of, or from"). The structural pattern that interacting or interrelated parts take. In most general cases, interchangeable with GESTALT, FORM, and WHOLE.

confirmation (L. *confirmare*, from *con*, "with," and *firmare*, "to make firm"). Partial or tentative evidence or VERIFICATION. Not all empirical statements can be verified (observationally or experimentally tested). Examples: "All crows are black." "All gases expand as their temperatures rise." Observation and experimental evidence for such statements are based on a limited or finite number of instances from which inductive generalizations such as the above are made. But the statements are universal and refer also to the many unobserved cases in the past and in the future. Other examples: "If *X* is a chemical compound, then when put under some specific pressure and temperature it will become a solid." "Salt is soluble in water." For statements such as these, for hypotheses, for unobservable entities in science, there can only be confirmation (partial evidence) but not verification. Probability theory is used as a quantitative procedure for confirmation of laws, hypotheses, or concepts. See HYPOTHESIS.

confirmation, principle of. Sometimes *confirmation principle, principle of confirmability, confirmability principle*. A weaker variation of the principle of verification (see VERIFIABILITY, PRINCIPLE OF). Some logical positivists, recognizing that statements (hypotheses, theories, etc.) can never be completely verified or completely refuted by observation, proposed the principle of confirmation in place of the principle of verification. A few of the main points involved in the principle of confirmability: (**a**) Statements are more or less confirmed (or disconfirmed) by observation evidence. (**b**) Statements are confirmed if the consequences deduced from them are true and if not as many true consequences can be deduced from competing statements. (c) Statements may not be directly testable but are confirmable if other observational statements tend to confirm them (or imply their confirmability). (d) Statements are confirmable if they can be defined precisely enough so that their degree of probability can be calculated.

conflagration (Stoics). (Gk., *ekpyrōsis,* from *ek,* "out of," and *pyr,* "fire," which meant "being burnt up or consumed entirely"). In the Stoic view, the universe eternally goes through cycles of being dissolved into fire. A new cycle in essential respects similar to all the previous cycles emerges to be eternally repeated. See RECURRENCE, ETERNAL.

connotation (L., *con,* "with," and *notare,* "to mark"). **1.** The associations (feelings, attitudes, emotions, images, thoughts) suggested by a word either to the user of the word or to the listener. Examples: "He isn't man enough to do it." The word *man* is not used for its literal meaning but for the expressive or emotional meanings that have come to be associated with it (such as courageous, responsible, mature). The word *snake* in its literal sense means a reptile without legs, but it carries associations of being slippery, devious, slimy, upsetting. **2.** The literal, actual meaning of a word. The SIGNIFICATION or designation of a word, which states the main characteristics that determine the things (referents) to which the word can be correctly applied. See CONNOTATION (INTENSION); DEFINITION, TYPES OF (2).

connotation (intension). The collection of characteristics (properties, qualities) common to all (and only to those) things referred to by a word. Those characteristics "intended" by the use of the word. The connotation of the word *dog* would consist of the specific characteristics applicable to, or common to, all dogs. This is the informative or descriptive meaning of CONNOTATION. See INTENSION.

conscience (L., *conscire,* "to know," "to be conscious," from *con,* "with," "together," and *scire,* "to know"). The sense, feeling, or awareness (a) of what one ought to do and what one ought not to do, and/or (b) of what is morally correct, right, good, permissible, etc., and morally incorrect, wrong, bad, prohibited, etc. This MORAL SENSE is (1) *intuitive* and/or *immediate,* that is, no argumentation or process of reasoning is involved, and (2) *urgent,* that is, there is a feeling of obligation to do its bidding. **1.** Traditionally conscience has been associated with: (a) an inner *restraining force*— an inner voice such as SOCRATES' *DAIMŌN* which prohibits some actions (and occasionally suggests some). The "Thou shalt not" aspect of human behavior; (b) an *individualism* in which the dictates of personal conscience supersede social sanctions (the inner moral law takes precedence over the secular order); (c) a *directing force* for moral behavior stemming from the core of a person's humanity, especially in situations where ethical codes may not provide an answer, expressed in such phrases as "Let your conscience be your guide." **2.** The FACULTY interpretation: The mind has different faculties that are the sources of man's different abilities. For example, the rational faculty is the cause of rational action. The willing faculty (the ability to do, to decide, to choose) is the origin of volition. The conscience faculty is used to distinguish between right and wrong, good and bad. It is the source of ethical behavior, deciding what is morally the best thing to do and impelling obedience. See ETHICS, **3.** The behavioristic interpretation: Conscience is the sum total of an individual's conditioned responses to internal and external stimuli. These responses have been reinforced basically by social and peer approval and are broken only with internal conflict and difficulty. The internalization of norms of behavior. See *DAIMŌN*.

consciousness (L., *conscire*, "to know," "to be aware of"). Consciousness and MIND are often used synonymously. Consciousness has been regarded as a "center" or focal point of AWARENESS, FEELING, PERCEPTION, and KNOWLEDGE. **1.** A relation between an object being known and a knowing subject. **2.** A relation existing among (**a**) an activity of knowing, (**b**) the content being known, and (**c**) the awareness of them both. See SELF-CONSCIOUSNESS. **3.** The constituents and operation of awareness (of the mind) at any given moment. **4.** The actual mental states as they occur (pain, jealousy, an image, a concept). **5.** The ability to (symbolically) identify mental states. See INTROSPECTION. **6.** Consciousness has ascribed to it characteristics such as: (**a**) It is a primitive—something that cannot as such be analyzed or traced further and that cannot be built up out of other more rudimentary concepts or states. (**b**) Consciousness is a *brute fact*—something that just happens and cannot be reduced to anything else similar to it as its source (although on another level of analysis it can correctly be said to be "caused" by cerebral functions). (**c**) Each consciousness is characterized by its uniqueness, individuality, unity, continuity in time, privacy (no one can know another's consciousness as it is in itself), intentionality, and self-reflection. (**d**) Consciousness has irreducible *modes* (levels, aspects, abilities, dimensions) such as: content (images, sensations, perceptions, feelings, emotions, cognitions, etc.), quality, mood, intensity, comprehensiveness, direction, volition, selectivity, attention, intention, memory, etc. See entries under EGO and SELF.

consequentialism (**ethics**). The view that the correctness (rightness, goodness) of moral conduct is judged in terms of its results (consequences). See ETHICS, TELEOLOGICAL.

consistent (L., *consistere*, "to stand still or firm," "to be stable," from *con,* "with," and *sistere,* "to cause to stand"). Concepts are consistent (**a**) if their meanings do not contain contradictory terms (e.g., "squared circle") which mutually exclude each other or (**b**) if they do not contain inherent contradictions (e.g., "A thing X can be wholly in two different spaces at the same time,") or (**c**) if they are not outright contradictions (e.g., "Adam is a male and he is not a male"). Compare with COHERENCE. Contrast with CONTRADICTION.

construct, theoretical. Sometimes *theoretical construction, theoretical fiction, hypothetical construct, hypothetical construction, hypothetical fiction.* **1.** An inferred, nonobserved entity. **2.** An entity or process whose existence is postulated (assumed, hypothesized, supposed) and used within a system of explanation to explain observable phenomena. Examples: meson, quanta, the subconscious.

contemplation (L., *contemplari,* "to contemplate," "to meditate," "to gaze at attentively"). **1.** In metaphysics, the life of thinking for the sake of thinking that results in happiness achieved through the actualization of the individuals's highest faculty, reason (see EUDAIMONIA). **2.** In epistemology, synonymous with knowledge or the act of acquiring knowledge; the activity of thinking or of pondering. **3.** In religion, synonymous with *meditation,* the act of attempting to behold some spiritual object or gain spiritual insight. **4.** In mysticism, "mystical contemplation" or "the contemplation of the mystic" are used with reference to the method of experiencing complete or partial absorption into the One (God; Nature; the Unity of all things). See entries under MYSTICISM.

context (L., *contexere,* "to weave together," from *con,* "with," and *texere,* "to weave"). The sum total of meanings (associations, ideas, assumptions, preconceptions, etc.) that (**a**) are intimately related to a thing, (**b**) provide the origins for and (**c**) influence our attitudes, perspectives, judgments, and knowledge of that thing.

contextualism (metaphysics). The view which rejects the distinction between APPEARANCE on the one hand and a REALITY supposedly behind the appearances on the other. Such distinctions are regarded as relative to, and making sense in terms of, the purposes of a specific line of inquiry (or language). There is no absolutely correct or real context.

contiguity, law of. In philosophical psychologies (such as atomistic and associationistic psychologies), the association of ideas or combination of ideas (**a**) that have coexisted or (**b**) that have succeeded one another so that one brings the other to consciousness. See ASSOCIATION, LAWS OF.

continence (L., *continere,* "to hold together," "to repress") **1.** Self-restraint, self-command, self-mastery, self-governance; especially with reference to strong passions. (Sometimes continence specifically refers to the exercise of sexual self-restraint, total or partial.) **2.** In ethics, that moral state of the individual in which irrational bodily desires are controlled by reason. Contrast with INCONTINENCE.

contingent (epistemology) (L., *contingere,* "to touch on all sides," "to happen," from *con,* "with," and *tangere,* "to touch"). Refers to knowledge that is obtained by empirical means (as opposed to logical means) and must thus be regarded as only probably true. Compare with *A POSTERIORI.* Contrast with *A PRIORI.*

contingent (logic). Refers to any statement that is not necessarily true (that is, its denial does not produce a self-contradiction), and is logically possible. Contrast with *TAUTOLOGY*.

contingent (metaphysics). In general, something that is liable to happen, but not certain to happen; it could happen or not depending on the circumstances. The contingent includes all those things that are not necessary and that are not impossible. **1.** An event which is not necessitated to happen. **2.** Refers to the causal or temporal dependence of an event upon the existence of other events (themselves not necessitated) without which the event will not occur. Contrast with entries under NECESSARY.

continuity, law of (Leibniz). The theory that all change in nature occurs in degrees; there are no discontinuous changes; no "jumps" anywhere in any process in the universe.

continuum. 1. That which has an uninterrupted sameness about itself within a process of change or growth. A continuity of common characteristics recognizable within an activity. **2.** That which **(a)** exhibits no change about itself but remains the same in some particular way relative to certain other features about itself which are changing, and/or **(b)** remains the same with itself relative to other things around it which change. **3.** That imperceptible and/or gradual change of a thing's characteristics in time. Example: the continuum of development of a seed to a plant. **4.** That area (often regarded as uninterruped or as gapless, except in abstraction) between different things or qualities. The greater the difference, the greater is the tendency to polarize the continuum with words such as "the end points," "the extremes," "the poles," "the opposites" of the continuum. Examples: the continuum between hot and cold; the continuum between illusion and reality.

contradiction (L., *contradicere,* "to speak against," from *contra,* "against," and *dicere,* "to speak"). **1.** Any statement that is necessarily (by logical definition) always false. **2.** Any statement whose final truth column contains all falses. **3.** The negation of a statement. See LAWS OF THOUGHT, THE THREE. Contrast with CONSISTENT.

contradiction, self-. A statement or concept that contradicts itself; that both affirms and denies its basic meaning. Examples: "The ball dropped upward." "Adam is one bachelor I know of who is married." "Self-caused." "Causeless event." "Uncaused effect."

contraries (metaphysics). See OPPOSITES (METAPHYSICS).

contrast, law of (L., *contrastare,* "to stand in opposition to," from *contra,* "against," and *stare,* "to stand"). In philosophical psychology, qualities such as hot and cold, light and dark, which are distinctive (different) in comparison to each other, tend to be associated together in consciousness; that is, they tend to bring one another to mind. Sometimes classified as one of the laws of association. See ASSOCIATION, LAWS OF.

convention (L., *conveniens,* "suitable," "fit," proper," "acceptable"). **1.** A convention is any commonly agreed-upon statement whose truth is based not upon the way things are in nature but upon that agreement itself. Examples: (a) Laws and moral rules are regarded as social contracts under, which people agree to live in order to procure safety, protection, order, an education, fulfillment of their needs, and so on. (b) That an object is called "red" is a convention since another name could have been chosen. 2. In Greek philosophy, convention (*NOMOS*, "law," "common agreement," "standard acceptance") was contrasted with nature or the natural (*PHYSIS*).

conventionalism. 1. In the philosophy of science, the view that physical laws (theories, hypotheses) are convenient shorthand expressions (conventions) for organizing and explaining experience. Other expressions can be found—and will be found—which perform similar tasks. Thus physical laws are postulates; they are not absolute. They are relative to our framework of knowledge and to our technology. They cannot reveal reality as it is in itself but reveal only what and how consciousness puts things in relationships. They are commonly accepted in scientific circles because they bring about simplicity of explanation, control, comprehensiveness of understanding, prediction, and ways to deduce further concepts than can competing laws. Physical laws are subject to revision and utlimately will be abandoned if they cannot perform these functions. Compare with INSTRUMENTALISM. **2.** In logic, the truths and principles of logic are arbitrary conventions agreed upon in order to build up a formal system. No one set of axioms (or rules of inference, or postulates, or conceptual method) is primary and fundamental to all logical systems. The truth of axioms in a logical system is a matter of conceptual agreement as to where to begin and how to proceed. **3.** Sometimes *linguistic conventionalism, pragmatism in language, linguistic pragmatism.* The view that languages or calculi can be syntactically set up in a number of ways. The decision to accept one language rather than another is a decision made on the basis of combinations of such things as convenience, simplicity of procedures, practicality, comprehensiveness, usefulness, applicability. See LANGUAGE, FORMAL.

corporeal (L., *corporeus*, from *corpus*, "body"). Sometimes *corporal*. **1.** Material. Consisting of MATTER. **2.** PHYSICAL. Having physical dimensions. **3.** Extended. That which occupies space. **4.** Bodily. Having a BODY as opposed to being a SPIRIT or SOUL. **5.** Tangible. Opposite to INCORPOREAL. See FORM, CORPOREAL.

correspondence. See TRUTH, CORRESPONDENCE THEORY OF.

corrigible (L., *corrigere*, "to correct"). **1.** Subject to error. **2.** Capable of correction. Opposite to INCORRIGIBLE.

cosmogony (Gk., *kosmos*, "world," "universe," and *gignesthai*, "to be born"). Sometimes used synonymously with COSMOLOGY. **1.** A theory of the origination of the universe. This may be expressed in the form of myths, speculation, or science. **2.** The systematic inquiry into the origin of the universe.

cosmological argument for God's existence. 1. Any of the arguments for God's existence which proceed from what are regarded as observed facts about the universe, such as motion, cause, contingency, order, to the conclusion that God exists as the origin of and ground for these facts, such as PRIME MOVER, FIRST CAUSE, NECESSARY BEING, orderer. Proceeds from an analysis of the existence of things to the existence of God and to one or more of His characteristics. (This is in contrast with the ontological argument (see entries under ONTOLOGICAL ARGUMENT FOR GOD'S EXISTENCE), which proceeds from the acceptance of the definition of God (His essence) to His existence. **2.** The cosmological argument may refer to any argument for God's existence based on the derivative and dependent nature of the universe upon something other than itself; based on the contingency of the universe and its utter dependence on a necessary being (God) who begins, supports, and maintains it (as the sound of a harp is dependent on a harpist).

All cosmological arguments stress (a) the behind-the-scene activity of this necessary being and (b) how different from the universe in essential characteristics that necessary being (God) is. God is nondependent, whereas the universe is dependent upon God. God is self-moving, whereas the universe has motion imparted to it. God is eternal, whereas the universe has a beginning in time. God is self-actualized, whereas the universe is in a state of potential being partly actualized in time. God is immutable (unchanging), whereas the universe is in continual change. See GOD, ARGUMENTS FOR THE EXISTENCE OF.

cosmology (Gk., *kosmos,* "world," "universe," and *logos,* "the study of," "the underlying reasons for," "an account of"). **1.** The study of the universe as a rational and orderly system. **2.** Sometimes used synonymously with METAPHYSICS: The study of the most general and pervasive concepts that can be applied to the universe (such as space, time, matter, change, motion, extension, force, causality, eternity). **3.** Often used to refer to that branch of science, specifically a section of astronomy, which attempts to hypothesize about the origin, structure, characteristics, and development of the physical universe on the basis of observations and scientific methodology. See COSMOGONY.

cosmos (Gk., *kosmos,* "order," "the form or structure of a thing." One meaning of *kosmos* was the ordered adornment, the harmonious ornamentation, such as necklaces and earrings, that women wore to beautify themselves. An early use of the word was applied to the starry heavens designating that they were created to adorn and beautify the earth). **1.** The order (or harmony) of the universe. Contrasted with CHAOS. **2.** The ordered universe. **3.** The universe itself as a single, integrated whole or system. Used as a synonym for UNIVERSE.

counterexample, method of. 1. The method of refuting something by pointing out an instance that denies it or is in some way contrary to it. Example: A black swan is a counterexample to the assertion that "All swans
are white." **2.** In logic (also called "refutation by logical analogy"), the
method of arguing by which the validity of an argument-form is refuted
by showing an instance in which the same argument-form can be given
true premises yet have a false conclusion.

courage (L., *cor,* "heart"). That state of mind or action that enables one to
face a danger without being overcome by the attendant fear. In Greek
philosophy, courage was one of the cardinal virtues. See VIRTUES, CAR-
DINAL. A courageous person is not one who has no fear, and not one
who is overcome by fear, but one who is able to control fear and act according to a sense of duty or rational judgment. It was regarded by Aristotle as the mean between (the excess of) foolhardiness and (the defect
of) cowardice. See MEAN, THE (ARISTOTLE).

creatio ex nihilo (L., "creation out of nothing"). See CREATIONISM. Contrast with *EX NIHILO NIHIL FIT.*

creation (L., *creare,* "to create," "to cause to exist," "to bring into being").
1. The bringing something new into existence out of something previously
existing. This is the sense of creation in Plato's *Timaeus;* the rational
guiding principle of the universe (see DEMIURGE) shapes eternally existing matter into new forms by following the eternally perfect ideal Forms.
See FORMS, PLATO'S THEORY OF IDEAL. **2.** The activity of constructing,
making, building, shaping, or the product of such activity.

creationism. 1. The view that the universe and its life forms were produced
(and are being produced) by a supernatural agent. **2.** All things begin
and continue to exist only through the decision, plan, and activity of a supernatural being (God). **3.** Matter (the universe) was created instantaneously by God out of nothing. **4.** The human soul is separately created
and presented by God at birth (or at conception).

credo quia absurdum est (L., "I believe because it is absurd"). Sometimes
expressed: *Credo quia impossible est* ("I believe because it is impossible"). Often referred to as *Tertullian's dictum.*

credo ut intelligam (L., "I believe in order that I may understand"). The
dictum that serves as the basis of Anselm's ONTOLOGICAL ARGUMENT,
and expressed in the first part of Chapter 2 of his *Prologion* (also spelled
Proslogium): "I do not seek to understand in order that I may believe,
but I believe in order that I may understand. For this I also believe; that
if I did not believe, I could not understand." See FAITH; *FIDES PROECEDIT
INTELLECTUM.*

criterion (Gk., *kritērion,* "a means for judging," from *kritēs,* "judge," "one
who decides"). **1.** A standard (rule, test, method) for judging or measuring something. For example, in ethics, one of the principal concerns is to
find the criterion (or criteria) by which we can call acts moral or immor-

al, good or bad, right or wrong. **2.** That which enables one to know (discriminate, classify, decide) such things as: whether a statement is analytic or synthetic, true or false, etc., whether a thing exists or not (and what type of existence it has); whether a linguistic usage is correct; whether a concept is applicable; whether certain characteristics define a thing, etc.

cybernetics (Gk., *kybernētēs,* "steersman," "pilot," "controller," "governor"). **1.** The study of feedback mechanisms, communication systems, and controls found in machines and in living organisms. **2.** The study of how mechanical systems can be regarded as adaptive. **3.** The study of the self-regulatory features of artificial automata (and living organisms) which display "purposiveness" and other functions that have been traditionally assigned to the activity of a mind.

cynic. Words such as *cynic, cynicism, cynical* have pejorative connotations of: moroseness; pessimism; doubt; belittlement; contempt for other's opinions; lack of faith in ideals and humanity; a belief that humans are selfish, hypocritical, insincere, and self-indulgent.

Cynics, the. A school of Greek philosophers whose founders included Antisthenes of Athens (a friend of Socrates) and Diogenes of Sinope (who, according to legend, carried a lighted lantern around in the daytime to seek an honest man). The traditions of the sect lasted from the fourth century B.C. well into the Roman sixth century A.D. The Greek word for dog (transliterated as *kyōn* or *cyōn*) may have been derogatorily applied to them; hence their name "cynics," "the dog philosophers," since they appeared to live freely like dogs, roaming, scrounging, and begging, unfettered by cultural restraints. The sect may have been named after the gymnasium Cynosarges, which was its first gathering place and which was probably founded by Antisthenes. The Cynics taught that virtue is the highest good. Its essence is self-control and independence. Happiness comes from acting virtuously, which to them also meant using one's native intelligence to survive. They distinguished between natural values (conformity with the rhythms of nature) and artificial values (those imposed by individuals upon individuals). Ignorance of one's simple nature and its simple needs (but instead following the corrupt ways of society) leads to unhappiness. Embracing unnatural values (external and material things) such as fame, wealth, success, achievements, pleasures, reputation, academic degrees leads to unhappiness. Desires lead to unhappiness. Individuals should live in a state of nature with a minimum of desires and needs. The individual who wants nothing, lacks nothing, has a minimum of needs is like the gods who have no needs to be satisfied. Lack of moderation, lack of the power to abstain, overindulgence lead to unhappiness. Self-sufficiency can be achieved only through self-discipline, which involves training the body and disciplining the mind. Only then can the individual have the rational presence to act virtuously, fulfilling his highest capacities. In general the Cynics were ascetics, antinomians (against the established norms, customs, traditions, laws of society), anti-intellectuals, nonacademic, nonsystematic, highly individualistic. They ridiculed luxury and sensual pleasures and idolized poverty. They despised the speculative theories of the academics, which they thought had no practical benefit for the individual but enslaved him with false obligations (such as duty to family; care of property; loyalty to the rulers, the wealthy, and the military; patriotism).

cyrenaics. A Greek hedonistic philosophy founded by Aristippus of Cyrene; hence the name Cyrenaics. The Cyrenaics believed that the highest good in life is obtaining pleasure for oneself—intense pleasure of the moment, regardless of any consequent pain. Live for present pleasures; there may not be any future. Pleasure is the only good desirable for its own sake. Pleasure is the only criterion for deciding right and wrong. Intense, immediate physical pleasure is the best. Manipulate anything and anyone by shrewdness, intelligence, and wit in order to secure these intense pleasures. All things—wealth, power, fame, luxury—are not good in themselves or desirable in themselves but are for the attainment of pleasure. See HEDONISM (ARISTIPPUS) and compare with other entries under HEDONISM.

D

daimōn (Gk., sometimes transliterated as *daemon* or *demon*. Also found as *daimonion* or *daemonion*). Some of the variety of meanings: **1.** *Daimōn* was used interchangeably with *theo,* "a god," or *thea,* "a goddess." In a general way it meant "deity" or "divine power." **2.** A divinity whose characteristics are somewhere between the traditional gods and the most idealized of humans, which serves as an intermediary (similar to a guardian angel) between humans and the gods. (In Plato's *Symposium* the *daimon* communicates to the gods the prayers of humans and reveals to humans the commands of the gods. Socrates refers to a *daimonion ti,* "a divinelike something or other," that wants him to refrain from, or engage in certain actions.) See CONSCIENCE; SOCRATES' DAIMŌN. **3.** *Daimōn* also referred to "one's genius," "one's fortune or lot," and to "one's tendency of spirit." **4.** Used as a synonym for PSYCHE to mean "soul" ("self," "spirit") attached to an individual at birth that determines his fate or fortune. See EUDAIMONIA.

Darwinism, social. The theory that society is a state of struggle for existence in which the fittest (strongest) wins. The strongest is characterized by EGOISM, ruthlessness, competition, ambition, manipulation, scheming, intelligence, energy, wealth, power. "Might makes right." "Social selection" operates in society much the same way as NATURAL SELECTION operates in nature, whereby the unfit (weakest) is eliminated. The unfit are characterized as being noncompetitive, altruistic, idle, lazy, powerless, poor. The good of society as a whole is served in this social struggle for existence. The self-made millionaire has traditionally been regarded as the exemplar of the fittest.

dasein (Ger.) Used in a number of senses: **1.** Fact or factuality. **2.** Being. Existence, usually of any kind. (Used interchangeably with the German *Existenz*). **3.** That kind of existence applicable to things (as opposed to individuals that initiate activity). The third meaning is identical with the French *être-en-soi* and is used by Heidegger. See *EN SOI* (SARTRE).

data, empirical. See EXPERIENTIAL.

data, experiential. See EXPERIENTIAL.

datum (L., *datum,* "given"). Plural *data.* Sometimes *presentment* or *presentational immediacy.* **1.** In logic, that which is given, presented, or admitted as a fact from which inferences can be made. **2.** In epistemology, the specific content that appears in CONSCIOUSNESS. That which is given in consciousness as fundamental to knowledge.

dealienation. The process of denying the tendency toward SELF-ALIENATION (self-estrangement) in which the "self" emotionally and intellectually feels itself removed from and uninvolved in its surroundings and actions. The process of feeling that one's "self" is self-directed and self-relating in a meaningful and consenting way. Compare with ALIENATION; ESTRANGEMENT.

deduction (L., *deducere,* "to lead from," from *de,* "from," "away," "down," and *ducere,* "to lead," "to draw"). **1.** Reasoning from a general truth to a particular instance of that truth. Example: All dogs are mortal. Charlie is a dog. Therefore Charlie is mortal. **2.** The process of making explicit the logical implications of statements or premises. **3.** The process of inference from statements (premises) in which a necessarily true conclusion is arrived at by rules of logic. Contrasted with INDUCTION.

deduction, transcendental (Kant). The name given by Kant to the attempt to show that there is one set of categories basic and ultimate to all human understanding and experiencing. See CATEGORIES OF THE UNDERSTANDING (KANT).

definiendum (L., "that which is to be defined"). The word (expression, phrase, symbol) being defined.

definiens (L., "that which does the defining"). The words used to define something. That part of a definition that gives the meaning of the *DEFINIENDUM.*

defining, rules for. Many rules have been presented since Plato and Aristotle for constructing good definitions. There are many kinds of definitions used for different purposes and with different intentions. Most of the rules have exceptions. Rules for defining can be looked at as general guidelines to control extreme subjectivity and relativity in expressing meanings and to limit capriciousness and confusion in communication. Some of the rules: **1.** A definition must indicate the essential characteristics (the essential properties, attributes, qualities, or features, the true "nature," the "essence") of the thing being defined and not its accidental characteristics, that is, those which merely happen to apply, but need not apply, to the thing being defined. **2.** Wherever applicable, a definition should give the *GENUS* and *DIFFERENTIA* of the thing being defined. **3.** The *DEFINIENDUM* should not appear in the *DEFINIENS.* **4.** On initial contact with a word to be defined, the *definiens* in some sense must be more familiar and clearer than the *definiendum.* (In dictionary definitions that which is contained in the definition of a word is more readily understood by the use of relatively explicit and familiar terminology.) **5.** The *definiendum* must be logically equivalent to (synonymous with) the *definiens.* **6.** A definition should be precise and not too broad and not too narrow. (A definition is too broad if the *definiens* applies to things to which the *definiendum* does not. A definition is too narrow if the *definiendum* applies to things to which the *definiens* does not.) **7.** A definition must be concise, with no superfluity, irrelevancies, or redundancy. **8.** A definition must not be ambiguous. **9.** A definition must not be obscure, but must be expressed in terminology which can be easily understood. **10.** A definition must not be vague. **11.** A definition must not be expressed in metaphors or figurative language. **12.** A definition must not be defined in negatives. **13.** A definition must not be stated in opposite or correlative terms.

definition (L., *definire,* "to limit," "to end," "to be concerned with the boundaries of something"). **1.** The meaning of a word (either its ordinary, commonly accepted meaning, or the meaning stipulated [intended] by the user). **2.** The description of the essential characteristics (properties, attributes, qualities, features) of a thing or idea. The principal function of definitions is to present meanings for words that are not clearly understood in a context of other words (and their meanings) that *are* clearly understood. Definitions increase vocabulary and impart information. They attempt to prevent ambiguity, obscurity, unintelligibility, imprecision, vagueness, and complexity (by, for example, making it possible to substitute single words for long and sometimes cumbersome meanings). Definitions are, in a general sense, stipulative. They are resolutions—declared intentions as to (a) how to use words in a certain manner, and (b) how they are used.

definition, family resemblance view of. See FAMILY RESEMBLANCE (WITTGENSTEIN).

definition, Socratic theory of. See SOCRATIC THEORY OF DEFINITION.

definition, types of. The following twenty types of definitions are not exhaustive of the types of definitions that can be presented, nor have their nomenclature and classifications been standardized. Many fuse into one another. **1.** *Circular definition.* The Latin phrase is often used: *circulus in definiendo,* "circularity in defining." Presenting the meaning of a word either (a) by using the same word with the same meaning in the *DEFINIENS,* or (b) using a grammatical variation of the same word (the *DEFINIENDUM*) in the *definiens.* Examples: "A preacher is one who preaches." "A Medicare official is one who officiates in the Medicare program." Usually regarded as a fallacious method of definition, although most

types of definition contain this circular quality. See CIRCULARITY. **2.**
CONNOTATIVE definition. One in which the *definiens* presents or explains
the concept (idea) symbolized by the *definiendum.* A connotative definition gives meaning to a word by describing the common characteristics
possessed by all the things denoted by the word. Emphasis is put on implicitly or explicitly stating the GENUS and *DIFFERENTIA* of a thing. The
definiens attempts to present the unique characteristics of the *definiendum.* Example: A "bird" is "a vertebrate with feathers." **3.** *Contextual
definition.* Sometimes *definition in use.* A definition which defines a
word by establishing a context for it, or indicating the context which
gives it meaning. Example: "X is defined as soft when it yields easily to
my touch." **4.** *DENOTATIVE definition.* Gives a list of examples to which
the word in question can be correctly applied. Example: A "bird" means
such things as a "sparrow," "eagle," "cardinal," "kiwi," "penguin." **5.**
Essence definition. Also *essential definition, real definition.* Giving the
ESSENCE of a thing. From among the characteristics possessed by a thing,
one is unique and hierarchically superior in that it states **(a)** the most important characteristic of the thing, and/or **(b)** that characteristic upon
which the others depend for their existence. Example: "Human" is "an
animal that reasons." Other characteristics which depend upon reason
for their existence: (1) an animal that laughs, (2) an animal that creates
and uses tools, (3) an animal that creates and uses symbols and language,
(4) an animal that cooks its food, (5) an animal with an opposable
thumb. Definition by essence looks for a single, objectively existing essence. **6.** *Functional definition.* Defining in terms of the functions the
thing performs. Example: Defining a referee in connection with what he
does in the game he is refereeing (such as blowing the whistle to stop
play, applying penalties, enforcing rules, etc.). Words such as philosopher, president, charity, liver, student, manager, predator, gene can be
functionally defined. Functional definitions are extrinsic; they do not
stress the defining characteristics peculiar to the thing itself but the functions of the thing and its relations to other things. **7.** *GENUS ET DIFFEREN-
TIA* definition. Defining by giving the characteristics (*differentia*) of a
class that distinguish it from other subclasses that also fall within a more
general class (genus). Example: "Human" is an "animal (genus) that is
rational *(differentia).*" **8.** *Historical definition.* Defining in reference to
the history of the thing being defined. Example: Defining a graduate in
terms of his participation for a time in a series of events. A person would
not be called a graduate unless he participated in a history of events
which lead up to graduation. Other words that can be historically defined: sufferer, retiree, medical doctor, veteran, athlete. Historical definitions are extrinsic. They do not stress the characteristics peculiar to the
thing itself but present its external relations to other things and the se-
quential events involving it. **9.** *Lexical definition.* Sometimes *customary*

or *reportive definition*. Reporting the meaning that a word has in common (ordinary, established) usage. Example: "Nibble means to bite lightly or gently; also to eat in small bits." **10.** *Loaded definition*. Giving the meaning of a word in a prejudicial or biased way. Often associated with propaganda. Example: Dr. Johnson's definition of fishing as a fish on one end of a line and a fool on the other. **11.** *Nominal definition*. Sometimes *verbal definition*. Any definition which explains the meaning of a *word* or *symbol*, as opposed to a *real definition*, which gives the definition of a *thing*. Example: "A triangle is (names) a plane figure with three connected straight sides that form three angles that total 180°." **12.** *Operational definition*. Indicating the actions (operations, activities, procedures) which the word symbolically implies and which when performed serve as its meaning. Example: "The word length means taking a measuring stick such as a foot ruler, laying it on the object to be measured so that one end of the stick coincides with one end of the object. Mark the object where the other end of the stick ends, then move the stick along the object in a straight line until the first (previous) end point coincides with the previous position of the second end. Repeat the process as often as possible. Note the total number of times the operation has been performed. This total number constitutes the length of the object." See OPERATIONALISM. **13.** OSTENSIVE *definition*. Sometimes *demonstrative definition*. Defining by pointing to (demonstrating, showing, illustrating, feeling) actual examples of the thing being defined. Example: "The word bird means this" (*point to a bird*). **14.** *Persuasive definition*. Sometimes *rhetorical definition*. Giving the meanings of words in an emotive (expressive) way in order to influence the attitudes (feelings, emotions, goals) of others. Example: "The true meaning of a teacher is one who relates to his students on a personal level and enthusiastically guides them to sources of information." (Often associated with advertising.) **15.** *Precising definition*. Sometimes *restricting definition*. A specific form of *stipulative definition* whereby specific and explicit meanings are attached, and can only be attached, to a word. Example: "For the purpose of our discussion, the word 'argument' is to mean a conclusion drawn from more than one sentence according to the formal rules of inference presented in this book." **16.** *Real definition*. Sometimes used interchangeably with *essence definition* and on occasion with *connotative definition*. A definition which presents the essential characteristic (nature, structure, form, essence, property, attribute, etc.) of a thing as opposed to a *nominal definition*, which gives the meaning of a word or symbol. **17.** *Recursive definition*. Sometimes *inductive definition*. A definition in which a variation of the word defined occurs in the *definiens*, thereby avoiding the appearance of a circular definition. Example: "A mother is a female parent." **18.** *Stipulative definition*. Sometimes *legislative definition*. (a) The *definiens* is intentionally limited in meaning and/or is assigned a specific meaning for consistency and clarity of communication and as a matter of preference. Indicates how the user of the word intends to have that word understood. Example: "We propose to restrict the meaning of the word 'college' to four-year institutions of higher learning." (b) A new word chosen somewhat arbitrarily that is assigned a meaning for the sake of such things as brevity, expressing a new concept, secrecy, added precision, avoidance of emotive connotations, standardization. Example: When Norbert Weiner coined the word "cybernetics" he gave it the stipulative definition: "the science of communication and control systems." 19. *Synonymous definition.* Sometimes *dictionary definition.* A definition in which the *definiendum* and *definiens* are interchangeable. The giving of a list of cognate words, or identical meanings. The paradigm for synonymous definitions is the translation of words from one language to another language. Examples: "To hate means to loathe." "The word *kyōn* means dog." 20. *Syntactical definition.* That which defines the notational conventions that prescribe the ways in which certain signs (symbols, expressions) will represent, or be substituted for, particular items.

deism (Originally from the Gk., *theos,* "God," transliterated into Latin as *Deus*). In general, the belief in the existence of God. The term deism was first used in Christianity by the Calvinists during the latter part of the sixteenth century; in England, it appeared during the early seventeenth century. For the most part, deism holds to the following beliefs: **1.** God as the FIRST CAUSE created the universe. **2.** God created the unchangeable laws by which the universe is governed. **3.** God is in no way immanent in his creation, but totally different from it, transcending it as for example a watchmaker transcends the watch he has made and set in motion. **4.** Reason is in harmony with revelation (or revelation must conform to reason). **5.** The Bible must be analyzed according to reason and its doctrines should not be made into mysteries. **6.** God has a preordained plan for the universe; all things are predetermined. **7.** The highest duty and sole aim of human life is to fulfill the purpose of the natural laws God has created. **8.** In some versions: God occasionally suspends his physical laws in order to revitalize the natural system. **9.** In some versions: God can intervene in the lives of humans, and provide grace and/or moral guidance. See GOD CONCEPTS.

Demiurge (Sometimes *demiourgos:* transliterated from the Gk., *demiourgos,* meaning "one who does work for people," "a skilled workman," "craftsman," "a maker," "a creator"). A term used by Plato, principally in his dialogue on cosmology *The Timaeus,* to refer to the principle (force, power) of creation in the universe. The Demiurge follows the eternal, unchanging, perfect ideal Forms, shaping chaotic and recalcitrant matter into the best possible rational patterns. See *ANANGKĒ;* CREATION.

demonstration (L., *de,* "from," "down," "away," and *monstrare,* "to show"). Sometimes *derivation* or *justification*. In logic, the formal proof used in an argument (usually a deductive argument) that shows the inferences used to reach the conclusion.

denial. See NEGATION.

denotation (L., *denotare,* from *de,* "from," "down," "away," and *notare,* "to mark"). **1.** The application of the meaning of a word (term, symbol, etc.). **2.** The naming of instances that a word has. Citing the referents for a word. Giving examples of the thing to be defined or explained. Example: The characteristics of being a bird may not be entirely clear or agreed upon, but listing examples sometimes helps convey the meaning: sparrow, pigeon, eagle, vulture, kiwi, duck. The complete denotation of a word would be the entire list of all the things to which the word has applied or will apply. **3.** EXTENSION: The collection of all those things to which the word applies. The things (instances, items, objects, individuals) which can be subsumed under a word or conception and thereby be partly definable. See DEFINITION, TYPES OF (4).

deontology (Gk., *deon,* "moral duty," "that which is morally binding," "the morally right," "obligation," "imperative," "necessity," and *logos,* "the study of the underlying reasons of a thing," "the science of," "an account of"). The study of the concept of DUTY (obligation, responsibility, commitment) and its related concepts. See ETHICS, DEONTOLOGICAL. *Deontic* is occasionally used for deontological. *Deontic* in general refers to anything having to do with the concept of necessity (see LOGIC, DEONTIC), or with duty.

descriptivism (ethics). See ETHICS, DESCRIPTIVISM IN.

design, argument from. Sometimes simply the *design argument.* Kant refers to it as the *physico-theological argument.* Refers to any of the wide assortment of arguments for God's existence that rely on the apparently purposeful design in the universe, to prove the existence of a God that is a Cosmic Mind (Designer). See GOD, ARGUMENTS FOR THE EXISTENCE OF; TELEOLOGICAL ARGUMENT FOR THE EXISTENCE OF GOD.

destiny (L., *destinare,* "to decree beforehand, "to make fast, determine, settle"). One's predetermined lot, usually divinely foreordained. FATE. Sometimes personified as a power which cannot be resisted.

determinism. 1. The view that every event has a CAUSE. **2.** Given a set of conditions, *X,* it will always be followed by nothing other than a set of conditions *Y.* (And given that set of conditions *X, Y* could not have been preceded by anything other than that set of conditions *X.*) **3.** The view that (**a**) all things in the universe are "governed" by, or operate in accordance with, causal laws; (**b**) everything in the universe is absolutely dependent upon and necessitated by causes; (**c**) given sufficient knowledge of the workings of any particular thing, we would be able to see not only its future but the future of all things completely mirrored in it (see MONADS [LEIBNIZ]); or, as for example in Laplace (**d**) given sufficient knowledge of the mass, position, and direction of every particle in the universe at any given time, and an infinite mathematical ability, one could predict every future event. Compare with entries under FREE WILL; INDETERMINISM.

deus ex machina (L., "God from out of the machine"). Used derogatorily to mean that God or some other supernatural cause is artificially brought in to provide an explanation or resolution of a problem.

dialectic (Gk., *dialectikē*, "the art of conversation, discussion," or *dialectikos*, "one skilled in logical argument or debate." "Dialectic" originally referred to debating tournaments in which the primary aim was to refute an opponent's arguments or lead him to contradictions, dilemmas, or paradoxes. In general, a dialectician was one who left nothing unquestioned). **1.** The art (*TECHNĒ*) of asking and answering the proper questions in a discussion at the proper time and in the proper way so as to bring knowledge out into the open. **2.** The art of gaining better knowledge on a topic by exchanging reasoned views and arguments. **3.** The art of procuring true knowledge on a topic by the use of a formal reasoning process. (*Dialectics* is the term sometimes used to designate that branch of logic which presents the rules and modes of reasoning correctly; also to designate the systematic, logical analysis of concepts to show what they entail.) **4.** The method of arriving at a definition for a concept by means of examining the common characteristics found in a number of particular examples of that concept. **5.** The method of classification whereby there is a repeated division of a concept into its respective subclasses.

dialectic (eristic). See ERISTIC.

dialectic (Hegel). **1.** The process whereby a thought or an existing thing necessarily leads to or changes into its opposite (or contradictory) and thereby a new synthesis (unity) is arrived at. **2.** The process of change in thought and the universe where a higher level of knowledge (truth) and of existence (unity) is reached by means of the necessary opposition of contradictories. **3.** The process of necessary change involving a triad (three elements) consisting of (**a**) an existing thing or thought (*thesis*), (**b**) its opposite or contradictory (ANTITHESIS) and (**c**) the unity (SYNTHESIS) resulting from their interaction and which then becomes the basis (*thesis*) of another dialectical movement. Sometimes referred to as *triadic dialectic*. Hegel's dialectic is developmental and evolutionary in character and its end point is complete perfection. See LOGIC, DIALECTICAL; MATERIALISM, DIALECTICAL (MARX-ENGELS).

dialectic (Heracleitus). The process of change in the universe whereby all things pass over into what they are not, and were not (OPPOSITES).

dialectic (Plato). **1.** Used specifically in Plato's *Republic* to refer to the unique and complex education required of the philosopher-ruler from childhood on as he ascends to the vision of the Supreme Good by which all his decisions and behavior are thereafter guided. **2.** Plato also used "dialectic" to refer to the rational, philosophical method in general.

dialectic (Socrates). 1. Socrates' method of asking questions to bring out a point for elaboration and with others following the answers to their logical conclusions (which ultimately conform to the good, the true, and the beautiful). **2.** Socrates' question-and-answer method of getting his listeners to accept the truth of particular instances that have something in common, and from that acceptance to also assent to the true universal element, the generalization, or the ESSENCE evident in those particular instances. (The UNIVERSAL or essence that is found provides the basis for the definition of the concept or thing, and also gives insight into the ideal forms which it exemplifies.) **3.** The method of inquiry into and the finding of the real (essence) definitions of things. **4.** The method of separating (*dialegontas*) things according to their class, nature, or kind. **5.** The give-and-take in discussion whereby an opponent is made to admit a series of points only to find that acceptance of them leads to an inconsistency with what he believes. See SOCRATIC METHOD; SOCRATIC QUEST, THE; SOCRATIC THEORY OF DEFINITION.

dialectic (Zeno). That *REDUCTIO AD ABSURDUM* method of argumentation attributed to Zeno the Eleatic whereby a belief is refuted by showing how its acceptance leads either to (**a**) a logical contradiction or (**b**) to a logical conclusion which is in no way acceptable to reason (or common sense). See ZENO'S PARADOXES.

dialectic, transcendental (Kant). In Kant's *Critique of Pure Reason* one of the divisions of his Transcendental Logic (see CATEGORIES OF LOGIC [KANT]) was called "Transcendental Dialectic." The purpose of such a dialectic was to find those judgments which presume to go beyond the limits of finite human experience. Such judgments in Kant's view are not only presumptuous but also illusory. The four antinomies (see ANTINOMIES, THE FOUR [KANT]) and the notion of God as the FIRST CAUSE are cited by Kant as examples of such judgments.

dialectical materialism. See MATERIALISM, DIALECTICAL (MARX-ENGELS).

dialectics, historical (Marxism). The following are some basic views: **1.** Humankind and history are in tension yet in an inseparable harmony. **2.** Insofar as humans are in conflict with the historical dialectical forces operating in the universe, then these forces will be alienated, unexpressed, unrealized. **3.** Humankind is a product of the negating ideologies of its particular epoch. By means of revolution humans can eliminate the gap between themselves and these perfecting but alienated historical forces at work in the universe. **4.** People are humanized by transcending their immediacy, by overcoming the impersonality of social (class) forces, and by identifying themselves with those historical dialectical forces that are rational and person-oriented. **5.** The final state of development is social and ethical perfection. See LOGIC, DIALECTICAL.

dianoia (Gk., referring in general [a] to the act of thinking or [b] to the faculty of thought). **1.** In Plato, *dianoia* is a type of discursive knowledge between DOXA (mere opinion or faith) and NOĒSIS (true intuitive knowledge. See NOUS). **2.** In Aristotle, *dianoia* is used in general to mean intellectual activity that critically (**a**) appraises the differences among concepts, (**b**) is able to see them in combinations and relationships, and (**c**) can extrapolate from (**a**) and (**b**). *Dianoia* is subdivided into (1) THEORIA and EPISTĒMĒ (in their sense of knowledge sought for its own sake), (2) TECHNĒ (knowledge used to make something), and (3) PHRŌNESIS (knowledge wisely applied to conduct). **3.** In his works on logic Aristotle uses *dianoia* specifically to mean syllogistic reasoning. See VIRTUES, DIANOETIC (ARISTOTLE).

dichotomy (Gk., *dichotomia,* from *dicha,* "two," and *temnein,* "to cut"). **1.** The division of things into two basic parts that are regarded as fundamentally and/or irreducibly different. Examples: A human is composed of a soul and a body. Two realities exist: the supernatural and the natural. Sometimes the term is used pejoratively referring to divisions that are artificial or arbitrary. **2.** Refers to any mutually exclusive relationship of two things (classes, statements, entities, events). Frequently such relationships are also regarded as exhaustive. **3.** In logic, dichotomy (dichotomizing) refers to the method or process of classifying or dividing into a genus and species according to differentiae. See DIFFERENTIA. Compare with DISPARATE; DISTINGUISH.

dichotomy, is/ought. See IS/OUGHT DICHOTOMY.

dichotomy, mind/body. See MIND/BODY DICHOTOMY.

difference, method of. See METHODS, MILL'S INDUCTIVE.

difference in identity, principle of. 1. Regardless of how similar (identical) things are, any thing in the universe can be said to be different from any other thing in at least one respect, for example that they occupy different spaces (are numerically distinct), exist at different times, are distinct or different objects of thought or being, etc. **2.** No two things can be identical in all respects (otherwise they would not be *two* things). Compare with IDENTITY IN DIFFERENCE, PRINCIPLE OF.

differentia (L., "difference"). **1.** The distinguishing characteristic or specific difference of a thing from other things. **2.** The characteristic of a thing that (**a**) is used to make class divisions, or (**b**) that distinguishes one subclass from another subclass within a class. Example: having all three sides equal is the *differentia* between equilateral triangles and all other types. See GENUS ET DIFFERENTIA DISTINCTION.

dikaiosynē (Plato) (Gk., "justice") *Dikaiosynē* is the word most often used by Plato for what has been translated as justice but which in general means "an inner sense of righteousness; knowing when to do the fair and right thing." (There are connotations in this Greek word and its cognates of such concepts as rightness, lawful, judgment, justified, judicial, punishment, penalty.) Plato uses the word distinctively and in several senses:

1. That intuitive response (principally a characteristic of the philosopher-king, who has attained knowledge of the Ideal Forms) to a situation that automatically expresses a sense of what is good, correct, proper, the best, the most rational for that situation. **2.** Doing, within the context of a highly integrated community such as in Plato's *Republic*, **(a)** that for which one is best suited by heredity and training, and **(b)** that which will help achieve a functioning harmony of all parts of the community in order to produce the general good. **3.** Having the three faculties of the soul (reason, will, desires) integrated, not in conflict or tension, governed by rational principles, and thereby able to respond in a rational, tranquil, and morally correct way to all circumstances and problems. See VIRTUES, CARDINAL.

dilemma, moral. A situation in which mutually exclusive moral actions or choices are equally binding.

ding an sich, das. German expression used by Kant and Kantians, meaning the "thing in itself." **1.** Refers to anything beyond and hence unknowable to consciousness and to any possible experience. **2.** That transcendent, independent reality which is beyond any possibility of being known by humans. See DIALECTIC, TRANSCENDENTAL (KANT).

Dionysian spirit. The irrational impulse in humans that accepts and craves ecstatic, spontaneous experiences in life and is associated with the will to life and power. Its opposite is the APOLLONIAN SPIRIT. Both concepts were developed in Friedrich Nietzsche's *The Birth of Tragedy* (1872). Compare with ROMANTICISM.

discourse, universe of. See UNIVERSE OF DISCOURSE.

discursive. See REASONING, DISCURSIVE.

disparate (L., *disparatus*, from *dis*, "away," "between," and *parare*, "to prepare," or from *par*, "equal"). **1.** Dissimilarity in basic kind and/or quality. (For example, the sensations of color and cold are disparate.) **2.** Two ideas are disparate if neither calls up something of the other. **3.** Two things are disparate if they cannot be put into a genus/species relationship. Compare with DICHOTOMY.

disposition (L., *disponere*, "to dispose," from *dis*, "away," and *ponere*, "to place"). The tendency (propensity, bent, inclination) to behave in a certain way. Dispositions differ from emotions (feelings) in that they do not report on the mood a person is in at a given time, but report a general set of tendencies. Example: "She is afraid of crowded places" indicates a tendency to be in the emotional state of fear in crowded places. *Emotional dispositions* (such as emotional commitments to a person or idea; prejudices; preferences) are contrasted with *cognitive dispositions* (such as the tendency to believe; anticipations; expectations). See STATE, DISPOSITION. Contrasted with STATE, OCCURRENT.

dispute. See VERBAL DISPUTE.

distinction. See DISTINGUISH. Also *GENUS ET DIFFERENTIA* DISTINCTION;

SENTENCE/STATEMENT DISTINCTION; TYPE/TOKEN DISTINCTION; USE/MENTION DISTINCTION.

distinguish. **1.** To point out the differences between (or among) things. **2.** To recognize that one thing (quality, feature, predicate, object, etc.) is not another.

When either **1** or **2** is done, a *distinction* is made. A *real distinction* is one that distinguishes according to differences that exist in the qualities of the things being distinguished (such as mind and brain or animal and radios). An *abstract distinction* is one that distinguishes qualities or differences according to abstract principles, which in reality are not separable or distinguishable (except in abstraction) from the thing of which they are a part. For example, we may say that only an abstract distinction can be made between the qualities of mind and the qualities of brain, though the "objects" thus distinguished are not separable in reality. Abstract distinctions are sometimes referred to as *mental* (or *conceptual,* or *arbitrary*) distinctions. Compare with DICHOTOMY.

distributively. Considering each member of a class (group, set) singly. What can be said about a class distributively may not be true of the class taken as a whole. Opposite to COLLECTIVELY. See TERM, DISTRIBUTED.

division, fallacy of. See FALLACY, TYPES OF INFORMAL (**18**).

dogma (Gk., *dogma,* "that which seems to one," "an opinion," "a belief," "a public ordinance"). **1.** A doctrine (BELIEF, ideology, tenet, opinion) that has been formally and authoritatively proclaimed either by a leader or by an institution such as a church. **2.** That which one who accepts the authority must think about a specific thing.

dogmatism. **1.** Unmerited positiveness in asserting the truth of a doctrine. **2.** The rejection of any examination of an idea and the assertion that the idea is true by authority and is beyond questioning.

dogmatists (Kant). A term used somewhat pejoratively by Immanuel Kant to apply to philosophers, principally metaphysicians, who believed that: **(a)** the universe can be known by means of inferences derived from a few self-evident principles without recourse to observation, control, experimentation, testing; **(b)** humans have the ability to transcend experience and independently of sense experience arrive at truth about the real nature of things.

double-aspect theory of mind. See entries under MIND, DOUBLE-ASPECT THEORY OF.

double effect doctrine (ethics). The doctrine that an act done with good intentions and according to moral principles can have good results but also unintended repercussions and/or side effects that **(a)** are not themselves worthwhile or morally acceptable, or **(b)** are morally acceptable only because they are inextricably associated with that act.

doubt (L., *dubitare,* "to waver in one's opinion"). **1.** To hesitate or to be undecided about the truth of something. **2.** To question the veracity of an idea or to consider it questionable. **3.** To be inclined not to believe the truth of an assertion. Contrast with CERTAIN.

One is in doubt about the truth of an assertion whenever he does not commit himself to its truth (or to the truth of its negation).

doubt, Descartes' method of. The first of four rules presented by Descartes in Part II of his *Discourse on Method* contains the most succinct formation of his method of doubt: Nothing is to be admitted as true unless **(a)** it is free from all prejudicial judgments, and **(b)** it is so clearly and distinctly presented to the mind that in no circumstance can it ever be doubted. See METHOD (DESCARTES).

Descartes' method of doubt was to doubt anything and everything until he arrived at something which could not in any way be doubted by any rational being. (The idea so arrived at would be indubitably CERTAIN and universally true.) From this absolutely certain and true idea one could then derive in logical fashion other certainties and truths. A system so constructed would be an organized group of interdependent ideas each consistent with all others and each implying the others; thus the system would be comprehensive and flawless. See SKEPTICISM (DESCARTES).

doxa (Gk., "opinion," "seeming," "judgment"). In general, used to refer to an inferior type of knowledge, for example, in comparison to *EPISTĒMĒ*. See *DIANOIA;* ESSENTIALISM (PLATO).

dualism (L., *duo,* "two," "twofold"). Any philosophic view that insists on the existence of two independent, separable, irreducible, unique realms. Examples: Supernatural/Natural. God/Universe. Spirit/Matter. Soul/Body. Visible World/Invisible World. World of the Senses/World of the Intellect. Thinking Substance/Material Substance. Actual Reality/Possible Reality. Noumenal World/Phenomenal World. Force of Good/Force of Evil. The universe can be explained only by means of both realms. Contrasted with MONISM; PLURALISM. See GOD CONCEPTS **(4)**.

dualism, Descartes' soul/body. Descartes held that the human being is a union of two separable and distinct substances: body and soul. The body is part of the physical universe and mechanical in operation, as are all things in the physical universe. The body on its own can—and does—operate with its own "life," and many of its activities are not caused by the soul. The soul is connected to all parts of the body, but it performs most of its functions at the pineal gland in the brain. By acting upon the pineal gland, the soul produces such mental events as thinking, perceiving, willing, emoting, sensing. Compare with MIND/BODY INTERACTIONISM and other MIND/BODY entries.

dualism, mind/body. 1. The belief that minds are distinct from bodies. Human beings are not merely a collection of material particles. **2.** The belief that mind and body are two irreducibly distinct and separable substances whose essential attributes are different in every respect. See MIND, TYPES

OF THEORIES OF. Compare with MIND/BODY DICHOTOMY and other MIND/BODY entries.

dualism, theological. See GOD CONCEPTS (**4**).

duration (Bergson). For Henri Bergson every true duration (*durée réelle*) is (**a**) incomplete, (**b**) changing (dynamic), (**c**) unique (novel), and (**d**) continuous. Duration is a continuum of successive but heterogeneous movements. It is TIME conceived (perceived) as indivisible. Each moment contains an element of uniqueness or novelty; no moment completely reflects the past or the future. Nature is in a dynamic process of change; nothing is immutable. All change is continuous and congruous with all change "externally" related to it. Duration excludes the possibility of any discontinuity with other existing changes or movements.

duty (L., *debere,* "to owe," "to be in debt"). **1.** That which one is required and expected to do (or not to do) in reference to such things as one's humaneness, status, occupation, responsibilities. **2.** That which one ought to do, and/or one feels obligated to do. **3.** That which one feels morally compelled to do. Usually opposite to what one is inclined (wishes, desires) to do. Related to concepts such as CONSCIENCE, moral principles, VIRTUE, the GOOD, the RIGHT, OBLIGATION. See CATEGORICAL IMPERATIVE, THE (KANT).

duty (Kant). See ETHICS (KANT).

duty, *prima facie.* See *PRIMA FACIE* DUTIES (ROSS).

dyad/dyadic (Gk., *dyas,* "two"). "Dyad" means two units regarded as one; "dyadic" means binary, composed of two parts, or dual without necessarily implying a monism or identity of the two. Examples of dyadic thought: Reality is both One and Many; Unchanging and Changing; Moving yet Unmoving; Unified yet Varied; Same yet Different; Good and evil; Spontaneous and Necessitated.

***dynamis* (Aristotle)** (Gk., "power," "force," "strength"). **1.** That power (energy, force) which causes change, and/or **2.** that state of potential a thing has to produce change or to become other than what it is. Compare with *ENERGEIA.*

***dynamis* (Plato)** (Gk., "power"). Used by Plato to mean: **1.** the power of transferring or imparting activity or change to something else, **2.** the ability to receive power (force, motion, activity), and **3.** the capacity to be influenced by forces (change, movement, etc.).

dynamism (Gk., *dynamis,* "power," "strength," "the ability to do a thing"). **1.** The theory that everything in the universe is composed of FORCE (tendency, will, power) or forces. **2.** The universe is a totality of forces. Dynamism uses the concept of force as the fundamental unit of explanation in contrast, for example, to atoms, matter, mass, motion, ideas, souls.

dysteleological (Gk., *dys,* "hard," "ill," "bad," "difficult," and *telos,* "end," "goal," "purpose," and *logos,* "the study of"). Referring to processes of maladjustment in the universe such as inherent limits to organic adaptation, accident, disease, and death. Such processes thwart the achievement of purpose and/or indicate forces other than only adaptive (good) forces at work in the universe. Contrast with TELEOLOGY.

dystopia (Gk., *dys,* "bad," and *topos,* "a place"). A place or state not of ideal perfection, but of ideal imperfection in regard to individuality, humanness, dignity, uniqueness. Novels such as *Brave New World* and *1984* have been called *dystopian.* Opposite to UTOPIA.

E

eclecticism (Gk., *eklektikos,* "one who selects," from *eklegein,* "to pick out," "to choose from"). **1.** Choosing ideas (concepts, beliefs, doctrines) from a variety of systems of thought in the process of constructing one's own system. **2.** Selecting from diverse schools of thought that which is considered of value so as to create from the diversity an acceptable unified system.

economy, principle of. See OCKHAM'S RAZOR.

ecstasy (Gk., *ekstasis,* "being out of place," "displacement," "entrancement," "astonishment," "a trance," from *ek,* "out," and *estanai,* "to set," "to stand"—to stand outside oneself). A state **1.** of joy, rapture, exaltation; **2.** of being overpowered by an emotion; **3.** of being beyond the realm of reason and even self-control; **4.** a mystical, prophetic, or poetic trance.

The feeling involved is so intense and overwhelming that it is interpreted as an experience of "standing outside of" one's ordinary consciousness, and as a climactic focus or absorption of all the faculties into an undifferentiated unity in which there is no discrimination among things such as body, spirit, mind, intellect, will, desires, needs. See MYSTICAL EXPERIENCE.

eduction (L., *educere,* "to lead forth," from *e,* "out," and *ducere,* "to lead"). **1.** The eliciting (extracting, drawing out) of a point or an idea by ANALYSIS, or INFERENCE. **2.** Direct inference of a PARTICULAR from particulars. **3.** Arguing from particulars. **4.** In metaphysics, the drawing out (or the ACTUALIZATION) of a substantial form potentially in matter.

effect. See entries under CAUSE.

efficient cause. See CAUSES, ARISTOTLE'S FOUR.

effluences (effluxes), theory of (L., *efflux*, from *effluere*, "to flow out of," from *ex*, "out of," and *fluere*, "to flow"—"that which flows out of something"). Sometimes *theory of effluvia* or *theory of simulacra*. Pre-Socratic theory primarily found in Empedocles and Democritus. Physical objects shed (spurt out, give off) *aporroai*, films (images, effluences), which fit into sense-organ pores meeting with like effluences in the body. This process causes the sensations and perceptions which form the basis of our knowledge of the external world. This theory lasted in MATERIALISM throughout the medieval period. Compare with *EIDOLA*.

egalitarianism. The view that all humans are equal and should be treated equally in liberties, rights, respect, acceptance, opportunities, etc. See EQUALITARIANISM for a fuller discussion.

ego (Gk., *egō*, the pronoun of the first person, "I," "I at least," "for my part," "for myself"). Used as a synonym for SELF and some meanings of AGENT, PERSONAL IDENTITY, PERSON, SUBJECT, CONSCIOUSNESS.

ego, empirical (Kant). The active individual self (subject, ego) in its processes and contents as perceived by immediate INTROSPECTION, and which qualitatively distinguishes one person from another (or which provides his particular character). Contrasted with EGO, TRANSCENDENTAL (KANT).

ego, pure. That nonempirical (invisible, intangible, nonmaterial, unchanging, unverifiable) entity (soul, spirit) **(a)** which is the underlying cause of all human mental functions and (usually) **(b)** whose existence cannot be known directly by introspective analysis but must be *inferred* from the content of our introspection. (For Kant, a pure ego must be presupposed without empirical evidence in order to explain the unity of our consciousness.) See EGO, TRANSCENDENTAL (KANT).

ego, transcendental (Kant). That unfathomable subject (self) presupposed by (implied by, indicated by) the unity of our consciousness. In other philosophies usually referred to as pure ego (see EGO, PURE). Contrasted with EGO, EMPIRICAL (KANT).

ego of introspection, the. **1.** The intuitively felt (or perceived) unity of consciousness. **2.** That system of internal mental states (an individual self or identity) that endures throughout change and moments of time. **3.** The personal awareness of a series of interconnected, internal mental acts, or states, or contents. **4.** The cognition of a conceptual distinction **(a)** between one's own consciousness and a realm of nonconsciousness, and **(b)** between one's own consciousness as immediately given (and directly known), and all other things that can never be known in this unique way. See INTROSPECTION.

egocentric illusion (Gk., *egō*, "I," and *kentron*, "center," "pivotal point"). **1.** The apparent fact that each self cannot help perceiving itself as the focal point and center of the universe, though in reality no self is such. **2.** The view that everything in the universe is organized to satisfy our ego, our needs and goals, our wishes and desires.

egocentric predicament. 1. The apparent situation that each person can have knowledge only of his own experiences. One cannot get beyond his experiences to know anything about the world as it exists apart from him. One cannot know anything about another's experiences as they exist to him. **2.** All knowledge is a product of our own individual consciousness and no knowledge is possible of anything outside our consciousness. See entries under SOLIPSISM. **3.** The term was invented by Ralph Barton Perry to name the fact that we are all limited to and by our own unique and peculiar perceptual world. We cannot go beyond this world to know what the external world is like in itself since that knowledge would inevitably have to be structured in terms of our perceptions. See *DING AN SICH, DAS.*

egoism. 1. In general, excessive self-love and preoccupation with oneself, and excessive reference to one's own knowledge, experiences, manners, customs, or beliefs. **2.** Specifically, gratification of the self. The belief that the aim of life is to procure satisfactions (pleasures) for oneself, as humans are by nature selfish, self-seeking, self-interested, self-loving creatures. (In strong forms of egoism, humans act to fulfill only their own desires and interests even at the expense of others.) Opposite to AL-TRUISM. See DARWINISM, SOCIAL.

egoism, altruistic. Sometimes *egoistic altruism.* The view that self-interest is compatible with benevolent actions and motives. It is possible to satisfy our own interests in the act of seeking the best interests of others. The achievement of the happiness of others creates happiness in us. The loss of happiness in others diminishes the happiness in us. Thus benevolence (see ALTRUISM) is not to be regarded as a secondary motive in humans.

egoism, ethical. The view that (a) each person *should* aim to promote his own well-being and interests; (b) the *SUMMUM BONUM* of life should be to procure the most satisfactions (pleasures, goals, desires, needs) possible for onself; (c) one's own success and happiness should be of primary and ultimate worth and all other values should stem from this.

Some forms of ethical egoism are referred to as *enlightened* (or *rational*) *self-interest,* of which altruistic egoism (see EGOISM, ALTRUISTIC) is the exemplary form.

egoism, psychological. 1. The thesis that all individuals do *in fact* seek their own interests at all times. There is no purely unselfish act. See SELFISH-NESS. **2.** The theory that all human actions are consciously or unconsciously motivated by a desire for one's own well-being and satisfactions; it only appears that one acts for the benefit of others.

egotism. Connotes (a) offensive self-conceit, self-adulation, self-praise, and (b) offensive living for the selfish satisfaction of one's own interests, desires, needs, and appetites. Not necessarily to be equated with EGOISM.

eidetic (Gk., *eidos,* "that which is seen," "form," "shape," "figure," "appearance," "type," "species," "idea"). Referring to an idea or image that resembles the characteristic property or constitutive ESSENCE of a thing. (Husserl uses *eidos* to mean essence.)

eidōla. Also IDOLA (Gk., "images," "likenesses," "ideas," "phantoms," "idols"). Used in Greek philosophy primarily by the Atomists to refer to the groups of particles that flow as effluences (images, films, copies) from physical objects and stimulate the sense organs to produce sensations and perceptions which are the sources of our knowledge of the external world. Compare with EFFLUENCES (EFFLUXES), THEORY OF.

In Democritus, *eidōla* were emissions of material particles from an object that were like the form of the object. They imprinted themselves upon the sense organs and produced sense experiences of external objects. In Epicurus, *eidōla* were the physical images of external objects that perpetually peeled off from the surface of things and flew about at random imprinting themselves upon us to form perception of things.

eidōla (art). The term may refer to the human created pictorial images of actual things or to the representations of images. *Eidōla* imitate or are only a semblance (PHANTASMA) of their originals. This imitation of the original exists within two extremes: **1.** A likeness (*eikon* or ICON) that has many of the characteristics of the original such as in a model or sculpture of a thing, or **2.** a likeness that has only the appearance of being like the original, such as something painted in linear perspective on a two-dimensional canvas.

eidos. See IDEAS (PLATO).

einfühlung. German, most frequently translated as EMPATHY.

élan vital (Fr., "vital impetus," "vital principle," or "vital impulse"). In nonmechanistic and creative evolutionary theories (such as Bergson's) the *élan vital* is a term used to answer such questions as why living organisms have evolved into greater and greater complexity in the course of evolutionary time. The *élan vital* is (a) the driving force propelling life on to higher and higher levels of structure and organization and (b) the creative force giving direction to evolution. It is likened to a flow or current of consciousness, with which all the universe is imbued and which determines the direction of evolution. Bergson speaks of the *élan vital* as a supraconsciousness, a nonempirical, intangible, invisible, nonverifiable acting force. The term VITALISM is taken from this French term.

Eleatics, the. The school of philosophy founded by Parmenides in Elea (a city in what is now southern Italy). Melissus of Samos and Zeno of Elea are two famous disciples. Eleaticism is characterized by an extreme MONISM: reality is one, motionless, unchanging, undifferentiable, and eternal. Melissus defended the eternality of the One by showing that its denial implies the untenable position of the creation of something from nothing, or the destruction of something into nothing. See MATTER, PRIN-

CIPLE OF THE CONSERVATION OF. Zeno defended extreme monism by showing the contradictory nature of the language of change (motion, movement, activity, process); since the linguistic description of change is contradictory there is no change. See DIALECTIC (ZENO); ZENO'S PARADOXES.

elements (L., *elementa,* "the first principles of things," "the rudimentary nature of something"). **1.** The simple substances out of which (or by which) something comes to be. See ELEMENTS, THE FOUR. **2.** The simple constituents of a complex. In this sense used synonymously with "component." Elements are regarded as primary and irreducible.

elements, the four. Water, air, fire, and earth, which some Greek philosophers believed to be the ultimate irreducible primary simple constituents (or masses) of the universe.

emanation (L., *emanare,* "to flow out of," from *e,* "out," and *manare,* "to flow"). A creation theory that all reality proceeds (by necessity) from a central principle of perfect being which is one and eternally present. The emanation conception of creation often uses the analogy of the sun and the light that radiates from it. The sun is the source of the light; the One is the source of all existence. Light "emanates" from the sun and is dependent upon it but is not identical with it. Take away the sun, you then take away light. The universe is an outpouring of the One and is dependent upon it for its existence and order but is not identical with it. Take away the One, you then take away the universe. The farther you are from the sun the less bright the light. The farther away from the One a thing is, the less spirituality and perfection it possesses. Matter is the farthest away from the One; intelligence is the closest to the One, followed by pure psyche (soul, spirit). The theory of emanation is primarily associated with the neo-Platonic philosophy of Plotinus. See BEING, HIERARCHY OF; *HEN;* ONE, THE.

embodied mind. See MIND, EMBODIED.

emergent, an. Sometimes *gestalt property* of organized structures. The new qualitative synthesis produced by structures organized in certain patterns that cannot be predicted from the examination of the constituent parts of the whole. Examples: Water (liquidity, fluidity) is the quality which emerges from the combination of two parts hydrogen and one part oxygen under certain conditions. Both hydrogen and oxygen are gases that burn. The emergent quality (water) could not have been predicted from knowledge of the properties of hydrogen and oxygen. The mind (consciousness, awareness) is regarded as a new quality that emerges when certain neural processes become organized in a specific way; change the organization of these physical structures and another quality (mind) will emerge. See EVOLUTION, EMERGENT.

emergent mentalism. See MENTALISM, EMERGENT.

emotion (L., *emovere,* "to remove," "to shake," "to stir up," from *e,* "out," and *movere,* "to move"). **1.** A mode of feeling. **2.** A particular, irreducible, unanalyzable feeling; a quality of consciousness, immediately present, known only by having it, and not accessible as a felt quality to anyone else's consciousness. In general, any of the feeling, affective passion states referred to by emotion terms (love, hate, fear, anger, etc.).

Some characteristics of emotions: **3.** Emotions (**a**) are occurrent states (see STATE, OCCURRENT) of consciousness such as immediate feelings or moods that may be of short or long duration, and (**b**) may also be dispositional states (see STATE, DISPOSITION) which tend one toward other emotions, attitudes, or activities. An example of **a:** The joy of solving a puzzle. An example of **b:** Sympathy inclining you toward helping someone in need. **4.** All emotions involve covert and overt bodily changes whether recognizable or not, such as changes in digestion, heartbeat, blood pressure, hemoglobin count, adrenalin secretion, amounts and kinds of hormones, blushing, panting, trembling, paling, fainting, crying, nausea. **5.** Classifications of emotions may be made according to their being desirable or not desirable, harmful or not harmful, useful or not useful, etc. **6.** Emotions may be thought of in terms of whether or not they are related to an increase in the efficiency of and in the energy available for behavior such as thinking, perceiving, concentrating, selecting, acting. Examples: Fear may be associated with the prevention of learning, inhibited perception, decreased concentration. On some occasions it may be associated with certain kinds of learning, intensification of perception, and improved concentration about specific things in the environment. Grief may be associated with decreased efficiency in relating to people or desire to get things done; or it may be associated with the opposite effect in some personalities. See PATHOS. Compare with FEELING; SENSATION.

emotivism. See ETHICS, EMOTIVE THEORY OF.

empathy (Gk., *empathēs,* "being in a state of emotion," "being much affected by, or at, something." The English word was constructed out of the Greek *en,* "in," "into," and *pathos,* "suffering," "emotion," "feeling," "passion"). Sometimes referred to by the German *EINFUHLUNG.* **1.** The projection of one's own inner feelings upon an object or activity. Examples: "Those pillars are straining under the tension of the roof's weight." The feelings had while (empathetically) watching a boxing match and undergoing, physically and mentally, what is thought to be taking place in the combatants. **2.** The abstract understanding of the inner feelings of another consciousness but without oneself experiencing them at that moment. Example: Knowing a friend's grief but not being involved emotionally in the grieving. See ANIMISM; SYMPATHY.

empirical (Gk., *empeiros,* "experienced," "practiced in a thing," "directly acquainted with some knowledge"). Sometimes *empiric.* Referring to knowledge founded on experience, observation, facts, sensation, practice, concrete situations, and real events. *A posteriori* knowledge (see KNOWL-

EDGE, *A POSTERIORI*) as opposed to *a priori* knowledge (see KNOWLEDGE, *A PRIORI*). Contrast with EXPERIENTAL.

empiricism (Gk., *empeiria*, "experience," "concrete acquaintance, or familiarity with something"). **1.** The view that all ideas are abstractions formed by compounding (combining, recombining) what is experienced (observed, immediately given in sensation). **2.** Experience is the sole source of knowledge. **3.** All that we know is ultimately dependent on sense data. All knowledge is directly derived or indirectly inferred from sense data (except some definitional truths of logic and mathematics). **4.** Reason cannot of its own provide us with knowledge of reality without reference to sense experience and the use of our sense organs. Information provided by our senses serves as the basic building block of all knowledge. Contrasted with RATIONALISM.

empiricism, logical. Holds to views such as: **(a)** Modern logical analyses are applicable to the solution of philosophical and scientific problems. (The traditional problems of philosophy are divided into two classifications: (1) problems of fact, which science deals with, and (2) problems of methodology and conceptual analysis, which philosophy deals with. All other problems are either irrelevant or meaningless.) **(b)** There are limits to empiricism. The principles of formal systems of logic and of inductive inference cannot be proved by reference to experience. **(c)** All true propositions (except logical truths) are reducible to sense datum propositions (basic propositions) which are about immediately given sense data. See MEANING, EMPIRICIST THEORY OF; POSITIVISM, LOGICAL. Compare with ANALYIC PHILOSOPHY.

empiricism, radical. 1. The theory that relations as well as particulars exist in the external world. **2.** The theory that immediate experience is the only origin of and sanction for all knowledge. (Radical empiricism is called SENSATIONALISM when "immediate experience" is interpreted as "immediate sensations.")

empiricists, the British. Those traditionally included: Locke, Berkeley, Hume. Sometimes also included: Francis Bacon and Thomas Hobbes. Contrasted with RATIONALISTS, CONTINENTAL (EUROPEAN).

end. 1. The object (goal, PURPOSE, aim) whose attainment is intended by an agent. **2.** That ultimate state of ACTUALIZATION of a FORM, ESSENCE, or process beyond which there is no further need for development. **3.** The relative state of fulfillment that must be reached in order for a process to progress to another stage or to a final stage.

end, man as an (Kant). The ethical rule that all humans must be treated as ends in themselves, and not as means to ends. All persons are morally self-governing agents living under natural moral law. All are able to realize the good will which is the only thing good in itself without qualification. See ETHICS (KANT).

endeiktikon (Gk., "that which marks or points out, or indicates"). Referring to indicative words, signs, or symbols whose referents are not observed or experienced in a direct way. For example, words such as "soul," "spirit," "substance," "mind," "matter," "essence" are considered as *endeiktic* (indicative signs) when believed to refer to entities inaccessible to empirical testing or experience.

ends, heteronomy of (Kant). The condition of the will in which the will is guided (governed, directed, motivated) by ends that are sought for the benefit of oneself or another (such as reputation, pleasure) rather than for the development and betterment of one's own moral will, and/or obeys moral laws that are not its own. Opposite to WILL, AUTONOMY OF THE (KANT).

ends, kingdom of (Kant). The unity of all rational people under a universal moral law.

ends/means controversy, the. The dispute regarding dichotomous statements such as: "The end justifies the means"/"The end never justifies the means"; "Evil means lead to good ends"/"Evil means never lead to good ends"; "Actions must be judged only by their consequences"/"Actions cannot be judged on the basis of their consequences."

energeia (Gk., "energy," from *en,* "in," and *ergon,* "work," and from *energos,* "active"). A term used as in Aristotle to refer to "force," "the active exercise of," "activity," "the power of acting," "the process of becoming actualized," "the development of a thing's potentiality into its actualization." The *energeia* of things varies in duration. Contrasted with POTENTIALITY and POSSIBILITY. Compare with ACTUALITY; *DYNAMIS* (ARISTOTLE); ENTELECHY (ARISTOTLE).

energy. 1. The POWER, FORCE, strength exerted by a thing. **2.** The power to produce a change. **3.** The inherent capacity to act (move) and to cause action (motion).

The concept of energy entails concepts such as (**a**) space, (**b**) time, (**c**) a flow or transformation, (**d**) a quantity, (**e**) (often) a direction, and (usually) (**f**) a physical medium which "has" the first five characteristics. Often regarded as the basic physical reality upon which all phenomena depend for their existence; all phenomena are manifestations of the various processes, transformations, or levels of energy. In this sense, MATTER is not conceived of as a SUBSTANCE, or as the ultimate unchanging building block of the universe. Rather matter becomes *identical* or interchangeable with the concepts of (1) energy, (2) process, or (3) matter regarded as a *form* of energy.

In most cases energy is a more general term than MOTION, force, power.

energy, principle of the conservation of. See MATTER, PRINCIPLE OF THE CONSERVATION OF.

ennui (Fr., from the Latin *in odio,* "in hatred"). Boredom, tedium, weariness usually arising from overindulgence, satiety, or the lack of capacity to be stimulated. See EXISTENTIALISM.

ens (L., "being"; the present participle of *ESSE,* "to be"). **1.** Used interchangeably with the Latin RES. **2.** Sometimes used to refer to being-as-being, without any qualifications (properties, determining features. In theology, the ultimate *ens* refers to God in whom ESSENCE and EXISTENCE are identical. In metaphysics, the ultimate *ens* refers to the ABSOLUTE. See *A SE.*

en soi (Sartre) (Fr., "in itself," "in oneself"). A phrase used by Sartre to refer to existence in which one acts (is acted upon) as a mere existing thing, suppressing (or out of ignorance not realizing) the fact that authentic, free choices are open for one's every action. The quality of *être* (being)-*en-soi* belongs to things and to humans insofar as they act like inactive objects. Sartre contrasts *en soi* with *POUR SOI. En soi* is related to self-deception and inauthentic existence and in particular to an individual who lives avoiding responsibility, to himself and others, in order also to avoid the anxiety, distress, and malaise that accompany the act, or fulfillment, of responsibility. Individuals live *en soi* when they are involved in BAD FAITH (SARTRE). See EXISTENTIALISM.

entelechy (Aristotle) (Gk., *entelecheia,* "being complete"). **1.** In Aristotle's philosophy, synonymous with completed actuality where there is no further potentiality to be realized, where the thing's essence has been fulfilled. **2.** Also in Aristotle's philosophy, "entelechies" are regarded as the regulators of orderly activity causing things to do that which is natural to them and to seek their specific natural ends or completion. Compare with *ENERGEIA.*

entelechy (Leibniz). The dominant monad within a complex. The ultimate entelechy is the Dominant Monad or God. See MONADS (LEIBNIZ).

entity (L., *entitas,* from ENS, "thing"; the present participle of ESSE, "to be"). **1.** A being. **2.** An existent. **3.** That which has a real, substantial existence.

entity, neutral. Sometimes *neutral stuff.* A qualityless existent or being, usually one that has characteristics of neither mind nor matter. See MONISM, NEUTRAL.

entropic, anti-. Sometimes *antientropic* or *anabolic factor.* Those forces at work in the universe that tend to prevent an increase in the ENTROPY of a system or which make a system less entropic.

entropy (Gk., *entropē,* "A turning in," from *en,* "in," and *tropē,* "a turn" or "a transformation"). **1.** The disorganization of a physical system. **2.** The tendency of a closed nonequilibrium physical system toward a state of equilibrium or lack of potential. **3.** The transformation of energy in a closed system away from one level (kind, quality) where energy is available to do physical (mechanical) work. The *less* energy the system has ready to be used as work, the higher its entropy. Example: A bucket of ice melting to water. Energy must be brought into the system to make that water into steam or ice again. The water has reached an entropy level; a level of thermal equilibrium.

Epicureanism. See ATOMISM, GREEK; HEDONISM (EPICURUS).

epiphenomenalism (Gk., *epiphaneia,* "appearance," from *epi,* "on," "upon," "over and above," and *phainein,* "to appear," "to show," "to become evident"). A theory of the relationship of body and mind. (a) Consciousness is an epiphenomenon (an aftereffect, a by-product) caused by certain cerebral processes; (b) Consciousness does not affect the body but exists as a powerless neutral state; (c) Nor do conscious states affect other conscious states. The usual analogies given in epiphenomenalism: Just as the body causes its shadow and the shadow has no causal efficacy upon the body or upon other shadows, so the brain causes consciousness, but consciousness cannot affect the brain. Just as the locomotive produces steam or smoke, which do not causally affect the locomotive, so the body produces consciousness which has no causal connection with its source in brain processes. See MIND, TYPES OF THEORIES OF (5).

epistēmē (Gk., "true knowledge," "scientific knowledge," "systematic knowledge"). Opposite to *DOXA.* Contrasted with *POIETIKOS; TECHNĒ; THEORIA.* See *DIANOIA;* ESSENTIALISM (PLATO).

epistemic. Pertaining to knowledge.

epistemology (Gk., *epistēmē,* "knowledge," and *logos,* "the study of," "theory of"). Theory of knowledge. The study of (a) the origins, (b) the presuppositions, (c) the nature, (d) the extent, and (e) the veracity (truth, reliability, validity) of knowledge. That branch of philosophy which asks questions such as: "Where does knowledge come from—how is it formulated, expressed, and communicated? What is knowledge? Is sense experience necessary for all types of knowledge? What part does reason play in knowledge? Is there knowledge derived only from reason? What are the differences among concepts such as: belief, knowledge, opinion, fact, reality, error, imagining, conceptualizing, idea, truth, possibility, certainty?

epochē (Gk., "a check," "a cessation"). Used for example by the Greek Skeptics to mean: **1.** a provisional suspension of judgment about the truth or falsity, or the belief or disbelief in ideas until a better determination can be made, or **2.** a deliberate denial of knowledge in order to arrive at certainty from a clean slate. Compare with AGNOSTICISM; SKEPTIC; and entries under SKEPTICISM.

equalitarianism. 1. The belief that all humans are socially and politically equal (sometimes also favors economic equality). Each individual is to be counted as one. A common trait is seen to exist in all people that requires they be treated equally. This trait may be reason, or a soul, or a moral sense, or suffering, or being created by God. **2.** The view that everyone ought to be treated with the same consideration and concern. Each individual should receive equal treatment under law and equal opportunity for such things as an education, development of capacities, fulfillment of needs. This is to be taken as a regulative procedure of social and ethical conduct which in the end produces a more abundant good for humankind than alternative attitudes. **3.** The nondiscriminatory treatment of all persons regardless of race, religion, sex, sexual preference, status, wealth, intelligence, physical abilities, etc. See EGALITARIANISM.

equivocation (L., *aequivocus*, "calling something by the same name and same meaning," from *aequus*, "equal," and *vocare*, "to call"). **1.** Refers to the inconsistency of giving different meanings (or senses) to the same word. See entries under AMBIGUITY. **2.** An equivocation is committed when a word is used with one particular meaning in one part of a presentation and then deliberately or nondeliberately used with another meaning in another part of the presentation. Example: "A crime should be punished. It is a crime the way he wastes his money on alcohol. Therefore he should be punished." The two uses of the word *crime* are different. In the first it means "legal infraction or violation"; in the second it means "a pity; morally inexcusable and reprehensible." The fallacy of equivocation occurs when conclusions are reached by using words which have changed their meanings within the argument. See FALLACY, TYPES OF INFORMAL **(19)**.

Words (or actions) are *equivocal* when given two or more possible meanings without certainty as to which meaning is intended. Opposite to UNIVOCAL. To *equivocate* is to use language equivocally, and in the derogatory sense of the word, to use language in a willful way to mislead or deceive by the use of double, or varied, meanings. *Equivocator* means one who says one thing and really means another whereas a *hypocrite* is one who says one thing and does another, and a *prevaricator* (see PREVARICATION) is one who evades the truth by quibbling with words and/or shuffling their meanings to suit his purpose.

eristic (Gk., *eris*, "strife," "conflict"). Sometimes *eristic dialectic*. **1.** Argumentative. **2.** Characterized by spurious reasoning. **3.** Referring to the exchange of ideas in which the aim is not truth but the intentional use of any kind of argument and manipulation of language in order to win a dispute and/or to persuade someone of the truth of a point in question.

The phrase *eristic dialectic* is sometimes used pejoratively, specifically to refer to the Sophists' claim to debate in such a way as to make the worse appear the better and the better appear the worse. Opposite to APODEICTIC. See DIALECTIC; SOPHISTIC.

erōs (Gk., "love"). **1.** In Greek mythology the god of love. (Hesiod depicted *Erōs* as the first of the gods to emerge from Chaos, drawing all things together into an order. Later writers spoke of him as the son of Aphrodite.) **2.** The creative and binding force in the universe. **3.** The love of beauty. The source of inspiration for the search in life for beauty and the good. **4.** Possessive love. **5.** Sensual and/or sexual (erotic) attraction. Physical love. **6.** Desire. **7.** The passionate attachment to (or enthusiasm toward) another, or which is created in another. Compare with *AGAPĒ; PHILIA.*

erotetic. (Gk., *erōtēsis,* "a question," or "a questioning"). Referring to the asking of questions, or to the procedure of questioning. Some forms of DIALECTIC are erotetic.

In Aristotle's logic, an *erōtēma* was a question used as a premise in a syllogism that had to be responded to before the argument could proceed.

eschatology (Gk., *eschatos,* "the last," "the furthest," "the outermost," "the last time," and *logos,* "the study of"). The beliefs associated with last or final events such as death, a judgment day, the end of the earth, the final moment of history, and people's relationship to them.

esoteric (Gk., *esōterikos,* "inner," "interior"). Referring to private or secret doctrines (ideologies, beliefs) understood and shared only by the initiated. Opposite to EXOTERIC.

ESP. An acronym (initialism) for *extrasensory perception, extrasensory phenomena,* or *extrasensory powers.* See PARAPSYCHOLOGY.

esse (L., "to exist," "to be"). **1.** The *act* of being (as opposed to a *state* of being). **2.** Used to refer to the active expression of an ESSENCE. Compare with *ENS.*

esse est percipi (L., "to be is to be perceived"). Berkeley's phrase that was the cornerstone of his philosophy. The view that for something to exist it must either be perceived or be engaged in the act of perceiving. Berkeley called things that are perceived "sensible things," "sensible qualities"; sometimes he called them "ideas" or "sensations." Examples: pains, pleasures, itches, colors, sounds, tastes, smells, tangible shapes. These sensible qualities exist as passive products or objects of a mind (or a spirit). They cannot exist when they are not being experienced. Minds are active beings that will and perceive. (Perceiving is an activity.) Only active minds together with their sensible qualities exist. Only because the world is continuously perceived by God does it continue to exist when humans are not perceiving it. See IMMATERIALISM (BERKELEY).

essence (L., *essentia,* from *esse,* "to be"). **1.** That which makes a thing what it is (and without which it would not be what it is). **2.** That which makes a thing what it is rather than its being or becoming something else. **3.** That which a thing possesses and which makes that thing identifiable as the particular thing it is (and without which it would not be identified as that thing). **4.** The necessary and essential defining characteristic of a thing. **5.** The fundamental, prime, ultimate power of a thing. **6.** The abstract idea (or law) of a thing by which we can recognize further particular instances of it.

Essence is often contrasted in abstraction with EXISTENCE. But for philosophers who take the concept of essence seriously, a thing could not exist without having an essence. Essence and existence are said to be identical in such things as God, the Universe (Eternal Matter), the Absolute. Sometimes essence is used synonymously with FORM, IDEA. See *OUSIA.*

The plural, *essences,* is sometimes used to refer to the spirits, souls, immaterial agencies in things.

essence (Aristotle). 1. That something which the thing is to be in its final completed state. **2.** The essential nature (internal principle) of a thing which makes it what it is at any given state in its teleological development and makes it become what it will finally be. See FORM (ARISTOTLE.) **3.** That which is the underlying identity or nature of a thing throughout the process of change from potentiality to actuality. In this sense Aristotle is using essence (*OUSIA*) and substance synonymously (see entries under SUBSTANCE that refer to Aristotle). **4.** That which is necessary and unchanging about a concept or thing. Compare with DYNAMIS (ARISTOTLE).

essentialism. 1. The belief that things have essences. **2.** The theory that a definition describes or reveals the essence of a thing, and/or of the perfect ideal form of which it is an imperfect copy. To the extent to which it does this, it is indubitable, true, exact, precise, incontrovertible. To the extent that it does not do this, it is untrue, false, inadequate, inexact, imprecise, disputable.

essentialism (Plato). There are two general levels of knowledge: **(a)** that of the eternally perfect, immutable, invisible, abstract forms (ARCHETYPES, essences) and **(b)** that of visible, tangible (sensed) objects. The aim of philosophy is to gain an understanding of the real world of forms. This is achieved by means of pure rationality (contemplation, mathematical-type reasoning): the abstract intellectual grasp of the ideal forms of which particular objects are imperfect imitations. Plato called this knowledge *EPISTĒMĒ*. Common knowledge has to do with the understanding of the sensed world by means of sense perception, experience, observation of particulars. Plato called this knowledge *DOXA:* "opinion."

esthetics. See AESTHETICS.

estrangement (L., *extraneous,* "strange," from *extraneare,* "to treat or regard something as a stranger" [sometimes an unwanted and unknown stranger]). **1.** The act of keeping something at a distance, or withdrawing and withholding one's emotions and confidence in things, usually because the world appears unfriendly. See ALIENATION. **2.** The state of feeling produced by **1.** See SELF-ALIENATION. Contrast with DEALIENATION.

eternal (L., *aeternus,* from *aevum,* "age"). **1.** Everlasting. Of infinite duration. Endless continuation in time without beginning or end. SEMPITERNAL. Perpetual. **2.** Having no succession, but existing all at once, an unchanging timelessly present One. See AEVITERNITY.

eternal, *a parte ante.* The infinite extent of time before (*ante*) any present moment.

eternal, *a parte post.* The infinite extent of time after (*post*) any present moment.

eternal recurrence. See RECURRENCE, ETERNAL.

eternal return. See RECURRENCE, ETERNAL.

ethical imperativism. See IMPERATIVISM.

ethical intuitionism. See ETHICS, INTUITIVE.

ethical naturalism. See NATURALISM, ETHICAL.

ethical nihilism. See NIHILISM (ETHICS).

ethical relativism. See RELATIVISM (VALUE THEORY).

ethics (Gk., *ēthikos,* from *ĒTHOS,* "usage," "character," "custom," "disposition," "manners"). **1.** The analysis of concepts such as "ought," "should," "duty," "moral rules," "right," "wrong," "obligation," "responsibility," etc. **2.** The inquiry into the nature of morality or moral acts. **3.** The search for the morally good life.

ethics (Kant). Doing something out of a desire to do it and doing something out of a feeling of moral OBLIGATION (DUTY) to do it are different states. Moral merit cannot be given to actions done out of instinct or inclination. Moral merit can be given only to those actions done out of a sense of duty as prescribed by reason. The only unqualified good is the "good will." To have a good will is to act always from a sense of duty. Duty is awareness of the moral law and complete submission to the moral law. Moral law is in opposition to inclination and it is expressed in the form of a categorical imperative ("No matter what, you must . . ."). The moral law is unconditional. Desire is variable. The methods for obtaining the satisfaction of desires are variable. But the moral law applies at all times, in all places and to all people, and with respect to every moral instance. Duty, the good will, the moral law are *a priori* concepts. No one can ever know them merely by describing behavior. See CATEGORICAL IMPERATIVE, THE (KANT); ETHICS, FORMALISTIC (KANT); END, MAN AS AN (KANT); ENDS, HETERONOMY OF (KANT); ENDS, KINGDOM OF (KANT); POSTULATES OF PRACTICAL REASON, THE (KANT); WILL, AUTONOMY OF THE (KANT); WILL, FREE ELECTIVE (KANT).

ethics, axiological. The theory that the values inherent or involved in a moral act determine the act's worth and correctness. See AXIOLOGY.

ethics, casuistic (L., *casus,* "case," from *cadere,* "to fall," "to happen"). Sometimes simply referred to as CASUISTRY. **1.** The application (or stretching) of ethical rules to judge (favorably or adversely) a particular ethical situation. **2.** Using conniving or false arguments to morally defend an action insupportable by moral rules. **3.** Using dubious moral rules to defend an action. Compare with RATIONALIZE.

ethics, deontological. Sometimes, but rarely, simply *deontics* (see DEONTOLOGY). The theory (a) that the rightness or wrongness of a moral action is determined, at least partly, with reference to formal rules of conduct, rather than consequences or results of an action, and (b) that some actions in conformance with these rules are obligatory (compulsory, categorically imperative, necessary) regardless of their results. Sometimes called a "formalist" theory (see ETHICS, FORMALISTIC), since it is based on following the fixed, formal status of moral law. Related to *ethical intuitionism* (see ETHICS, INTUITIVE; INTUITIONISM [ETHICS]) when it is thought that the formal rules of conduct are obtained by intuition. Contrasted with approaches such as the pragmatic, the utilitarian, and the teleological, which stress the results of an act as determining the moral act's worth and correctness. Opposite to ETHICS, TELEOLOGICAL.

ethics, descriptive. Sometimes *descriptive morality.* Seeks to know (**a**) what ethical rules (or moral actions) are common among people, (**b**) whether they are universal, and (**c**) what effects their application has.

ethics, descriptivism in. Sometimes *ethical descriptivism.* The view that ethical statements (values) are obtained much as factual (descriptive) statements are obtained and are meaningful and utilizable much in the same way. For the most part related with ethical objectivism and descriptive ethics (see ETHICS, DESCRIPTIVE). Contrasted with *emotivism* (see ETHICS, EMOTIVE THEORY OF) and PRESCRIPTIVISM in ethics.

ethics, emotive theory of. Also *emotivism.* A noncognitive theory: ethical knowledge is different from other kinds of knowledge such as factual, scientific, conceptual, cognitive, logical. Words like "right," "wrong," "bad," "good," "should," "ought to," (**a**) do not refer to qualities in things, (**b**) cannot be said to be true or false (since they do not describe any states of affairs), (**c**) cannot be formally deduced or demonstrated by means of a logical system, and (**d**) cannot be empirically verified by such things as experimentation, observation, testing procedures. Ethical words function similarly to interjections ("Terrific!"), imperatives ("Do that!"), prescriptions ("Thou shalt . . ."), optatives ("Would that . . .!"), or performative utterances ("I apologize"). Ethical statements are expressions of such things as blame, praise, prohibition, derogation, used (1) to influence conduct and/or (2) to express emotions, feelings, attitudes, or (3) to evoke similar emotions. They request, exhort, command, persuade, advise, cajole. Ethical disagreement (disagreement about convictions or values) is actually disagreement about attitudes. For some emotive theorists, ethical statements may indirectly be cognitive, in that they may provide information about one's attitudes, beliefs, ideas, commitments, and convictions.

ethics, evolutionary. See DARWINISM, SOCIAL.

ethics, formalistic. Sometimes *ethical formalism,* or *deontological ethics.* Universal ethical rules are obligatory regardless of their consequences to us or to others. See ETHICS, DEONTOLOGICAL.

ethics, formalistic (Kant). Sometimes Kant's ethics is referred to as *ethical formalism.* Correct moral choices (action, behavior) can be made according to many motives and standards such as prudence ("If I wish this, then I must do such and such"), sympathy, goodness, benevolence, love, compassion. But the highest motive and standard must be a sense of duty—the unqualified submission to the universal, exceptionless moral law. See CATEGORICAL IMPERATIVE, THE (KANT); ETHICS (KANT).

ethics, intuitive. Sometimes *ethical intuitionism.* **1.** Moral values are intuitively apprehended, or given. **2.** (Usually): These intuitively apprehended moral values are (a) objectively real, universally obligatory, common to all human beings, and (b) the ability to discern them by INTUITION is latent in everyone. **3.** (a) Certain kinds of human actions are directly, intuitively, and self-evidently known to be intrinsically wrong or right, bad or good, and/or (b) certain ultimate, universal moral principles or rules are directly, intuitively, and self-evidently known as binding upon human nature.

Intuitively known moral universals and values are often claimed to be (**a**) unobservable, (**b**) nonnatural (underived from an examination of natural phenomena), (**c**) innate, (**d**) simple, (**e**) self-evidently true, (**f**) immediately and directly present to (or perceived by) conscience, and (**g**) requiring no justification.

ethics, is/ought dichotomy in. Sometimes *fact/value dichotomy*. From a description of facts it is impossible to assert moral strictures or arrive at ethical convictions. Example: you cannot deduce the moral dictum "Humans ought to speak the truth" from the fact that humans do speak the truth (or do not speak the truth). See IS/OUGHT DICHOTOMY; and entries under NATURALISTIC FALLACY.

ethics, monistic. Sometimes *ethical monism*. The theory that only one intrinsically worthwhile ethical good such as pleasure exists. All things are done for the sake of that good.

ethics, moral faculty theory in. 1. The theory that one can perceive the difference between good and bad, right and wrong, with the aid of an ethical FACULTY or sense, in the same way that one can perceive the difference between yellow and blue, a sound and a smell, with the aid of perceptual faculties. One can know that this paper is white by perceiving it. So one can know that something is ethical or not by perceiving the situation. **2.** The view that there is a faculty which directs us toward moral values such as benevolence, the common GOOD, DUTY, sacrifice, love of mankind. Compare with MORAL SENSE. See CONSCIENCE.

ethics, naturalistic. 1. The theory that ethics is empirical. Ethical statements have their source in what is occurring in nature and in human nature. Ethics can be derived from an examination of nonethical conditions such as the social interaction of people, their needs and drives. **2.** Ethical terms can be defined in nonethical (natural, descriptive, factual) terms. **3.** Ethical statements can be reduced to factual statements about natural processes or events. See NATURALISM, ETHICAL.

ethics, noncognitive. The position that statements containing implicit or explicit references to moral values do not contain descriptive knowledge, are not informative in that sense, and hence are neither true nor false.

ethics, normative. Moral philosophy that provides man with general guidelines or knowledge about such things as (**a**) what is good and right (bad and wrong), (**b**) what man ought to do (and ought not to do) in specific situations, (**c**) what should be pursued in life, (**d**) how life should be lived,

(e) what we should do to others and what they should do to us.

ethics, objectivism in. See OBJECTIVISM (VALUE THEORY).

ethics, perfectionism in. See PERFECTIONISM (ETHICS).

ethics, pluralistic. Sometimes *ethical pluralism.* The theory that (**a**) a number of intrinsically worthwhile ethical values or goods (such as charity, love, sharing, benevolence, kindness) exist, and (**b**) the SUMMUM BONUM of an individual is to participate in as many of them as he can.

ethics, subjectivism in. 1. The theory that ethical judgments such as "good" mean that I approve of certain actions and that I personally feel or think the same way. **2.** Moral values are expressions of human emotions, attitudes, reactions, feelings, thoughts, wishes, desires, and have no objective reference in the world. **3.** There is no way of rationally or objectively solving moral conflict, or arriving at moral judgments or values. Compare with SUBJECTIVISM (VALUE THEORY).

ethics, teleological. 1. The theory that the consequences (see CONSEQUEN-TIALISM [ETHICS]) of a moral act (as opposed to its intention, motive, moral principle, etc.) determine the act's worth and correctness. One may have the best of intentions, or follow the highest moral principles, but if the result of a moral act is harmful or bad it must be judged as a morally or ethically wrong act. PRAGMATISM, UTILITARIANISM, and other related theories presuppose teleological ethics. Opposite to ETHICS, DEON-TOLOGICAL. **2.** An ethics in which the moral worth of an act is judged in terms of the extent to which that act accomplishes its purpose or end (or the purpose or end of the ethical system adhered to). **3.** An ethics in which the rightness or wrongness of an act is judged with reference to some end result that is regarded as desirable and good. Whatever achieves this end result is morally good and whatever thwarts its achievement is morally bad.

ethnocentrism (Gk., *ethnos,* "nation," and *kentron,* "center," "central"). The belief of a people or group that their own ways (values, religion, race, nation, culture, language) are superior to all others.

ēthos (Gk., "character," "one's habitual way of living," "one's moral motivation or purpose"). **1.** The character, tone, disposition, values, and sentiments of a person, community, or people. **2.** In Plato, one's *ēthos* is the character produced by habitual responses. **3.** In Aristotle, one's *ēthos* is the character produced by moral as opposed to intellectual habits. (Aristotle describes different *ēthoi* (plural) found at different stages in human development. Aristotle also used *ēthos* to refer to a drama's presentation of character as opposed to action, incidents, suffering, thought, diction, etc. Compare with PATHOS. **4.** In Stoicism, *ēthos* refers to that which motivates behavior or conduct. (This is reminiscent of Heracleitus' saying that the *ēthos* of an individual is his DAIMŌN.)

etiology. See AETIOLOGY.

être en soi (Fr., "being-in-itself," "being-in-oneself"). See EN SOI (SARTRE).

être pour soi (Fr., "being for itself," "being for oneself"). See *POUR SOI* (SARTRE).

eudaimonia (Gk., "a vital spiritual well-being," "happiness," from *eu,* "well," "good," and *DAIMŌN,* "spirit," "god," "inner force," "genius"). Aristotle's word for the happiness attained when all of an individual's potentiality for a full rational life is realized to the utmost and the individual fully expresses all of his varied capacities. This striving for self-realization is the essence of being human. See GOOD (ARISTOTLE).

euphemism (Gk., *euphēmismos,* from *euphēmizein,* "to use words that have a good omen or appearance," from *eu,* "well," and *phēmē,* "voice," "speech," or *phanai,* "to speak," "to make appear"). Sometimes referred to as *eulogism.* An inoffensive or better-sounding word or expression substituted for one that is unpleasant, harsh-sounding, or insensitive.

event (L., *eventus,* from *evenire,* "to happen," "to come out," "to occur," from *e,* "out," and *venire,* "to come"). **1.** That which occurs (happens). **2.** A change in the properties (qualities, characteristics, attributes, relations) of a thing. **3.** A change (movement, activity, process) between or among things. (Contrasted with object, thing, state of.)

evidence (L., *e,* "out," and *videre,* "to see"). **1.** Proof or fact. **2.** That which tends or is used to prove or support something. **3.** That which is accepted as conclusive (clear, obvious, acceptable, confirmed) support of a statement (proposition, hypothesis, law).

evil. 1. That which is injurious, painful, hurtful, or calamitous. **2.** Morally bad or unacceptable. Sinful. Wicked. Vicious. Corrupt. **3.** That which impedes the achievement of goals, ideals, happiness, or general well-being. **4.** Misfortune.

evil, moral. Evil that is the result of deliberate human action. Contrasted with EVIL, NATURAL.

evil, natural. Evil that is the result of usual or unusual natural occurrences. Examples: diseases, famines, drought, volcanic eruption causing death. Contrasted with EVIL, MORAL.

evil, theological problem of. An ANTILOGISM that stems from assuming three things, only two of which are compatible (sometimes called the *incompatible triad):* (**a**) the omnipotence of God, (**b**) the omnibenevolence of God, and (**c**) the existence of evil.

Epicurus presented the problem this way:

Is God willing to prevent evil, but *not able* to prevent evil? Then he is not omnipotent.
Is God able to prevent evil, but *not willing* to prevent evil? Then He is not omnibenevolent.
Is God *both* willing and able to prevent evil?
Then why does evil exist?

Hume presented the same problem thus:

If evil in the world is the intention of the Deity, then He is not benevolent.

If evil in the world is contrary to His intention, then He is not omnipotent.

But evil is either in accordance with His intention or contrary to it.

Therefore, either the Deity is not benevolent, or He is not omnipotent.

evolution (L., *evolutio,* "an unrolling," "unfolding," "developing"). **1.** The
development of a thing into a more complex organization and/or different organization. **2.** The development of a thing's potential toward a further result, purpose, or end.

Evolutionism is the general name given to developmental views of life
or the universe. See NATURAL SELECTION (DARWIN).

evolution, emergent. As a speculative COSMOGONY, emergent evolution deals
with more than the evolution of living forms on earth. It presents the general outlines of the evolutionary process of the universe (the totality of
spatio-temporal existence). Its principal aim is to delineate the succession
of levels in the universe that show such characteristics as unity, variety,
and progressive increase in complexity. The basic categories or concepts
used in its analysis are: (**a**) discontinuity (emergence), (**b**) levels (qualities), (**c**) novelty, (**d**) creative advance. **1.** *Discontinuity:* Differs from the
gradualism (the continuity of changes among life forms) of Darwinism.
Evolutionary events are *discontinuous* with previous events. Novelty,
that which comes into existence for the first time, does so abruptly. **2.**
Level: That part of the universe having related qualities (properties, aspects, characteristics) which have emerged from previously existing levels. Each succeeding level contains the constituents of the preceding level.
3. *Novelty:* The evolutionary process "produces" existents which have
never in any way been in existence before. Those novel features produced
can neither be reduced in explanation to their constituent parts nor predicted from them. They are cumulative features of a creative advance
(NISUS). Examples: life, mind, fluidity, translucence, conscience, sensation. Each novel quality may be thought of "holistically" as more than
the sum of its parts (see *GESTALT;* HOLISM). In a sense, this is allied with
the notion that there is more in the effect than that which is contained in
the cause. **4.** *Creative advance:* There are small accumulative advances in
the rearrangements and reorganizations of the constituents at each level,
but there is also a broad, general creative direction toward an all-encompassing, interrelated perfect whole. (For most emergent evolutionists that
perfect whole will never be completely realized but is the infinite goal
toward which the universe strives.) Emergent evolution is associated with
such names as C. Lloyd Morgan, Jan Christiaan Smuts, Samuel Alexander, Henri Bergson. See EMERGENT, AN; VITALISM.

excluded middle, law of. See LAWS OF THOUGHT, THE THREE.

existence (L., *existere,* "to appear," "to exist," "to emerge," "to have actual being," from *ex,* "out of," and *sistere,* "to cause to stand"). **1.** That which exists. **2.** That which has actuality (being). **3.** Anything that is experienced.

Asserting *that* a thing is, in contrast with ESSENCE, which asserts *what* a thing is (what a thing truly is according to its inherent nature). See OBJECTIVE EXISTENCE (REALITY).

existential. In EXISTENTIALISM, refers to: **1.** the vivid experience of the reality and varied dimensions of the present, **2.** the awareness that one *is* and that one is an acting, choosing being creating and expressing one's self-identity in the process of acting and choosing responsibly, **3.** the experience of being intensely involved in living, its fulfillments and predicaments.

existential import. Refers to statements that assert or assume the real existence of the objects that they denote.

existentialism. Also *existential philosophy, existentialist philosophy.* A relatively modern view in philosophy (although with historical roots as far back as Greek and medieval philosophy) associated in its inception with Søren Kierkegaard and Friedrich Nietzsche. Its primary and best-known exponent in contemporary philosophy is the French philosopher Jean-Paul Sartre. Other existentialists: Camus, Jaspers, Heidegger, Marcel. There are many varieties of existentialism ranging from atheism to theism, from phenomenalism and phenomenology to forms of Aristotelianism. Some of the following themes are common to existentialists: **1.** EXISTENCE precedes ESSENCE. Forms do not determine existence to be what it is. Existence fortuitously becomes and is whatever it becomes and is, and that existence then makes up its "essence." **2.** An individual has no essential nature, no self-identity other than that involved in the act of choosing. **3.** Truth is subjectivity. **4.** Abstractions can never grasp nor communicate the reality of individual existence. **5.** Philosophy must concern itself with the human predicament and inner states such as alienation, anxiety, inauthenticity, dread, sense of nothingness, anticipation of death. **6.** The universe has no rational direction or scheme. It is meaningless and absurd. **7.** The universe does not provide moral rules. Moral principles are constructed by humans in the context of being responsible for their actions and for the actions of others. **8.** Individual actions are unpredictable. **9.** Individuals have complete freedom of the will. **10.** Individuals cannot help but make choices. **11.** An individual can become completely other than what he is. See *ANGOISSE;* BAD FAITH (SARTRE); COMMITMENT (SARTRE); *ENNUI; EN SOI* (SARTRE); ONTOLOGY (EXISTENTIAL PSYCHOLOGY); *POUR SOI* (SARTRE).

existentialism, humanistic. Some of the beliefs: **1.** The universe (**a**) is not in itself intelligible (humans make it intelligible), (**b**) does not conform to any rational, logical order or process, (**c**) is not created, supported, or designed by an omnipotent, benevolent God. **2.** All things are contingent;

nothing is necessarily decreed to occur as it occurs. **3.** All meaning, order, explanation, classification is given to reality by consciousness and is not part of any reality other than the reality of consciousness. **4.** Reality cannot be reduced to a neat system since it is inherently unintelligible, noncategorizable and amorphous. **5.** There is no objective moral realm; moral values do not exist ouside of consciousness. Compare with HUMANISM, PHILOSOPHICAL.

ex nihilo nihil fit (L., "nothing comes out of nothing," or "out of nothing, nothing can come," or "nothing can be made out of nothing"). Sometimes simply *nihil ex nihilo* or *creatio ex nihilo nihil fit*. Contrasted with *CREATIO EX NIHILO*.

exoteric (Gk., *exōterikos,* "being outside something," from *exōteros,* "outer," "utter," "exterior"). **1.** Open to everyone. Pertaining to that which is not secretive and understood only by a selected few, but is easily comprehended by the public. **2.** Referring to the public, or popular, presentation of ideas (doctrines, beliefs) easily understood by laymen (noninitiates, nonexperts). **3.** Specifically, exoteric refers to some of Aristotle's (mostly early) writings (*exōterikoi logoi*), which were written for general, popular reading outside his school and contained ideas easily grasped by the populace (in contrast to the *esōterikoi logoi* or technical writings intended for student use within his school). Contrast with ESOTERIC.

experience (L., *experientia,* "trial, experience"). **1.** Living through events, feelings, emotions, sufferings, happenings, states of CONSCIOUSNESS. **2.** Knowledge derived from personal activity, practice, practical skills. **3.** The capacity or talent to perform something derived from the above. **4.** States of consciousness such as being in pain, imagining a unicorn, doubting a belief, thinking about the sum of 2 and 2, enjoying a musical composition. (There is philosophic controversy as to whether or not there is a difference between such immediate experiences and the AWARENESS that one is having them.) Compare with EXPERIENTIAL; PERCEPTION; SENSATION.

experience, mystical. See MYSTICAL EXPERIENCE.

experience, pure. See PURE EXPERIENCE.

experience, religious. See RELIGIOUS EXPERIENCE.

experiential. Referring to any kind of experience, in contrast to EMPIRICAL, which is confined to sensation/perception/observation types of experiences that are shared by people. For example, *experiential data* includes the knowledge (understanding, intuitions, insights, information) obtainable by such means as INTROSPECTION, self-analysis, private conscious states, etc., whereas *empirical data* is limited to the knowledge obtained through the senses and/or checked by the senses.

experientialism. The theory that immediate, concrete experience is the only source of knowledge and the only method of testing the value and truth of knowledge (theories, hypotheses, etc.).

explanation (L., *explanare,* "to flatten," "to make level or plane," "to explain"). In general, making something intelligible, rational, or familiar. An explanation of phenomena differs from a proof of phenomena in that if one requests an explanation, this assumes the existence of the phenomena to be explained, whereas if one requests a PROOF, this assumes that the phenomena may have not occurred and some evidence of their occurrence must be presented.

explanation, functional. Explanation of phenomena in terms of describing the interrelated activities (functions, actions) that elements of a thing undergo during its existence. A functional explanation of "Why does the heart beat?" would be in terms of the further activities that depend upon the heart's activities such as the circulation of blood, and/or the physical, chemical, and possibly artificial processes (functions) of those parts of the heart and body upon which the beating of the heart depends. Opposed to explanations in terms of "purposes," "intentional striving for goals," "drives to fulfill an end." Contrasted with EXPLANATION, TELEOLOGICAL.

explanation, holistic. See HOLISTIC EXPLANATION.

explanation, mechanistic. The description of how parts mechanically interact with other parts within a complex. Opposite to EXPLANATION, TELEOLOGICAL. See MECHANISM.

explanation, organismic. See ORGANISMIC EXPLANATION.

explanation, scientific. Making something intelligible by describing *what* the structures and processes of a thing are, and/or showing *how* a thing does what it does. Contrasted with EXPLANATION, TELEOLOGICAL.

The foundation of scientific explanation: (**a**) the forming of generalizations (theories) from facts (empirical observations) by the use of inductive-deductive methods; (**b**) connecting these facts with a consistent and systematic body of generalizations and related facts already accumulated and accepted (confirmed, verified); (**c**) drawing out the logical and empirical implications and consequences the facts may have for the body of generalizations itself, (**d**) constructing a JUSTIFICATION (CONFIRMATION, VERIFICATION) for the facts and for the generalizations; and (**e**) showing that facts can be calculated (deduced), quantified, or predicted from the body of generalizations. See METHOD, SCIENTIFIC.

explanation, teleological 1. Explanation in terms of some purpose (end, goal) for which something is done. **2.** Explanation in terms of goal-directed or purpose-directed activity. Usually the goal or purpose is preset or planned. **3.** Explaining the present and past with reference to something in the future (a goal, purpose, end, result) that is being striven for or for the sake of which the process takes place. Opposite to mechanistic explanation (see EXPLANATION, MECHANISTIC), which explains the present, and any future event, in terms of conditions prior to it. **4.** Explanation in terms of the structures and activities of the parts of a whole being adapted (coordinated, adjusted, fitted, suited) to each other toward the fulfillment of the purposes or needs of that whole. See ANIMISM; CAUSES, ARISTOTLE'S FOUR; ORGANISMIC EXPLANATION; and entries under TELEOLOGICAL.

explication (L., *explicatus,* present participle of *explicare,* "to unfold," "to display," from *ex,* "out of," "from," and *plicare,* "to fold"). **1.** Explanation. **2.** The process of making obvious (explicit) and (sometimes) precise, what is implied or implicit in a statement. **3.** In categorical logic, showing how the meaning of the predicate is contained in the meaning of the subject. See STATEMENT, ANALYTIC. Opposite to SYNTHETIC. **4.** The giving of a full and detailed account of something.

expressive. See MEANING, EXPRESSIVE.

extension. 1. DENOTATION. The sum total of things to which a word applies. The extension of the common noun "human" is all those things that possess the (intensional) characteristics of humans such as being a rational mammal that is a biped. The extension of a word is determined by its CONNOTATION (INTENSION.) **2.** The range of things to which a concept refers or over which it has meaning.

In general, extension refers to the objective world, as opposed to intension, which refers to how we *mean* to see or look at the world. Also, for the most part extension has to do with classes and intension with qualities (properties, attributes, characteristics, etc.). See LAW OF INVERSE VARIATION (INTENSION/EXTENSION); MEANING, EXTENSIONAL. Compare with INTENSION.

extension (metaphysics) (L., *ex,* "out," and *tendere,* "to stretch out"). Also *extended.* Occupying physical space and existing in time. That which is tangible, can be divided, has shape or figure and is capable of being changed and/or moved. See entries under SUBSTANCE.

extension, empty. Refers to words that have meaning but do not denote anything. Example: The word *centaur* does not denote; it has no extension; it has an empty extension.

extensionality, thesis of. 1. The theory that every (empirical) statement is either an elementary propositon of fact (a logically simple statement) *or* a truth-function of such statements. **2.** The theory that every intensional statement can be translated into an extensional statement; all intensionality can be reduced to extensionality; there is no intensional logic since all extensional statements contain no intensionality. See EXTENSION; INTENTION.

external relations. See RELATIONS, EXTERNAL.

externalization. Sometimes *extrojection* or *external reference.* The tendency or the act of the mind to regard sensations as externally real objects.

extrapolation. The process of assigning probability values for events, or of predicting events that extend beyond the patterns established by the known empirical data, but which are suggested, or which can be inferred from such data.

extraspection. The ability to have, or the feeling that one has, direct and immediate communication with or understanding of external minds. Compare with INTROSPECTION; RETROSPECTION; TELEPATHY.

extrasensory phenomena or perception. See ESP; PARAPSYCHOLOGY.

extrinsic (L., *exter,* "outside," and *secus,* "beside," "otherwise"). **1.** External. **2.** Unessential. Opposite to INTRINSIC.

extrinsic good (value). See GOOD, EXTRINSIC.

extrinsic-intrinsic good (value). See GOOD, INTRINSIC-EXTRINSIC.

F

fact (L., *facere,* "to do"). **1.** An actually occurring event, quality, relation, state of affairs. That which is actual, real. That which is. **2.** A situation or state of affairs that has taken place. **3.** A true description of what is happening or of what has happened. A fact in the sense of **1** or **2** makes such a description true or false. These views assume that facts exist independently of our thoughts about them. **4.** The meaning contained in true statements. **5.** A judgment (interpretation) of what we regard reality to be like. The view in **4** and **5** assumes that facts do *not* exist independently of our thoughts about them. **6.** That which corresponds to a true statement. See TRUTH, CORRESPONDENCE THEORY OF.

fact, atomic. See ATOMIC FACT.

fact, brute. An ultimate fact for which no further explanation (reason, account) need or can be given. Example: That the universe is eternal.

fact/value dichotomy. See IS/OUGHT DICHOTOMY.

faculties of the soul (Plato). The soul is divided into three faculties: **(a)** The APPETITIVE, **(b)** the spirited, and **(c)** the rational. When the faculties are in harmony about ideals and knowledge of the good, an individual has peace of soul. When they are divided, an individual is in a state of disorder and conflict. See SOUL (PLATO).

faculty (L., *facultas,* from *facilis,* "easy," and *facere,* "to make"). A power (ability, endowment) of the mind (soul or body) that produces certain operations or functions. A general list of faculties: **(a)** *Vegetative* or *nutritive:* causes activities such as metabolism, respiration, nutrition, growth, reproduction. **(b)** *Locomotive:* causes movement, directional change. **(c)**

APPETITIVE: causes our basic wants, drives, desires, and bodily needs. (**d**) AFFECTIVE or *sensory:* causes sensation, perception, feelings, emotions, pleasures, pains, and is the basis of most forms of memory and imagination. (**e**) *Volitional:* causes our will to live and our drive (energy) to attain our desires, wants, needs, and interests. See VOLITION; WILL. (**f**) RATIONAL, *cognitive,* or *intellectual:* causes knowledge and activities such as abstract thinking, conceptualizing, judging, interpreting, using language, knowing the good and directing the will toward it. See CONSCIENCE.

faculty psychology. The theory that: **1.** consciousness, or mental states such as those of willing (VOLITION), thinking, imagining, feeling, are caused and explainable by the faculties of the mind that correspond with those states of consciousness, such as the faculty of volition, the faculty of reason, the faculty of imagination or fancy, the spirited faculty, the appetitive faculty, etc. **2.** The mind (or soul) operates according to the faculties in **1.** Taken together they form the entity or substance called the mind, soul, spirit, which in some mode of interaction with the body is the source of our consciousness or mental states. Contrasted with FUNCTIONAL PSYCHOLOGY.

faith (L., *fides,* "faith," "trust," "loyalty"). **1.** Acceptance of a system of beliefs believed to be true. **2.** Belief in the creeds of a religion **3.** Steadfast belief and trust in God, (usually one who has revealed Himself and can be known). **4.** Belief in something despite the evidence against it. **5.** Belief in something even though there is an absence of evidence for it. **6.** Belief in something because of past evidence for it. Confidence based on reliability. **7.** Trust in the truth of something which cannot be rationally or empirically supported but which is presupposed by some form of empirical knowledge. See BELIEF; *CREDO UT INTELLIGAM; FIDEISM.*

faith (ethics). Used mostly in the sense of "keeping faith" (as opposed to "keeping the faith") which implies such things as keeping promises, being loyal, trustworthy, fair, reliable, etc.

faith (Kant). The acceptance of regulative principles or ideals that cannot be demonstrated theoretically or empirically but nevertheless are needed and used efficiently in scientific, practical, and moral affairs.

faith, bad. See BAD FAITH (SARTRE).

fallacy (L., *fallax,* "deceitful," and *fallere,* "to deceive"). **1.** A logical error; reasoning that does not follow the rules of inference or that violates them. **2.** An argument that is misleading in the sense that it is incorrect but may, or is used to, convince people of its correctness. **3.** A defective (false, incorrect, erroneous, mistaken) argument in which the conclusion is not justified by the statements supporting it. Fallacies can be divided into two broad groupings: *formal fallacies* and *informal fallacies.* See further entries under FALLACY. Compare with INVALID; PREVARICATION; SOPHISM.

fallacy, classification of informal. Informal fallacies (see FALLACY, INFOR-

MAL) may be classified in a variety of ways. Three general categories: **(a)** *Material fallacies* have to do with the facts (the matter, the content) of the argument in question. Two subcategories of material fallacies are: (1) *fallacies of evidence,* which refer to arguments that do not provide the required factual support (ground, evidence) for their conclusion, and (2) *fallacies of irrelevance* (or *relevance*) which refer to arguments that have supporting statements that are irrelevant to the conclusion being asserted and therefore cannot establish the truth of that conclusion. **(b)** *Linguistic fallacies* have to do with defects in arguments such as ambiguity (in which careless shifts of meanings or linguistic imprecisions lead to erroneous conclusions), vagueness, incorrect use of words, lack of clarity, linguistic inconsistencies, circularities. **(c)** *Fallacies of irrelevant emotional appeal* have to do with affecting behavior (responses, attitudes). That is, arguments are presented in such a way as to appeal to one's prejudices, biases, loyalty, dedication, fear, guilt, and so on. They persuade, cajole, threaten, or confuse in order to win assent to an argument.

fallacy, formal. 1. An invalid argument. An error in deductive logic (reasoning) in which the conclusion does not follow with necessity from the premises. See INVALID. **2.** An invalid inference. A misconstrued or wrong inference that may seem to follow a correct rule of inference but does not, such as denying the antecedent of a conditional statement in order to deny its consequent. **3.** An error of logical form (see FORM, LOGICAL), a violation of a rule of inference or the principles of logic.

Formal fallacies are committed only by deductive arguments.

fallacy, informal 1. Any error in reasoning to conclusions which does not follow the formal structures and rules of logical validity. **2.** An argument whose conclusion **(a)** is not adequately supported and/or **(b)** does not necessarily have to be the conclusion that can be drawn.

Informal fallacies are committed by inductive reasoning or arguments.

fallacy, types of informal. Sometimes *semiformal* or *quasi-formal* fallacies. The following is a list of 40 informal fallacies which is by no means exhaustive. No attempt has been made to subsume them under general categories such as in FALLACIES, CLASSIFICATION OF INFORMAL. **1.** *Black-and-white fallacy.* Arguing **(a)** with the use of sharp ("black-and-white") distinctions despite any factual or theoretical support for them, or **(b)** by classifying any middle point between extremes ("black-and-white") as one of the extremes. Examples: "If he is not an atheist then he is a decent person." "He is either a conservative or a liberal." "He must not be peace-loving, since he participated in picketing the American embassy." **2.** *Fallacy of argumentum ad baculum* (*argument from power or force.*) The Latin means "an argument according to the stick," "argument by means of the rod," "argument using force." Arguing to support the acceptance of an argument by a threat, or use of force. Reasoning is replaced by force, which results in the termination of logical argumentation, and elicits other kinds of behavior (such as fear, anger, reciprocal use of force, etc.). **3.** *Fallacy of argumentum ad hominem* (*argument against the man*). The Latin means "argument to the man." **(a)** Arguing against, or rejecting a person's views by attacking or abusing his personality, character, motives, intentions, qualifications, etc., as opposed to providing evidence why the views are incorrect. Example: "What John said should not be believed because he was a Nazi sympathizer." **4.** *Fallacy of argumentum ad ignorantiam* (*argument from ignorance*). The Latin means "argument *to* ignorance." **(a)** Arguing that something is true because no one has proved it to be false, or **(b)** arguing that something is false because no one has proved it to be true. Examples: **(a)** Spirits exist since no one has as yet proved that there are not any. **(b)** Spirits do not exist since no one has as yet proved their existence. Also called the *appeal to ignorance:* the lack of evidence (proof) for something is used to support its truth. **5.** *Fallacy of argumentum ad misericordiam* (*argument to pity*). Arguing by appeal to pity in order to have some point accepted. Example: "I've got to have at least a B in this course, Professor Angeles. If I don't, I won't stand a chance for medical school, and this is my last semester at the university." Also called the *appeal to pity.* **6.** *Fallacy of argumentum ad personam* (*appeal to personal interest*). Arguing by appealing to the personal likes (preferences, prejudices, predispositions, etc.) of others in order to have an argument accepted. **7.** *Fallacy of argumentum ad populum* (*argument to the people*). Also the *appeal to the gallery, appeal to the majority, appeal to what is popular, appeal to popular prejudice, appeal to the multitude, appeal to mob instinct.* Arguing in order to arouse an emotional, popular acceptance of an idea without resorting to a logical justification of the idea. An appeal is made to such things as biases, prejudices, feelings, enthusiasms, attitudes of the multitude in order to evoke assent rather than to rationally support the idea. **8.** *Fallacy of argumentum ad verecundiam* (*argument to authority or to veneration*). **(a)** Appealing to authority (including customs, tradition, institutions, etc.) in order to gain acceptance of a point at issue and/ or **(b)** appealing to the feelings of reverence or respect we have of those in authority, or who are famous. Example: "I believe that the statement 'You cannot legislate morality' is true, because President Eisenhower said it." **9.** *Fallacy of accent.* Sometimes classified as an *ambiguity of accent.* Arguing to conclusions from undue emphasis (accent, tone) upon certain words or statements. Classified as a *fallacy of ambiguity* whenever this emphasis creates an ambiguity or AMPHIBOLY in the words or statements used in the argument. Example: "The queen cannot but be praised." **10.** *Fallacy of accident.* Also called by its Latin name *a dicto simpliciter ad dictum secundum quid.* **(a)** Applying a general rule or principle to a particular instance whose circumstances by "accident" do not allow the proper application of that generalization. Example: "It is a general truth that no one should lie. Therefore, no one should lie if a murderer at the point of a knife asks you for information you know would lead to a further murder." **(b)** The error in argumentation of applying a general statement to a situation to which it cannot, and was not necessarily intended to, be applied. **11.** *Fallacy of ambiguity.* An argument that has at least one ambiguous word or statement from which a misleading or wrong conclusion is drawn. **12.** *Fallacy of amphiboly.* Arguing to conclusions from statements that are amphibolous—ambiguous because of their syntax (grammatical construction). Sometimes classified as a *fallacy of ambiguity.* **13.** *Fallacy of begging the question.* **(a)** Arriving at a conclusion from statements that themselves are questionable and have to be proved but are assumed true. Example: The universe has a beginning. Every thing that has a beginning has a beginner. Therefore the universe has a beginner called God. This assumes (begs the question) that the universe does indeed have a beginning and also that all things that have a beginning have a beginner. **(b)** Assuming the conclusion or part of the conclusion in the premises of an argument. Sometimes called *circular reasoning, vicious circularity, vicious circle fallacy.* Example: "Everything has a cause. The universe is a thing. Therefore, the universe is a thing that has a cause." See PETITIO PRINCIPII. **(c)** Arguing in a circle. One statement is supported by reference to another statement which statement itself is supported by reference to the first statement. Example: "Aristocracy is the best form of government because the best form of government is that which has strong aristocratic leadership." **14.** *Fallacy of complex question* (or *loaded question*). **(a)** Asking questions for which either a yes or a no answer will incriminate the respondent. The desired answer is already tacitly assumed in the question and no qualification of the simple answer is allowed. Example: "Have you discontinued the use of opiates?" **(b)** Asking questions that are based on unstated attitudes or questionable (or unjustified) assumptions. These questions are often asked rhetorically of the respondent in such a way as to elicit an agreement with those attitudes or assumptions from others. Example: "How long are you going to put up with this brutality?" **15.** *Fallacy of composition.* Arguing **(a)** that what is true of each part of a whole is also (necessarily) true of the whole itself, or **(b)** that what is true of some parts of a whole is also (necessarily) true of the whole itself. Example: "Each member (or some members) of the team is married; therefore the team also has (must have) a wife." Inferring that a collection has certain characteristics merely on the basis that its parts have them erroneously proceeds from regarding the collection DISTRIBUTIVELY to regarding it COLLECTIVELY. **16.** *Fallacy of consensus gentium.* Arguing that an idea is true on the basis **(a)** that the majority of people believe it and/or **(b)** that it has been universally held by all men at all times. Example: "God exists because all cultures have had some concept of a God." **17.** *Fallacy of con-*

verse accident. Sometimes *converse fallacy of accident.* Also called by its Latin name *a dicto secundum quid ad dictum simpliciter.* The error of generalizing from atypical or exceptional instances. Example: "A shot of warm brandy each night helps older people relax and sleep better. People in general ought to drink warm brandy to relieve their tension and sleep better." **18.** *Fallacy of division.* Arguing that what is true of a whole is (a) also (necessarily) true of its parts and/or (b) also true of some of its parts. Example: "The community of Pacific Palisades is extremely wealthy. Therefore, every person living there is (must be) extremely wealthy (or therefore Adam, who lives there, is [must be] extremely wealthy)." Inferring that the parts of a collection have certain characteristics merely on the basis that their collection has them erroneously proceeds from regarding the collection collectively to regarding it distributively. **19.** *Fallacy of equivocation.* An argument in which a word is used with one meaning (or sense) in one part of the argument and with another meaning in another part. A common example: "The *end* of a thing is its perfection; death is the *end* of life; hence, death is the perfection of life." **20.** *Fallacy of non causa pro causa.* The Latin may be translated as "there is no cause of the sort which has been given as the cause." (a) Believing that something is the cause of an effect when in reality it is not. Example: "My incantations caused it to rain." (b) Arguing so that a statement appears unacceptable because it *implies* another statement that is false (but in reality is not). **21.** *Fallacy of post hoc ergo propter hoc.* The Latin means "after this therefore the consequence (effect) of this," or "after this therefore because of this." Sometimes simply *fallacy of false cause.* Concluding that one thing is the cause of another thing because it precedes it in time. A confusion between the concept of succession and that of causation. Example: "A black cat ran across my path. Ten minutes later I was hit by a truck. Therefore, the cat's running across my path was the cause of my being hit by a truck." **22.** *Fallacy of hasty generalization.* Sometimes *fallacy of hasty induction.* An error of reasoning whereby a general statement is asserted (inferred) based on (a) limited information or (b) inadequate evidence, or (c) an unrepresentative sampling. **23.** *Fallacy of ignoratio elenchi* (*irrelevant conclusion*). An argument that is irrelevant; that argues for something other than that which is to be proved and thereby in no way refutes (or supports) the points at issue. Example: A lawyer in defending his alcoholic client who has murdered three people in a drunken spree argues that alcoholism is a terrible disease and attempts should be made to eliminate it. *IGNORATIO ELENCHI* is sometimes used as a general name for all fallacies that are based on irrelevancy (such as *ad baculum, ad hominem, ad misericordiam, ad populum, ad verecundiam, consensus gentium,* etc.) **24.** *Fallacy of inconsistency.* Arguing from inconsistent statements, or to conclusions that are inconsistent with the premises. See the *fallacy of tu* *quoque* below. **25.** *Fallacy of irrelevant purpose.* Arguing against something on the basis that it has not fulfilled its purpose (although in fact that was not its intended purpose). **26.** *Fallacy of "is" to "ought."* Arguing from premises that have only descriptive statements (is) to a conclusion that contains an ought, or a should. See IS/OUGHT DICHOTOMY. **27.** *Fallacy of limited* (or *false*) *alternatives.* The error of insisting without full inquiry or evidence that the alternatives to a course of action have been exhausted and/or are mutually exclusive. **28.** *Fallacy of many questions.* Sometimes *fallacy of the false question.* Asking a question for which a single and simple answer is demanded yet the question **(a)** requires a series of answers, and/or **(b)** requires answers to a host of other questions, each of which should be answered separately. Example: "Have you left school?" **29.** *Fallacy of misleading context.* Arguing by misrepresenting, distorting, omitting, or quoting something out of context. **30.** *Fallacy of prejudice.* Arguing from a bias or emotional identification or involvement with an idea (argument, doctrine, institution, etc.). **31.** *Fallacy of red herring.* Ignoring a criticism of an argument by changing attention to another subject. Examples: "You believe in abortion, yet you don't believe in the right-to-die-with-dignity bill before the legislature." **32.** *Fallacy of slanting.* Deliberately omitting, deemphasizing, or overemphasizing certain points to the exclusion of others in order to hide evidence that is important and relevant to the conclusion of an argument and that should be taken account of in an argument. **33.** *Fallacy of special pleading.* **(a)** Accepting an idea or criticism when applied to an opponent's argument but rejecting it when applied to one's own argument, or **(b)** rejecting an idea or criticism when applied to an opponent's argument but accepting it when applied to one's own. **34.** *Fallacy of straw man.* Presenting an opponent's position in as weak or misrepresented a version as possible so that it can be easily refuted. Example: "Darwinism is in error. It claims that we are all descendants from an apelike creature, from which we evolved according to natural selection. No evidence of such a creature has been found. No adequate and consistent explanation of natural selection has been given. Therefore, evolution according to Darwinism has not taken place." **35.** *Fallacy of the beard.* Arguing **(a)** that small or minor differences do not (or cannot) make a difference, or are not (or cannot be) significant, or **(b)** arguing so as to find a definite point at which something can be named. For example, insisting that a few hairs lost here and there do not indicate anything significant about my impending baldness; or trying to determine how many hairs a person must have before he can be called bald (or not bald). **36.** *Fallacy of tu quoque* (you also). **(a)** Presenting evidence that a person's actions are not consistent with that for which he is arguing. Example: "John preaches that we should be kind and loving. He doesn't practice it. I've seen him beat up his kids." **(b)** Showing that a person's views are inconsistent with what he previously believed and therefore (1) he is not to be trusted, and/or (2) his new view is to be rejected. Example: "Judge Egener was against marijuana legislation four years ago when he was running for office. Now he is for it. How can you trust a man who has changed his mind on such an important issue? His present position is inconsistent with his earlier view and therefore should not be accepted." (c) Sometimes related to the *fallacy of two wrongs make a right*. Example: The Democrats for years used illegal wiretapping; therefore the Republicans should not be condemned for illegal wiretapping. **37.** *Fallacy of unqualified source*. Using as support in an argument a source of authority that is not qualified to provide evidence. **38.** *Gambler's fallacy*. (a) Arguing that since, for example, a penny *has* fallen tails ten times in a row then it will fall heads the eleventh time or (b) arguing that since, for example, an airline *has not* had an accident for the past ten years, it is then soon due for an accident. The gambler's fallacy rejects the assumption in probability theory that each event is independent of its previous happening. The chances of an event happening are always the same no matter how many times that event has taken place in the past. Given those events happening over a long enough period of time then their frequency would average out to ½. See entries under PROBABILITY. Sometimes referred to as the *Monte Carlo fallacy* (a generalized form of the *gambler's fallacy)*: The error of assuming that because something has happened less frequently than expected in the past, there is an increased chance that it will happen soon. **39.** *Genetic fallacy*. (a) Arguing that the origin of something is identical with that from which it originates. Example: "Consciousness originates in neural processes. Therefore, consciousness is (nothing but) neural processes." Sometimes referred to as the *nothing-but fallacy*, or the REDUCTIVE FALLACY. (b) Appraising or explaining something in terms of its origin, or source, or beginnings. (c) Arguing that something is to be rejected because its origins are known and/or are suspicious. **40.** *Pragmatic fallacy*. Arguing that something is true because it has practical effects upon people: it makes them happier, easier to deal with, more moral, loyal, stable. Example: "An immortal life exists because without such a concept men would have nothing to live for. There would be no meaning or purpose in life and everyone would be immoral."

For a few of the other remaining informal fallacies see PATHETIC FALLACY; and entries under NATURALISTIC FALLACY.

false. 1. To say that an idea (belief, proposition, opinion) is false is to say that the FACT to which it refers does not exist (has no being). **2.** Not conforming to reality or truth. **3.** Not having good supporting evidence. **4.** Wrong. **5.** The member of a two truth value set that denies the truth value assigned to a statement. Contrasted with entries under TRUTH.

In science, to *falsify* is to show that the evidence in support of an empirical statement is not verified or confirmed by scientific methodology.

family resemblance (Wittgenstein). The phrase used to refer to an approach in defining that opposes the traditional method of searching for the real ESSENCE or the defining characteristic of a thing. Meanings are associated by a number of elements (features that have family resemblances) **(a)** each of which is possessed by several things, and **(b)** several of which are possessed by each thing without there being any one element (or definite set of elements) possessed by all the things defined in the same way.

fatalism. 1. The belief that all events are necessitated (determined) to happen the way they do in fact happen no matter what we do to try to avoid them or prevent them. Even our attempts to countermand FATE are inevitably thwarted. "What will be will be." **2.** The individual is the product of predeterministic forces operating in the universe. He cannot in any way direct his behavior or his destiny, or that of history. No one can help being what he is and acting as he does. **3.** Certain events will inevitably come to pass in our existence at a particular time and at a prescribed place. See PREDETERMINISM.

fatalism (theology). 1. The belief that God as all-knowing and all-powerful foresees and necessitates according to His foresight how every event in the universe will occur. **2.** All that the individual is and becomes is caused by God's rational power operating in conformity with God's will. Nothing that one can do will alter that fixed plan. Only that which God has decreed to happen happens and that which happens is that which God has decreed to happen. **3.** God necessitates certain events to happen to each individual according to His foreknowledge of the individual's faith and merit as a believer. These events are fated to occur in this life or as salvation in an afterlife. See PREDESTINATION (THEOLOGY).

fate (L., *fatum,* "an oracle," "that which is ordained to happen by the gods"). **1.** PREDESTINATION. The necessity in things compelling them to happen as they do. **2.** DESTINY. One's appointed lot. **3.** Divine Providence. In this sense fate is regarded as the rational, purposeful, good, and necessary outcome of an intelligence. **4.** One's fortune as shaped by forces over which there is no control.

Sometimes fate is regarded as an arbitrary, capricious, impersonal and menacing force, will, or agency. Sometimes fate is personified and pictured as an agent external to the universe determining (necessitating) its processes by an act of intelligence and/or will.

feeling. 1. Sentience. Sensating. Experiencing a sensation in itself apart from any direct reference to the object producing it or to the PERCEPTION (COGNITION, CONATION) of which it is a part. Feelings are regarded as pure subjective states that reveal aspects of the subject's CONSCIOUSNESS but not (necessarily) the qualities of its source. **2.** Used to refer to any experience, or any quality of experience whatever. ("I feel hot." "It feels hot." "I feel neglected." "I feel a thought coming on." "It feels like rain.")

Feelings can be classified as (**a**) occurrent states (see STATE, OCCURRENT) of consciousness happening at a given moment ("I feel morose"), or (**b**) disposition states (see STATE, DISPOSITION) which express tendencies towards something ("I feel that Adam will win this bout").

fictionism. See ALS OB.

fideism (L., *fides,* "faith"). **1.** The doctrine that religious truth is founded on FAITH and not on reason or empirical evidence. **2.** Faith is superior to reason or science as a source of knowledge. **3.** All other sources of knowledge (**a**) must conform to and support knowledge obtained by faith, or (**b**) are based on a faith in presuppositions that cannot be justified by reason or evidence.

fides proecedit intellectum (L., "faith precedes understanding," "faith must be had before one can understand"). An expression used since the time of Augustine to assert the primacy of FAITH; the subordination of the intellect to faith; the subservience of reason to revelation. See *CREDO UT INTELLIGAM.*

final cause. See CAUSES, ARISTOTLE'S FOUR.

fine arts. Those arts whose primary function is to produce an aesthetic experience of beauty without regard to what economic or practical use they may be put. Some of the arts that may fall under this category: architecture, poetry, painting, music, sculpture.

The general contrast to fine art may be called *useful* or *mechanical art.* This refers to products having definite practical human uses (such as chairs, automobiles, houses, umbrellas), which may be made to possess aesthetic qualities yet serve principally a nonaesthetic function. See *TECHNĒ.*

finite (L., *finere,* "to finish," "to limit," "to arrive at an end," and *finis,* "end," "boundary," "limit"). **1.** Having a limit or end point, for example in a series. **2.** Being bounded or contained. Having a magnitude. **3.** Being limited in such qualities as power, abilities, imagination, size. Opposite to INFINITE.

first cause. 1. The uncaused being usually called God, which is the initial cause of the universe's existence. Before this first causal event there was either (**a**) no universe in existence and God created the universe out of nothing (see *CREATIO EX NIHILO*), or (**b**) the universe existed statically without any causal series or interrelationships activating it. **2.** That uncaused being which is the continual causal ground for the particular cause-effect patterns that occur at any given time in the universe. This being may be as in **1**, or it may be the support at each moment of events that stretch back infinitely. Compare with PRIME MOVER; UNCAUSED CAUSE; UNMOVED MOVER. See COSMOLOGICAL ARGUMENT FOR GOD'S EXISTENCE.

first mover. See PRIME MOVER.

first philosophy (**Aristotle**). Translation of Aristotle's *prōtē philosophia,* which had to do with **1.** the study of being as being; the study of the general and pervasive characteristics of all types of existence, the causes and first principles of being, and with **2.** the study of that kind of being that is IMMUTABLE and TRANSCENDENT. **1** is nearly synonymous with modern conceptions of METAPHYSICS and ONTOLOGY. **2** is nearly synonymous with modern conceptions of THEOLOGY. Compare with METAPHYSICS (ARISTOTLE).

first principles. 1. Statements (laws, reasons, rules) that are self-evident and/or fundamental to the explanation of a system and upon which the system depends for consistency and coherence. They are thought to need no explanation. **2.** Those basic laws that cause things to be what they are. They are brute facts and have no cause. **3.** The rudimentary and ultimate truths which serve as the foundation of moral action.

five ways, the (Aquinas). Sometimes *quinque viae*. Refers to the five proofs or arguments that Aquinas presents in his *Summa Theologiae* for the existence of God: **1.** UNMOVED MOVER; **2.** FIRST CAUSE; **3.** The ultimate source of necessity; **4.** The hierarchy of perfections in the world and their source in something completely perfect; and **5.** The governance of the world or teleological direction. See GOD, ARGUMENTS FOR THE EXISTENCE OF.

flux (L., *fluere,* "to flow"). **1.** Change or that which changes. **2.** Motion (flow) or that which moves (flows). Generally associated with Heracleitus' philosophy. *Flux* is one of the translations of the Greek *hroē,* "a river," "a stream," "a flood," "a flowing," "a changing," as for example found in the famous statement attributed to Heracleitus, *panta hrei:* "all things change (are in a state of flux)." See CHANGE (HERACLEITUS).

force (L., *fortis,* "strong"). **1.** That which is able to affect something else. **2.** Any activity (action, power, ENERGY, strength) that changes the condition (characteristics, qualities, motion, spatial relationship) of a thing. **3.** Any action that overcomes resistance or suppresses another action. **4.** The cause of CHANGE (MOTION, activity, action). Compare with entries under POWER. See DYNAMISM.

form (L., *forma,* "form," "shape," "figure," "pattern," "imprint," "organization," "plan," "mold," "stamp"). **1.** An image of the shape or structure of a thing. **2.** The shape, structure, CONFIGURATION of a thing. **3.** The orderly arrangement of things. **4.** That aspect under which a thing is conceptualized or appears and by which it is classified. **5.** The ESSENCE of a thing.

form (Aristotle). 1. ESSENCE. *OUSIA.* **2.** That which is in matter and makes (forms) it into the object it is. See CAUSES, ARISTOTLE'S FOUR. For Aristotle, form could not exist independently of matter except in abstraction. See *HYLE* (ARISTOTLE).

form (Kant). The *A PRIORI* ingredient in all experience whereby what is presented to us as raw sensation by "sensuous intuition" is categorized and unified by the mind into perceptions and judgments. Nothing is meaningful unless structure (form) is imposed upon it by the mind.

form, accidental. That which is secondary but dependent upon the essential form of a thing and which leads the essential form into a nonnecessary mode of existence. Example: The essential form of man is reason. That he becomes a mathematician rather than a dramatist is *forma accidentalis* (accidental form), a mode secondary to the *forma essentia* (essential form) yet dependent on it. Contrasted with FORM, ESSENTIAL OR SUBSTANTIAL.

form, corporeal. That which gives a thing its bodily (material) configuration and characteristics and which is the source of its tendency to continue in existence and to struggle to survive. See CORPOREAL.

form, essential or substantial. 1. That which makes a thing exist as it is. That which causes an existing thing to be what it is. **2.** That which makes a thing become what it becomes. That which gives a process the pattern it has in its becoming or being something. **3.** Matter and change in themselves are indifferent to what composition, configuration, or direction they take. It is substantial or essential form which gives them the particular activity, organization, and purpose they have. **4.** That aspect of a thing which enables us (**a**) to recognize the class (species, order, family) to which it belongs and (**b**) to differentiate it from other things. Contrasted with FORM, ACCIDENTAL.

form, immaterial. That form (spirit, soul) which can, and at times does, exist independently of matter and material objects but which is created by God to manifest itself in a material object (the body) in order to fulfill its essential nature (or form).

form, logical. 1. The pattern (structure) of a statement or an argument, or a process of reasoning, as opposed to its content (subject matter). **2.** The pattern found in the relations of variables and in their truth values. **3.** The inferential relations among statements or arguments independent of their meanings.

form, material. That form which needs matter (*materialis*) for it to exist and to be active as a form.

form, pure immaterial. That form (pure spirit) which exists independently of matter and which at no time relates to matter, neither affecting matter nor needing to have its essence revealed through a material manifestation.

formal. Referring to that which has to do with the abstract pattern, structure, or principle of a thing as opposed to its parts, subject matter, or contents.

formal cause. See CAUSES, ARISTOTLE'S FOUR.

formal language. See LANGUAGE, FORMAL.

formal logic. See LOGIC, FORMAL.

formalism. Any system that stresses FORM (principles, rules, laws) as the significant or ultimate ground of explanation or evaluation.

forms, Plato's theory of ideal. Also *Plato's theory of ideas.* There are two worlds: **(a)** The transcendent (noumenal) world of Absolute, Perfect, unchanging Ideal Forms of which The Good (see *AGATHON*) is the primary one (usually interpreted as including BEAUTY and TRUTH) and the source of all the others such as Justice, Temperance, Courage, and **(b)** the phenomenal world (the world of appearances) composed of things in a state of flux attempting unsuccessfully to emulate (imitate, participate in, partake of) the Ideal Forms. The love (attraction, affinity) that things have for the perfection inherent in these Ideal Forms inspire (cause, motivate) things in the phenomenal world to change, move, act, seek goals. The phenomenal world is the world of our sensuous, ordinary, everyday experiences which are changing, illusory, unstable, erroneous, finite. The world of eternal Forms is the real, true, permanent world of which reason after proper discipline occasionally gives us a glimpse. Abstractions, such as of equality, circularity, redness, humanness, that one can conceive and recognize in a variety of things provide simple indications that Forms exist. The Forms exist independently of consciousness. See ARCHETYPES; IDEAS (PLATO); KNOWLEDGE (PLATO); MOTION (PLATO).

four causes, Aristotle's. See CAUSES, ARISTOTLE'S FOUR.

four elements. See ELEMENTS, THE FOUR.

free will, sense of. 1. The feeling **(a)** of making uncaused, uncompelled choices, or **(b)** initiating uncaused actions. **2.** The feeling that given the same circumstances I could have done otherwise than that which I did in fact do. **3.** The feeling that I can will something, can exert energy in some desired direction, and have it successfully implemented. **4.** The feeling that alternative courses of action are open to me at any given moment and that the future is not fated.

free will, theory of. 1. The belief that, given again the same conditions, humans can will to do otherwise than what they did do. **2.** Acts of free will are caused by inner mental states (willing) of an agent but **(a)** *not* by material changes in the brain and **(b)** *not* by external stimuli. **3.** The will is free in the sense of not being caused or determined by anything else. That is, it is independent of antecedent physiological, neurological, psychological, environmental conditions. Acts of free will are alleged to be "uncaused events," such as uncaused assents, dissents, choices, decisions. See INDETERMINISM (ETHICS). Opposite to DETERMINISM; PREDESTINATION (THEOLOGY); PREDETERMINISM.

free will problem, the. 1. If all human actions are caused, then how can concepts found in our everyday experience such as blame, responsibility, duty, obligation, commitment, dedication to ideals, self-control, self-direction, self-determination, freedom, be made meaningful? **2.** If every human act is caused, then how can this be made compatible with a human's sense of free will? See FREE WILL, SENSE OF. **3.** If each human decision is caused, then how can this be made consistent with humans' common and universal feeling that had they an opportunity to do it over again (a) they *could* have decided to do the opposite, or to do something else, or (b) looking at the past situation with present hindsight they *would* have decided differently, and hence *can* if the situation arises again?

free will problem, the (theology). 1. God is omniscient and therefore knows beforehand as an eternal truth each choice (action) that each human will decide upon. If this is the case, then humans cannot "freely" choose (act) otherwise than the way in which God knows they will (and if they do act contrary to God's knowledge then God cannot be omniscient). If God knows humans' sins before they commit them, and they must occur according to God's knowledge, then how can humans avoid those sins, and how can humans be said to have free will? **2.** If God has complete foreknowledge of everything that will happen, and is also omnipotent, then He must have organized with His power all things to happen the way in which He has foreknowledge of them happening. If this is the case then how can it be maintained that humans have free will?

freedom. 1. Self-determination. Self-control. Self-direction. Self-regulation. **2.** The ability of an agent to act or not to act according to his dictates (willingness, commands) and/or preferences (desires, drives). Being able to act in conformity with that which one wills. Being the cause of one's own actions. **3.** Being compelled or directed by desirable internal motives, ideals, wishes, and drives as opposed to external or internal compulsion, coercion, or constraint. **4.** The ability to choose and the opportunity to satisfy or procure that choice. Compare with LIBERTY.

freedom (Plato). 1. Being governed (mastered, determined) by reason enlightened by knowledge of the ideal Good. Obeying reason rather than being a servant to passions, to involuntary and ignorant actions. **2.** Having the will guided by righteousness (*DIKAIOSYNĒ*). Lack of freedom is being guided by the bad, being subservient to evil. The evil tyrant is to be pitied because being ignorant of the good, he is a slave to evil. Plato and Platonism assumed as an ideal (a) the primacy of man's reason, and (b) the subordination of man's will to reason. God's will is perfectly free because it is directed by perfect goodness.

freedom for. See LIBERTY.

freedom from. 1. The absence of undesirable external or internal interference, containment, coercion, or restraint, imposed by other people, society, institutions, natural forces, or one's inner self, in the realization of desired goals or interests. **2.** The absence of undesirable conditions in life, such as freedom from pain, freedom from hunger, freedom from poverty, freedom from anxiety, freedom from fear, freedom from responsibility.

freedom of. See RIGHTS.

freedom to. The opportunity to achieve the desired goals (ideas, objectives,

purposes, ends) that one has selected for oneself without being obstruct-
ed.

function (L., *functio,* from *fungi,* "to perform," or from *fungor,* "I ex-
ecute," "I perform an operation of some kind"). **1.** The usual (proper,
normal, characteristic) activity of a thing within a system. **2.** The power
or faculty of acting in a certain way unique to that class of things. **3.** The
conceptual operation of relating ordered sets of things that have some
correspondence or dependency between them.

functional explanation. See EXPLANATION, FUNCTIONAL.

functional psychology. The doctrine that conscious processes or states such
as those of willing (volition), thinking, emoting, perceiving, sensating are
activities or operations of an organism in physical interrelationship with a
physical environment and cannot be given hypostatized, substantive existence. These activities facilitate the organism's control, survival, adaptation, engagement or withdrawal, recognition, direction, etc. The entire
organism can be analyzed as a feedback and stimulus response system.
See CYBERNETICS. Consciousness is not produced by faculties, a soul or a
mind, but is the variety of functions found in the human considered as a
biological, physical creature interacting with an environment. Functional
psychology opposes the FACULTY view in psychology (see FACULTY PSY-
CHOLOGY) that, for example, the WILL is a faculty of the self (mind,
personality, consciousness) that *causes* us to make decisions or exert energy toward a goal. Acts of choice and striving are not acts that "obey" a
will. Compare with BEHAVIORISM.

functional unity. Any self-regulating, self-directing, self-organizing, or self-
maintaining unit (system). Such integrated systems are regarded as organic wholes as in biology, or as unitary wholes as in CYBERNETICS, in
which parts of the whole interrelate with each other **(a)** enabling the system to accomplish a specific activity (function, task), and/or **(b)** enabling
the system to persist in its activity merely as an ordered system. That activity which a part within the whole plays in its interrelationships with
other parts in support of **a** and/or **b** is called its "function" within the
system.

fundamentum divisionis (L., "fundamental division"). The method or criterion by which a genus is subdivided.

future (L., *futurus;* used as the future participle of *esse,* "to be"). **1.** That
which is to be. **2.** That which is to come after any "now" moment, or instant of time. **3.** That time yet to come.

future, the. That part of eternity which includes all events that are not occurring and have not occurred but that will occur.

G

gambler's fallacy. See FALLACY, TYPES OF INFORMAL (**38**).

geist (Ger., "spirit," "ghost," "soul," "mind," "that which gives life to a thing"). In German idealistic philosophy the term is used to refer to the ultimate reality and source of all things.

generalization. **1.** That general or universal concept arrived at by an examination of particular things. **2.** A statement referring to something that is regarded as (**a**) true about all members of a class ("All men are mortal") or (**b**) true about a number of the members of a class ("Some artists are wealthy").

generalization, inductive. Sometimes *generalization from experience.* Inductive reasoning that proceeds from the experience or observation of characteristics found in some things to a statement about all members of that class.

generation (L., *generare,* "to generate"). **1.** Origination. **2.** Production. **3.** Formation. **4.** The process of beginning an activity. **5.** In Aristotelianism, the name for the process of change from some particular substance (or form) to another substance so different that another name must be given to it. Example: a caterpillar changing into a butterfly.

genesis (Gk., *genesis,* "origin," "source," "the productive cause of a thing," "the beginning," "the generation of something." Used as a suffix the term signifies development, evolution, a growth process). **1.** The mode of coming into being such as biological growth, or artistic creation. **2.** The origin of a thing's existence, such as its manner of birth, its descent, or its beginning.

genesis (Aristotle). Aristotle's view of genesis (becoming, change, beginning, growth) involves three fundamental concepts: (**a**) the existence of a permanently existing *substratum* or underlying support which he called HY-POKEIMENON or *HYLE;* (**b**) the changing of qualities into their opposites *(enantia),* or into what they were not before, and (**c**) the absence of *sterē-sis,* or the lack of the opposing (or differing) qualities. See CHANGE (AR-ISTOTLE); SUBSTANCE (ARISTOTLE); NATURE (ARISTOTLE).

genetic fallacy. See FALLACY, TYPES OF INFORMAL (**39**).

genus (L., "birth," "rare," "kind," "sort"; the plural is genera). **1.** Any CLASS of objects that can be divided into subclasses or subordinate SPE-CIES. **2.** That class of things being divided into species. Example: In the statement, "dogs are animals," "animals" is the genus. But in "animals are living things," "living things" is the genus, and "animals" becomes the species.

genus, summum (L., "the highest class [category, set, substance]"). **1.** Refers to a supreme genus that is not a member (not a species) of any higher genus; the most inclusive class in any classification and which is not a subclass of any more inclusive class. Example: Being may be regarded as a *summum genus* that includes within it the general classes of: things, objects, bodies, organisms, animals, humans (which general classes can be further divided). **2.** *Summum genus* may be used to refer to what is to be regarded within a context as the highest genus (or one of the highest genera). Example: Quality, which includes: color, blue, azure, teal, turquoise.

genus et differentia **distinction.** The *genus* possesses features that can be predicated of, and are essential to, other kinds (types, classes) of things. The *differentia* is that which is possessed by, or can be predicated of, the members of only one class. Example: "People are animals that laugh." "Animal" is the *genus* and can apply to several other classes such as whales, cats, horses. "Laughing" is the *differentia.* It is a property limited to the class of "people." See DEFINITION, TYPES OF (**7**).

genus/species (Aristotle). One of the principal tasks of science is to divide objects into the classifications of genus and species that are the real kinds or categories in which by their nature they belong and strive to stay. Example: All objects that are colored belong to the genus "color" because they all have in common the property of being colored. Particular red objects belong to a species of that genus. Particular yellow objects belong to another different species of that same genus. They belong to different species because they have different properties; one has the property of being red and the other has the property of being yellow. See SPECIES.

gestalt (Ger., "form," "configuration," "organized WHOLE," "pattern"). **1.** A unified whole, such as an organism (**a**) that has parts that act in an integrated fashion, (**b**) that is greater than the sum of its parts, (**c**) that has a substantive existence over and above the interaction of its individual parts, and (**d**) that is able to affect the behavior of its parts. **2.** In a non-metaphysical sense, *gestalt* merely refers to the CONFIGURATION or sense of totality that a perception has. Example: When a melody is heard (perceived), a dynamic unity or wholeness appears to perception, yet its tones are in themselves diverse and succeed each other in a particular time sequence. Change the time sequence and its *gestalt* is altered. See EMERGENT, AN.

Gestalt philosophy. Three of its basic philosophical tenets: (**a**) Our environment is seen as organized wholes (tables, chairs, houses) that can be broken down further into their constituent parts or sensa rather than being built up out of basic, irreducible, discrete impressions. (**b**) Consciousness has the same essential form *(GESTALT,* structure) as does its correlated psycho-neural-physical source. (**c**) Reality is any world to which the physical organism responds in the process of organizing perceived structures or wholes.

given, the. 1. Anything that is immediately presented to consciousness. **2.** The direct, immediate, irreducible sense data (presentments, appearances, impressions) or feelings, which serve as (**a**) the ultimate foundation of and reference point for what is known and (**b**) the material from which inferences and judgments are made. Compare with PROTOCOLS; SENSA.

gnōsis (Gk., "a knowing," "knowledge," "an inquiry to ascertain knowledge about what happened").

gnothi se auton (Gk., "know thyself" or "knowledge of oneself"). An injunction found inscribed on the Greek temple at Delphi (and others) which served as the basis of Socrates' philosophy of self-analysis and self-realization in order to arrive at better knowledge and conduct.

God. A term variously conceived but used to apply to that which is considered to be a (or *the*) fundamental source of one's existence and/or values.

God, arguments for the existence of. See COMMON CONSENT ARGUMENT FOR GOD'S EXISTENCE; COSMOLOGICAL ARGUMENT FOR GOD'S EXISTENCE; DESIGN, ARGUMENT FROM; FIVE WAYS, THE (AQUINAS); TELEOLOGICAL ARGUMENT FOR THE EXISTENCE OF GOD. Also see entries under ONTOLOGICAL ARGUMENT FOR GOD'S EXISTENCE.

God concepts. God concepts fall into a general classification that refers to the *number* of gods and the *degree* to which it is believed God is *identical with,* or is an IMMANENT or TRANSCENDENT force operating in the universe. The following is a list of some of the God concepts adhering to this classification: **1.** *Polytheism* (Gk., *polys,* "many," and *theos,* "God"). The belief in the existence of many gods. **2.** *Kathenotheism* (Gk., *kath-'hen,* "one by one," and *theos,* "God"). A form of *polytheism,* or, depending on the perspective, a form of *monotheism,* or *monism.* Of the many gods named and believed in, each in turn ("one by one") at a designated time of the year is worshiped and given the allegiance and respect customary to a supreme deity, in the realization that each god symbolizes only one of the innumerable facets of a more complex and fundamental reality or God that is the source of all things. **3.** *Henotheism* (Gk., *heis* or *enos,* "one," and *theos,* "God"). A form of polytheism. Of the many gods that exist, one is their supreme ruler to whom the others must give their loyalty and obedience. **4.** *Dualism* (L., *duo,* "two"). The belief that two gods exist, one a force for good, the other a force for evil, vying for control of the universe. See DUALISM. **5.** *Monotheism* (Gk., *monos,* "one," "single," "alone," "one-and-only," and *theos,* "God"). The belief that there is one-and-only-one God. **6.** *Pantheism* (Gk., *pan,* "all," and *theos,* "God"). The belief that God is identical with the universe. All is God and God is all. The universe taken as a whole is God. God and nature (universe, the totality of all that there is) are synonymous, or two words for the same thing. **7.** *Panentheism* (Gk., *pan,* "all," and *en,* "in," and *theos,* "God"). All things are imbued with God's being in the sense that all things are *in* God. God is more than all that there is. He is a consciousness and the highest unity possible. **8.** *Panpsychism* (Gk., *pan,* "all," and PSYCHĒ, "soul," "spirit," "mind"). The belief that God is completely immanent *in* all things in the universe as a psychic force (mind, consciousness, spirit, soul). See PANPSYCHISM (METAPHYSICS). **9.** *Theism* (Gk., *theos,* "God"). On most interpretations: God is partly immanent in the universe and partly transcendent. See THEISM. **10.** *Deism* (L., *deus,* "God"). On most interpretations: God is totally transcendent, "wholly other" to the universe and none of his being is immanent in the universe. See DEISM.

golden mean, the. See MEAN, THE (ARISTOTLE).

golden rule, the. 1. Do unto others as you would want others to do unto you. **2.** Do not do to others what you would not want done to you.

good. 1. Any object of interest, value, or desire. **2.** That which is the object of, or valued by, the rational will. **3.** That desired by the will. **4.** The product of contemplative activity or the feelings surrounding such activity. The word good conveys laudatory qualities such as approval, commendation, excellence, admiration, appropriateness, and has meanings such as virtuous, beneficent, beneficial, favorable, genuine, praiseworthy. Compare with entries under PLEASURE; UTILITARIANISM.

good (Aristotle). The good is that which in fact a thing aims to achieve in accord with its inherent nature. Example: The good for the individual is that which one is, by one's essential nature, committed to seeking. This is the full actualization of his essence (reason), the development of his rational faculties to the utmost, that Aristotle calls EUDAIMONIA, which is translated as "happiness" but which means the vital well-being that comes from exercising one's potentialities for a rational life. The good is not always identified with what one wishes since wishes are not based on one's essential rational nature. Only when one wishes to express one's essential nature and seeks to do this are the two then coherent with each other.

good (G. E. Moore). Good is like yellow: a simple, indefinable property. The terms differ in that yellow is known by the use of our senses whereas good is intuited. See OPEN-QUESTION ARGUMENT (G. E. MOORE).

good (Plato and Pythagoreans). The good of anything is (**a**) its existence in an intelligent (rational) order (proportion), and in the case of the individual (**b**) his being activated by the highest intellectual (rational) ideas. See *AGATHON.*

good, contributory. That which is desired or valued because of (**a**) the part it plays within an activity or whole which is itself desired or valued (considered a good), and/or (**b**) the part it plays in a process that is developing toward something that is desired.

good, extrinsic. That which is desired or valued not for its own sake but for the sake of something else, for the beneficial consequences it brings. Example: enduring the discomfort of having a decayed tooth removed in order to be relieved of pain. See EXTRINSIC.

good, inherent. 1. The quality in an object or experience that provides the basis for our seeing it as desirable or to be valued. **2.** An ideal objectively existing quality common to all good things and good experiences. Example: aesthetic form.

good, instrumental. That which is desired or valued as a means of obtaining another good. Example: money. See INSTRUMENTALISM.

good, intrinsic. 1. That which is desired or valued in and for itself. **2.** An end sought for its own desirability. Example: pleasure. See INTRINSIC.

good, intrinsic-extrinsic. That which is desired or valued both for its own sake (in and for itself) as well as for the sake of something else, for the beneficial consequences that it brings. Example: listening to a Bach fugue for the sheer enjoyment of it but also in order to pass a music test the next day.

good, the (Plato). See *AGATHON.*

good, the highest. See *SUMMUM BONUM.*

good will, the (Kant). See ETHICS (KANT).

greatest happiness principle. See UTILITARIANISM.

Greek atomism. See ATOMISM, GREEK.

H

habit (L., *habitus,* "state," "appearance," "dress," from *habere,* "to have"). Behavior, associations, or inclinations (**a**) acquired by repetition, (**b**) activated and expressed with little or no thought, and (**c**) performed without much resistance. Compare with *HEXIS* (ARISTOTLE); INSTINCT.

happiness. 1. The pleasurable feeling-tone, which may vary in intensity, associated with one's life, or with certain activities in one's life. The sense of being pleased, joyous, content, satisfied, fortunate, blessed, favored, graced. **2.** The achievement of the highest value or goal in life (that which all individuals strive for) but interpreted variously as the procurement of pleasure, the realization of one's potential, exercising one's duty, being virtuous, following natural law, living a life of moderation, complete freedom to rationally determine one's own destiny, etc.

happiness (Aristotle). See *EUDAIMONIA.*

happiness (Kant). Happiness is an ideal that cannot be realized (at least in this life). It consists of three fundamental aspects which themselves cannot be fully realized in practice: (**a**) self-sufficiency, (**b**) integration (harmony) of the self, and (**c**) self-determination (freedom of the will).

happiness (Mill). Identical (**a**) with pleasure and (**b**) with the absence of pain. Contrast with UNHAPPINESS (MILL).

happiness (Plato). See *ARETĒ.*

hedonic. Refers to (**a**) the pleasure-producing quality of a thing, or (**b**) the tendency of a thing to produce pleasure, or (**c**) the state of pleasure actually produced.

hedonics. That aspect of ethics which deals with the relationship of DUTY to pleasure.

hedonism (Aristippus). The aim of life should be the pursuit by any means whatever of as much physical pleasure for each moment as possible without taking heed of the consequences that might follow. See CYRENAICS.

hedonism (Epicurus). The highest good in life is the absence of (a) pain and (b) vexing pleasures that bring pain or discomfort as their consequence. The aim of life should be *ATARAXIA:* tranquillity (imperturbability) of body, mind, and spirit.

hedonism, egoistic (psychological). The theory that all human actions should be motivated by the desire to secure one's own pleasure, and by the desire to avoid pain to oneself, even if the pleasure or good of others has to be sacrificed.

hedonism, ethical (Gk., *hēdonē,* "pleasure," and *hēdys,* "sweet," "pleasant"). The doctrine that (a) pleasure is the highest good (or the sole good) in life, (b) pleasure is an intrinsic good (or the only intrinsic good), (c) pleasure should be sought, and (d) the ethical worth (value, good) of human actions is determined by whether or not they produce pleasure. Ethical hedonism insists that each individual is obligated to himself to live so as to obtain as much pleasure and as little pain as possible.

hedonism, psychological. The theory that all human actions are in fact motivated by the desire to secure pleasure, and by the desire to avoid pain, and it is impossible to do otherwise.

hedonistic calculus (Bentham). Sometimes *hedonic calculus, utility calculus,* or *felicity calculus.* Jeremy Bentham devised a method of choosing an action, based on the amount of pleaure (as opposed to pain) that the action would provide. The quantity of pleasure was determined by the following units: intensity, duration, propinquity (nearness), certainty, fecundity (fruitfulness or fertility), and purity (not mixed with unappealing feelings such as pain or boredom and not followed by such feelings). See UTILITARIANISM.

hedonistic paradox. 1. The person who constantly seeks pleasure for himself will not find it, yet the person who helps others find pleasure will in the process find pleasure for himself (or has a greater chance of finding it). **2.** Pleasure is not something to be sought after directly; it is not to be thought of as an end in itself separate from an activity or an experience. It is attainable only as an attitude or feeling accompanying other things.

Heisenberg's principle of uncertainty. See UNCERTAINTY, HEISENBERG'S PRINCIPLE OF.

hen (Gk., "one"). The Single One, that which includes all other things and is not included in anything, the source of all being, change, or emanation, the nondependent First, the ultimate reality. Also: a unit, a unity, an individuality (in contrast to multiplicity, manifold, aggregate, having parts, etc.). See EMANATION; ONE, THE.

henotheism. See GOD CONCEPTS (3).

here. An indexical sign (such as "this," "I," "now," "that") (a) used to refer to spatiotemporal position and (b) having no descriptive content unless accompanied by further meanings. See SIGN, INDEXICAL.

heterogeneity (Gk., *heterogenēs,* from *heteros,* "other," and *genos,* "kind"). **1.** Having unlike qualities or parts throughout. **2.** The theory that things have unlike qualities or parts present in them no matter how similar they are. Opposite to HOMOGENEITY.

heterological. Refers to an expression whose meaning does not characterize (apply to) itself. Example: The word *Greek* is not a Greek word. Contrasted with HOMOLOGICAL.

heuristic (Gk., *heuriskein,* "to discover"). Providing assistance in discovering (or in presenting) a truth or solving a problem, for example a model or a useful hypothesis. Contrasted with PROOF.

heuristic principle. A principle that is neither asserted nor evaluated as true but that is assumed for specific purposes at hand (such as to inquire into, explain something) because of its previous success or usefulness as an investigative tool.

heuristics. The name for the discipline that studies the methods by which truth (fact, ideas, etc.) are discovered and (sometimes) communicated.

hexis **(Aristotle)** (Gk., "a habit," "a state," "a characteristic"). Those predispositional structures in a thing that influence its activity and/or wellbeing and are not easy to change. They may be acquired (habits) or an inherent condition and are usually associated with emotions and feelings.

hierarchy of being. See BEING, HIERARCHY OF.

historicism. Occasionally *historism.* **1.** The theory that things are what they are because of their historical development. The descriptive account of a thing's history is a sufficient explanation for it. **2.** The theory that inexorable laws determine all historical events, which are what history attempts to understand and use for prediction.

holism. Sometimes *wholism.*The theory that there is a real fundamental and irreducible difference between living and nonliving, between organic and inorganic, activity. The parts of living (organic) wholes function differently within the whole from the way they do outside it. Organic wholes must be studied as wholes since knowing how parts act outside a whole does not enable us to know how those parts will act within a whole. See EVOLUTION, EMERGENT.

holistic explanation. 1. Explaining phenomena in terms of the functions (purposes, properties, activities) of a whole (form, totality, unity) that is the guiding principle of its parts. **2.** Explaining the activity of the parts of a whole in terms of the functions of that whole. See ANIMISM, TELEOLOGICAL. Compare with entries under EXPLANATION.

homogeneity (Gk., *homogenēs,* from *homos,* "same" and *genos,* "kind"). **1.** The state of having the same qualities or parts throughout. **2.** The theory that things have a similar quality or part present in them no matter how unlike they are. Opposite to HETEROGENEITY.

homoiomeries (Anaxagoras). The basic building blocks *(homoioi)* of the universe that can be divided, yet remain of the same kind. All things possess parts, and are constructed from parts that are similar to their whole, to the whole from which they are taken. These homoiomeries may be divided infinitely and they will continue to resemble each other. Example: Bone is made up of elements that look like bone. Those elements may be divided into parts that themselves look like bone.

homoiomeries (Aristotle) (Gk., *homoiōma,* "a likeness," "an image," "a resemblance," "a counterfeit"). Those parts of a whole that resemble one another when separated from the whole. (On some interpretations the parts also resemble the whole.) Examples: wood, metal, hair, liver tissue. Aristotle did not believe this division can go on indefinitely. He thought that there is a point of division at which the part no longer resembles other parts taken from the whole.

homological. Sometimes *autological.* Refers to that whose meaning characterizes (applies to) itself. Example: The word *polysyllabic* is itself a polysyllabic word. Contrasted with HETEROLOGICAL.

homo mensura **theory.** The theory that man *(homo)* is the measure *(mensura)* of all things. See RELATIVISM, PROTAGOREAN.

humanism, philosophical. A philosophy that (**a**) regards the rational individual as the highest value; (**b**) considers the individual to be the ultimate source of value; and (**c**) is dedicated to fostering the individual's creative and moral development in a meaningful and rational way without reference to concepts of the supernatural. Compare with EXISTENTIALISM, HUMANISTIC NATURALISM.

human rights. See RIGHTS, HUMAN.

hybris. Sometimes *hubris* (Gk., "overbearing pride," "insolence," "wanton violence," "arrogance," "going beyond one's abilities and making a fool of oneself," "attempting to emulate the gods"). *Hybris* was regarded as an evil that tended to result in a disaster or one's downfall.

hylē (Gk., "matter," "material," "the primary substance of change"). Sometimes used synonymously with HYPOKEIMENON. Originally *hylē* meant "wood" and especially the wooden structures holding a ship together or holding up a building. Also, any material from which something could be made. In later, philosophic Greek it came to mean the "substance" underlying reality, or the "matter" of which something is composed. *Hylism* is used to mean materialism.

hylē **(Aristotle).** The common material stuff found in a variety of things. In itself it had no distinct characteristics **1.** until form was *imparted* to it (on one interpretation of Aristotle), or **2.** until the form inherent in that matter began to become actualized (on another interpretation of Aristotle). This latter interpretation holds that no matter can exist without form being in some way associated with it, and no form can exist without its being imbued in matter. See FORM (ARISTOTLE); GENESIS (ARISTOTLE).

hylomorphism (Gk., *hylē,* "matter," and *morphē,* "form," "figure," "shape"). **1.** The theory that the universe is composed of matter and form in inseparable unity throughout. Wherever matter exists, form will also exist. Wherever form exists, matter will also exist. **2.** The view that form as directing energy gives matter its activity and pattern. Matter is that which is being structured into a process or pattern. **3.** The view that form is that which endures throughout change and does not itself change, thereby guaranteeing a continuity and identity to the individual thing. Matter is the changed and continually changing ingredient which without form could have no substantial or individual existence. Compare with ANIMISM.

hylozoism (Gk., *hylē,* "matter," and *zōē,* "life"). **1.** The theory that all matter possesses some degree of life qualities and all life possesses a material basis. Matter and life are inseparable (except in abstraction). **2.** The theory that the universe is everywhere alive; all matter is innately life-active. Reality can be best understood as a self-sustaining, living organism. Compare with PANPSYCHISM (METAPHYSICS).

hypokeimenon (Gk., "substratum," "underlying ground," "that which stands as the support for something"). See GENESIS (ARISTOTLE). In logic, used to mean that which is presupposed by something else.

hypostasis (Gk., "standing under as support," "substance," "subsistance," from *hypo,* "under," and *histanai,* "to cause to stand"). That substance (ultimate ground, subsistent principle, essential nature, self-subsistent reality, subject) **(a)** in which attributes inhere and/or **(b)** which supports a subsisting personality. See *SUBSTANTIA* and entries under SUBSTANCE.

hypostatization. Sometimes *abstractionism.* Often used interchangeably with REIFICATION/REISM. **1.** Attributing actual existence to something that is only a name or an abstraction. **2.** Regarding an abstraction or a relation as if it were an existing object. Example: Treating the concept "nation" as an entity over and above the relations, structures, activities, etc. that it designates.

hypothesis (Gk., *hypothesis,* "supposition," "assumption," "foundation," "that which is laid down as a rule of action," "a principle"). **1.** That which is assumed (or conjectured) without direct empirical evidence for the purpose of accounting for some fact or facts. **2.** A provisional or tentative proposal for the explanation of phenomena that has some degree of empirical substantiation or probability.

In science, a hypothesis describes what will (or would) occur under certain conditions. Observations are made and/or experiments are conducted to determine if the hypothesis is accurate or tenable (relative to other proposed hypotheses) in accounting for the facts, and/or to determine if what the hypothesis can be made to predict does come about. A predictive hypothesis is of great importance in science and is confirmed if its predictions come about. If its predictive and/or explanatory power is high, a hypothesis may be elevated to the status of a theory or law. If the prediction is not substantiated, this is good reason for not accepting the hypothesis, at least not without modification. An ideal hypothesis not only predicts but explains all the facts that have to be explained about a particular phenomenon. A hypothesis often serves also to suggest further investigations, observations, or experimentation. All hypotheses are subject to change as additional factual information is gathered and/or as new theories and laws are advanced. See CONFIRMATION; METHOD, SCIENTIFIC. Compare with THEORY, SCIENTIFIC.

hypothetical construct. See CONSTRUCT, THEORETICAL.

hypothetical-deductive method. Sometimes *hypothetico-deductive method.* See EXPLANATION, SCIENTIFIC.

hypothetical imperative (Kant). An imperative, and that system of morals based on such an imperative, which is conditional on a wish to possess a desired value or good. *If* you wish to have health, *then* you must (or ought) to do such and such. An imperative directing one to act on the basis of prudence and/or self-interest and not on the basis of DUTY or obligation to moral principles. Contrasted with CATEGORICAL IMPERATIVE, THE (KANT).

I

I. An indexical sign (see SIGN, INDEXICAL) such as "now," "this," "here," "that," **(a)** used by someone to refer to himself without reference to any particular aspect of himself, and **(b)** containing no descriptive content.

icon. Sometimes *ikon* (Gk., *eikōn,* "image"). **1.** An image, likeness, or representation of something. See *EIDOLA* (ART). **2.** A picture or a sign that is like in image to the thing it indicates or represents. See SIGN, ICONIC.

idea (Gk., *idea,* "concept," "class," "kind," "idea," "mode," "sort," "species," "form," "nature," from *eidos,* "visual appearance," "form," and *idein,* "to see," "to grasp conceptually"). **1.** Anything that is a content (object, item) of consciousness. Any act of awareness. **2.** A mental image or picture of something. **3.** The real likeness, representation, or essence of a thing embodied in an object and grasped by intelligence. **4.** Any general notion, thought, mental impression, or concept. **5.** Anything fantasized, fictionalized, or imagined. **6.** A belief, opinion, supposition, or doctrine held. **7.** Something designed or intended to take place, such as a plan. **8.** An archetype, ideal, or pattern to be followed.

idea, abstract. See ABSTRACTION.

ideal. 1. A standard of perfection, excellence, beauty, goodness. **2.** A perfect type. Embodying a perfect exemplar. **3.** Archetypal idea. See ARCHETYPES. The perfect form grasped simply, consistently, and comprehensively. **4.** The perfect object or goal of our desire and willing.

ideal of reason, the (Kant). Refers to reason's (unattainable) search for **(a)** knowledge of the totality of things, its conditions, structure, and possibilities, and **(b)** knowledge of its unconditioned and absolute ground. Kant

119

calls this search the "transcendental illusion." See ILLUSION, TRANSCEN-
DENTAL (KANT).

idealism. Sometimes *mentalism* or *immaterialism*. **1.** The theory that the
universe is an embodiment of a mind. **2.** Reality is dependent for its existence upon a mind and its activities. **3.** All reality is mental (spiritual,
psychical). Matter, the physical, does not exist. **4.** No knowledge is possible except of mental states and processes, and that is all that exists. Reality is explained in terms of such psychic phenomena as minds, selves,
spirits, ideas, Absolute Thought, etc., rather than in terms of matter. **5.**
Only mind-type activities and their idea-type content exist. The external
world is not physical.

idealism (Berkeley). See IMMATERIALISM (BERKELEY).

idealism (Plato). The true, absolute reality is the realm of the perfect, independently existing, unchanging, timeless forms (Ideas), and the true object of all knowledge. See FORMS, PLATO'S THEORY OF IDEAL.

idealism, absolute. The theory that the Absolute (see ABSOLUTE, THE) regarded as a Mind, Ego, Self, Spirit, Soul is the fundamental, undetermined reality in the universe: **(a)** upon which all things depend for their
existence but which depends on nothing else for its existence, **(b)** from
which all things can be rationally deduced, **(c)** from which all finite things
flow in a progressive development of its thought, and **(d)** in which all
things exist as a thought. A monistic or pantheistic philosophy.

idealism, absolute (Hegel). Hegel denied the Kantian distinction between
that which is given in our experience (such as sense impressions) and the
categories used to structure and understand it. Things exist in our consciousness but in interrelationship to other things that also exist there.
These relationships and connections of things are real, as real as qualities, as real as attributes. They can be understood as parts of a monistic
system of an evolving substance in which the essential self-subsisting core
is Absolute Spirit. The essence of this Absolute Spirit is **(a)** self-actualization into perfection and **(b)** its all-encompassing determining nature. See
ABSOLUTE, THE.

idealism, critical (Kant). Refers to Kant's theory of knowledge. The essence
of critical idealism is Kant's sharp distinction between what is given to us
in our experience (sense impressions) and the structures (forms of intuition and the categories) which the mind uses to arrange, interpret, and
evaluate that which is given. See entries under CATEGORIES (KANT).

idealism, epistemological. The theory that **(a)** nothing can be known except
minds (selves) and their mental content. The extreme version of this is:
nothing can be known except the operations of our mind and its content
(see entries under SOLIPSISM); **(b)** knowledge of the mind is the fundamental and only source for constructing knowledge of anything else at all;
and **(c)** all knowledge exists as a content in, and is caused by, a mind.

idealism, metaphysical. The theory that **(a)** no object can exist without a mind (subject, self, ego) perceiving it (see ESSE EST PERCIPI), and (b) only minds and their content (ideas, images, perceptions, etc.) exist. Metaphysical idealism assumes an epistemological idealism. See IDEALISM, EPISTEMOLOGICAL.

idealism, pantheistic. Sometimes *monistic idealism.* The theory that all finite minds (foci of psychic activity) are inseparable parts or aspects (modes, features, attributes) of the Absolute Thought (God, Mind, Spirit, Soul), which can be separated only in abstraction.

idealism, personal. Synonymous with PERSONALISM.

idealism, pluralistic. The theory that all finite minds or foci of psychic activity (a) are autonomous, unique, and irreducible, (b) interrelate, (c) are singular, private activities, and (d) may or may not relate to an Absolute One or Mind.

idealism, subjective. The theory that (a) the knower and the thing known do not have independent existence; all knowledge is knowledge of our conscious states and processes and not of any external world; (b) that which is known is created by the human mind; matter is not real; (c) the Absolute (God) creates the human mind to know that which the human mind creates for itself to know; all that is known exists for and in our minds; (d) that creative act of the Absolute in c results from an act of thought by the Absolute itself, (e) the only reality is mind and its processes and content, and (f) mental reality is all that can ever be known.

idealism, transcendental (Kant) Knowledge of the external world is produced by our transcendental unity (logical ego) of apperception. Rational thought processes *per se* cannot give us synthetic knowledge of the external world. Sensation *per se* cannot give us knowledge. Our perceptions are organized by the pure *a priori* intuitions of space and time and by the categories of our understanding. They, and not how things are in themselves, are the conditions that make experience possible and intelligible. The transcendental unity (self, ego) is the source of these intuitions and categories and is that which applies them to raw "experience." Nothing can be known of this transcendental unity. It is the *condition* for knowledge but not an *object* of knowledge. All we can know about it is *that* it is but we cannot say *what* it is. See APPERCEPTION, TRANSCENDENTAL.

ideas (Berkeley). Ideas are the content of sense experience (perception) or the act of perceiving, and are totally dependent on a soul (mind) and ultimately dependent on God's thought or perception. See IMMATERIALISM (BERKELEY).

ideas (Descartes). Descartes distinguished three types of ideas: 1. *innate ideas* that proceed form the structure, activity, or potential (capacity, ability) of thought (the mind) itself. The three principal innate ideas are of (a) God, (b) the self (mind, ego, thinking substance) and (c) matter (body, external physical objects, material substance); 2. *factitious ideas* that are constructed by the mind in order to understand what things are (or might be) like (such as a scientist's physical or chemical model of a material object); and **3.** *adventitious ideas* that come as stimuli from the external world (such as of sound [a note], of sight [the moon], of heat [a fire]); adventitious ideas do not come into the mind from the outside as qualities or entities but are formed by the mind from physical motions that affect the brain. See IDEAS, CLEAR AND DISTINCT (DESCARTES).

ideas (Hume). Less intense and vivid images or copies of sense impressions retained in memory. See KNOWLEDGE (HUME).

ideas (Kant). Those necessary, formal, and regulative concepts of reason to which no corresponding object can be given in sensation (such as that of the unity of the ego). See IDEALISM, TRANSCENDENTAL (KANT).

ideas (Locke). Objects of understanding; anything that the mind attends to, is aware of, concentrates upon, *has* as a representation, or is *given*. This includes that which the mind perceives **(a)** as its activity such as willing, thinking, doubting, tending, feeling, and **(b)** as the immediate content of its perception or thought. See KNOWLEDGE (LOCKE); and entries under IDEAS (LOCKE) which follow.

ideas (Plato). 1. Timeless, perfect, unchanging, immaterial, eternal ARCHE-TYPES (forms) of which existing things are imperfect copies. **2.** The eternal perfect Forms used by the DEMIURGE as blueprints to be followed in its act of organizing matter into things. **3.** The essences (forms, universals) found in all things that resemble (imitate) the perfect forms and which when compared with our innate knowledge of the perfect forms make them recognizable (intelligible, namable) to us. **4.** Universals (such as redness, circularity) that apply to more than one thing, as opposed to particulars (such as this red ball, that circular table). **5.** The ideal standard by which particular things are judged to be an approximation. **6.** Any object of pure intelligence as opposed to objects of sensation. **7.** That enduring state of something as opposed to its becoming, or changing state.

Plato's word for idea was *eidos,* translated as idea or form, sometimes as "constitutive nature" or ESSENCE, and occasionally "type," or "species" (see FORMS, PLATO'S THEORY OF IDEAL). Every major general word such as good, beauty, justice, equality, circularity, has a corresponding abstract Idea (FORM OR ARCHETYPE) that is an eternal, unchanging, incorporeal spiritual substance grasped only by the highest form of reasoning. All the many particular instances of these Ideas (general classes) "imitate," "participate in," "emulate" their corresponding Idea. This Idea is the ideal standard by which its particular instance is identified and judged as to its shortcomings. Also it is the *cause* of their being what they are since all things are urged on (activated) by a desire (longing, love) to be like their ideal. See *ANAMNĒSIS;* BEAUTY; *MIMĒSIS;* SOUL (PLATO).

ideas, clear and distinct (Descartes). An idea is "clear" if it can be conceived as a whole and without inconsistency (for example, the conception of a circle); an idea is "distinct" if it is never confused with another idea (for example, a circle is never confused wtih a square). Descartes believed that **1.** those ideas and only those ideas that are perceived clearly and distinctly are to be accepted as true, and **2.** an idea may be clear without being distinct but cannot be distinct without also being clear. The three clear and distinct (self-evident) ideas about reality that provide the basis of his philosophy: (**a**) *extension* (matter occupying space), (**b**) *figure* (shape, size, spatial dimensions) and (**c**) *movement* (motion). See IDEAS (DESCARTES); METHOD (DESCARTES).

ideas, complex (Locke). Ideas that are built up into combinations out of simple ideas. See IDEAS, SIMPLE (LOCKE). Complex ideas include abstract ideas, general ideas, universals, abstractions, some ideas of reflection and introspection, etc. Complex ideas are divided into (**a**) *modes,* (**b**) *relations,* and (**c**) *substance.* (The latter two are called *mixed modes;* they are arbitrary mental constructions and do not correspond to real entities.) A *simple mode* refers to the forms a particular simple idea can take (such as unity, spatiality) and a *complex mode* refers to the combination of simple ideas into a complex idea (such as that of number or amount). *Relations* consist of the contrasting (associating, etc.) of ideas (such as cause/effect, identity/diversity, oneness/multiplicity, place/time). *Substance* refers to the recognition that external objects continue to exist independently of consciousness, and includes (1) the general idea of substance (matter, an underlying physical ground), (2) the particular idea of substances, and (3) the collective idea of substances.

ideas, innate. 1. Ideas (knowledge, concepts, beliefs) that are not derived in any way from our sense organs (experience) but preexist and originate in the mind intself. **2.** Ideas that are potentially present in the mind at birth and that are brought to consciousness under certain conditions. **3.** Ideas that are present to the mind as a tendency or predisposition to think a certain way.

Theories about innate ideas assume that innate ideas efficiently apply to, and provide an insight into, reality unobtainable from any other source.

ideas, simple (Locke). Ideas that cannot be broken down any further into component parts. They are irreducible, primitive, indefinable, unmixed (such as red, pain, point, a sound, a smell, etc.). Usually associated with the immediate objects of our perception. Simple ideas appear to (or in) the mind as a unity; the mind of its own cannot in any way create, imagine, invent, or construct them, but needs them in order to have knowledge. The mind has the ability to store them in memory, remember (recall) them, contrast and associate them in new combinations (see IDEAS, COMPLEX [LOCKE]) that are not found in our experience of them as simple ideas. According to Locke, on most occasions we do not have experiences of simple ideas as discrete, autonomous, independent units. Simple ideas are found in integrated clusters that are broken up by the mind into their unique components. For example, the experience of a hot piece of metal combines such simple ideas as that of heat, hardness, smoothness. Some simple ideas such as of heat, touch, sight, smell, come only from one corresponding sense. Others such as of shape, space, figure, numbered amounts, come from the intermingling of senses.

ideas of practical reason (Kant). Ideas that have no empirical foundation but which are necessary for the function of morality, such as the ideas of God, freedom, and immortality. See ETHICS (KANT).

ideas of pure reason (Kant). Sometimes *ideas of theoretical reason.* Ideas that have no corresponding objects but are necessary to the function of reason, such as the ideas of a soul, of the existence of an external world, and of God. See entries under CATEGORIES with reference to Kant.

ideas of reflection (Locke). 1. Those ideas had whenever we introspect upon what we are doing when we engage in such activities as thinking, willing, doubting, hearing, touching, seeing. **2.** What the mind perceives in an awareness of, or reflection upon, its functions. Compare with REFLECTION (LOCKE).

ideas of sensation (Locke). 1. The immediate quality (content) of perception, such as that the table is green, heavy, and tall. **2.** That which is given in sensation.

identical. 1. Two things are identical if all the characteristics of one are also possessed by the other and vice versa. **2.** Two things are identical whenever the totality of what can be said to be true about one is also the totality of what can be said to be true about the other. (All objects that are identical belong to the same class and all identical classes belong to the same class. Identical objects belong to a class if-and-only-if the others do also.)

identify. 1. To recognize or establish *what* a thing is, or *that* it is what it is. **2.** The process of recognizing or claiming that a thing is the same (in at least one respect) at a given moment in time as it was at a previous moment in time.

identity (L., *idem,* "the same"). **1.** Exactly the same, as in "identical houses." A relation of complete and absolute sameness or resemblance between two things. Referred to as *strict* identity. See IDENTICAL. **2.** Not a relation of complete sameness or resemblance between two things, but a meaning relation that remains the same in our application of it, between the name (sign, symbol) of a thing and that thing being named. **3.** Neither 1 nor 2 but a relation of sameness that exists among those names themselves that refer to the same meanings or things. See "IS" OF FORMAL EQUIVALENCE.

identity (metaphysics). 1. Permanence. **2.** Relative permanence. **3.** That which endures throughout change. **4.** That which endures throughout change relatively longer than other things that can be seen to change. **5.** Oneness. That which endures as a self-regulating unity throughout change. **6.** Sameness. That which can be identified as being the same from among a diversity or plurality of things. **7.** That which is the same with itself.

identity, law of (logic). See LAWS OF THOUGHT, THE THREE.

identity, numerical. One and the same thing. That which is the same with itself. Self-sameness. Example: The Vice-President of the United States and the officer presiding over the U.S. Senate are identical. Things that share the same place (space) and time are numerically identical. If things are identified as being numerically identical they have all their characterisitcs in common.

identity, personal. See PERSONAL IDENTITY.

identity, principle of (logic). See LAWS OF THOUGHT, THE THREE.

identity, problem of. 1. Change exists. All things become other than what they were. In spite of this we experience something about things that we can identify as remaining the selfsame thing. What is that enduring selfsame thing? **2.** Things within a class are all different, yet something about them can be classed as being similar. There is difference yet at the same time sameness. There is sameness yet at the same time difference. What is it that is the "same" among the differences? See UNITY IN VARIETY AND VARIETY IN UNITY, PRINCIPLE OF (METAPHYSICS).

identity, theory of mind/body. See MIND/BODY, IDENTITY THEORY OF.

identity in difference, principle of. 1. Regardless of how different things are, any thing in the universe can be said to be identical with (similar to) any other thing in at least one respect (that they exist, occupy space, exist in time, are objects of thought, etc.). **2.** No two things can be different in all respects. Compare with DIFFERENCE IN IDENTITY, PRINCIPLE OF.

identity of indiscernibles, principle of (Leibniz). Sometimes *Leibniz's Law*. **1.** No two things in the universe are exactly alike in all respects. When they are looked at closely enough, some differences will always be found. Thus no two things are indiscernible from one another. **2.** No two things can be exactly alike in every respect except numerically. (No two things can differ only numerically.) Thus no two things are identical, since each thing in the universe possesses something which no other thing in the universe possesses. **3.** All things that differ numerically (are spatially separated) have discernible differences. All things that have discernible differences are numerically distinct.

Leibniz's metaphysical inferences from his Principle: **(a)** If things differ only spatially, this difference indicates the necessity of a further difference within their essential being (otherwise they would be identically the selfsame nature and therefore need not be different even spatially; **(b)** Difference is one of the most fundamental aspects of every existing thing (as is force, activity, and a unique rate of change); **(c)** All properties (characteristics, attributes) of a thing are necessary, essential, and unique to that thing; (**d**) There are no accidental attributes of a thing; a thing is what it is because of all the attributes it possesses and would be something else if it possessed attributes different from those. See REASON, PRINCIPLE OF SUFFICIENT (LEIBNIZ).

ideology (Gk., *idea*, "idea," and *logos*, "the study of," "the science of"). **1.** Literally and as used in classical metaphysics, the science of ideas, the study of their origins. **2.** In modern usage, it has a pejorative sense, as dogmatic, visionary theorizing or speculation that is false or unrealistic. **3.** In a nonpejorative sense, any system of ideas regarding philosophic, economic, political, social beliefs and ideals.

idola. See EIDŌLA.

idols (Bacon). Described in Francis Bacon's *Novum Organum*. They are the four hindrances (preconceptions, prejudices, predispositions, biases) that Bacon believed prevent the proper use of the inductive method to obtain scientific knowledge. **1.** *The Idols of the Tribe:* anthropomorphic projection and wishful ways of thinking that are inherent in the very nature of all human beings, all tribes, and all races, whereby their way of viewing things is regarded as the standard by which things really are. **2.** *The Idols of the Den (Cave):* private, unique personal prejudices. **3.** *The Idols of the Market:* failure to use language correctly and to define terms precisely. **4.** *The Idols of the Theatre:* the blind acceptance of tradition and authority. See BACONIAN METHOD.

ignoratio elenchi (L., "arguing or refuting by ignoring the issues at hand"). Refers to any fallacy of irrelevance whereby a conclusion is proved that does not have anything to do with the question at issue and thereby in no way refutes the argument it opposes. For further discussion see FALLACY, TYPES OF INFORMAL **(23).**

illocutionary expression/act (illocution) (L., *il*, the assimilated form of *in*, "in," and *loqui*, "to speak," "to utter"). Sometimes simply *illocutionary*. **1.** Something that is done *in* the very (or *by* the very) utterance of some statement or by an act. Something over and above the utterance of the statement, or the act, is implied. Examples: "Where have you been all this time?" "I think that is enough." A great diversity of things are classified under illocutionary expressions/acts as predictions, promises, requests, orders, commands, questions, pleas, persuasions, expressions of feeling, etc. **2.** The act that is performed in performing a LOCUTIONARY EXPRESSION/ACT (such as the act of stating what I just stated). See PERLOCUTIONARY EXPRESSION/ACT (PERLOCUTION).

illumination (L., *illuminare*, "to enlighten"). Intellectual or spiritual enlightenment usually described as a sudden flash of insight or understanding.

illusion, egocentric. See EGOCENTRIC ILLUSION.

illusion, transcendental (Kant). The illusion which is a consequence of the belief that such things as the *a priori* forms of intuition and the categories of understanding are descriptions of the true nature of reality in itself, not merely ways by which our consciousness structures that unknowable reality. See IDEAL OF REASON, THE (KANT); SKEPTICISM (KANT).

image, mental (L., *imago,* "an image," "a representation"). **1.** Any mental occurrence, such as a conception, an idea, or a picturing of something. **2.** Abstract mental pictures (copies, representations) of external objects, much as a map is a "picture" of an area. **3.** An imitation or representation of a mental occurrence, as of an idea, a sensation, a product of the imagination or of fancy. Compare with CONCEIVE.

imagination. 1. The power (faculty) of producing images and recombining them in new combinations apart from their actual occurrence in reality. **2.** The process of reviving perceptions as images, altering them, and merging them into new patterns or unities. **3.** The ability to idealize or to objectify experiences. **4.** The activity of constructing ideas (concepts, images, models) that give insight into and help explain phenomena.

The pejorative use in such phrases as "It was only a product of my imagination" implies some mental construction that is totally unreal, the formation of imagery that does not accurately or in any way represent what has taken place. None of the above definitions necessarily implies such a use, though they may imply a creative fictionalizing or reconstruction of reality.

imitation. See MIMĒSIS.

immanent (L., *immanere,* "to remain in"). Indwelling. Inherent. Operating from within. Being actually present in something. Opposite to TRANSCENDENT.

immaterial (L., *im,* an assimilated form of *in,* "not," and *materialis,* "matter," "the stuff of which things are made"). Not consisting of matter. Synonyms are: incorporeal; spiritual; nonmaterial; nonphysical. Things that have been regarded as immaterial: God, spirits, angels, the soul, daimons, ghosts, the formal cause or principle in things, the *ELAN VITAL,* the mind, consciousness, the will, the intellect, emotions, feelings, sensations. A few of these (such as the latter nine or so) have sometimes been considered as immaterial things but as dependent upon material activity of some sort for their existence or activity.

immaterialism. Sometimes MENTALISM. The doctrine that **1.** matter does not exist. Only ideas (immaterial or nonmaterial entities) and the psychic sources of these ideas exist. **2.** Nothing exists or can ever be known to exist except in terms of ideas and the minds having them. (It is impossible to have an idea of something existing apart from its being thought of by a mind since only in the very act of its being thought of is it an idea.) **3.** Matter without any mind qualities existing independently of a mind perceiving and bringing it into existence is a contradiction in terms. (It is self-contradictory to hold that the universe consists of relations and qual-

ities that are independent of a mind.) Immaterialism is a form of idealism. See entries under IDEALISM.

immaterialism (Berkeley). **1.** The objects of our perception (mind) are ideas
(sensibles, sensations). **2.** Ideas are mental. See IDEAS (BERKELEY). **3.**
The essence of ideas is to be perceived (see *ESSE EST PERCIPI*) and to be
caused by a mind. (Ideas can never exist without a mind receiving them
or producing them.) **4.** What we call physical things (such as tables, marbles, grass) are orderly collections of mind-dependent ideas. (They exist
insofar as they are perceived by a mind and cannot exist unless they are
perceived.) **5.** Like causes like. Minds (spirits) exist to cause ideas (sensations, sensibles, perceptions). Matter, being totally unlike ideas, cannot
cause ideas. It is meaningless to talk about matter apart from the presence of a mind perceiving it or causing a perception of it. The word *matter* is like the word *universal*—only a name (see NOMINALISM) standing for a collection of ideas (sensible qualities). **6.** We cannot
have general ideas of things in abstraction or abstracted from their particular existing qualities. For example, I cannot have an idea of "redness" but always only of a particular red object such as a red handker-
chief, a red ball, a red sunset, a red patch, a red surface (so with
"matter"). **7.** There is no physical (material) reality that exists behind
our ideas causing them. (Both primary and secondary qualities depend on
a mind.) **8.** All knowledge except that of God and of one's own existence
is derived from sense perception (experience) of particular things. **9.** Although we as minds (spirits) are the immediate cause of ideas produced
by our imagination, God is the ultimate cause of all our ideas and sensations. **10.** Physical things (matter) are really ideas in God's mind and we
perceive these ideas as tables, marbles, grass. **11.** Things (ideas) that we
perceive are signs or symbols in God's language as he attempts to communicate with us. The universe is God's expression in a language. The order, pattern, and regularity of all things indicate this. **12.** Reality and its
immediately felt unity cannot be reduced to a series of mindless, discontinuous, unrelated, nonmental aggregates. See MOTION (BERKELEY).

immediacy, presentational See PRESENTMENT/PRESENTATION.

immoral (L., *im,* "not," and *moralis,* "manner," "custom," "conduct").
Not moral. Acting contrary to morality and/or conscience. Not conform-
ing to the accepted rules of right conduct. Unvirtuous. Contrast with
AMORAL; MORAL.

immoralist. One who refuses to accept the binding conditions or claims of a
moral system.

immortality (L., *im,* "not," and *mortalis,* from *mors, mortis,* "death," and
mori, "to die"). **1.** The unending continued existence of a life in some
form. **2.** Personal survival after death. The belief that the individual in
some form and in some kind of existence survives the death (dissolution,
destruction, total degeneration) of his body. This may be thought of in

terms of the REINCARNATION, TRANSMIGRATION, or METEMPSYCHOSIS of a soul or the passing of a soul into an eternal realm such as Heaven or Hell or Nirvana. Most forms of immortality hold to the prior existence of the soul in bodies or objects.

immutable (L., *im*, "not," and *mutabilis*, from *mutare*, "to change"). **1.** Absolutely unchanging. Constantly the same. Invariable. **2.** Not capable of changing. **3.** Not capable of being changed.

imperative, categorical. See CATEGORICAL IMPERATIVE (KANT).

imperative, hypothetical. See HYPOTHETICAL IMPERATIVE (KANT).

imperativism. Sometimes *ethical imperativism.* The view that morality is directive language: a set of commands or recommendations to act or not to act in certain specified ways.

implication, logical. 1. Sometimes *definitional implication.* Deducibility of one statement from another. Example: "Adam is married" logically implies that Adam has a wife or that Adam is a husband. **2.** Sometimes synonymous with *logical entailment.* The relationship of two statements whereby if the first is true then the other is also necessarily true. **3.** The necessary relationship between the premises and the conclusion of a valid argument. Used in this sense it is synonymous with *logical inference.*

impossible, logically. Refers: **1.** to that which is a self-contradiction (such as a polygon with only two corners, or a thing being wholly present in two different spaces at the same time, or **2.** to logically false statement forms (such as p and not-p). All nonself-contradictions are logically possible. Contrast with POSSIBLE/POSSIBILITY.

impression (L., *im*, "in," "on," "upon," and *premere*, "to press," "to stamp upon"). **1.** The immediate and momentary conscious effect produced by stimulation of the senses. **2.** An indistinct, general notion, remembrances, opinion, or idea.

impression (Hume). The immediate, noninferential, noninterpretive sense datum presented to consciousness, or which appears in consciousness. Sensation. Sense image. That direct irreducible and primitive experience upon which all knowledge is based. See KNOWLEDGE (HUME).

improbabilism. The theory that it is not possible for the empirical sciences to assign positive probability values to hypotheses or theories in order to show their degree of confirmation. They can show only the improbability and the falsifiability of hypotheses or theories. Compare with PROBABILISM.

inauthenticity. See BAD FAITH (SARTRE).

inclination (L., *in*, "in," and *clinare*, "to hand," "to lean toward"). **1.** A disposition, propensity, or tendency (**a**) to act in a particular way or (**b**) to be favorable toward something. **2.** Used (for example in Kant) to refer to the sum total of personal states and tendencies, such as feelings, moods, motives, intentions, attitudes, emotions, desires, wants, drives, etc.

incoherence (L., *in*, "not," and *cohaerere*, "to adhere together"). Not connected logically and/or conceptually. Incongruity in thinking. Inconsistency. Opposite to COHERENCE. Compare with COMPATIBLE. See INCOMPATIBLE.

incompatible (L., *in*, "not," and *compati*, "to have compassion," from *com*, "with," and *pati*, "to bear," "to suffer"). **1.** Not compatible. Not capable of coexisting in harmony. Discordant. **2.** Mutually inconsistent. Referring to statements that cannot be consistently related logically and/or conceptually. Opposite to COMPATIBLE. Compare with INCOHERENCE.

inconsistency, fallacy of. See FALLACY, TYPES OF INFORMAL (24).

inconsistent triad. See ANTILOGISM; EVIL, THE THEOLOGICAL PROBLEM OF.

incontinence (L., *in*, "not," and *continere*, "to hold together," "to repress"). **1.** The inability to control one's lust (base physical desires) for the attainment of more rational and higher values. **2.** The desiring and choosing of an evil in the presence of a conflict between (a) knowledge of what is good (right, correct) and (b) those uncontrolled passions (desires, appetites, cravings, drives) for something that is recognized as evil (bad, incorrect, destructive). In the context of Aristotle's philosophy, an incontinent man feels the conflict between his tendency to immoral or depraved conduct and his tendency to follow rational moral principles and allows the base part of himself to win out, whereas the licentious man feels no such conflict. Compare with CONTINENCE; LICENTIOUS. See *AKRASIA*.

incorporeal (L., *in*, "not," and *corporeus*, from *corpus*, "body"). Not corporeal. Immaterial. Nonmaterial. Bodiless. Matterless. Unextended. Nonspatial. Having no physical dimensions. Intangible. Opposite to CORPOREAL.

incorrigible (L., *in*, "not," and *corrigere*, "to correct"). **1.** Not capable of correction. **2.** Not subject to error. **3.** That against which nothing would count as evidence. **4.** Absolutely certain. Example: The assertion (claim, affirmation) *that* we are having a feeling or a thought (mental claims) is incorrigible. Opposite to CORRIGIBLE.

independence, logical. See STATEMENT, LOGICALLY INDEPENDENT.

indeterminacy, principle of. See UNCERTAINTY, HEISENBERG'S PRINCIPLE OF.

indeterminism (ethics) (L., *in*, "not," and *determinare*, from *de*, "from," "down," "away," and *terminus*, "limit"). Sometimes referred to as LIBERTARIANISM. **1.** The theory that the mind (consciousness, self, soul, personality) is an agent free to cause effects such as moral decisions. **2.** A rational being has freedom of the will to choose without being compelled (determined) to this choice by causes independent of that act. **3.** Ethical choices are not influenced, and/or not caused by antecedent events. See entries under FREE and FREEDOM.

indeterminism (metaphysics). 1. The theory that some events do not have causes. **2.** The theory that some events (a) cannot be explained by being subsumed under general, universal laws or principles and (b) cannot be predicted, not because of our lack of knowledge but because of an inherent characteristic in the universe such as chance, randomness, uncertainty, spontaneity, novelty, an undetermined openness for possibilities to happen in the future.

indifference, principle of (probability theory). Sometimes *principle of insufficient reason, principle of nonsufficient reason.* If there are *X* possibilities for combinations (events) to occur, and no reason can be given why one should be more likely to occur than another, then the probability of each combination occurring is *1/X*. Example: If this principle is assumed, the probability of throwing double-six would be calculated at $\frac{1}{36}$ since there are 36 ways in which two dice can fall and only one is favorable for that double-six occurrence (based on the assumption that no reason can be given why any particular one of the 36 possibilities is any more likely than any other to occur). Also referred to as the principle of *nonsufficient reason.* See REASON, PRINCIPLE OF NONSUFFICIENT. Compare with REASON, PRINCIPLE OF SUFFICIENT.

indiscernible. Not recognized in any way as being different; recognized as being exactly alike. See IDENTITY OF INDISCERNIBLES, PRINCIPLE OF (LEIBNIZ).

individual (L., *individuus,* "indivisible," from *in,* "not," and *dividuus,* "divisible"). 1. An entity, existing as a distinct unity (unit) incapable of being divided actually or conceptually without losing its identity. 2. A PARTICULAR. Opposite to general, UNIVERSAL. 3. A single thing. 4. PERSON; SELF; EGO.

individualism (political theory). 1. The theory that the principal concern of all political and social groupings is to preserve the rights, guarantee the independence, and enhance the development of the individual person. The state is a means used by individuals in the attainment of these goals and is never an end in itself. Society exists for the sake of its individual members. 2. Government must never interfere with the individual's pursuit of his wishes unless this can be shown to produce harm to other individuals. The best form of government is the least amount of government. 3. All government must stem from the self-directing and self-regulating powers of individuals and must not be imposed by regulations and external coercion.

individuate 1. To discriminate (distinguish, identify, single out) from among others of a class or species. 2. To give something individuality or a particular character.

individuation (metaphysics). 1. The development of a particular (individual) thing from its corresponding universal or form. 2. The determination of the particular (individual) from its universal or general type. The *principle of individuation* refers to the cause (such as matter, or form, or God) of 1 or 2.

indubitable (L., *in,* "not," and *dubitare,* "to waver in opinion," "to be undecided," "to hesitate in belief"). **1.** That which cannot be doubted because there are no reasons that can be found to doubt it. **2.** Not doubtful in any way. **3.** Unquestionably true. Absolutely certain. Incontrovertible. Undeniable. Irrefragable. Sure beyond a doubt. Indubitable and INCORRIGIBLE are sometimes used synonymously. See CERTAIN.

An *indubitable statement* is one that cannot be doubted (rejected, disbelieved), such as "I exist," "I am now thinking."

induction (L., *in,* and *ducere,* "to lead"). Sometimes *inductive reasoning, inductive generalization, empirical generalization, enumerative induction.* **1.** Reasoning from a part of a whole, from particular instances of something to a general statement about them, from individuals to universals. **2.** Reaching a conclusion about all (or many) members of a class from statements describing only some of them. Example: "All observed X's have had the characteristic Y, therefore all X's are Y's." It is often believed that in this procedure the probability of the truth of the generalization is increased by each instance that verifies it. **3.** A form of nondeductive inference in which the conclusion expresses something that goes beyond what is said in the premises; the conclusion does not follow with logical necessity from the premises. Contrast with DEDUCTION.

induction, ampliative. Reasoning from a limited number of observed instances to a general causal relationship.

induction, eliminative. The process of supporting or confirming a statement or hypothesis by falsifying those competing with it. An indirect method of CONFIRMATION.

induction, intuitive. The view that we can experience necessary truths about the world, that something is essentially of a certain and necessary pattern and existence. Experience can show us what physically *must* happen. All necessity is not logical necessity. See UNIVERSALS (ARISTOTLE).

induction, intuitive (Aristotle). See UNIVERSALS (ARISTOTLE).

induction, perfect. Also *formal induction, induction by complete enumeration.* Stating a truth about all members of a class on the basis of having observed that truth in every member of that class. (In Aristotle, perfect induction is the process of arriving at a *genus* from an examination of all its *species.*)

induction, principle of (metaphysics). The belief that things that have happened regularly in the past will continue to happen in the future. The future will resemble the past. Compare with UNIFORMITY OF NATURE, PRINCIPLE OF THE.

induction, problem of. The problem of inferring a true statement about all members of a class on the basis of observing only some members of that class. Example: The truth of the statement "All crows are black" is based (a) on our seeing a great number of black crows, and (b) also on our not having seen any crows of another color. How is one logically justified in proceeding from "some" to "all" since not all crows have been observed?

inductive methods, Mill's. See METHODS, MILL'S INDUCTIVE.

ineffable (L., *in,* "not," and *effablis,* "capable of being expressed," from *ex,* "out," and *fari,* "to speak"). **1.** Incapable of being expressed or communicated. Unutterable. Indescribable. **2.** That about which nothing at all can be said (such as God or reality in itself) due (a) to its inconceivability by the finite mind and/or (b) to its existing permanently outside the realm of human consciousness.

inert (L., *inertis,* "unskilled," "idle," from *in,* "not," and *ars,* "art"). **1.** Unable to move itself (as in the phrase "inert matter"). **2.** Unable, actively and on its own, to resist motion from being impressed on it. **3.** Not having its own active powers. **4.** Powerless. Not being able to produce the expected or required effect. **5.** Idle. Not active (as in the phrase "inert personality"). **6.** The inherent or habitual indisposition of activity.

inertia, principle of (Newton). Newton's First Law of Motion. See MOTION, NEWTON'S THREE LAWS OF.

in esse (L., "in being," "in existence," "actually existing").

in facto (L., "the final, complete product that has been actualized or caused," "that which has been produced or taken place"). Example: A house is *in facto* when it has been finished and ready to be moved into. Compare with *IN INTELLECTU.*

inference (L., *in,* "in," and *ferre,* "to bring"). **1.** The logical or conceptual process of deriving a statement from one, or more statements. **2.** A CONCLUSION reached. **3.** DEDUCTION. Deriving a conclusion from premises that are accepted as true. **4.** INDUCTION. Deriving a conclusion from factual statements taken as evidence for the conclusion. See EDUCTION.

inference (deductive logic). **1.** The procedure by which a statement is affirmed or denied on the basis of other statements that are accepted as true or false. This aspect of deductive logic is concerned (a) with the possible true/false relationships of statements for which a true or false claim is made: (b) in the context of the truth values of the logical connectives by which they are related. The interest is not in whether statements are in fact true or false, but whether, if they are claimed as true (or false), then how their true-false combinations can be related to other statements in true-false combinations. **2.** The procedure of establishing the validity of a conclusion from premises accepted as true by the use of principles of inference. Compare JUSTIFICATION; PROOF.

inference, invalid. See INVALID.

inference, valid. See VALID.

in fieri (L., "in the process of becoming" or "in the act of beginning to be what it will be when completed"). Example: A house is *in fieri* during the time it is being worked on by the builders.

infinite (L., *in,* "not," and *finire,* "to limit," "to end," "to finish," "to complete"). **1.** Unlimited. Inexhaustible. Endless. **2.** Having no boundary. Indefinitely large. Opposite to FINITE.

infinite, actual/potential (Aristotle). Aristotle denied **(a)** that there can be any physical object that can be divided indefinitely; **(b)** that there is any physical object infinite in number; **(c)** that there is any physical object infinite in extent. He denied Zeno's notion that a line segment can actually be divided into an infinite number of indivisible units or unextended points. Aristotle believed that this could be done only theoretically or "potentially." There is no actual infinite class; the members of a class may be increased without limit, but the class never reaches a completed totality (and in this sense there are classes that are "potentially" infinite). Many finite things are "potentially" infinite in that they will appear again and again without end (and have appeared without a beginning point).

infinite, the actual. The infinite considered as a whole.

infinitesimal. Immeasurably and/or incalculably small. Indefinitely small.

informal fallacies. See entries under FALLACY.

ingression (L., *ingredi,* "to enter into," from *in,* "in," and *gradi,* "to walk," "to go"). **1.** The coming together of potential occurrences, thereby creating existing complexes. **2.** The developing together, or growing together, of diverse things, thereby creating concrete wholes. A term used by Alfred North Whitehead and by process philosophers. See PROCESS PHILOSOPHY.

in intellectu (L., "existing in the intellect," or "existing in the mind"). Referring to a thing's existing as an abstract idea or concept but without excluding the possibility that it also exists in reality. Compare with *IN FACTO.*

innate ideas. See IDEAS, INNATE.

inner sense. See SENSE, INTERNAL.

in res. Sometimes *in rebus, in re* (L., "existing in reality," "existing in an actual material way or thing," "existing in the external world even apart from any consciousness of it"). Used by medieval philosophers in the context of an Aristotelian realism (see REALISM, ARISTOTELIAN) whereby universals were regarded as existing "in things," "in reality," not in an ideal world of forms prior to reality (see REALISM, PLATONIC) and not only as names for similarities (see NOMINALISM; *ANTE RES; POST RES).*

in se (L., "in itself"). When applied to God (or Substance, or Ultimate Being, or the Universe) it refers to an eternal, self-subsisting ultimate being in which all things are found. Compare with *A SE.*

instinct (L., *instinguere,* "to incite," "to instigate"). **1.** An unlearned, natural impulse to act in a certain way. **2.** An involuntary, unreasoned, inherited tendency to act or to perform a specific action under the proper internal and external stimuli. **3.** Predilection. A natural (innate, spontaneous) and/or ingrained aptitude or knack for doing something.

instrumentalism. The philosophic position that ideas (laws, theories, hypotheses, etc.) are tools (instruments, devices, means) by which certain conceptual manipulations and calculations can take place in resolving the puzzles in life and scientific inquiry. Ideas are used to control, predict, explain, organize, and create possibilities for human experience. Whether ideas are true or false is not a serious question; rather, whether they are useful or powerful enough to explain and cause change and satisfy human needs and purposes. Thinking is to be judged according to its success in helping an organism adjust and thus survive socially and environmentally. The term is associated with the philosophy of John Dewey and has affinities with CONVENTIONALISM; PRAGMATISM; OPERATIONALISM. Also *experimentalism* (which is the word John Dewey himself preferred and used).

insufficient reason, principle of. See INDIFFERENCE, PRINCIPLE OF (PROBABILITY THEORY).

intellect (L., *intelligere,* "to understand," from *inter,* "between," and *legere,* "to collect," "to choose"). **1.** The cognitive faculty; the faculty of knowing (as opposed in FACULTY PSYCHOLOGY to the faculty of willing and the faculty of feeling). **2.** That function of reason that makes ideas (concepts, abstractions) possible. **3.** The ability (or capability or power) **(a)** to know, to conceptually understand, and **(b)** to relate that which is known or understood. See FACULTY and entries under REASON.

intellect, active/passive. See REASON, ACTIVE/PASSIVE (ARISTOTLE).

intellectual virtues. See VIRTUES, DIANOETIC (ARISTOTLE).

intellectus. See RATIO.

intellectus agens (L., "the active intellect"). Referring to the intellect as an agent affecting sensations (or phantasms) and perceptions and making them abstract so that they can be handled and known as universals.

intellectus possibilis (L., "the possible intellect"). Referring to the passive intellect (as opposed to the active intellect) whereby concepts (ideas, universals) are received (or developed or recognized) from the abstraction presented by the active intellect.

intelligence. 1. The activity of an organism in adjusting to situations by the use of combinations of functions such as perception, memory, conceptualizing, abstracting, imagining, attending, concentrating, selecting, relating, planning, extrapolating, predicting, controlling, choosing, directing. Contrasted with instinct, habit, rote, custom, tradition. **2.** The process of coping with problems (issues, perplexities) by means of abstract thinking. Higher levels of intelligence contain elements such as **(a)** symbolization and communication of abstract thinking, **(b)** its critical analysis, **(c)** its reconstruction to apply to further possibilities and/or to related situations, either practical or theoretical.

intension. 1. The way in which something is intended to be understood. **2.** The way in which something is understood. (Compare with COMPREHENSION. **3.** Sometimes used synonymously with CONNOTATION. See LAW OF INVERSE VARIATION (INTENSION/EXTENSION); MEANING, INTENSIONAL. Compare with EXTENSION.

intent (L., *intendere,* "to intend," "to attend," from *in,* "in," and *tendere,* "to stretch"). **1.** The meaning (import, purpose, motive) of a thing. **2.** The directional activity (plan, design) toward purposely accomplishing something. **3.** Being disposed to act in a certain way toward a specific object in order to achieve some desired result.

intention. 1. Meaning. Import. **2.** PURPOSE. Design. See INTENT. **3.** A predisposition to act to change something. **4.** A tendency to perform a specific act in order to attain some END.

intentionalism. The view that the essential and defining characteristic of consciousness is (**a**) that it is able to have (understand) meanings (INTENSION) and (**b**) that it is able to direct itself conatively by intending.

intentionality. 1. The ability of consciousness to (**a**) create a mental object which need not exist in the external world, (**b**) refer (apply) its content to reality, and (**c**) direct activity toward results. **2.** The ability of consciousness to refer to something that is not like itself or that is not like its own activity. **3.** The condition in which something directs, points to, or refers to something beyond itself.

In phenomenology, the *thesis of intentionality* (or *intentionality thesis*) refers to the belief that every act of consciousness possesses the above-listed qualities—all consciousness is consciousness of objects. The act of consciousness is called the *intentional act* and the object is called the *intentional object.* Bretano and Husserl are the leading exponents of this view.

interactionism, mind/body. See MIND/BODY INTERACTIONISM.

interjections, pure (L., *interjicere,* "to throw into," from *inter,* "among," "amid," "between," "together," "into," and *jacere,* "to throw"). Words such as "Ugh!" "Terrific!" "Out of sight!" "Hi!" "Alas!" Usually these words do not call up specific objects or images in the listener. See LANGUAGE, FUNCTIONS OF (**10**).

internal (L., *internus,* "in," "within"). **1.** Inherent. Intrinsic. **2.** That which is within consciousness as opposed to that which is external to consciousness. **3.** The inner or essential nature of a thing such as its qualities or characteristics. **4.** (**a**) The activity (or relationships) of the parts within a whole and/or (**b**) that which is contained within a whole.

internal relations, doctrine of. See RELATIONS, DOCTRINE OF INTERNAL.

intrinsic (L., *intrinsecus,* "inward," from *intra,* "within," and *secus,* "otherwise," "beside"). **1.** Inherent. In and of itself. **2.** Essential. **3.** Internal. Opposite to EXTRINSIC.

introjection (L., *intro,* "inwardly," "within," "into," "in," and *jacere,* "to throw"). **1.** The process whereby external objects are internalized as representational images of reality. **2.** The theory that the mind is composed of a complex of ideas (images, concepts) that have been internalized, and that it knows the external world by projecting this internal complex upon the world.

introspection (L., *intro,* "inward," "within," "into," and *specere,* "to look").

1. Looking into—giving mental attention to—one's mind, self, or consciousness. **2.** Examining (observing) one's mental states and functions in an attempt to describe, study, or enjoy them. When introspection attends to previous happenings as opposed to immediately occurring mental states it is called RETROSPECTION. Compare with REFLECTION (LOCKE). See EGO OF INTROSPECTION, THE.

intuition (L., *intueri,* "to look on," from *in,* "on," and *tueri,* "to see," "to watch"). **1.** Immediate noninferential apprehension or cognition of something. **2.** The power (ability) to have immediate, direct knowledge of something without the use of reason. **3.** Innate, instinctive knowledge or insight without the use of our sense organs, ordinary experience, or reason.

Intuition has been regarded as a true and certain source of knowledge, and as the only source of knowledge of some realms of being such as of the Ideal Forms, of God, or of the essences of things.

intuition (Kant). In general, the process of sensing, or the act of having a sensation. See SENSIBILITY (KANT). Intuitions are of two kinds: **1.** *empirical* (*a posteriori*) intuition of things by means of our sense organs, and **2.** *pure* or *formal* (*a priori*) intuition that structures what is given by the empirical intuition into sensations that have the quality of being in space and time. *Anschauung* is the German word for intuition, used by Kant, and has the connotations of "insight," "perception," "that which is directly and immediately provided to and organized by the mind." See KNOWLEDGE (KANT).

intuitionism (ethics). See ETHICS, INTUITIVE.

invalid (L., *invalidus,* "not strong," "inadequate"). Referring to a deductive argument that is not valid: The conclusion does not necessarily and with certainty follow from the premises. The premises do not establish undeniable logical support for the conclusion. It is possible for the premises to be true yet the conclusion false. Denial of the conclusion leads to no contradiction about what is claimed in the premises. Contrast with VALID.

inverse variation, law of (intension/extension). See LAW OF INVERSE VARIATION (INTENSION/EXTENSION).

involuntary act. See VOLUNTARY ACTION; VOLUNTARY-INVOLUNTARY ACTIONS.

ipso facto (L., "in accordance with fact itself").

irrational (L., *ir,* the assimilated form of *in,* "not," and *rationalis, ratio,* "reason"). **1.** Not in accordance with, or contrary to, reason. Absurd. Foolish. Nonsensical. **2.** Not endowed with reason (rational powers, rational faculty). **3.** Not exercising reason or rational judgment. Not acting rationally. **4.** Chaotic. Inexpressible as a sensible order or arrangement. **5.** Having no realistic or rational foundation (ground or explanation).

"is." A syntactical form of the phrase "to be." The third person singular present indicative of the verb *be.*

Is may be used in a number of ways: **1.** to relate things such as a subject and its predicate (as in "The rose is red"); **2.** to point things out (as in "This is a sparrow"); **3.** to classify or put into a list (as in "A whale is a mammal, and a snake is a reptile"); **4.** to provide identification for something (as in "He is a police officer"); **5.** to identify (as in "This is Mary Nagelmann"); **6.** to establish a meaning (or definition) relation (as in "The definition of bachelor is 'an unmarried man' "); **7.** to show an identity relation (as in "Lauri is Lauri" or "The Bard is Shakespeare"); **8.** to refer to what a thing is made up of (as in "This is pure butter, chocolate, and sugar); **9.** to express a tenseless meaning or sense (as in "The sum of four and four is eight"); **10.** to refer to something in a present sense (as in "He is breaking up the porch"); **11.** to refer to a past condition (as in "What Aristotle believed about substance is the backbone of his entire philosophy"); **12.** to refer to the future (as in "It is going to be a terrible sight").

"is" of formal equivalence. The identity of meanings or truth-values related by the word *is,* as in "Lightning *is* an electric discharge between clouds or a cloud and an object on earth."

"is" of identity. 1. Numerical identity. A relationship of selfsameness or one-and-the-same thing, as in "This marble is this marble," "I am that which I am," "That (moon) is the moon," "The USSR is Russia." **2.** Isomorphic identity. A relationship of things being *exactly the same* in every respect (except spatiotemporally), such as in "Marble *x* is identical to marble *y*." Or in a weaker form: "Jane is the identical image of her twin sister Beth."

"is" of predication. Sometimes referred to as the *copulative is.* Identifying (applying, referring, relating) a quality (predicate, characteristic, attribute) to a subject, as in "The grass *is* green," "Water *is* a liquid," "School *is* a bore."

isomorphism (Gk., *isos,* "equal," and *morphē,* "form"). **1.** Likeness of form (pattern, order, structure). Structural similarity. **2.** The one-to-one correspondence of similarity between the structure of one thing and that of another. That which establishes the identity relationship among things.

is/ought dichotomy. Also *fact/value dichotomy.* Statements containing the verb *is* are related to descriptive or factual claims and are of a different order from those containing the verb *ought* (*should*), which are related to judgments, evaluations, or commands. It is impossible (logically, formally, conceptually) to derive an "ought" (or "should") statement from an "is" (factual) statement, a NORMATIVE statement from a statement of facts; it is impossible to have a valid deductive argument in which the premises state descriptions and the conclusion states prescriptions or imperatives. See ETHICS, IS/OUGHT DICHOTOMY IN.

J

joint method of agreement and difference. See METHOD, MILL'S INDUCTIVE.

judgment (L., *jus,* "law"). **1.** That deliberate function of consciousness involving such activities as identifying, comparing, discriminating, and evaluating whereby values and/or knowledge are asserted or interpreted. **2.** Good sense. The power (ability, faculty) of judging wisely or correctly. **3.** Decision. The result of an appraisal that results in an opinion or decree. **4.** The assertion (or denial) of something. (In traditional categorical logic, the asserting or denying a predicate of some subject.) **5.** JUSTIFICATION. The process by which the truth or falsity of statements is determined. **6.** The process of forming or the state of a belief, opinion, assertion, conclusion. Used interchangeably with words such as knowledge, statement, proposition, concept, evaluation, decision.

judgment, analytic (Kant). Knowledge in which what is thought (said, meant) in its predicate has already been thought in its subject. Examples: "Matter occupies space and exists in time." "A thing cannot be both true and false at the same time in the same respect." All analytic judgments are necessarily true or necessarily false. Contrast with JUDGMENT, SYNTHETIC (KANT).

judgment, *a priori* (Kant). Knowledge that is necessary, universal, transcendental to experience, not derived from experience yet applicable to all experiences. Examples: "Every cause is followed by an effect." "There are no uncaused events."

judgment, logical (Kant). See CATEGORIES OF LOGIC, THE (KANT).

judgment, synthetic (Kant). Knowledge in which what is thought in its predicate has not been thought in its subject. Examples: "Bananas are green and then turn yellow." "Lead is heavy." Contrast with JUDGMENT, ANALYTIC (KANT).

judgment, synthetic *a priori* (Kant). See KNOWLEDGE, SYNTHETIC *A PRIORI* (KANT).

jus naturalis (L., "natural law"). Also *jus naturale*. Also *jus naturae*, "law of nature." The *jus* is also found as *ius*.

justice (L., *justus*, "just," and *justitia*, "justice"). **1.** Fairness. Equitableness. **2.** Correct treatment. Merited reward or punishment. **3.** Rectitude. Correctness and impartiality in the application of principles of rightness and of sound judgment. **4.** The embodiment of the virtues (ideals, values, principles) of a society. **5.** The establishment of a harmony between one's rights and the rights of others (society, the public, government, or individuals). See VIRTUES, CARDINAL.

justice (Plato). See *DIKAIOSYNĒ* (PLATO).

justice, commutative (Aristotle). Acceptable and uncoerced exchange of goods (values, benefits) as contrasted with undesired and excessive manipulation, profiteering, exploitation.

justice, corrective/rehabilitative. Justice whose aim, for example, is not punishment for the sake of punishment or for revenge but for the purpose of changing the character and the environment of the offender so that similar actions will not occur again.

justice, distributive. Proportionate or equal distribution. EGALITARIANISM. Allocating fairly to members of a community such things as money, property, privileges, opportunities, education, rights.

justice, distributive (Aristotle). That proper proportion determined objectively by reason, such as between a person's actions and its reward and between a person's status (abilities, performance) and its compensation.

justice, retributive. Sometimes *retaliative* or *retaliatory justice*. Justice whose principal aim is revenge and/or vindictiveness as indicated in the statement "An eye for an eye and a tooth for a tooth."

justification. 1. Defense. That which is offered as the sufficient grounds for an assertion (claim, statement, conclusion) or for one's conduct. **2.** Logical proof. In logic, the procedures applied to the premises of an argument that show the proof for the conclusion. Compare with EXPLANATION; PROOF.

K

kakos (Gk., "bad," "mean," "ugly," when applied to persons and when opposed to *KALOS*). When opposed to *AGATHOS* it means "ill-born," "ignoble," "of mean disposition or temper." *Kakos* has a variety of further meanings and interpretations such as: evil, worthless, poor, something to be pitied, wicked, baneful, unlucky. The neuter form *kakon* means *evil*.

kalos (Gk., "beautiful in outward appearance or in form," "excellent"). The neuter form *kalon* means "moral beauty," "virtue," "virtuous," "excellence." See *AGATHOS*..

katharsis (Gk., *katharsis*, "a cleansing from guilt or defilement," "purification," "PURGATION"). Also transliterated *catharsis*. **1.** The purification, or cleansing, or purgation of emotions by means of the aesthetic experience. **2.** The elimination, sublimation, or transformation of one's emotions, especially destructive emotions.

katharsis (Aristotle). In the *Poetics,* Aristotle used tragedy as an example of katharsis whereby feelings such as pity and fear are gotten rid of (purged) or cleansed (purified) by a vicarious experience of them in a controlled form (the tragedy) and setting (the theater). The emotion of pity is produced when we see an excellence destroyed, when we see a person of noble stature, with great promise and strong character, fall from a state of happiness and fortune to a state of unhappiness and misfortune. The feeling of fear is aroused when we recognize that a similar downfall may take place in our own lives. See TRAGEDY (ARISTOTLE).

kathēkon (Gk., "duty," "that which is fit or proper or one's due"). Used by the Stoics to refer to that which is the best course of action in accordance with the rational necessity inherent in nature. See STOICS, THE.

kathenotheism. See GOD CONCEPTS.

kind. 1. A natural CLASS. A group or division whose members have many natural qualities or functions in common, some of which are regarded as the defining characteristic of the class. **2.** A class. That classification which designates a common characteristic among its members, distinguishing those members from other things. Sometimes used synonymously with *species, genus,* a collection, a grouping, a set.

kinēsis (Gk., "change," "motion," "movement," "activity," "process," "development," "any kind of disturbance," even "dance." From *kinein,* "to move"). In general refers to any kind of change: spatial, temporal, qualitative, biological (such as growth, decay), etc. See CHANGE (ARISTOTLE).

knowledge. 1. Recognition of something. **2.** Familiarity or acquaintance with something from actual experience. **3.** That which is learned. **4.** Clear perception of what is regarded as fact, truth, or duty. **5.** Information and/or learning that is preserved and continued by civilizations. **6.** Things had in CONSCIOUSNESS (beliefs, ideas, facts, images, concepts, notions, opinions) that become justified in some way and thereby are regarded as true.

knowledge (Aristotle). 1. Knowledge may be divided into three parts: **(a)** *Theoretical:* Knowledge pursued for its own sake as in the study of metaphysics (FIRST PHILOSOPHY), physics, and mathematics. **(b)** *Practical:* Knowledge pursued for the sake of actions as in the study of ethics and politics. See *PRAXIS.* **(c)** *Productive:* Knowledge pursued in order to make, produce, or create something, as in the study of architecture, engineering, the crafts. See *POIESIS/POIETIKOS* (ARISTOTLE). **2.** Only knowledge of the form in things can be directly known by reason (the intellect). Matter that is imbued with form is not as such an object of direct intellectual apprehension. Knowledge is based on a process of uninferred experience or perception (intuitive induction) that grasps the necessary connections among the forms in the particular things experienced. This process provides the self-evident axioms, or first principles, for demonstrative knowledge; the organized deductive system called science.

knowledge (Descartes). Knowledge **(a)** must be certain; **(b)** must be objectively real; and **(c)** must be necessary, impossible to doubt (if denied, a contradiction ensues). Knowledge is possible only on condition that there is something (or that there are some things) about which we can never be wrong. All knowledge is derived by a deductive process similar to that in axiomatic geometry from this primitive and absolutely infallible truth. See METHOD (DESCARTES); SUBSTANCE (DESCARTES).

knowledge (Hume). All knowledge comes from **1.** *impressions:* the immediate, sensory, perceptual content of consciousness and **2.** *ideas:* the vague copies of these impressions that linger as content in our memory and imagination. Ideas may be divided into **(a)** *simple ideas:* every simple idea is a copy of a corresponding impression, and **(b)** *complex ideas:* simple ideas that are recombined and reorganized into new combinations (for example, ideas of a unicorn or of a human). There are two kinds of relationships among ideas: (1) relations that completely depend upon the ideas that are related, such as the necessary truths of logic and mathematics which when denied involve one in a contradiction, and (2) relations that can be changed without contradiction, and without changing the ideas themselves, such as matters of observed fact or descriptions of actual connections. The first may be called *ideas of reflection* and the second *ideas of sensation.* See IDEAS (HUME); IMPRESSION (HUME); SKEPTICISM (HUME).

knowledge (Kant). All knowledge is related to experience, but not all knowledge is derived from experience. That which is experienced must conform to fundamental structures of thought if it is to be intelligible. (Or, knowledge *is* the conformity of that which we experience with certain fundamental structurings of thought.) *A PRIORI* knowledge makes experience intelligible; it provides the structures with which experiencing must be organized if it is to be objectively real and not merely a product of fancy or imagination. See entries under JUDGMENT with reference to Kant. Also KNOWLEDGE, SYNTHETIC *A PRIORI* (KANT); KNOWLEDGE, TRANSCENDENTAL (KANT); SKEPTICISM (KANT).

knowledge (Locke). All knowledge is the perception of simple and complex ideas and of their relationships (such as of agreement/disagreement, affinity/disaffinity, similarity/dissimilarity). There are three kinds of knowledge: **1.** *Intuitive.* Examples: Knowledge of our own existence; knowledge that we think; knowledge that a sound is not a color. See INTUITION (LOCKE). **2.** *Demonstrative.* Examples: knowledge of God's existence; knowledge of moral principles; knowledge of mathematics. **3.** *Sensitive.* Examples: knowledge of the existence of specific, particular things external to us. The first two are certain, indubitable kinds of knowledge. See IDEAS (LOCKE); SKEPTICISM (LOCKE).

knowledge (Mill). Inductive inference is the major source (if not the only source) of knowledge. See METHODS, MILL'S INDUCTIVE. Mathematical inference itself is based on induction. Abstract thinking such as mathematics is composed of very highly confirmed generalizations based on (or derived from) experience. Mill's theory of knowledge is a form of PHENOMENALISM, whose central theme is that matter is the permanent possibility of sensation and that things, objects must be considered as phenomenal existents.

knowledge (Plato). There are two general realms of knowledge: **1.** The nonnatural realm of Eternal Ideal Forms (Ideas) that are transcendent, unchanging, perfect, intelligible with certainty, and **2.** the natural realm of ordinary sensations and particular things that are temporal, changing, unstable, unintelligible, and uncertain. The first is the realm of true being grasped by the intellect. The second is the realm of becoming grasped by our fallible senses. The everyday world of our senses does not give us knowledge since sense knowledge is erring, uncertain, fallible, imperfect, illusory, changing, imprecise, relative. Knowledge to be true knowledge must be unerring, certain, infallible, perfect, precise, absolute. True knowledge, as opposed to the illusory knowledge of the senses, is derived from an awareness of the eternal Forms. See FORMS, PLATO'S THEORY OF IDEAL.

knowledge, analytic. See JUDGMENT, ANALYTIC.

knowledge, *a posteriori*. Knowledge derived from sense experience. To know something *a posteriori* is to know it by experiencing it by one's senses as an aspect of the world, as something existing and found in reality. In principle, the truth or falsity of *a posteriori* knowledge can be checked against sense experience. Since however, sense experience is relative, inconsistent, variable, and thus not fully reliable, *a posteriori* knowledge is not regarded as necessary or certain knowledge; it is rather probable knowledge that can be denied without pain of contradiction. (This is in opposition to *a priori* knowledge, which is regarded as certain knowledge based on reason alone and which cannot be denied without contradiction.) *A posteriori* knowledge is not true in all possible worlds but is true under specific conditions of existence: that is, at particular times and places and for particular types of experiences. *A posteriori* truths are called *truths of fact* or *sense experiences* (as opposed to the *a priori truths of reason*) and are based on the veracity of our experiences of the world around us. Example: Adam has brown eyes. See A POSTERIORI. Compare with CONTINGENT; EMPIRICAL; PROBABLE; INDUCTION. Contrast with A PRIORI; CERTAINTY; DEDUCTION; NECESSARY; TAUTOLOGY.

knowledge, *a priori*. 1. Knowledge derived from the function of reason without reference to sense experience. Nonempirical knowledge. To know something *a priori* is to know it prior to experiencing anything like it in the external world. The truth of *a priori* knowledge (**a**) is not derived from sense experience, (**b**) cannot be checked against sense experience, (**c**) cannot be refuted by any sense experience. It is regarded as certain knowledge which if denied leads to a contradiction. (This is opposite to *a posteriori* knowledge, which is probable knowledge whose truth is based on sense experience and which can be denied without contradiction.) Since *a priori* knowledge cannot be invalidated, it is true under all conditions and at any time and place: that is, it is true in all possible worlds. *A priori* truths are called *truths of reason* (as opposed to *a posteriori truths of fact* or *sense experience*). *A priori* truths may be regarded as expressing the definitional relationships among ideas (concepts, meanings) such as those found in formal logic and in mathematics. They are truths based on definitionally identical (synonymous, equivalent) statements, which may be correctly substituted for each other. The truth of an *a priori* statement can thus be ascertained by examining the statement itself (or it can be logically deduced from such statements). The statement is true in itself because of its own inherent meanings. Example: All triangles have 180°. **2.** Knowledge that is necessary, universal, transcendental to experience, not derived from experience yet applicable to all experiences (Kant's *a priori* judgments). Examples: "There are no uncaused events." "Every cause is followed by an effect." **3.** Used synonymously with "self-evident": innate knowledge which is not derived from sense experience but which is imposed upon reality (such as the categories of understanding) so that reality can be organized and thereby understood and coped with. **4.** Sometimes used in the context of innate, self-evident moral truths such as "Killing is wrong." See A PRIORI. Compare with CERTAINTY; DEDUCTION; NECESSARY; TAUTOLOGY. Contrast with CONTINGENT; EMPIRICAL; INDUCTION; PROBABLE.

knowledge, explicative. See EXPLICATION.

knowledge, private. See PRIVACY, EPISTEMIC.

knowledge, public. See PUBLICITY, EPISTEMIC.

knowledge, synthetic. See JUDGMENT, SYNTHETIC (KANT).

knowledge, synthetic *a priori* (Kant). Also *synthetic a priori judgment.* Knowledge **(a)** that is prior to the experiencing of something, **(b)** by which that experience is structured and made possible, and **(c)** into which all experiences can be structured. Examples: "Every event has a cause." "Every cause has an effect." Such statements are not true because of the meanings of the words that are being related (see TAUTOLOGY); they are not true on the grounds of their logical form alone; they are not true because we experience them as true. They are known to be true independently of all empirical evidence. The knowledge contained in such statements is informative but nonempirical, necessary but not tautological (not analytic, not purely definitionally true—its denial does not produce a contradiction according to Kant). Synthetic *a priori* knowledge is found in the physical sciences and in mathematics. See entries under JUDGMENT with reference to Kant. See also REASON (KANT).

knowledge, theory of. See EPISTEMOLOGY.

knowledge, transcendental (Kant). 1. The knowledge of those conditions (categories, forms, structures) that make conscious experience possible. For Kant, knowledge of a reality transcending our experience is impossible (see SKEPTICISM (KANT), but transcendental knowledge *is* possible. **2.** That *in* experience, or that *about* experience, which can be ascertained *a priori.* Transcendental knowledge transcends empirical knowledge, but it does not transcend all human knowledge or human experience: that is, it does not become TRANSCENDENT. See KNOWLEDGE (KANT).

knowledge by acquaintance. Sometimes *immediate knowledge, direct knowledge.* Contrasted with KNOWLEDGE BY DESCRIPTION. **1.** Personal knowledge gained through the actual experience of something (as opposed to obtaining it, for example, vicariously by means of its description from someone else). Example: If I have been drunk I have some knowledge of drunkenness by direct acquaintance. If I have never been drunk but I have been told what it feels like to be drunk, then I have knowledge of drunkenness by description. **2.** Immediate perception or sensation of an object or event. Example: seeing or touching an eel.

knowledge by description. Sometimes *indirect knowledge, vicarious knowledge*. Contrasted with KNOWLEDGE BY ACQUAINTANCE. **1.** Having an indirect experience or knowledge of something by means of someone relating it in some way such as verbally. Example: never having been drunk but being told how it feels to be drunk. **2.** Having knowledge of something based on inference or imagination but not on direct familiarity or experience of that thing. Example: knowing that a person is drunk not because we have experienced drunkenness but because he is swaying, he cannot walk in a straight line, he cannot enunciate properly, he reeks of alcohol, his blood has a high percentage of alcohol.

koinai ennoiai (Gk.). A phrase primarily associated with Stoic philosophy (see STOICS, THE) that designates concepts such as good, evil, beauty, the existence of God that are *common (koinai)* to all men **(a)** as natural tendencies of thought, **(b)** as innately present as part of the universal LOGOS in man; and **(c)** as imparted by humanity or civilized society which was a reflection of the Logos.

kosmos. See COSMOS.

L

laissez-faire. Sometimes *laisser faire, laisser passer* (Fr., "allow things to proceed without interference," "let [people] do or make [what they wish]"). A philosophy of governmental noninterference in the economic activities of individuals (such as in production, marketing, trading, financing, investing, advertising); a philosophy of free enterprise founded on private ownership of goods, property, resources, and services, which asserts that an individual is more efficient and productive when allowed to seek his self-interest without governmental regulation or restriction. Principally associated with the philosophy of Adam Smith.

language (L., *lingua,* "tongue," hence "speech," "language"). **1.** That body of words, their standardized meanings, and the forms of speech used as a method of communication. **2.** Any means of expressing the contents of consciousness (feelings, emotions, desires, thoughts) in a consistent pattern of meaning.

Language requires *symbols* (such as words, sounds, gestures, signs) that are organized and related in a complex system for the purpose of communicating meanings. This system of symbols can be manipulated in such a way as to be able to construct an indefinite combination to which meanings may be attached and by which meanings can be expressed. Such a system has rules specifying how such combinations can take place and how standardized meanings are to be assigned. Some further elements in a language are: (a) an intelligence producing it, to (b) intentionally affect (communicate with, transmit something to) some other form of intelligence, (c) hoping for a reaction or a similar response and exchange, (**d**) about some content (concepts, meanings, ideas) that has some common ground of understanding and/or apprehension. Language is a system of symbols that can be used to express or refer to such things as: (1) external material objects; (2) internal mental existents: (3) qualities; (4) relations; (5) logical-mathematical signs; (6) functions; (7) states; (8) processes; (9) events.

language, conventionalism in/pragmatism in. See CONVENTIONALISM.

language, formal. Sometimes *artificial, formalized, symbolic,* or *ideal language.* A language deliberately constructed according to specific conceptual and logical rules and used to accomplish a specific purpose consistently, precisely, and completely. Formal languages are contrasted with "natural" languages such as English, Greek, German, etc. (Formal languages are not classified with the "artificial" languages such as Esperanto, which are languages invented in order to correct and replace what is regarded as inadequate natural languages. Formal languages are not primarily intended as substitutes for natural languages.) A formal language has characteristics such as: **1.** *Symbolism.* **2.** *Syntactical rules* (or *formation rules*) that determine how these symbols are to be connected; what grammatical connections (syntax) are possible within the system. Syntactical rules allow us to transform, replace, and substitute symbols. **3.** *Semantical rules* (including any rules of definition) by which the formal language is to be translated. Semantical rules enable us to assign and to interpret the meanings given to the vocabulary (terms) of the language. **4.** *Rules of logic* such as the principles of inference for deductive purposes. **5.** *Terms* (vocabulary) that include such items as variables, constants, signs for grouping or punctuation, etc. Formal languages are used for purposes such as: (**a**) to symbolize scientific theories and laws; and (**b**) to symbolize languages such as logic and mathematics.

language, functions of. Language has many functions. The following are some of the principal ones: **1.** *Cognitive.* This includes such functions as referring, conveying information, communication of meanings (concepts, ideas, usage), and the construction of symbolic systems to accomplish such functions. Examples: "Marian has black hair" functions to communicate something about a referent, something claimed to be true about an objective world that can be judged to be true or false. "A statement cannot be both true and false at the same time in the same respect" functions to communicate the meanings of a procedural rule used in logic irrespective of whether or not there is a referent for it. **2.** *Emotive.* Here language functions to express and/or to evoke emotions, feelings, moods, sensations, attitudes, images, values, actions, prejudices, often in order to influence conduct. Examples: "You are a disgusting slob." "That was very embarrassing to me and you should feel ashamed of yourself." For the most part emotive language does not refer to a referent, does not directly communicate information about a referent, and is not directly concerned with asserting that something is actually true or false. **3.** *Imperative* (*directive*). Language that functions to command (advise, exhort, obligate, bind). Examples: "Open the door." "Please do as I say." "Thou shalt not steal." **4.** *Evaluative* (*appraising, judging*). Language that functions to analyze the value (worth, merit) of something. Examples: "I believe that our government is the best system of government in the world." "The paintings of Picasso are far more beautiful than those of Cézanne." Many of these functions are found together in language. They are not the only functions that can be pointed out. Some others: **5.** *Questioning.* **6.** *Performative* (see LANGUAGE, PERFORMATIVE). **7.** *Magical.* **8.** *Ceremonial.* **9.** *Expressive.* **10.** *Interjectional* see (INTERSECTIONS, PURE).

language, object. 1. Object language is that language used to talk about things of which we are conscious, as opposed to METALANGUAGE, which is language used to talk (and/or theorize) about such a language or about other languages. The expressions used in an object language have no linguistic or syntactical reference. The expressions used in a metalanguage do. Examples: "Doug is a male" is a statement in an object language. " 'Doug' is a proper noun with four letters" is a statement in a metalanguage. **2.** To study the structures of a language one must use a language to study it with. The language that is being systematically analyzed is called the *object language*—the object of the analysis; the language being mentioned. The language that is being used in the analysis of this object language is called its *metalanguage*—the language in which the investigation of the language is being carried out; the language being used.

language, ordinary. See ORDINARY LANGUAGE PHILOSOPHY.

language, performative. Sometimes *performatory language.* Language that is used in specific contexts (**a**) whose meaning is derived from its being used to act out (perform) the meaning (activity) it is informing us about, or (**b**) whose meaning consists in the very act of uttering it. Examples: "I promise." "I congratulate you on winning." "I offer you this as a token of my esteem." "With this bottle of champagne, I christen thee SS Elizabeth I." "I apologize for my rude behavior." See TRUTH, PERFORMATIVE THEORY OF.

language, philosophy of. The conceptual analysis of language in all its dimensions such as raised in SEMANTICS, PROBLEMS OF and in such further problems as: **1.** What (if any) are the unique characteristics of religious language, moral language, poetic language, scientific language, mathematical language, computer language, language of gesture, language of body image? **2.** What is the relationship between language and knowledge, language and intuitive understanding? Can we have knowledge without language? **3.** What is the relationship between what our language helps us to conceptualize and that reality which it conceptualizes? **4.** For what purposes and in what ways can language be used? **5.** What are linguistic acts? How do they differ from linguistic uses? **6.** What is a symbol (sign)? **7.** What kinds of symbols are there? How are they invented or constructed? **8.** What is communication? **9.** How is communication of meaning possible? **10.** What are the varieties of ways of communicating? **11.** Are there ways of perfecting language? How are (perfect) formal languages constructed? **12.** Are there presuppositions that natural, or ordinary, language brings with it that give us an insight into the nature of the mind and/or of reality? See ANALYSIS, LINGUISTIC.

language philosophy, ordinary. See ORDINARY LANGUAGE PHILOSOPHY.

latent (L., *latere,* "to lie hidden"). **1.** Present but not visible or apparent. Hidden. Concealed. **2.** POTENTIAL. Capable of developing into something. **3.** Having possibility. Able to be used in some way or for some purpose.

law, natural (ethics). 1. The set of obligations or principles (laws, maxims, duties, codes, commands, etc.) binding upon one's conduct which are obtained by reason from an examination of the universe (nature) in contrast to those obtained by revelation, intuition, innate moral conscience, authority, feelings, inclinations. **2.** The moral rules of conduct, the sense of fairness and justice, which humans possess by the pure activity of their reason (or moral conscience) and which is obligatory independently of, and in spite of, what other forms of law prescribe. Example: It is a natural law that when a person is using his property resourcefully for the community it should not be taken away from him. **3.** The universal rules of conduct found in all humans and societies as basic aspects of their nature and activity. **4.** The description of what should be or ought to be binding upon all humans discovered by a rational examination of human nature and successful human relationships.

law, natural (Stoics). The universe is a rational whole. All things follow the inexorable necessity of the rational principle in all things (natural law). Humans are unique in that they can either obey or not obey the rational and moral structure of the universe. Morality, justice, virtue have to do with humanity's accepting and following the direction of this rationality. Common phrases depicting this in Stoicism: "conformity to nature," "adherence to the *LOGOS*," "following the natural law in all things."

law, natural (theology). A set of codes (rules, precepts) (a) intended by nature and grounded in some "higher" or "transcendent" reality, (b) which prescribes what should or should not be done, (c) which is universally binding upon all humans, and (d) which can be found by a rational examination of nature. Example: It is immoral to have intercourse and mechanically or artificially prevent a sperm from meeting with the ovum. Such a natural union of sperm and ovum is intended by nature and any deliberate interruption of this process goes against what is intended by nature and by God.

Natural law is contrasted with notions of civil law, secular law, positive law, common law, public law, state law, etc. In theology, natural law supersedes these forms of law and is used to judge them.

law, scientific. A general statement describing an invariable order or regularity that exists among phenomena under certain specific conditions. Such a description is regarded as an explanation of how things in fact occur. The description may take the form of: **1.** A simple observation of an experience (such as "Hydrochloric acid dissolves iron filings"). **2.** A complex statement (such as "Every body perseveres in its state of rest, or of uniform motion in a straight line, unless it is compelled to change that state by forces impressed thereon"). **3.** A highly complex mathematical-deductive statement (such as "If $F = 0$, then $\frac{d(mv)}{dt} = 0$"). Some further characteristics, in most cases, of scientific laws: **4.** They have a wide range of applicability. **5.** They are expressed in some form of universal statement. **6.** They are expressed in some form of a timeless present tense, whereby they can be considered as true at all times that exemplify their stated conditions or order. **7.** They are subject to confirmation or verification by testing procedures. (Or there are conditions that can be presented at least theoretically under which it would be possible to *falsify* them.) **8.** They contain data that can be observed. **9.** They are stated in as precise a definitional and mathematical way as possible relative to the complexity of the situation they are attempting to describe. **10.** They have predictive power. They are able to tell us how things will behave under certain specific conditions. **11.** They assume a hypothetical or conditional stance whereby *if* these conditions occur *then* such and such will be the case. **12.** They are stated in ideal terms and in highly general and ideal contexts, but can with a margin of error be applied to concrete situations that are empirically examinable. **13.** They are exceptionless (primarily because if any counterinstance is discovered, the law is changed into an exceptionless form, or if there are enough exceptions it ceases to be regarded as a law). See METHOD, SCIENTIFIC; THEORY, SCIENTIFIC.

law of excluded middle. See LAWS OF THOUGHT, THE THREE.

law of identity. See LAWS OF THOUGHT, THE THREE.

law of inverse variation (intension/extension). Words may be ordered in increasing INTENSION. Example: animal, vertebrate, mammal, canine, dog, poodle. When this is done their order can be seen to be arranged in decreasing (or at least nonincreasing) extension. EXTENSION and intension vary inversely with each other (or: if the extensions vary at all, they vary inversely with the intensions).

law of noncontradiction. See LAWS OF THOUGHT, THE THREE.

law of three stages (Comte). See POSITIVISM (COMTE).

laws, moral (as regulative principles). The view that moral laws are rules or ideals which regulate conduct, by which conduct can be organized and limited, and which remind us of what we are seeking and/or what we ought to do (much as a police officer's uniform reminds us that we should obey the speed limit or traffic light).

laws, moral and social. 1. Prohibitions, commands, obligations imposed by authority (or custom, reason, etc.) for the purpose of directing and controlling behavior, as in laws of custom, laws of society, laws of morality, common laws, statute laws, civil laws, religious laws, etc. **2.** Objective, universally applicable and binding rules to be followed in conduct for such purposes as group cohesion, stability, interpersonal relations, protection, expression of sentiments, standardization of conduct.

laws as conventions. The view that scientific laws are conventions which provide explanations of the physical world and that other conventions could be used to describe it. One convention is accepted over another because it is more useful, simpler, more convenient, explains a greater variety of phenomena. Laws are not "true" in the sense that they describe the physical world; they are mathematical/logical ways of ordering our perceptions of the world, and the way we describe the world is due to the linguistic conventions our culture has adopted. "Truth" is thus relative to our mathematical/logical and linguistic framework. Many "pictures" or frameworks of a reality can be constructed; some are better than others but none can really be said to be truer. There is no *one* true set of laws describing the universe. Any consistent and highly sophisticated comprehensive system of analysis can be applied to the study of nature. The order (patterns, identities, wholes) we find in the physical world is dependent upon how our mind and how our mathematical/logical/linguistic systems see it, organize it, and present it. Compare with CONVENTIONAL-ISM.

laws as physical necessities of nature. The view that natural laws express the necessary connection among events that irrevocably binds them together and necessitates them to happen as they do happen and in no other way. Physical necessity of this kind is believed to be an irreducible and fundamental aspect of all nature and is what natural law describes.

laws as procedural rules. The view that scientific laws are rules that allow inferences from events to events, or from statements about events to other statements about events.

laws as regularities. The view that scientific laws describe an order about reality in terms of such basic concepts as: (**a**) the *coexistence* of events (things happening together), (**b**) the *cosuccession* of events (things happening together in a series) and (**c**) the *invariant connections* (such as cause and effect relations) among events.

laws of nature (antinecessitarian view). Necessity does not exist in nature. Things could have been other than what they are. Nature need not have been as it was; it might have been otherwise. The necessity that is seen in natural (physical) laws is the *logical* necessity stemming from the system of interrelated concepts with which these natural laws are formulated and expressed and the theoretical structure of which they are a part. See ACCIDENTALISM.

laws of nature (descriptive view). The laws of nature are general statements which describe regular sequences of events which are observed to occur. Example: If water is heated at sea level to 100°C, then we also observe that it boils. The law pertaining to this merely points out that as a matter of fact (as a matter of our experience) these connections seem to hold and describe (explain) in a general way what is actually taking place.

laws of nature (necessitarian view). Also the *governance* or *prescriptive view*. The laws of nature are principles (directions, commands, rules) which make things happen, govern or prescribe things to happen, in a certain way and which necessitate that they happen exactly in that way. Their necessity applies everywhere in the universe and in all possible universes. They are prior in reality and power to what they cause to happen. Example: When water is heated at sea level to 100°C, there is a law which these conditions obey and by which they are governed so that water *must* boil at that temperature and atmospheric pressure. Any water which did not behave in this way would be "violating" a law of nature. In theology, God creates these laws which govern the activity of all things. His will is expressed by means of the laws of nature which are signs of His omnipresence and omnipotence. Compare with PREDETERMINISM.

laws of thought, the three. Also *the three principles of thought*. The formulation of what have been called the Three Laws of Thought goes back to Plato and Aristotle. They have been regarded as *ontologically real* (describing the ultimate features of reality); as *cognitively necessary* (no consistent thinking is possible without their use; all coherent thought, and all logical systems, rely upon them for justification; their denial presupposes their use in denying them); as *uninferred knowledge* (the immediate and direct result of a rational examination of the relations of timeless universals). In modern times, they have been regarded as only three among many *principles,* or *rules of inference* that can be invented and used in logic; or as definitionally true (tautologous) and hence irrefutable. **1.** *The Law of Identity:* If p is true, then p is true. (If p is false, then p is false.) If a thing A is A, then it is A. A is A. Everything is what it is (and cannot, at the time it is what it is, be something else). **2.** *The Law of Noncontradiction* (also *The Law of Contradiction*): p cannot be both true and false (at the same time and in the same respect). A thing A cannot be both A and not A (at the time it is A). **3.** *The Law of Excluded Middle:* Either p is true or p is false; one or the other but not both at the same time and in the same respect. A thing A is either A or it is not A.

Leibniz's law. See IDENTITY OF INDISCERNIBLES, PRINCIPLE OF (LEIBNIZ).

liar paradox. See PARADOX, LIAR.

libertarianism. 1. In ethics, the view that humans have free will interpreted as an uncaused event. See INDETERMINISM (ETHICS). **2.** In metaphysics, the view that there are uncaused events in the universe.

liberty (L., *liber*, "free"). **1.** The right of a person to choose from among alternative courses of action or goals without being restricted by authority.

2. The right of a person not to be interfered with in pursuit or possession of what he wills or values. **3.** The right of individuals to express themselves however they wish, without constraint, and to employ the means they wish to obtain their interests. **4.** The absence of (FREEDOM FROM) external restraints, obstructions, constraints, or impediments, and without fear of punishment or reprisal. **5.** The freedom (ability) or opportunity to act in accordance with one's choice.

Liberty has traditionally been thought of in the political and social context of being free to do that (**a**) for which there is no normal or other good reason against doing it (any interference by authorities must be justified by good reasons such as a danger to public health, damage to the safety or well-being of others, etc.), and (**b**) which does not infringe upon (interfere with, harm, restrain, coerce) the activities of others and their rights. Liberty has been regarded as an inalienable natural right (together with life, property, and the pursuit of happiness). Compare with entries under FREEDOM and RIGHTS.

licentious (L., *licentia,* from *licere,* "to be permitted"). **1.** Immoral. Deviating from moral principles. **2.** Uncurbed. Taking excessive liberty, or freedom of action in regard to what is proper, good, or enough. **3.** Lawless. Compare with INCONTINENCE.

licentious (Aristotle). One who feels no conflict between base physical desires (passions, cravings, yearnings) and rational promptings (urges, impulses) toward the attainment of higher values. This is in contrast with the incontinent person (see INCONTINENCE), who does feel the conflict but nevertheless allows the desires to win out.

like causes like, principle of. The principle that the qualities in the cause are also qualities present in the effect, and vice versa: Cause and effect can never be qualitatively disparate or dichotomous. For example, on the basis of this principle, mind cannot come from something that does not contain mental characteristics; life cannot come from something that does not contain life.

like perceives like, principle of. The principle used in Greek philosophy by philosophers such as Empedocles and Plato: (**a**) that what is perceived resembles (in quality and/or in form) that which is perceived and (**b**) that knowledge is possible only if such a resemblance exists. This principle, together with the principle of like causes like (see LIKE CAUSES LIKE, PRINCIPLE OF), is the foundation of the metaphysical assumption that nature *is* as we perceive (and construct) it, and *acts* monistically as an integrated unity.

limit, the. See *PERAS.*

limitless, the. See *APEIRON.*

linguistic analysis/philosophy. See ANALYSIS, LINGUISTIC.

locutionary expression/act (locution). The act of uttering a statement and using a language (or utterance) with a somewhat definite reference and sense and/or meaning; the act of uttering a meaningful statement. Example: "The house is on fire." Compare with ILLOCUTIONARY EXPRESSION/ ACT (ILLOCUTION); PERLOCUTIONARY EXPRESSION/ACT (PERLOCUTION).

logic (Gk., *logikē,* or *logikos,* "that which belongs to intelligent speech or to a well-functioning reason," "ordered," "systematized," "intelligible"). **1.** The study of the rules of exact reasoning, of the forms of sound or valid thought patterns. **2.** The study and the application of the rules of inference to arguments or to systems of thought.

logic (Aristotle). Logic as the science of making correct inferences was regarded by Aristotle as the indispensable foundation for all types of knowledge. Logic is an instrument, or tool, for the unlocking of the intelligible connections found in concepts and in things. (*To Organon* was the name given by later editors to the compilation of Aristotle's works on logic. It means "the tool," "the instrument," "the method" for obtaining philosophical and scientific knowledge. Aristotle himself most frequently used a variation of the word *analysis,* from *ana,* "up," and *lyein,* "to loosen," to apply to what we now label his works on logic.) For Aristotle, the main part of logic was the categorical syllogism. His syllogistic methods remained the basis for the development of formal logic through the medieval period, when it was studied intensively and considerably enlarged in a systematic way, to the beginning of the twentieth century, when new symbolic techniques and principles for logic were invented.

logic, deductive. The systematic attempt (**a**) to formulate rules of inference that are consistent and complete and (**b**) to apply them to formally presented arguments and (**c**) to determine whether or not their conclusions can be validly inferred from the premises. See DEDUCTION.

logic, deontic. Logic that deals with and formalizes concepts such as obligation, permissibility and nonpermissibility, ought, should, could into a coherent system. Some of its basic principles: "If something is obligatory, then it should be permissible." "If something is not permissible, then it is not obligatory." "If something is done because it is obligatory, then it itself is something obligatory that should be done." "It is not true that that which is obligatory is (necessarily) done." "It is not true that that which is done is permissible." "It ought to be the case that that which is obligatory should be done." "It is the case that for a thing to be obligatory it must be possible for it to be done."

logic, dialectical. Sometimes simply *dialectics* (see entries under DIALECTIC). The general term given to the logic of philosophers such as Hegel, Marx, Engels, who attempted to refute the Three Laws of Thought (see LAWS OF THOUGHT, THE THREE) and develop a logic of becoming that attempts to present the ever-changing processes of things. For example, contradiction exists in reality. It is possible for the selfsame thing to be and not to be—the same thing is and is not. It is thought that this process can be seen in the polarities of change (thesis and antithesis) found in all activity. Contradiction is the driving force in all things. (It would have been more linguistically accurate for them to have used the words contrast, contrary, opposition, rather than contradiction. The concept of noncontradiction, together with the other two Laws of Thought, is definitionally and irrevocably true.)

Hegel viewed logic as a process (the dialectical process) and not as an analysis of how form could be applied to content (or of how content could be put into a form). Form and content are inseparably united in a movement that not only describes human thought patterns but also describes the three states by which natural events take place. The movement involves what has been commonly named a thesis, an antithesis, and a synthesis. The categories or principles of reason (ideas, notions, concepts) are exemplified in this process of movement from a THESIS to an ANTITHESIS and on to their unity in a SYNTHESIS. The principles of reason, or the categories, cannot be enumerated completely since the dialectical process has not yet fully actualized itself in reality. See DIALECTIC (HEGEL).

logic, formal. Logic that constructs valid patterns (forms) of inference as opposed to dealing directly with content (meanings).

logic, inductive. The attempt (a) to formulate rules (such as Mill's Methods of Induction) by which statements can be established as empirically confirmed or probable; (b) to formulate systematic procedures for presenting nondeductive inferences or arguments; and (c) to determine a degree of CONFIRMATION or PROBABILITY for the conclusion based on the degree of confirmation or probability that it is possible to establish for the premises.

logic, informal. The study of those inferences that (a) do not follow a precise logical form (and if they do, their truth does not depend on such a form), (b) are based on the meanings rather than the validity of the forms involved in the argument, and (c) may be true or false depending upon considerations (such as empirical evidence) other than the form of their argument.

logic, many-valued (multivalued). Logic that attempts to employ more than the two (usually three) truth values of "true" and "false" in analyzing some types of arguments. Some values other than true or false: (a) known as true/known as false/not known (or unknown); (b) true/false/undetermined (or undeterminable); (c) true necessarily/false necessarily/possible (contingent); (d) true certainly/false certainly/true probably/false probably.

logic, modal. Logic that deals with and formalizes into a coherent symbolic system concepts such as necessity, possibility (and impossibility). Some of its basic principles: "If something is necessary then it should be possible." "If something is necessary then it is not impossible." "If something is impossible then it is necessarily false." "If something is necessarily false then it is impossible." "If something is necessitated by something necessarily true, then it itself is necessarily true." "That which is necessary is both truly actual and possible."

logic, symbolic. Sometimes *formalized logic*. Logic presented in abstract symbolization consisting of well-defined elements such as (**a**) symbols, (**b**) signs, (**c**) connectives, (**d**) rules for the combination of symbols, (**e**) rules for substitution, (**f**) rules of inference, (**g**) rules of derivation.

logic, traditional categorical. Sometimes *Aristotelian logic*. **1.** The logic of the categorical SYLLOGISM. **2.** The logic of classes. **3.** The study of the rules and procedures by which terms related as subject and predicate lead to conclusions that follow with necessity (certainty).

logic, transcendental. See CATEGORIES OF LOGIC, THE (KANT).

logical atomism. See ATOMISM, LOGICAL.

logical empiricism. See EMPIRICISM, LOGICAL.

logical form. See FORM, LOGICAL.

logical implication. See IMPLICATION, LOGICAL.

logical independence. See STATEMENT, LOGICALLY INDEPENDENT.

logical paradox. See PARADOX, LOGICAL.

logical positivism. See POSITIVISM, LOGICAL.

logical table of judgments, the (Kant). See CATEGORIES OF LOGIC, THE (KANT).

logicism. 1. Generally, the theory that mathematics is an extension of logic: (**a**) mathematics can be deduced from the concepts and the deductive procedures of logic; (**b**) all mathematical proofs are forms of deductive reasoning; (**c**) mathematics can be reduced to logic. **2.** Specifically, (**a**) pure mathematics deals with concepts all of which can be defined in terms of a few fundamental logical concepts; and (**b**) the statements of mathematics can all be derived from a few logical rules (principles). **3.** The theory that all necessary statements (truths, logical forms) can be seen to be logically analytically true.

Logos (Gk., "speech," "discourse," "thought," "reason," "word," "meaning," "study of," "the account of," "the science of," "the underlying reasons for why a thing is what it is," "the principles and methods used to explain phenomena in a particular discipline," "those features in a thing that make it intelligible to us," "the rationale of a thing"). *Logos* is used in English as a combining form in such words as embryo*logy,* (the study of the embryo), psycho*logy* (the science of behavior), geo*logy,* (an account of the features of the earth), philo*logy* (the love of words). In Greek religion, *Logos* referred to the divine Word of a God or gods that provided spiritual inspiration, wisdom, and guidance. A prophet (*prophētēs*) was one whose speech (*logos*) communicated that divine Word.

Logos (**Heracleitus**). **1.** The immanent cause of the pattern and identity that is evident in the constant flux of all things. Heracleitus may have believed the *Logos* to be a material existence like fire (*pyr*). **2.** The underlying reason for the existence of any particular thing in the universe. **3.** Cosmic necessity, law, fate, or destiny. **4.** That about the universe which remains the same whereas all other things change. Those features about the universe which can be identified, talked about, named, and remain relatively unchanged.

Humans possess a fragment of the universal *Logos* as exhibited in their reasoning powers and in their continued existence as identities. Compare with CHANGE (HERACLEITUS).

Logos (Stoics). **1.** The underlying, cosmic principle of intelligence or reason (God) that produces the rationally ordered activity in the universe. As in Heracleitus, it was identified with a material force, and specifically with the eternal fire, which permeates all things as their causal agent. **2.** The active principle of intelligence or reason as exhibited in us which we can use (**a**) to understand the rational purpose and direction of the universe; (**b**) to perceive the necessary way of conducting our lives so as to conform with nature (synonymous for the Stoics with the rational); and thereby (**c**) to cultivate an acceptance and endurance of all things as they happen because they are rationally necessitated (fated) by the *Logos*. The *Logos* was *heimarmenē,* "predeterministic," a "fating" intelligence. **3.** The *Logos* providentially regulated all things (**a**) toward their own good (insofar as they, being what they were, could express their good) and (**b**) toward the overall harmony and good of the universe as a whole. The *Logos* was called *pronoia,* which meant "divine providence," "foreknowledge," "premeditation," "purposefulness." **4.** The *Logos* was the source of all moral values. Regardless of their physical or cultural differences, all individuals are members of humanity because each possesses a part of that eternal *Logos* into which all humans dissolve without distinction at death. **5.** The soul (*logos*) of humans is immortal, as is the Cosmic *Logos* of which the soul is a part.

Logos orthos (Gk., "right reason," "correct reasoning," "straight talk or truth," "right argument," "validity," "soundness of argumentation." *Orthos* is found in English words such as *ortho*dox, *ortho*genesis, *ortho*pedics, and is a combining form meaning "correct," "straight," "right," "upright," "regular"). **1.** *Logos orthos* was used for example by the SOPHISTS in their development of logic and rhetoric to signify those arguments and logical principles that could be (**a**) used correctly for proper inferences and (**b**) used to present correctly the strongest case possible for a point of view. **2.** Also used by the Greek Stoics and Roman Stoics, who used the Latin phrase RECTA RATIO to designate the intelligent and correct (*recta*) rationale (law, necessity, reason, order) in the universe to which human actions and law must conform.

Logos Spermatikos (Gk., "the life-giving word"). The Stoic name for the rational sperm (*sperma*), seed, semen dispersed throughout the universe that was the cause of the generation, development, and change of all things within it. It could be thought of as the forms (Platonic) or the universals (Aristotelian) immanent in nature and giving passive matter the shape and activity that it has. The STOICS looked upon the universe as a living organism. The *Logos Spermatikos* contains within it an infinite amount of individual sperm, (*spermatikoi*), each a rational agent or form creating purposing entities all harmoniously interrelated.

love. See *AGAPĒ; ERŌS; PHILIA.*

love, Platonic. Commonly understood as a spiritual comradeship or fellow-love without the presence of sexual desire or sexual contact.

M

macrocosm (Gk., *makros,* "long," "great," and *kosmos,* "the cosmos," "the universe," "the world"). **1.** In general, any large complex or whole contrasted with some small part of it (its MICROCOSM). They may be contrasted in order to show such things as (**a**) their similarities, (**b**) their differences, (**c**) their interdependence, (**d**) their fundamental oneness or unity. **2.** Specifically, the universe considered in its totality or as an active, structured whole.

maieutic (Gk., *maieutikos,* "one who acts like a midwife," from *maia,* "midwife"). Applied to Socrates' method of serving as the (intellectual) midwife to the birth of ideas from his listeners' pregnant minds; the ideas are there ready to be given birth, but require someone to assist by asking the proper questions and prodding the intellect. See SOCRATIC METHOD.

mania (**Plato**) (Gk., "madness," "inspiration," "frenzy," "enthusiasm"). Possession by a divinity which inspires a poet or artist to a truth, or to an expression of beauty.

manifold, sensory (Kant). **1.** The unorganized content presented to our senses which the mind structures into perception by means of concepts. **2.** The sense data of our experience, such as sounds, tastes, colors, regarded as discrete, unconnected units, before they are organized by the mind.

material cause. See CAUSES, THE FOUR (ARISTOTLE).

material object. Sometimes *material body,* or simply BODY, *physical object,* or *physical body.* A thing: **1.** that can be identified as a unity (unit); **2.** that has physical characteristics such as position, size, shape, structure, existence in time and space, mass, inertia, movement, and (sometimes) the sensed qualities of color, hardness, softness, sweetness, heat, weight, solidity, rigidity, etc.; **3.** that exists independently of our perception, although it is our perception of it that brings it to consciousness; **4.** that undergoes physical change; and **5.** that causally interacts and/or interrelates with other independently existing things. Examples: table, chair, plant, animal.

Usually it is admitted that material objects are perceived indirectly by inference from something more immediate and direct such as SENSA. Whereas we are always certain that we are having, or being presented with sensa, we do not have that certainty about material objects. Many sensa are associated with particular material objects. Material objects are often thought to persist independently of the sensa and/or persist as the sensa change. See MATTER; OBJECT.

materialism. The following are some main views of materialism. **1.** At one extreme it is the belief that nothing but matter in motion exists. The mind (spirit, consciousness, soul) *is* matter in motion. At the other extreme, it is the belief that mind does exist but is caused by material changes (see EPIPHENOMENALISM) and is completely dependent upon matter; mind has no causal efficacy, nor is it necessary to the functioning of the material universe. **2.** Matter and the universe do not in any way possess characteristics of mind such as purpose, awareness, intention, goals, meaning, direction, intelligence, willing, striving. **3.** There are no nonmaterial entities such as spirits, ghosts, demons, angels. Immaterial agencies do not exist. **4.** There is no God or supernatural (supranatural) realm. The sole reality is matter and everything is a manifestation of its activity. **5.** Every change (event, activity) has a material cause, and material explanations of phenomena are the only correct explanations. Everything in the universe can be explained in terms of material (physical) conditions. **6.** Matter, and its activity, is eternal. There is no First Cause or Prime Mover. **7.** The material configurations of things may be altered, and matter itself may exist in varied and complex dimensions, but matter can be neither created nor destroyed. **8.** No life, no mind, is immortal. All phenomena change, eventually pass out of existence, returning back again to a primordial, eternal material ground in an eternal retransformation of matter. **9.** Some materialists are predeterminists (see PREDETERMINISM) and some are determinists (see DETERMINISM). **10.** Some materialists are monists in the sense that they regard the universe as being a material unity and/or materially interrelated. Some are monists only in the sense that the sole ("mono") reality is matter in motion. **11.** Values do not exist in the universe independently of the activities of humans.

materialism, dialectical (Marx-Engels). 1. The theory that **(a)** social progress occurs through struggle, conflict, interaction, and opposition (in particular of economic classes), and **(b)** the development (or emergence) of one level of society from another does not happen gradually but by sudden and occasionally catastrophic jumps. **2.** The type of thinking process which attempts **(a)** to perceive how all things are inexorably interrelated as a whole, and **(b)** to accept the absolute necessity of that interrelated whole (which is the essence of freedom), and **(c)** to accept the inevitability of struggle, conflict, contradiction, change, and emergence of novelty in the universe.

Dialectical materialism holds to the concept of *struggle* (tension, change, opposite forces) as the most fundamental drive in all things. All things (1) struggle to become other than what they are or were, (2) struggle to avoid being overcome, and (3) struggle to overcome other things. Nothing remains exactly as it is. Nothing is self-sufficient. Nothing can exist in isolation from other things. Dialectical materialism also holds to the concept of *unity,* the necessary and rational interrelationship of all things in the universe. Complete truth consists in knowing the truths about the existence of any particular thing and knowing how it is related to all other things that exist and have existed in the universe. See DIALECTICS, HISTORICAL (MARXISM).

materialism, mechanistic. Sometimes simply *mechanism.* The theory that the universe is a machine and can be completely explained in terms of the mechanical operation of its parts upon each other. All phenomena are the outcome of the mechanical motions of matter. The traditional view holds that anything that produces a material (physical) effect must itself be a material object. Material objects can affect one another solely by direct mechanical contact (impact). There is no action at a distance. There are no final causes or purposes in the universe.

materialism, reductive. The theory that everything in the universe, including consciousness, can be explained in terms of matter in motion.

materialization. Sometimes *particularization, concretization, individuation, actualization.* **1.** Prime matter receiving form from a substantial form (see FORM, ESSENTIAL OR SUBSTANTIAL) and thereby becoming secondary matter: a BODY. **2.** The individuation of prime matter into a "this"; the actualization of form into a "this": "this dog," "this tree," "this cream."

matter (L., *materia,* "matter," "material," "the stuff of which something is composed"). **1.** The PHYSICAL or material constituent of something. That of which any physical object is composed. **2.** That which occupies space, for the most part is tangible, is empirically observable, and can be acted upon by other matter or forces. Together with ENERGY, it is regarded as the basis of all natural phenomena. Some of the further characteristics that have been associated with matter: atomic or corpuscular in nature (or a continuity of waves), impenetrable, indivisible (or divisible), having the potential to exhibit physical activity or change, having inertia, being eternal, self-moving (or not self-moving), having mass (although there are some levels of matter such as light to which mass is not attributed). **3.**

The (indeterminate) ground of all reality. **4.** The basic cause of experience. See MATERIAL OBJECT.

matter (Aristotle). See entries under SUBSTANCE with reference to Aristotle.

matter (atomists). See ATOMISM, GREEK.

matter (Descartes). Matter (material substance, body) has the essential attribute of *extension*, which undergoes sensible change. Matter fills all space (there is no empty space in the universe) and is incompressible. All properties of matter are quantifiable *modes* of extension that are a necessary part of our conception of any existing material object. These modes are: **(a)** *duration* (to conceive of a material thing is to conceive of it as continuing to exist from one moment in time to another moment in time), and **(b)** *time* as a measure of that duration. Our conception of material substance is not in any way derived from our senses but is a product of the ideas of our reason (as are God and mind). See VORTEX THEORY (DESCARTES.)

matter (Stoics). See STOICS, THE.

matter, prime. 1. Matter in a state of pure potentiality devoid of any properties or characteristics (whose only "property" may be said to be not having any property). **2.** That matter which is in itself the same in all physical things and which is being formed by active principles. **3.** What matter would be like without any form whatever to give it individual, positive qualities. **4.** The common substratum (stuff) that is thought to remain the same, such as when cream becomes butter, or when grapes become wine. See POTENCY, PURE.

matter, principle of the conservation of. 1. One of the oldest principles in philosophy, based on the concept that no thing can come from nothing. See ELEATICS, THE. If something comes into existence it must come from something previously existing. The universe is eternal; its energy is never lost or created. The theory that the matter (energy, mass, force, momentum, motion) in the universe is neither created nor destroyed, but remains quantitatively the same as potential or as actual. In this sense, referred to as the *Principle of the Conservation of Energy* (or *of Matter and Energy,* or *Mass and Energy*). **2.** *The First Law of Thermodynamics:* In any closed system—one that is isolated from the rest of the universe—the sum total of matter (mass) and energy remains constant (remains conserved) in any of its changes. This is expressed in the formula $E = mc^2$, where E = energy, m = matter, and c = the velocity of light, or Maxwell's constant.

matter/form (Aristotle). 1. Matter is the capacity to receive form, the capacity to be formed. **2.** Matter is that permanence (identity) present in anything that changes—that is changing in form. Form is that novelty, uniqueness which appears in things that are changing. **3.** Every material thing is composed of primary (formless) matter (see MATTER, PRIME) and a form. All material objects are embodied forms. See CHANGE (ARISTOTLE); GENESIS (ARISTOTLE).

mē agan (Gk., "nothing in excess").

mean, the (L., *medius,* "middle"). The moderate. The middle position, or the intermediate position between two points.

Mean, the (Aristotle). Also *Aristotle's Doctrine of the Mean* or the *Aristotelian Mean.* Sometimes *The Golden Mean.* Associated with moderation, temperance, the avoidance of extremes. The ethical principle that virtue consists in following a course of action somewhere between the extreme of too much (excess) and that of too little (defect). COURAGE, for example, avoids foolhardiness, recklessness (excess), and cowardice, timidity (defect). Hitting the right balance (moral goodness, virtue) between the extremes of excess and deficiency can be accomplished only through education, training, and experience. The mean is not an absolute centerpoint but is something adjustable and shifting; it is not arithmetical or quantifiable but is relative to the situation at hand and the personality involved. For example, we should in time of war expect the courage mean to be more toward the excess extreme for the soldier and more toward the defect extreme for the grocer. See VIRTUES, MORAL (ARISTOTLE).

meaning. 1. Signification. That which a thing designates or is intended to express. **2.** Explanation. The reason why a thing is what it is.

meaning (behavioristic view). Meaning is the behavioral responses to stimuli such as symbols, sounds, images, gestures, body positions.

meaning (sentences). The meaning of a sentence (statement, propositon) is not derivable **(a)** only from the meanings of its individual components, or **(b)** only from the pattern given the words but also from such things as **(c)** the context, **(d)** the accent (emphasis) upon certain of its features, **(e)** the attitudes and emotions conveyed through its utterance, **(f)** the promptings toward certain types of behavior such as requesting, commanding, promising, suggesting, advising, correcting, praising, blaming.

meaning, cognitive. Sometimes *assertive, informational, descriptive, factual, declarative meaning.* **1.** Referring to statements that give information and claim that information as true (or false). **2.** The meaning conveyed by statements that assert facts or describe.

meaning, connotative. See CONNOTATION.

meaning, definitional. Sometimes *lexical meaning.* Meaning that is derived from understanding the definitional meaning of the words themselves and/or how they may be put together into a sentence.

meaning, denotative. See DENOTATION.

meaning, descriptive or literal. The referents of a word. The variety of things to which a word may be applied.

meaning, emotive. 1. The emotions, feelings, attitudes, commands, etc., that things (words, sentences, symbols, images, gestures) communicate, express, or evoke. **2.** Our emotional and attitudinal responses to something. **3.** The interpretation of a statement (**a**) on the level of its intended emotional meaning and/or (**b**) on the level of the emotional meanings associated with the statement.

meaning, empiricist theory of. 1. The theory that words (sentences) get their real meaning from some kind of direct or indirect reference to concrete experiences. See EMPIRICISM. **2.** The theory that words have meaning only if rules about their application and/or VERIFICATION are based on (or derived from) experience. See EMPIRICISM, LOGICAL.

meaning, expressive. Meaning obtained from contexts that express, and hence elicit, such things as mood, feeling, emotion, values. For example, the meaning derived from poetry, commands, insults, exclamations, pleadings. Expressive meaning may also have cognitive or other kinds of meanings associated with it.

meaning, extensional. Sometimes *denotative* or *referential meaning* (see DENOTATION). The collection of *things* referred to by a word; the class of things to which a word may be applied. This concept of meaning stresses the notion that to understand a word is to know how to apply it correctly, to know how to identify its referent. (It is not necessary to know the entire list of all the things to which the word applies.) Criteria are presented to determine whether or not the thing can be subsumed within the extension (list of referents or class) of the word. All things included in the extension of a word have some common characteristics (properties, qualities) which thereby allow us to use the same term to "denote" them. The extensional meaning of a word is determined by its INTENSION. See EXTENSION.

meaning, factual. Referring to cognitive assertions that purport to be true about the world independently of our statements about them.

meaning, intensional. Sometimes *connotative meaning* (see CONNOTATION). **1.** The collection of characteristics (properties, qualities) common to things by which general (class) words are formed and in terms of which they are understood and applied correctly. **2.** The intended meaning of a word. The intensional meaning of a word determines its EXTENSION. See INTENSION.

meaning, linguistic (behavioristic view). The theory that meaning is the tendency of a linguistic expression to produce (elicit, evince, manifest) psychological, cognitive, emotive, sensory effects in the listener by means of a complex conditioning process of learning the use of a language and its associations in the act of communicating.

meaning, logical. Sometimes *formal meaning.* Meaning derived from the very form of a statement, from the relationships of the components themselves in a statement of logic.

meaning, operational theory of. The meaning of a word (concept) is the sum total of operations (procedures, activities, usually of a scientific sort) that must be performed in exemplifying (or understanding) it. See OPER-ATIONALISM (OPERATIONISM).

meaning, referential theory of. Words have meaning only if there is some-thing to which they refer, and that something constitutes their meaning. For example, the statement "Barbara is in the process of finishing her model airplane" must have objectively existing referents for each word in the statement for the statement to be meaningful. Thus "is," "in," "pro-cess," "of," are regarded as objective existents having extralinguistic ref-erence as much as "Barbara," "model," "airplane."

meaning, representative theory of. Also *correspondence theory of meaning.* Words symbolically represent or correspond to something in the external world, and their meaning is derived from the representation or correspon-dence.

meaning, verifiability theory of. 1. The theory that the meaning of a state-ment and its method of verification are identical. The conditions which verify a statement constitute its meaning. **2.** A statement is meaningful only if it is possible (at least in principle) to present empirical evidence that could verify it, that would support the factual truth of the statement. **3.** The meaning of a statement is equivalent to the sense experiences that we would have to have in order to determine that the statement is true. A statement means nothing more than the collection of sense experiences that taken together constitute the truth of the statement. **4.** A statement has cognitive meaning in direct relationship to how it is verified and whether or not it can be verified. If a statement is (a) not verifiable at least in principle, and is (b) not a tautology, then it is cognitively mean-ingless. Only logic and mathematics, which are tautologous, and the nat-ural sciences, which lead to verifiable empirical statements, can give cog-nitive meaning. **5.** A statement is meaningful (a) insofar as it can be determined to be true (b) either as an analytic (tautologous) statement or (c) as an empirically verifiable statement. See POSITIVISM, LOGICAL; VERI-FIABILITY, PRINCIPLE OF.

meaning as communicating of ideas. Meaning consists in using symbols to convey our inner and private ideas (thoughts) to others.

meaning as naming. The meaning of a statement is the object named by it and/or the act of naming.

meaning as usage. The theory that meaning consists in how a language is used by a speaker and how he behaves in that context. Meaning consists in what the speaker does when he speaks, what the person is doing when he uses a language. Meaning has to do with what people do with words and sentences.

mechanism (Gk., *mēchanē,* "an instrument or machine for lifting weights," "devices or contrivances for doing a thing," and from *mēchos,* "the means," "the way by which something is expedited"). **1.** The view that the interaction of parts with other parts within a whole (or system) unintentionally produces purposive activity and/or functions. The whole is neither ontologically prior to the parts nor causally efficacious upon them but merely the sum total (quantitatively and perceptually) of the interacting parts. Opposite to ANIMISM. **2.** The theory that all phenomena can be explained in terms of the principles by which machines (mechanical systems) are explained without recourse to intelligence as an operating cause or principle. Opposed to VITALISM and TELEOLOGY. **3.** The theory that all phenomena (natural, biological, psychological) are physical and can be explained in terms of material changes (matter in motion). See MATERIALISM; MATERIALISM, MECHANISTIC; PHYSICALISM. Opposite to ORGANICISM; SUPERNATURALISM.

meditation. See CONTEMPLATION.

meliorism (L., *melior,* "better"). **1.** The strong version: The belief (a) that the world tends to become better and better (more harmonious, more creative, more nearly perfect) and (b) that humanity (1) must identify itself as copartner in this creative thrust, and/or (2) *is* a part of this growth of values and betterment. **2.** The weak version: There is evil in the world and there is good in the world. There can be more good in existence than evil. In all probability evolution is tending toward more good than that which is now present. Humankind can assist in this progress toward more good. If it does not, for some meliorists the universe will do it on its own.

meliorism (theology). The belief that God is omnibenevolent (all-good) but not omnipotent (all-powerful). Humanity must work together with the forces of God in creating a universe with less evil and more good.

memory (L., *memoria,* from *memor,* "mindful"). **1.** The recalling (reproduction, recognition, remembering) of experiences. **2.** The ability to retain the past in the present. **3.** That which is retained of an experience (perception, sensation, conception). **4.** The sum total of the mind's actual and possible experiences which can be remembered. Memory is considered the *SINE QUA NON* of CONSCIOUSNESS. Some of the characteristics ascribed to memory: **(a)** Memory is immediately given. It can be used in inferential mediate knowledge, but is not itself inferred. **(b)** Memory involves the concepts of (1) recording of experiences; (2) recalling (reviving, reproducing, remembering) experiences; (3) recognizing experiences as experiences that have occurred in a past (or remembering that they will occur or are occurring); (4) recognizing that the content of the recalled experiences is qualitatively different from immediate experiences; (5) (sometimes) recognizing that some of that content may not be veridical; (6) (sometimes) having a sense of the recalled experiences' temporal-spatial locality—of when and where the experiences took place; (7) inferring from past experience; (8) extrapolating experiences. See RECOLLECTION.

mentalism. The belief that only minds (spirits, souls) and their contents exist. Synonymous with many varieties of IDEALISM.

mentalism, emergent. That aspect of the theory of emergent evolution in which mental states (mind, consciousness) are a new quality emerging from a nonmental (physical-chemical-biological) state that does not possess this quality. See EVOLUTION, EMERGENT.

mention. See USE/MENTION DISTINCTION.

meta (Gk., "after," "beyond," "between," "with," "over," "over and above"). Used as a prefix in English implying (in its philosophical use) transcendence or "on a higher level." In most cases, "meta" may be translated as "the study of the characteristics of" whatever it is prefixed to. Example: METALANGUAGE is the study of the characteristics possessed by language; language is that object being studied.

metaethics. 1. The study of the characteristics of (the nature of) ethics. **2.** The study of the methods, language, logical structure, reasoning used to arrive at and justify moral decisions and knowledge. **3.** The study of the source, meaning, and justification of ethical inquiry and judgments. **4.** The study of what ethics does and how it does it, as opposed to (**a**) what might be called *substantive ethics* such as utilitarianism, hedonism, Stoicism, which designate in a general way what the ethical good is, and (**b**) *normative ethics,* which studies and prescribes what one *should* do, how one *should* act, based on moral principles.

metalanguage. 1. That language in which the theory about a language which is being studied is formulated. **2.** The language used to talk about a language—about what it is and does. A language about a language. A logic or a syntactical language is an example of a metalanguage. Contrasted with *object language* (see LANGUAGE, OBJECT) which is that language that is being studied. A *metalinguistic* statement says something about something said or done by the object language. Contrasted with *referential* (*nonverbal*) *reality* about which a language communicates.

metalinguistic. When not used as a cognate of METALANGUAGE, it refers to a source of knowledge that is beyond (*META*) language, or that is not derived from language.

metaphor (Gk., *metaphora,* from *metapherein,* "to carry over," "to transfer," from *meta,* "beyond," "over," and *pherein,* "to bring," "to bear." In Aristotle's *Rhetoric, metaphora* meant "a word used in a changed sense"). A figure of speech by which a word (phrase, statement) that denotes one thing is applied (transferred) to another thing to suggest a likeness between them. Examples: "A sea of troubles." "The destroyer plowed the sea." "Agnes is a sly fox." Opposite to *literal.* Synonymous with *figurative.* Compare with ANALOGY; ANIMISM; PERSONIFICATION.

Metaphors contain a primary and a secondary term. The primary term is the thing being described. The secondary term is the description given to the thing being described. The usefulness or quality of a metaphor is judged by criteria such as: (**a**) the number of similarities (resemblances, correspondences) that exist between the things compared, and **(b)** the number of similarities brought to awareness which were previously unnoticed.

metaphysics (Gk., *meta ta physica,* "after the physics," from *meta,* "after," "beyond," and *physikos,* "pertaining to nature," or *physis,* "nature," "natural," "physical"). The origin of the word *metaphysics* is uncertain. Aristotle did not use the term, although there is a compilation of his works called *The Metaphysics.* There is no general agreement as to how to define metaphysics. The following are some of the main definitions: **1.** Metaphysics is the attempt to present a comprehensive, coherent, and consistent account (picture, view) of reality (being, the universe) as a whole. In this sense it is used interchangeably with most meanings of SYNOPTIC PHILOSOPHY and COSMOLOGY. **2.** Metaphysics is the study of Being as Being and not of "being" in the form of a particular being (thing, object, entity, activity). In this sense it is synonymous with ONTOLOGY and with FIRST PHILOSOPHY. **3.** Metaphysics is the study of the most general, persistent, and pervasive characteristics of the universe: existence, change, time, cause-effect relationships, space, substance, identity, uniqueness, difference, identity, unity, variety, sameness, oneness. **4.** Metaphysics is the study of ultimate reality—reality as it is constituted in itself apart from the illusory appearances presented in our perceptions. **5.** Metaphysics is the study of the underlying, self-sufficient ground (principle, reason, source, cause) of the existence of all things, the nondependent and fully self-determining being upon which all things depend for their existence. **6.** Metaphysics is the study of a transcendent reality that is the cause (source) of all existence. In this sense metaphysics becomes synonymous with THEOLOGY. **7.** Metaphysics is the study of anything that is spiritual (occult, supernatural, supranatural, immaterial) and which cannot be accounted for by the methods of explanation found in the physical sciences. **8.** Metaphysics is the study of that which by its very nature must exist and cannot be otherwise than what it is. **9.** Metaphysics is the critical examination of the underlying assumptions (presuppositions, basic beliefs) employed by our systems of knowledge in their claims about what is real. In this sense metaphysics is synonymous with important definitions of PHILOSOPHY and also with EPISTEMOLOGY. All these definitions of metaphysics with the possible exception of **9** are *rationalistic* (see RATIONALISM): By the process of thinking we can arrive at fundamental, undeniable truths about the universe (reality, the world, existence, God, Being). Experimental and scientific methods are not essential in obtaining metaphysical knowledge.

metaphysics (Aristotle). 1. Metaphysics is the study of Being-as-such (Being-in-itself) as distinct from the study of particular beings that exist in the universe. Biology studies the "being" of living organisms; geology studies the "being" of the earth; astronomy studies the "being" of the stars; physics studies the "being" of natural change, movement, and development. But metaphysics studies the properties that all of these "beings" have in common. In this sense of metaphysics the most important questions are: "What is Being?" "What is Substance?" "What is Reality?" **2.** Metaphysics is the study of what it means to say that something "is," what it means "to be." Metaphysics is the study of those properties (characteristics) a thing must have to be in change and to have an identity. **3.** Metaphysics is the study of the eternal First Principles (Laws) in accordance to which all things act. **4.** Metaphysics is the study of the separate realm of eternal, unchanging Being. In this sense metaphysics becomes identical with the traditional definition of THEOLOGY. **5.** Metaphysics is the study of nonsensible (insensible, not sensed) substance as opposed to the sciences that deal with sensible substances. Aristotle specifically referred to **4** and **5** as FIRST PHILOSOPHY. **6.** Metaphysics is the cataloging of (**a**) the general levels, or realms, of things that exist which are dealt with by the sciences, and (**b**) the study of how such levels of existence relate to one another and how they provide the framework in which activity occurs and by which it is limited. **7.** Metaphysics is (**a**) the study of the interrelationships of all types of knowledge, (**b**) the study of how their concepts apply (or can be intelligently applied) to what exists, and (**c**) the study of their ontological *and* logical status in providing us with truth about reality. Metaphysics as understood in **6** and **7** deals especially with such things as the ontological and logical status of universals, the relationship of particulars to universals and universals to particulars, the status of the concepts of unity, energy, change, form, mathematical points, lines, geometric forms, etc.

metempsychosis (Gk., *metempsychōsis,* from *meta,* "beyond," and *empsychoun,* "to animate," from *em,* "in," and *psychē,* "soul"). Also REINCARNATION, TRANSMIGRATION. The passing of an eternal soul at death from its body to another body.

method (Bacon). See BACONIAN METHOD; TABLES OF INVESTIGATION, THE THREE (BACON).

method (Descartes). In his *Discourse on Method,* Descartes presents four rules which provide us with knowledge and are the bases of all philosophic inquiry. They are: **1.** Never accept anything as true unless you can recognize it to be self-evidently true. Avoid all preconceptions and include nothing in your conclusions unless it presents itself so clearly and distinctly that there is no circumstance under which you can doubt it. See DOUBT, DESCARTES' METHOD OF. **2.** Divide a problem (difficulties) into as many distinct parts as possible or as might be needed to provide an easier solution. **3.** Think in an orderly (systematic) manner by beginning with the simplest elements in the problem and the easiest things to understand, and gradually reach toward more complex knowledge (synthesis). In this process you may have to assume an order among the elements that is not really there. **4.** Finally, make sure that everything has been taken into consideration and that nothing has been omitted from review.

method (Newton). The four *Rules of Reasoning in Philosophy* found in his *Mathematical Principles of Natural Philosophy, Book III,* serve as the foundation of Newton's method: **1.** Do not admit any more causes to explain things than are true and sufficient. **2.** Assign the same causes to the same effects. **3.** Assume that the qualities commonly observed in things are universally present. **4.** Consider the statements obtained by inductive procedures as true, or very nearly true, until (**a**) they are corrected and made more accurate by further observations (or experimentation) or (**b**) shown to have exceptions.

method, scientific. An empirical, experimental, logicomathematical conceptual system which organizes and interrelates facts within a structure of theories and inferences. In most cases scientific method presupposes that whatever happens has a specific cause followed by a specific effect; that effects can be deduced (predicted) from an empirical knowledge of causes; and that knowledge of causes can be derived from knowledge of effects. Scientific method begins in the formulation of a tentative, working HYPOTHESIS that explains some phenomena. See EXPLANATION, SCIENTIFIC; and entries under LAW.

methodology (Gk., *methodos,* "method," and *logos,* "the study of"). **1.** The study of the methods (procedures, principles) employed in an organized discipline, and/or used in organizing it. **2.** The principles themselves of any organized system. **3.** That branch of logic that formulates and/or analyzes the principles involved in making logical inferences and forming concepts. **4.** The procedures used in a discipline by which knowledge is obtained.

methods, Mill's inductive. Sometimes *Mill's Canons of Induction,* or *Mill's Experimental Methods.* Mill himself used the phrase *eliminative methods of induction.* In his *System of Logic,* Mill propounded five ways for discovering the causal relationship between phenomena: **1.** *The Method of Agreement:* "If two or more instances of the phenomenon under investigation have only one circumstance in common, the circumstance in which alone all the instances agree is the cause (or effect) of the given phenomenon." A cause of phenomena must always be present; is present whenever the phenomena occur. **2.** *The Method of Difference:* "If an instance in which the phenomenon under investigation occurs, and an instance in which it does not occur, have every circumstance in common save one, that one occurring in the former; the circumstance in which alone the two instances differ, is the effect, or the cause, or an indispensable part of the cause, of the phenomenon." Any event that occurs when phenomena of a certain sort do not, cannot be their cause. **3.** *The Joint Method of Agreement and Difference:* "If two or more instances in which the phenomenon occurs have only one circumstance in common, while two or more instances in which it does not occur have nothing in common save the absence of that circumstance, the circumstance in which alone the two sets of instances differ, is the effect, or the cause, or an indispensable part of the cause, of the phenomenon." **4.** *The Method of Concomitant Variations* (also known as *The Method of Isolation by Varying Concomitants):* "Whatever phenomenon varies in any manner whenever another phenomenon varies in some particular manner, is either a cause or an effect of that phenomenon, or is connected with it through some fact of causation." The cause of phenomena must be present to a similar degree as the phenomena. **5.** *The Method of Residues:* "Subduct from any phenomenon such part as is known by previous inductions to be the effect of certain antecedents, and the residue of the phenomenon is the effect of the remaing antecedents." See KNOWLEDGE (MILL).

microcosm (Gk., *mikros,* "small," "little," and *kosmos,* "the cosmos," "the universe," "the world"). Generally, any small part of a complex or whole contrasted with the larger complex of which it is a part (its MACROCOSM). The microcosm is often regarded as an epitome or analogue of the greater whole.

mimēsis **(Plato)** (Gk., "imitation," "representation by means of art," "a portrait." Some of its cognates in Greek mean "counterfeit"). The name for art that represents (imitates) objects in the sensible world and thereby does not reveal insight into the real and eternal world of forms of which objects are merely imperfect copies. *Mimēsis* is thus a copy of a copy of reality, twice removed from truth. Plato uses *mimēsis* to refer to the imitative relationship of objects in this world that imperfectly copy the ideal form. See IDEAS (PLATO).

mind. 1. Consciousness. Awareness. **2.** Human rational powers. Thought. The capacity to think. **3.** Psyche. Self. Ego. Personal identity. **4.** SOUL. Spirit. Spiritual substance. **5.** That which endures throughout changes of consciousness (experience, awareness). **6.** That entity which performs such functions as sensing, perceiving, remembering, imagining, conceiving, feeling, emoting, willing, reasoning, extrapolating into a future, judging. **7.** The name for those functions listed in **6** but not possessing any ontological reality as an entity or substance. **8.** The name for the adaptive responses of an organism to its environment in the struggle for survival. The dynamic, attending, and selective functionings of the organism upon items in its internal and external world that have possible survival value (and in the higher forms of mind have intrinsic interest).

mind, bundle theory of the (Hume). The mind is "nothing but a bundle or collection of different perceptions, which succeed each other with an inconceivable rapidity, and are in a perpetual flux and movement." The mind is not a mental substance but merely a bundle of experiences which occur in succession from birth to death. The entire series constitutes the bundle and this bundle may be named "mind" (or "the self"). Events in each bundle are related by such features as (**a**) resemblances of perceptions, (**b**) contiguity of experiences in time and place (**c**) regularity of succession among perceptions, and (**d**) memory. If these elements are not present, then we cannot be said to have a "mind" (or a "self"). The mind does not at any time exist as a self-subsisting entity apart from the above features.

mind, disembodied. A mind that continues to possess mental qualities such as feeling, thinking, perceiving, willing, without being in a body. Contrasted with MIND, EMBODIED.

mind, double-aspect theory of. 1. The theory that mind and body are distinguishable but inseparable features of one underlying reality (process, substance); two modes of the same substance. Mind and body are separable in abstraction but not in actuality; they ultimately can be reduced to the activities of this one, unitary substance but they cannot be reduced to each other. Example: The head side and the tail side of a coin are distinguishable but inseparable. Looked at from one perspective we can see the coin's head side (mind). Looked at from another perspective we can see the coin's tail side (body). Yet they are "aspects" of one and the same reality, facets of a common substance, the coin itself. Compare with MIND, DOUBLE-ASPECT THEORY OF (SPINOZA) **2.** Mind and body can each be seen as one of the facets or manifestations of a common substance which itself cannot be known. A variety of neutral monism. See MONISM, NEUTRAL.

mind, double-aspect theory of (Spinoza). A human is composed of two fundamental essences: mind (a human as a thinking thing) and body (a human as a thing occupying space). These are only two of the infinite aspects of the universe (God), and the only two humans can know in a direct, immediate way. Many of the other facets of God and of humans can be known, but not in their "essence." All things in the universe can be explained in terms of the essence of mind. Each essence contains potentially all the universe within it as a reflection of a deductive system. All things in the universe can be explained in terms of the essence of body (matter). It makes no difference which aspect of reality we care to use as our basis of explanation. But those two levels of explanation, the mental and the physical, must not be mixed. Looked at from their unique and different perspectives they appear as being two. But mind and body are attributes of one and the same thing (a manifestation or aspect of a common substance called God, nature, the universe). And for Spinoza: "Thinking substance and extended substance are one and the same thing." Spinoza's double-aspect view of mind/body ends up as a form of extreme MONISM.

mind, embodied. 1. In metaphysics, the theory that the universe is imbued with a cosmic mind as its operating principle of order and change. The universal mind IMMANENT in all things. **2.** In the philosophy of mind, the denial of a separate soul or mental agency that produces thought. Consciousness is that activity identified with the whole ordered structure of physiochemical and neurological processes. **3.** Body (or matter) imbued with a mind. **4.** Mind has mental qualities such as feeling, thinking, perceiving, willing only while immanent within a body. Contrasted with MIND, DISEMBODIED.

mind, emergent theory of. Mind is that quality that emerges from the particular organization (structure, arrangement) of the constituents of living forms. See EVOLUTION, EMERGENT.

mind, types of theories of. The theories that attempt to explain the nature of mind fall somewhere along a continuum of *extreme dualism:* mind and body are entirely separate and separable substances (entities) with utterly different characteristics, and *extreme monism:* mind (mental states) and body (physical states) are one and the same thing. **1.** *Mind as an Eternal Transmigrating Soul:* The mind is an eternal, immaterial, self-moving, self-activating soul or spirit that uses bodies as the vehicles through which it expresses its functions. The body is regarded as the temple of the soul or as the prison of the soul, depending on the attitude taken toward the body. See METEMPSYCHOSIS; TRANSMIGRATION. **2.** *Mind as a Product of the Action of the Soul upon the Body:* The soul as an eternal and immaterial agent acts upon the body and in so doing mental effects are produced such as perceiving, thinking, feeling, willing, imagining, remembering, etc. See DUALISM, DESCARTES' SOUL/BODY. **3.** *Mind as Mental* (or *Spiritual*) *Substance:* The mind (or soul) is a substance totally unlike matter or body, which endures throughout the changes of its body and **(a)** has such nonmaterial functions as: (1) self-direction, (2) thinking, (3) feeling, (4) willing, etc., and **(b)** has such nonmaterial characteristics as (1) intangibility, (2) not occupying space, (3) being indestructible (except in some theories by God), (4) being created and placed in a body by God, (5) being immortal as a disembodied entity in a heaven or hell, etc. **4.** *Mind as a Succession of Mental Events:* The mind is the rapid succession of mental states in continual change and not a self-subsisting entity (soul, spirit, substance, self) in its own right. There are forms of Idealism that view the rapid succession of mental events as caused not by activities of the body but by a spiritual agent. In a form of neutral monism, the cause is something unknown but nevertheless unlike body. **5.** *Mind as the By-product of the Body* (EPIPHENOMENALISM): The mind is caused by changes of the body (in particular by brain processes). Mental events are effects of the body or the brain. Mind is an appearance, an epiphenomenon completely dependent upon body and without causal efficacy of its own even upon subsequent mental events. The body causes the mind but the mind is a suspended noncausal existence. **6.** *Mind as the Function of the Form of the Body:* Mind is the form of the body, the functioning of the body. Mind is that which a body does and can do in fully expressing (actualizing, realizing, fulfilling) its forms, its capacities, that which it is able to express and by its nature "intends" to express. An analogy taken from Aristotle may be used to illustrate this position: As vision is to (the structures of) the eye, so the mind is to (the structures of) the body. Some of the implications in this analogy: (a) Change the structures and functions of the eye and you change vision. Change the structures and functions of the body and you change the mind. (b) Mind and body are organically interrelated, holistically integrated, and interdependent. One cannot be said to be the main cause affecting the other. (c) Vision as a function of the eye is the expression of the "form" (and matter) of the eye; so too the mind is a function of the body expressing the "form" (and matter) of the body. 7. *Mind as a Function of the Organism as a Whole:* Mind is that which an organism (mechanism) does and can do under the influence of internal and external stimuli. Mind is an integrated, self-directing, self-governing organism (mechanism) that has the ability to do such things as store knowledge, learn from this knowledge, prepare hypothetical situations based on this knowledge, adapt to novel situations in the light of this knowledge, predict, develop methods of solving perplexities, etc. See CYBERNETICS. 8. *Mind as the Behavior Patterns of the Body:* Mind is identical with the physical behavior that a body undergoes. Mental processes are behavioral activities such as laryngeal movements, muscular responses, bodily movements, skin responses, eye movements, etc. See BEHAVIORISM. 9. *Mind as Identical to Brain Processes:* Mental events are one and the same with specific neural processes of the brain. Since they are identical there is no interaction. See MIND/BODY, IDENTITY THEORY OF; PHYSICALISM (MIND/BODY). 10. *Mind as Matter, Mind as Material:* Mind is a level of material (physical) manifestation in the universe. All statements that contain references to mental phenomena can be reduced to statements about material (physical) events or processes. Not only is mind caused by physical forces, it is itself a form of energy or matter in motion. See MATERIALISM.

mind/body, God acting on. See OCCASIONALISM (MIND/BODY THEORY).

mind/body, identity theory of. Sometimes simply *identity theory,* or PHYSICALISM. Mind (sensations, perceptions, consciousness in general) is identical with certain brain processes and certain brain processes are identical with mind. A monistic philosophy.

mind/body dichotomy. Statements about mental states (events, qualities) are different from statements about physical states. The following is a partial list of the fundamental ways in which the characteristics attributed to mind are different from those attributed to body: 1. Mind is private; body is publicly observable. 2. Mind, both as a unity and in its various states, is immediately known, as opposed to body (matter) that is known by inference from perception and memory. 3. Mind is intentional; body has no intentionality. 4. Mind is intangible, nonspatial and nonlocatable;

body is tangible, spatial, and locatable. **5.** Mind does not occupy space; body occupies space. **6.** Things said about states of mind are INCORRIGIBLE; things said about states of a body are not incorrigible and can be denied without contradiction.

mind/body dualism. See DUALISM, MIND/BODY.

mind/body interactionism. Usually associated with the commonsense theory that mind and body are two separate and distinct realities, each causally affecting the other; mental events can change bodily states and bodily events can affect mental states. Examples: Worry, tension, fear, anxiety (mental events) can affect the body (ulcers, hair standing on end, increase in temperature). Carbon monoxide, too much alcohol in the bloodstream, a hit on the head (bodily events) can affect mental events (headache, unconsciousness, derangement, etc.). Compare with DUALISM, DESCARTES' SOUL/BODY.

mind/body relationships, theories of. 1. *Interactionism:* The body acts upon the mind; the mind acts upon the body. A variety of interactionistic theories exist: (**a**) The body produces the mind (mental events) but the mind once in existence can cause bodily changes. (**b**) The mind (as soul, spirit) is prior in existence to the body but interacts with it being affected by it and affecting it. See MIND/BODY INTERACTIONISM. **2.** *One-Way Causal Action by the Mind:* The mind (as soul, spirit) acts upon body causing it to perform the functions it does. **3.** *One-Way Causal Action by the Body:* The body produces the mind but then neither acts upon it, nor interacts with it. Mental events are effects of bodily causes. See EPIPHENOMENALISM. **4.** *Parallelism without Interaction,* also *Psycho-Physical Parallelism:* Mind and body are correlated but do not affect each other causally or in any other way. They accompany each other in time (are synchronized). Whenever a particular mental event occurs, a particular bodily event occurs which simultaneously and regularly accompanies it. Whenever a particular bodily event occurs, a particular mental event occurs which simultaneously and regularly accompanies it.

mind-stuff theory of mind. All things from human beings to the smallest particle are imbued with some amount of "mind-stuff," or psychic material. The less mind-stuff it possesses, the less is its complexity and intelligence. The human mind is the result of the combining together of this psychic matter into a particular continuing unity. A form of materialistic PANPSYCHISM.

misplaced concreteness. See CONCRETENESS, FALLACY OF MISPLACED.

modality (Kant). Refers to Possibility/Existence/Necessity and to Impossibility/Nonexistence/Contingency in Kant's Table of Categories. See CATEGORIES OF LOGIC (KANT); CATEGORIES OF THE UNDERSTANDING (KANT); MODE (KANT).

modal logic. See LOGIC, MODAL.

mode (L., *modus,* "a measure," "form," "the manner in which"). **1.** The manner in which relations or qualitites are combined. Usually considered as an entity apart from the thing to which it belongs. **2.** The condition (state of being or existence) in which a thing is at a given moment; its form of arrangement as manifested in existence. **3.** The particular form of existence given to (or acquired by) pure being, thereby limiting it and giving it an identity or individuation. See MATERIALIZATION. **4.** The form (way) in which something is understood. **5.** The form by which something is understood and with which a thing is identified as that thing and distinguished from other things. **6.** The way in which a quality (attribute, property) is, or can be, possessed by a thing, as in "Green is a mode (or can be a mode) of the quality color."

mode (Kant). Kant used the word *Modalität*, usually translated as *modality*, which meant the manner—as *actual*, as *possible*, or as *necessary*—in which something existed. These three modes were considered by Kant as A PRIORI and necessary for all experience.

mode (Locke). A mode is the manner in which an idea is known. A *simple mode* refers to the compounding of an idea in the same manner. Examples: double, dozen, decade, century. A *mixed mode* is the combining of several different simple modes into a complex idea (usually not representing an entity or substance). Examples: responsibility, loyalty, conniving.

mode (Spinoza). "That which exists in, and is conceived through, something other than itself." Of the substance (God) containing infinite attributes, humans can know only two: mind (thought) and matter (extension). Each of these attributes is infinite when looked at NATURA NATURANS. and finite when looked at NATURA NATURATA. Each attribute has modes by which it can be understood. The principal modes for mind are: intelligence (intellect) and volition (will). The principal modes for matter are: change (MOTION) and stasis (rest). See MONISM, NEUTRAL (SPINOZA).

mode, formal. Statements that are about words themselves. Examples: *"Cat* is a noun." *"Cat* has three letters." Contrasted with MODE, MATERIAL.

mode, material. Statements that are about things (entities, objects, relations, qualities). Example: "Tables are hard" is a sentence in the material mode. Contrasted with MODE, FORMAL.

monadology (Gk., *monas,* "a unit," and *logos,* "the study of"; literally, "the study of monads"). The term was first used by Leibniz to designate his metaphysical system. A speculative analysis of an infinite number of self-determining monads at different levels of actualization operating in a rational PREESTABLISHED HARMONY in accordance with the Prime Monad (God).

monads (Leibniz) (Gk., *monas,* "a unit," "a single entity," "a one," from *monos,* "alone"). The simple, discrete, irreducible, indestructible units regarded as the fundamental substances of the universe composed of active forces and relationships that mirror the universe as a whole but do not interact with other units. Regarded as analogous to psychic centers of activity. Some further characteristics of a monad: indivisible, impenetrable, teleologically oriented, self-contained, self-sufficient, self-activating, self-directing, having its own source of energy, being the individual center of force (power, energy, process), nonmaterial, unextended, a simple substance without parts, eternal (but can be caused to begin or cease to act by God, the Prime Monad), "windowless" (does not *interact* with other monads but contains within itself all the causes of its own activities, in a PREESTABLISHED HARMONY with the self-determining activity of all other monads). Each monad contains as a part of its inherent nature its own unique program for the rate of its activity and manifestation at any given moment in time; its own unique program for all that has happened to it, is happening to it, and will ever happen to it. All that happens to a monad happens to it because of its nature (program). Nothing outside a monad, nothing that is not a part of its internal self-actuating process, affects it. The nature of all monads is programmed by God (the Dominant or Prime or Supreme Monad) so that they all express themselves in a preestablished harmony with the activities of all other monads. See ENTELECHY (LEIBNIZ). Since all things are part of a preestablished harmony, anything that happens anywhere in the universe will (must) have a relationship with everything else in the universe, but not a causal relationship. The relationship is expressed in terms of such metaphors as the monads "mirroring," "echoing," "reflecting" the Simple Pure Monad (God). Since each monad contains all the properties of the universe, it is possible to logically deduce from any monad (a) all of its predicates (all that can ever be said of it) and (b) all that it will ever manifest.

monism (Gk., *monos,* "single"). **1.** The theory that all things in the universe can be reduced to (or explained in terms of) the activity of one fundamental constituent (God, matter, mind, energy, form). **2.** The theory that all things are derived from one single ultimate source. **3.** The belief that reality is One, and everything else is illusion. Contrasted with DUALISM and PLURALISM.

monism, ethical. See ETHICS, MONISTIC.

monism, neutral. 1. The theory that none of what we think of as the ultimate constituents of the universe, such as mind, God, or matter, is ultimate. The fundamental reality of all things is a netural element ("stuff") to which we can give no definite characteristics. See ENTITY, NEUTRAL. **2.** The theory that mental and material states and processes are the effects of the interrelationships among "neutrally" subsisting entities that are themselves neither mental nor material. See MIND, DOUBLE-ASPECT THEORY OF (2).

monotheism. See GOD CONCEPTS.

moral (L., *moralis,* from *mos, moris,* "manner," "custom," "conduct"). **1.** Having to do with human activities that are looked upon as good/bad, right/wrong, correct/incorrect. **2.** Conforming to the accepted rules of what is considered right (virtuous, just, proper conduct). **3.** Having **(a)** the capacity to be directed by (influenced by) an awareness of right and wrong, and **(b)** the capacity to direct (influence) others according to rules of conduct judged right or wrong. **4.** Pertaining to the manner in which one behaves in relationship with others. Compare with ETHICS. Contrast with AMORAL; IMMORAL.

moral act. Some of the characteristics involved in a moral act: **1.** A motive or intention to act. **2.** An agent choosing or deciding on some course of action. **3.** The choice must be uncompelled, or self-determined (self-desired). **4.** Moral qualities such as good/bad associated with any element in **1, 2, 3. 5.** Some consequence, intended or not, that results to oneself or others.

moral postulates, the (Kant). See POSTULATES OF PRACTICAL REASON, THE (KANT).

moral principles. 1. Principles that indicate what ought to (should) be done; that indicate obligation and responsibility. Examples: "Lying is wrong." "Stealing is wrong." "One ought to be kind." **2.** Principles **(a)** upon which one's moral conduct is consciously or subconsciously based or motivated, or **(b)** by which it can be explained or interpreted.

morals. 1. The manner of behaving of groups or individuals according to what is regarded as good, right, virtuous, proper, correct. **2.** The study of what is to be considered right conduct.

moral sense. 1. An innate, intuitive faculty or power **(a)** which is able to recognize right from wrong, **(b)** which motivates us toward right and **(c)** which gives us the standards with which we can make moral judgments. **2.** A "sixth sense" sensitive to qualities of good/bad, virtuous/invirtuous, that are found (sensed, responded to) in human activities. See CONSCIENCE.

mores (L., *mos, moris,* "a way of behaving," "a custom as determined by usage or practice and not by law"). The practices, behavior patterns, customs, attitudes, values held in common by a group.

motion (L., *motio,* from *movere, motum,* "to move"). **1.** Generally any CHANGE. (In the classical sense, motion [*KINĒSIS*], included all forms of change such as change in quality, quantity, position, shape, potency.) **2.** Specifically, movement. Change of the spatial location of bodies relative to each other. The process (act or state) of changing place (position). See ENERGY.

Concepts of motion serve as the essential ground for explanation of physical phenomena. (Opposite to rest. Motion has been defined negatively as anything that is not at rest.)

motion (Aristotle). See CHANGE (ARISTOTLE).

motion (atomists). Self-movement is the essential characteristic of all atoms. Motion is eternal. All things in the universe can be accounted for in terms of the distribution and redistribution of these self-moving atoms moving within voids (empty spaces). Just as atoms are irreducible and unexplainable in terms of anything more fundamental, so motion is irreducible and needs no further source of explanation. See ATOMISM, GREEK.

motion (Plato). Motion is of two kinds: **1.** motion externally imparted upon a thing, matter imparting motion to matter by contact, and **2.** self-propelling motion, motion originating in the thing itself and not imparted by an outside thing. Only souls (spirits) have their own internal source of motion; only souls originate their own motion. Externally imparted motion is ultimately dependent upon the self-propelling eternal motion of souls (spirits). In the final analysis all motion in the universe is dependent on the activity of a World Soul. Plato held that matter of itself is inert. The only thing that can move other nonmoving things is the soul, which can move itself (is eternally self-moving). Because it can move itself it can also move nonmoving things. SOUL is the primary cause of motion (change). The real world of Forms is not in motion. The Forms are perfect, immutable, and unchanging (see FORMS, PLATO'S THEORY OF IDEAL). The illusory sensible world is in continual motion (flux, change).

motion, continuum of (problems). The problems of continuous motion stem from conceptualizing motion in terms of an object that is at successively different points (positions, states) at successively different times. Some of the problems: **1.** How are the two points relatable and/or related in space? **2.** Can there be points between these two points? (Can there be states of motion between successive states of motion?) **3.** How does the object get from one point to the other—or does it? **4.** What are those points like? **5.** Are there "gaps" between these points? **6.** What is motion doing (what is motion like) at these "gaps"? **7.** If there are no "gaps" but only further points (an infinity of points between any two points) then how is motion possible? See ZENO'S PARADOXES.

motion, Newton's three laws of. 1. *The Principle of Inertia:* All bodies continue in a state of rest, or of uniform motion in a straight line, unless they are compelled to change that state by other forces acting upon them. **2.** The change of motion of a body is directly proportional to the force acting upon it and such change occurs in the direction of the straight line from which that force is acting. **3.** To every motion (action) there is an opposed and equal motion (reaction); the mutual motions (actions) of two bodies upon each other are always equal (and are directed to contrary parts).

motion, paradox of. A body in motion changes and yet sometimes can be seen to endure as that thing throughout the change. It changes place (position, space) and/or quality but it also retains its identity. See ZENO'S PARADOXES.

motion, relative. Motion that is understood in terms of reference to some other motion outside itself.

multiplicity, doctrine of (L., *multiplicitas,* from *multiplex,* "manifold," "multifarious"). The universe is composed of a variety of existents that can never be reduced to a Unity or a One. See PLURALISM.

multiplicity, principle of. That which causes variety in the universe as opposed to that which causes unity.

mundus intelligibilis (L., "the intelligible world"). Usually referring to a Platonic realm of Perfect Forms or Ideas that serve as the models for the imperfect existences in the sensible world. Contrasted with *MUNDUS SENSIBILIS.*

mundus sensibilis (L., "the world of sensibles" or "the world of existing objects"). Referring to the things perceived by our senses (as opposed to the abstractions of our intelligence) that are imperfect copies of the realm of Perfect Forms, or the Perfect Ideas in God's mind. Contrasted with *MUNDUS INTELLIGIBILIS.*

mystical experience. 1. The enraptured and ineffable state of union with a higher reality (such as the realm of Perfect Forms) or with God. **2.** The ecstatic identification of the self with the totality of all things, expressed by such phrases as "The All is One and the One is All." See ECSTASY. The mystical experience may be a contemplative union or identification, and/or it may be a state of pure overwhelming feeling. See NUMINOUS EXPERIENCE; RELIGIOUS EXPERIENCE.

mystical experience, characteristics of the. The following are some of the characteristics of the mystical experience. **1.** Joyous; ecstatic. **2.** Indescribably intense and unique. **3.** The most momentous, important, significant experience of one's life. **4.** Has a lasting and total effect upon one's life, providing one with "salvation," "serenity," "light," "bliss," "blessedness," which were not there before. **5.** Transforms one's moral nature, values, and intuitions. **6.** The experience is transient (yet it reveals the eternal and while one is having it, it may seem to last a long time). **7.** The experience is passive; it comes upon one suddenly, at unexpected times and places (although there are forms of mystical experiences that can be induced by such means as rational contemplation, meditation, ascetic practices, drugs). **8.** A feeling, and/or a vision of an encounter (confrontation) with some unusual reality never felt or seen in any ordinary experience. That reality is a Oneness or Unity **9.** A sense of identification (and sometimes communication) with that extraordinary reality (Unity) in which the self is dissolved or merged. **10.** The experience is NOETIC; a knowledge is gained about a reality unobtainable by any other means. **11.** That knowledge is ineffable, uncommunicable, and can never be put into language or conceptual schemes of understanding. **12.** The mystical experience itself and the knowledge thereby gained can never be described or conceptualized (nevertheless attempts are made by means of metaphors, analogies, paradoxes, poetic imagery that do not hope to communicate the quality of the experience or the content of the knowledge obtained, but seek to evoke, excite, spark intimations of the experience, an experience latent in all people).

mystical intuition. Where "mystical intuition" is not used synonymously with MYSTICAL EXPERIENCE, it is used to mean that latent or active faculty of the mind by which, and only by which, a knowledge of a higher reality is disclosed (revealed, perceived).

mysticism (Gk., *mystērion,* from *mystēs,* "one initiated in the mysteries or secrets of a truer reality"). **1.** The belief that the ultimate truth about reality can be obtained neither by ordinary experience nor by the intellect but only by the MYSTICAL EXPERIENCE or by a nonrational MYSTICAL INTUITION. The nature of reality is inexpressible and cannot be experienced in any ordinary experiential and rational way. **2.** The nonrational, nonordinary experience of all-inclusive reality (or often of a transcendent reality) whereby the separateness of the self is merged with that reality usually regarded as the source or ground for the existence of all things. Mysticism believes that rational knowledge stresses differentiation, distinctions, separation, individuation; it distorts reality, and is therefore illusory. See CONTEMPLATION.

mysticism (complete absorption). The experience of total identification or union with all things or with a higher reality in which there is no distinction between the individual having the experience and that which is experienced. The I is completely absorbed into the All (the One) and there is no subject/object separation.

mysticism (partial absorption). The experience of oneness with all things or with a higher reality in which there is an awareness at the time of the experience of a distinction between the self (the individual) having the experience and that which is experienced. The individual stands as a distinct perceiver before the All. The I encounters (confronts, is in the presence of) the All.

myth (Gk., *mythos,* "myth," "fable," "tale," "legend," "talk," "speech," "conversation," "rumor," "anything delivered by word of mouth"). A story whose origin is forgotten which: **1.** presents a nonscientific history of the thought of a people explaining in an anthropomorphic, animistic form such things as the creation of the universe (COSMOGONY), the structure of the universe (COSMOLOGY), the source and nature of human and natural phenomena (pride, jealousy, sin, trees, rivers, etc.); **2.** expresses the socially significant events of a people as well as their social consciousness; and **3.** expresses and reinforces, by ritual and other means, the social bonds, customs, and cultural ties of a people. Sympathetic modern interpretations of myths do not regard them as true or false, but as possessing poetic insight into reality (to the extent to which it does so, to that extent it can be called a "good," "relevant," "correct," or "proper" myth). Also, myths are looked upon as expressing archetypal symbolisms that recur because of humankind's collective unconscious. Compare with METAPHOR.

mythical thinking. Prerational thinking. The human mind casting its perceptions of reality in the form of artistic intuition and imagery.

N

naive realism. See REALISM, NAIVE.

name, negative. See CLASS, COMPLEMENTARY.

name, privative. See PRIVATIVE TERM (WORD, NAME).

natura naturans (L., "nature maturing," "nature naturing," "nature nurturing"). Refers to the active, creative processes of nature that are being manifested at any given moment. For Spinoza, nature as a causal agent of modes and attributes. In Scholasticism, a phrase designating God. Compare with *NATURA NATURATA*.

natura naturata (L., "nature matured," "nature natured," "nature having been nurtured"). Refers to the things created by (or in) nature. For Spinoza, the reality created by *NATURA NATURANS*. In Scholasticism, nature as created by God. See MODE (SPINOZA); SUBSTANCE (SPINOZA).

natural (L., *natura,* from *natus,* "born," "produced"; the past participle of *nasci,* "to be born"). **1.** Innate: inborn. **2.** In accordance with the inner nature (essence, predispositions) of a thing. **3.** Referring to physical phenomena. In accordance with, or pertaining to, the phenomena of nature and of human nature. **4.** Referring to conduct that seems instinctively right. **5.** Performed instinctively, without thinking or willing, usually in accordance with ordinary common experience. **6.** Normal. **7.** Not artificial.

natural law. See entries under LAW, NATURAL.

natural philosophy. Originally used to indicate the study of nature in general. With the development of mechanistic systems in early modern science, it referred specifically to the field of physics.

natural rights. See RIGHTS, NATURAL.

natural selection (Darwin). The process in nature that brings about the survival of the fittest in a struggle for existence. Those animals and plants survive which are best adjusted to the conditions in which they exist. The process of natural selection depends in large measure on the variability of the forms of life over a long period, gradually resulting in structural changes that are adaptive. Darwin held that in every population of living organisms there occur random variations that have differing degrees of adaptive value. Those variations that increase the chances of survival or the rate of reproduction persist in existence. They are thereby preserved and then genetically transmitted to subsequent generations. Those variations which do not have a high survival value decrease or pass out of existence. See DARWINISM, SOCIAL.

naturalism. Some of the tenets of naturalism: **1.** *Monistic:* The universe (nature) is the only reality. It is eternal, self-activating, self-existent, self-contained, self-dependent, self-operating, self-explanatory. The universe is not derived from nor dependent upon any supernatural or transcendent being or entities. Natural phenomena cannot be "interfered" with, "violated," "suspended." There is no supernatural realm. There are no souls, spirits, disembodied minds, immaterial forces. There is no immortality, reincarnation, transmigration. **2.** *Antisupernaturalistic:* All phenomena can be explained in terms of the inherent interrelationships of natural events without recourse to any supranatural or supernatural explanation. No reality exists other than processes (events, objects, happenings, occurrences) in space and time. There are no nonnatural causes. The universe has its own structure and originates its own structure. Many levels of reality or manifestations of the universe may exist (see PLURALISM), but none are supernaturally caused. **3.** *Proscientific* (put into a progressively stronger version): **(a)** Natural phenomena can be adequately explained by the improving methodology of the sciences. **(b)** All phenomena are in principle explainable by scientific methods. **(c)** All phenomena can be explained by scientific methodology. **(d)** Knowledge can be obtained only by the logical-empirical methodologies of the sciences. Intuition, the mystical experience, faith, revelation are rejected as direct and proper means of arriving at truth about reality. **4.** *Humanistic:* Humans are one of the many (natural) manifestations of the universe (and usually regarded as of no special hierarchical importance from the point of view of the universe). Human behavior is to be explained in terms of and seen to be related to **(a)** behavior similar to, but more complex than, the behavior of other animals, and **(b)** the social and environmental influences creating and conditioning human needs and awareness. The human ethical and aesthetic nature has its ground in natural phenomena. An empirical study of humans' place in nature and of human nature can provide us with ethical and aesthetic values by which humans can live cooperatively and happily. Values are human-made but realistically based upon natural conditions. Values do not have a supernatural source or sanction. **5.** *Tendencies toward:* (**a**) nonteleological explanations, (**b**) nonanthropomorphic, nonanimistic explanations, (**c**) reliance on experience and rational methods of inquiry, (**d**) individualism (in cooperative endeavor with other individuals), (**e**) the maximization and realization of human potentials, (**f**) freedom of inquiry and opportunity, (**g**) viewing humans in an organic relationship with their environment, society, and the universe. Opposite to SUPERNATURALISM. Compare with HUMANISM, PHILOSOPHICAL; MATERIALISM.

naturalism, critical. A form of naturalism that considers a purely mechanical or materialistic interpretation of reality as insufficient. Mind, life, values are other significant and efficacious levels of reality that cannot be interpreted purely as matter in motion. Some critical naturalists hold to the notion of a creative thrust in evolution towards the expression of higher and more integrated values. See EVOLUTION, EMERGENT.

naturalism, ethical. The view that no sharp demarcation exists between facts about the world and judgments (evaluations) about the world and how humans ought to act in it. Moral evaluations contain facts about natural phenomena. Examples: To determine the rightness or wrongness of an act one must refer to the facts as to whether or not pleasure will be obtained by such an act, or whether or not specific needs will in fact be achieved, or whether or not it will produce cooperation, unity, harmony. See ETHICS, NATURALISTIC.

naturalistic fallacy. Used interchangeably with REDUCTIVE FALLACY.

naturalistic fallacy (ethics). **1.** The fallacy of reducing ethical statements to factual statements, to statements about natural events. **2.** The fallacy of deriving (deducing) ethical statements from nonethical statements. Compare with ETHICS, IS/OUGHT DICHOTOMY IN. **3.** The fallacy of defining ethical terms in nonethical (descriptive, naturalistic, or factual) terms.

naturalistic fallacy (G. E. Moore). The fallacy of identifying goodness with a natural characteristic (property, attribute) such as pleasantness, being the object of desire, or promoting the general well-being of a community. What "good" means is different from designating what things are good. Moore regarded moral goodness as an indefinable, nonnatural property that cannot be derived from natural properties. See OPEN-QUESTION ARGUMENT (G. E. MOORE).

nature (L., *natura,* from *natus,* "born," "produced"; the past participle of *nasci,* "to be born"). **1.** The universe. The existing system of all that there is in time and space. Everything that happens (good and bad). **2.** The powers (forces) that cause (produce, create) existing phenomena. **3.** The origin (or foundation) of everything. **4.** The ground for the explanation of things. **5.** The essence of a thing; its essential characteristics. **6.** The natural endowments of a thing. **7.** The physical constitution of a thing. **8.** An original, primitive state of things unadulterated and uncultivated by humans. That which happens without human interference.

nature (Aristotle). 1. That which is not made by humans is called *PHYSIS*, "nature," in contrast to *TECHNĒ*, which refers to all the things made by humans. **2.** Nature is a teleological system and makes nothing without a purpose in two senses: **(a)** natural objects serve purposes other than their own purposes which interrelate as part of larger purposive schemes, and **(b)** there exists in the universe an overall pattern or order (purpose or design) that is being imitated throughout nature. **3.** The cause (principle, law, source) of all change (motion, movement). An understanding of nature entails an understanding of the characteristics and kinds of motion. **4.** The innate, immanent impulse for activity in all things (in contrast with *TECHNĒ*, which is a transcendent or external impulse for activity). This includes the material in which and through which this impulse (active form) expresses itself. See GENESIS (ARISTOTLE).

nature, state of. The condition of humanity without (or before) government. Its hypothetical description ranges from Hobbes' portrayal of anarchy with brutal and continual war of "all against all," to Rousseau's concept of the "noble savage" living in a condition of moral purity, happiness, and health.

necessary (L., *necessarius*, from *necesse*, "necessary"). **1.** Characterized by the impossibility of being otherwise. **2.** Indispensable, that without which something cannot be done or cannot exist. **3.** Inevitable. **4.** Unavoidable. **5.** Certain. **6.** Involuntary; compelled. **7.** Determined. **8.** Imperative. Must be. Opposite to CONTINGENT.

necessary being (theology). The independent, indestructible, incorruptible, uncaused eternal Being (God): **1.** which is the cause of the existence of everything else, **2.** which can never become something other than what it is, and **3.** can never be caused not to be. That Being upon which all things depend for their existence and sustenance, but which depends upon nothing for its existence and continuance. The self-sufficient Being. See entries under ABSOLUTE; COSMOLOGICAL ARGUMENT FOR GOD'S EXISTENCE.

necessary condition. See CONDITION, NECESSARY.

necessary existence. Also *necessary existent*. **1.** That which does not depend for its existence upon anything else. That uncaused eternal existence which does not owe its existence to something other than its own being. Absolute causal independence in its origin from all other things. **2.** That whose essence is to exist. That existent whose essence cannot be conceived as not existing. The universe, nature, or matter may be thought of as a necessary existence. Opposite to CONTINGENT existence, contingent existent. Compare with CONDITION, NECESSARY; SELF-EXISTENCE.

necessitarianism. The theory that all events in the universe are determined (necessitated) by causes and these causes themselves are necessitated to happen. Synonymous with PREDETERMINISM. Opposite to ACCIDENTALISM.

necessity, historical. See MATERIALISM, DIALECTICAL (MARX-ENGELS).

negation (L., *negatio,* from *negare,* "to say no," "to deny"). **1.** A contradiction. **2.** A denial or the act of denying. **3.** Assertion of the falsehood (unreality, untruthfulness) of something. **4.** A state of being or a making void, empty. **5.** Annihilation; obliteration.

In logic, the negation of a term (sentence, statement, proposition) is its contradiction; to negate a term is to contradict it; negating a term is replacing it with its contradictory.

neikos. Opposite to PHILIA.

neologist (Gk., *neos,* "new," "youthful," and *logos,* "the study of"). **1.** In general, one who introduces a new word and/or a new meaning into a language or discipline. **2.** In theology, used pejoratively to refer to one (a heretic) who introduces a new doctrine (dogma, decree) that is contrary to the desired and accepted doctrine.

neo-Platonism. See BEING, HIERARCHY OF; BEAUTY; EMANATION.

nescience (L., *nescientia,* from *nesciens,* present participle of *nescire,* "to not know," from *ne,* "not," and *scire,* "to know"). **1.** In general, a state of not knowing. **2.** Specifically refers to AGNOSTICISM and **(a)** its suspension of judgment, or **(b)** its declaration of ignorance about the existence and/or the characteristics of God.

neutral monism. See MONISM, NEUTRAL.

Newton's three laws of motion. See MOTION, NEWTON'S THREE LAWS OF.

nihil ex nihilo. See EX NIHILO NIHIL FIT.

nihilism (L., *nihil,* "nothing"). Literally, nothingness. **1.** In epistemology, the denial of any objective and real ground or state of truth. **2.** The theory that nothing is knowable. All knowledge is illusory, worthless, meaningless, relative, and insignificant. **3.** No knowledge is possible. Nothing can be known. **4.** The psychological and philosophical state in which there is a loss of all ethical, religious, political, social values. **5.** The skeptical denial of all that is regarded as real/unreal, knowledge/error, being/nonbeing, illusory/nonillusory; the denial of the value of all distinctions.

nihilism (ethics). The theory that moral values cannot be justified in any way—not by reason, by a God, by intuition, by conscience, or by the authority of the state or law. Moral values are **(a)** expressions of arbitrary and capricious behavior or **(b)** expressions of loose feelings and reasonless, social conditioning; and **(c)** they are worthless, meaningless, and irrational.

nihilism (Gorgias). See SKEPTICISM (GORGIAS).

nihilism (metaphysics). The theory that **(a)** the universe is meaningless and without purpose; **(b)** human life and its activities are of no value or significance; **(c)** nothing is worth existing for. See ENNUI.

nihilism (political). The belief that social organization is so corrupt that its destruction is desirable. Sometimes coupled with a form of ANARCHISM whereby no constructive alternative form of organization is deemed possible and terrorism, violent revolutionary activities, assassination are advocated.

nisus (L., from *nisus,* past participle of *niti,* "to strive"). **1.** A striving. An effort. The conative state of a thing. See CONATION. **2.** A creative tendency in the universe toward the production of qualitatively new emergents. See EVOLUTION, EMERGENT.

noēsis (Gk., "intelligence," "thought," "understanding," "mind"). In Greek philosophy, *noēsis* is the knowledge that results from the operation of *NOUS,* the mind, reason, intellectual faculty.

noetic (Gk., *noētikos,* "intelligent," from *noein,* "to perceive," "to know," and from *noētos,* "perceptible to the mind," "thinkable," [as opposed to visible, *horatos*]). **1.** Having to do with reason and the intellect. **2.** Cognitive. That knowledge (a) which is a consequence of the function of our cognitive faculties or (b) which is an innate content of our cognitive faculties. Usually refers to knowledge that is independent of sensation. **3.** Ontological cognition. That knowledge of reality had by the pure function of reason alone. Contrasted with ANOETIC.

nomic/nomological. 1. Lawlike. (Applied principally to physical occurrences.) **2.** Having to do with laws. (This includes physical, legal, moral laws.) See *NOMOS.*

nominal definition. See DEFINITION, TYPES OF (11).

nominalism (L., *nominalis,* from *nomen, nominis,* "a name"). Occasionally *terminism.* **1.** The theory that things do not have essences. **2.** Definitions, and languages in general, do not refer to things but deal with the names (terms) we attach to things. **3.** All universal terms, such as those indicating genus/species distinctions, and all general collective terms are only fictional names (artificial and arbitrary symbols) and have no objective, real existences that correspond to them. **4.** Only particular existents (particulars) exist. Abstractions, universals, ideas, essences are only products of our language and/or of how our mind understands reality. They do not communicate what reality is like. **5.** Abstractions such as "human" (a) are merely names that can be used to refer to more than one particular, (b) have no objective existence as an entity "human" or "humanhood" shared by all particular humans, and (c) cannot even be present in consciousness as an abstract idea or concept of "human," "humanhood." Compare with entries under REALISM. See UNIVERSALS (NOMINALISM).

nomos (Gk., "convention," "custom," "law"). Contrasted in Greek philosophy with *PHYSIS,* "the natural," "the necessarily innate." The word *nomos* has had a long history of varied meanings. Here are a few: (a) a feeding place (for example for cattle); (b) a district or province; (c) the abode assigned to one, a dwelling place; (d) anything assigned; (e) a usage, custom, law; (f) the law of force or of warring. **1.** In epistemology, the plural, *nomoi,* refers to those qualities of things such as color, smell, taste that are only appearances, or secondary qualities, in our mind and do not exist in the external world of objects. This is contrasted with *physis,* which refers to the qualities found in things such as size, shape, figure, arrangement that belong to the things themselves. See QUALITIES, PRIMARY/SECONDARY. **2.** In ethics, *nomos* refers to actions performed in accordance with the customs and human-made laws of society as opposed to actions performed according to one's nature or to natural law. See CONVENTION.

nonbeing. 1. The nonexistent. Nonexistence reified. **2.** The lack (privation, absence) of existence or of an existent. **3.** The nonpresence of a reality essential to the natural activity of a thing and to its identification (or the presence of a reality not natural to the thing). **4.** The lack of any determinate form or order, especially that form or order which is natural to it. **5.** Unreality. Nonreality. **6.** Matter. The lowest in the hierarchy of reality. Complete stasis. That state of no innate potential to be actualized, and no innate tendencies to actualize itself. (In Platonism identified with "evil," "darkness," "ignorance," "ugliness," "the furthest removed from the divine ground of being.") Contrast with BEING.

nonbeing (Plato). Plato attempted to strike a compromise between two extremes: (**a**) The extreme of Heracleitus' philosophy, in which all things are in a state of continual change and in which it is possible for the same thing to be (Being) and *not* to be (Nonbeing), and (**b**) the extreme of the Eleatic philosophy, in which nothing changes but is in reality always the selfsame thing (One) which cannot help but *be.* For Plato, the sensible world of particular objects, sensations, perceptions can be thought of as the confused if not illusory realm between the realm of true eternal unchanging Being (the true reality of the Perfect Ideal Forms) and the realm of Nonbeing that has no existence whatever. See FORMS, PLATO'S THEORY OF IDEAL.

non causa pro causa. See FALLACY, TYPES OF INFORMAL **(20).**

noncognitivism. See ETHICS, NONCOGNITIVE.

noncontradiction, principle of. See LAWS OF THOUGHT, THE THREE.

nonmoral. See AMORAL.

nonnatural property (G. E. Moore). A property **1.** that is not natural (as yellow is), **2.** that is not externally real (as objects are), and **3.** that is not supernatural (as being caused or given by God). A nonnatural property is "had" **4.** not by sensation, **5.** not by cognitive faculties, **6.** not by introspection, but **7.** by an intuitive grasp. Nonnatural intuitive properties are **8.** immediate, **9.** ineffable, indescribable, and **10.** associated with (accompanying) other properties.

A concept used by many ethical intuitionists. See NATURALISTIC FALLACY (G. E. MOORE); OPEN-QUESTION ARGUMENT (G. E. MOORE).

non sequitur (L., "it does not follow"). **1.** Used generally to refer to concepts or expressions for which a rational connection is asserted or implied but for which there is none. **2.** Used specifically to refer to any conclusion (inference) that does not follow from its premises. See FALLACY.

normative (L., *norma,* "a rule," "a pattern," "a precept"). **1.** That which is

(a) regulative of human conduct (according to an ideal, norm, or standard), (b) preferential (expressing felt attitudes, values, biases), and (c) prescriptive (expressing a command or an obligation). 2. Referring to that which "should" be done, "ought" to be done; that which one is "obliged to do," or "responsible" for; that which "must" be done because it ought to be done.

normative ethics. See ETHICS, NORMATIVE.

nothing. Not any thing. The denial of existence or of an existent. Opposite to "something," "a thing," "anything," "everything."

nothing-but fallacy. See REDUCTIVE FALLACY.

notion (L., *notio,* from *noscere,* "to know"). 1. Idea. Conception. Mental apprehension. 2. A view, theory, or opinion. 3. Personal belief or inclination. 4. Existing only in idea. 5. The state or process of an idea in its being formed into a better idea or concept. 6. Visionary idea. 7. Vague idea.

notion/*Begriff* (Hegel). The German *Begriff,* translated as "notion," was used by Hegel in several interrelated senses: 1. The essence of an object, 2. the essence of the thought of that object, and 3. the synthesis of Being and Essence (basically the synthesis of 1 and 2 as Idea).

noumenon (Gk., *noumenon,* "the thing perceived," related to *noein,* "to perceive," and to *nous,* "mind"). 1. That which is apprehended as an object by our reason (our understanding, our intellect) without any involvement of our senses, intuition, or other levels of apprehension. 2. That real but in itself unknowable reality (substance, object) which reason must postulate as the cause (ground, basis) of all phenomena. 3. A thing as it actually exists in itself apart from how it appears to us, as opposed to PHENOMENON, which refers to how a thing appears to us. The plural is *noumena. Noumenalism* is the doctrine of the existence of noumena (things-in-themselves) or of a noumenon (a thing-in-itself). *Noumenal* refers to either the singular or plural meaning.

noumenon (Kant). That reality (power, substance) which transcends experience and all rational knowledge. Reason must assume its existence as a beginning point for all science and philosophy (including ethics). Reason can know *that* it exists but not *what* its existence is like. That there is a noumenon is apprehended by reason alone. See KNOWLEDGE (KANT).

nous (Gk., "mind," "reason," "intellect"). In some philosophies used to indicate God as the Cosmic or World Mind (Reason, Intelligence). See *DIANOIA; NOĒSIS.*

nous (Anaxagoras). Anaxagoras used the word *nous* for the Universal Intelligence (Reason, Mind) that arranges the universe into a rational order. That all-pervading Mind which imposes (brings about) an intelligible pattern in an intrinsically nonintelligible universe. According to Anaxagoras, *nous* is not to be found as a constituent (mixture) *in* things. *Nous* is an intangible being affecting the constituents of all things and patterning them into the order that they have.

nous (Aristotle). 1. The Mind of the Eternal Divine Being in which all the intelligible forms are found and according to which all form actualizes itself. **2.** The single, unitary cosmic Intelligence or Reason which can be looked at in two ways (roughly corresponding to Aristotle's form and matter distinction): (**a**) that which becomes all things (matter) and (**b**) that which is an active force making all things (form). **3.** The rational part of the human mind which includes the intellectual and intuitive understanding of the fundamental ideas about reality in contrast to perceptual, sensible understanding. Often divided by Aristotelians into two parts separable only in abstraction: (**a**) NOUS PATHETIKOS, and (**b**) NOUS POIETIKOS.

nous pathetikos (Aristotelianism) (Gk.). That aspect of the mind (NOUS) able to apprehend and make sense of that which is given in experience. Passive Reason. Passive Intellection. Contrasted with Active Reason or Active Intellection. See REASON, ACTIVE/PASSIVE (ARISTOTLE).

nous poietikos (Aristotelianism) (Gk.). **1.** That (divine) aspect of the mind (NOUS) able to comprehend the eternal, first principles of all phenomena (the forms or intelligible substances), as opposed to that aspect of the mind which deals with passing phenomena. Compare with SUB SPECIES AETERNITAS. **2.** Active Reason. Active Intellection. Contrasted with Passive Reason or Passive Intellection. See REASON, ACTIVE/PASSIVE (ARISTOTLE).

now. 1. At the present time. Used to refer to that moment of time simultaneous with its utterance: "I exist at this very moment." **2.** At the time immediately to follow, used in expressions such as "Get it done now." **3.** Refers to the time immediately preceding a present moment used in expressions such as "Now that I have finished. . . ." "Now" is regarded as an indexical sign (see SIGN, INDEXICAL), such as "this," "here," "I," that has no descriptive content.

null (L., *nullus,* "not any," from *ne,* "not," and *ullus,* "any," a diminutive of *unus,* "one"). **1.** Empty. Void of. **2.** Nonexistent. **3.** Equivalent to nothing. Used in English as a prefix in phrases such as null-class, null-set.

numinous experience. A sense of some transcendent reality or presence that has qualities associated with it such as awesomeness, the sublime, the terrifying, infinite power, grandeur. This reality is often called God. The experience is of a Total Other that is so utterly different from anything in our experience that it is impossible to grasp rationally and impossible to communicate. The numinous experience evokes an inescapable sense of our finiteness, of our complete and total dependence upon this transcendent reality, and of our insufficiency as we stand in contrast to the glory and power of that reality. See entries under MYSTICAL; MYSTICISM.

O

object (L., *objectus,* past participle of *objicere, obicere,* "to throw before," "to oppose," from *ob,* "against," and *jacere,* "to throw"). **1.** That which is presented to one or more of our senses. Something visible, tangible, tactile, etc. **2.** That which is presented to consciousness and of which consciousness becomes aware. "Object" may refer to either (**a**) the thing in the external world independently existing to which our senses or consciousness have been stimulated to attend (see MATERIAL OBJECT), or (**b**) the mental content itself being attended to in consciousness. **3.** Anything at all that can be talked about (hence named), and especially as a noun having substantive existence.

object, conative. That thing (end, goal, ideal) being desired or willed.

object, epistemological. Sometimes *ostensible object.* That which is being known or experienced, whether VERIDICAL or not; anything sensed, perceived, conceived, imagined, etc.

object language. See LANGUAGE, OBJECT.

object, material. See MATERIAL OBJECT.

object, physical. See MATERIAL OBJECT.

objective. **1.** Refers (**a**) to the ability to make an evaluation of a situation without being affected by feelings, emotions, and preconceived notions, and (**b**) to the support of a statement (idea, judgment, knowledge, decision) with proof and evidence based on actual events. **2.** That goal, end, ideal, or object sought after by an activity or feeling.

objective existence (reality). Existence of an entity or an object in the external world (**a**) that is known, or (**b**) that can be known, and (**c**) that exists independently of our perception, conception, or judgment of it, as opposed to being merely a subjective existence in our mind or to being known in terms of our biases, feelings, and personal judgments.

Often implies something (1) that is publicly observable, or (2) that is the same for all those that experience it, or (3) that is commonly assented to and therefore unlike an individual's own peculiar reaction to it. See EXISTENCE; REALITY, OBJECTIVE AND FORMAL.

objectivism (epistemology). 1. The theory that a world (a) exists in itself independently of and external to our comprehension of it and (b) that it is a world which we can come to know about independently of any subjective viewpoint. **2.** The view that knowledge is based on factual evidence that (a) is discovered by objective methods of science and reasoning and (b) describes things as they are. **3.** The view that the only meaningful (true) knowledge is that which is derived from and/or confirmed by sensory experience. Opposite to SOLIPSISM, EPISTEMOLOGICAL.

objectivism (value theory). The view in aesthetics and ethics that (a) values exist in the external world independently of and external to our comprehension of them; (b) they can be found and known; (c) they must be used as principles for human judgments and conduct; (d) objects or activities are valuable or right because of some objectively existing quality in them which when perceived or experienced makes them desirable. Opposite to RELATIVISM (VALUE THEORY); SUBJECTIVISM (VALUE THEORY).

obligation (L., *obligare,* "to bind one to something"). **1.** A formal agreement, contract, or bond usually accompanied by the implication of a penalty for not fulfilling it. **2.** A DUTY. A necessity to act in some specified way imposed by law, moral sense, ethical principle, promise, social commitments, etc.

observation (L., *observare,* "to observe," "to save," "to keep"). **1.** Taking notice. Recognizing (and often systematically noting as in science) some feature (fact, occurrence). **2.** The result (conclusion, judgment) of **1.**

Observables are those items of reality derived from observation, especially sense perception. *Nonobservables* are items of reality unobservable in principle or at present, but which have observable effects (such as photons).

Occam's Razor. See OCKHAM'S RAZOR.

occasion (L., *occasio,* "a happening," from *occidare,* "to fall down"). A favorable opportunity for an activity; its timely chance. In this sense an occasion is an occurrence or a state of affairs that is a contributory or incidental cause of an event. The specific cause of an event is that which actually brings it about. The occasion of an event is the general set of causal conditions that provide an opportunity for the specific causes to act (or sets them going). Example: The increased level of bacteria caused the milk to sour; the occasion was the milk being allowed to stand at room temperature.

occasionalism (mind/body theory). An offshoot of the philosophy of Descartes. The apparent reciprocal action of mind and body is caused by an intervention of God, producing on the occasion of a change in one a corresponding change in the other. The main points in this general thesis: **1.** Mind and body are two separate and distinct realities so different in kind that they cannot causally interact. **2.** Each functions according to its own laws. **3.** God interconnects and synchronizes their activities. An event in one is an occasion for God's making an event happen in the other. For example, when I think, God has produced that thought on the occasion of some corresponding material movement. When I will to lift a weight, God causes me to move my arm to lift the weight on the occasion of my act of willing. When I see a landscape before me, God (and not the external world) has brought that perception into existence on the occasion of the actual existence of that landscape. Compare with entries under MIND/BODY.

occurrent state. See STATE, OCCURRENT.

Ockham's (Ockam's or Occam's) Razor. Also *principle of parsimony, principle of simplicity, principle of economy.* A methodological principle developed by William of Ockham expressed in Latin as *Entia non sunt multiplicanda praeter necessitatem,* translated as "Entities are not to be multiplied beyond necessity," or "The number of entities used to explain phenomena should not be increased unnecessarily." The principle implies: **1.** Of two or more possible explanations for phenomena choose the one that **(a)** explains what is to be explained with the fewest assumptions and explanatory principles; and **(b)** explains all, or most, of the facts that need explaining as satisfactorily as any of the other theories. **2.** The simplest explanation is the one most likely to be true, to depict reality as it is. See PARSIMONY, PRINCIPLE OF.

omnibenevolent (L., *omnis,* "all," and *benevolens,* from *bene,* "well," and *volens,* "willing"). Applies to God to indicate that He is all good, a pure moral Being capable only of love, mercy, compassion, and charity, and incapable in any way of willing evil. See EVIL, THEOLOGICAL PROBLEM OF.

omnipotence. See PARADOX OF GOD'S OMNIPOTENCE.

omnipotent (L., *omnipotens,* "all powerful," from *omnis,* "all," and *potens,* "powerful"). Usually applied to God to indicate that he is **(a)** all-powerful and/or **(b)** of infinite power. (The former need only imply that he is the most powerful and nothing is more powerful than He. Traditionally both **(a)** and **(b)** are meant.)

   Some of the variety of meanings for omnipotent that can be found in theology: **1.** God can do anything. He is able to bring about anything He wills or wants. **2.** God can do anything provided that it is logically possible to do; that is, provided that it is not self-contradictory. For example, His power cannot create a squared circle no matter how intensely He wills or wants that to happen, since self-contradictions cannot be brought into existence. **3.** God can do anything provided that it is worth while to do and (which amounts to the same thing) provided that it is an expression of His necessary essence as God.

The focal implication in these definitions is that God is the absolute controller (and in most cases also creator) of all things. See PARADOX OF GOD'S OMNIPOTENCE.

omnipresent (L., *omnis,* "all," and *praesens,* "that is before one," present participle of *praeesse,* "to be before," from *prae,* "before," and *esse,* "to be"). Usually applied to God to indicate (a) that He is wholly present in all things at all times or (b) that His influence is present and may be felt in all things. The main implication in the concept of God's omnipresence is that He is intimately related to all things as an efficient cause is related to that on which it acts.

omniscience. See PARADOX OF GOD'S OMNISCIENCE.

omniscient (L., *omni,* "all," and *sciens,* present participle of *scire,* "to know"). Usually applied to God to indicate that He is all-knowing: that He has infinite knowledge. Some of the variety of interrelatable interpretations for omniscient, omniscience: **1.** God perceives all things as they happen, and hence knows of their occurrence. **2.** God knows everything that has happened, is happening, and will happen. **3.** In addition to 1 and 2 God knows everything that it is possible to know.

The three primary implications in these definitions are: (a) All truths (knowledge) are eternal. (b) They are all known (eternally) by God, and (c) nothing can occur unless it accords with these eternal truths. See PARADOX OF GOD'S OMNISCIENCE.

omnitemporal (L., *omnis,* "all," and *temporalis,* from *tempus, temporis,* "time"). Something that exists (as itself) at all times: throughout eternity. Usually used to refer to God or to an Eternal Perfect Form, but it can be used to refer to the eternal unchanging atoms of the atomists. See ATOMISM, GREEK.

one, the. 1. The Eternal Perfect Form which all things imitate (act according to, participate in). **2.** The Absolute (Mind, Spirit, Soul). **3.** The Divine Being from which all things emanate (see EMANATION). **4.** The universe itself as a self-sufficient being. **5.** God. **6.** The World Spirit (Soul, Psyche, Reason, Mind).

In all these meanings the following points are emphasized. The One is (a) the first principle (the primary being, the underlying ground, the causal and ultimate origin) for the existence of all things, (b) the true reality as opposed to the appearances of phenomena, (c) self-dependent in that its nature is not derived from anything else, (d) a necessary existent, and (e) present in some way throughout its flow of processes. See *HEN.*

one and many, problem of. See IDENTITY, PROBLEM OF; UNITY IN VARIETY AND VARIETY IN UNITY, PRINCIPLE OF (METAPHYSICS).

ontological argument for God's existence (Anselm). The following from the *Proslogion* is the main version of the ontological argument for God's existence found in Anselm: **1.** God is "that than which nothing greater can be conceived" (*aliquod quo nihil maius cogitari possit*). **2.** God cannot be "that than which nothing greater can be conceived" only *in intellectu* (in our mind, in the intellect, in our understanding); otherwise God would not be "that than which nothing greater can be conceived" (since that which exists *both* in reality and in our mind is greater than that which exists only in our mind). **3.** If God as "that than which nothing greater can be conceived" can be thought of as part of our understanding, He must also be conceived to exist in reality, which is something greater, otherwise that something "that than which nothing greater can be conceived" thought of as existing in reality as well, would be greater than the one conceived only in our understanding—and that conception would thus be God, since He is "that than which nothing greater can be conceived."

ontological argument for God's existence (Descartes). Several ontological arguments for God's existence can be found in Descartes' writings. Of the three presented here the first and second are pure forms of the ontological argument (the first being a condensed and simplified version of Anselm's ontological argument) and the third has a tinge of the causal argument mixed with it. (The third argument is presented in two parts.) **1.** God is the completely perfect Being. Existence is necessary for anything to be completely perfect. Therefore, God exists as the completely perfect Being (for if He did not exist He would not be the completely perfect Being which He is). **2.** The essence of God is existence, just as the essence of a triangle is a plane figure composed of three straight lines joined together to form three angles equal to 180°. You cannot think of a triangle without thinking of that essence. You cannot think of that essence without thinking of a triangle. The two go together necessarily. So whenever you think of God you think of His existence and whenever you think of existence you think of God. The two go together necessarily. Whenever we think of God without existence we contradict ourselves. Therefore, God must exist (any other conclusion leads to a contradiction in terms). **3.** *Part I:* I have an idea of God as a Perfect and Infinite being. As a finite being, I could not have caused this idea in me. The cause of this idea is greater in reality and power than its effect. Therefore, God exists as this greater reality and power to produce upon my finite mind the idea of an infinite and completely perfect Being. *Part II:* I could not have caused myself. (It requires more reality, power, and perfection to create substance than, for example, to create attributes, qualities, properties.) If I could have created (caused) myself, I would have given myself perfect attributes (which no finite being has). I have not existed eternally, nor do I have the power to maintain existence from moment to moment. I cannot say that I was caused only by my parents (who were caused by other parents, etc.). It is therefore necessary to assume that an eternal, infinitely powerful, perfect God exists who is both the cause of my being and who implants the idea of Him in my mind as well as in the minds of my parents, their parents, etc.

ontology (Gk., *onta,* "the really existing things," "true reality," and *logos,* "the study of," "the theory which accounts for"). **1.** The study of the essential characteristics of Being in itself apart from the study of particular existing things. In studying Being in its most abstract form it asks questions such as "What is Being-in-itself?" "What is the nature of Being-as-Being?" **2.** That branch of philosophy which deals with the order and structure of reality in the broadest sense possible, using categories such as being/becoming, actuality/potentiality, real/apparent, change, time, existence/nonexistence, essence, necessity, being-as-being, self-dependency, self-sufficiency, ultimate, ground. **3.** That branch of philosophy which attempts (**a**) to describe the nature of ultimate Being (The One, The Absolute, The Perfect Eternal Form), (**b**) to show that all things depend upon it for their existence, (**c**) to indicate how this dependency is manifested in reality, and (**d**) to relate human thoughts and actions to this reality on an individual and historical basis. **4.** That branch of philosophy (**a**) which asks the question "What does 'to be,' 'to exist' mean?" (The same question is asked of the other categories or concepts used in **2**), and (**b**) which analyzes the variety of meanings (ways) in which things can be said to "be," "exist." **5.** That branch of philosophy (**a**) which inquires about the reality status of a thing (for example, "Are the objects of our sensations or perceptions real or illusory?" "Are numbers real?" "Are thoughts real?"), (**b**) which inquires about what sort of reality (or quality of illusion) things possess (for example, "What kind of reality do numbers have? Perceptions? Thoughts?"), and (**c**) which inquires about those other realities or Reality, upon which what we call reality and/or illusion depend (for example, is the reality—or illusory quality—of a thought or object dependent upon our mind, or upon an independent external source?).

Ontology has been used as a synonym for METAPHYSICS, or has been regarded as a branch of metaphysics. But it can be seen to be close to other branches of philosophy as well, such as to EPISTEMOLOGY, philosophical analysis, SEMANTICS. Its similarities to THEOLOGY are also obvious. What Aristotle refers to as FIRST PHILOSOPHY is ontology.

ontology (existential psychology). The study of the inescapable psychic and structural features (predicaments) of life such as death, fear, dread, suffering, responsibility, anguish, alienation. For example, the fear of extinction is ontological in the sense that it is possessed by all human beings, it is part of the human condition, it is inescapable and must be faced by all. The anxiety about death can be, and is, repressed, but it remains a part of our unconscious being affecting our behavior in sometimes unaccountable ways. See EXISTENTIALISM.

open-question argument (G. E. Moore). "Good" is an immediate, indefinable nonnatural property. See NONNATURAL PROPERTY (G. E. MOORE). Whatever definition of good is given it can always be asked (it remains an "open question") whether that which the definition refers to *is* good or *does* possess the property good. If a set of natural properties can be found for the word *good* such that we can say "Good is (natural properties)," we can ask the question, "Are those natural properties good?" Thus merely possessing this quality is not what is meant by "good." See GOOD (G. E. MOORE); NATURALISTIC FALLACY (G. E. MOORE).

operational definition. See DEFINITION, TYPES OF (**12**).

operationalism (L., *operari,* "to work," from *opus, operis,* "work," "labor"). Sometimes *operationism.* The theory that the meaning of a scientific idea (concept, term, symbol) is identical with the set of activities (operations) that have to be performed in order to understand it, and to which it refers. See DEFINITION, TYPES OF (**12**). Compare with INSTRUMENTALISM.

opinion (L., *opinio,* "suspicion," "belief," "conjecture," "imagination," "notion," "thinking," "judgment," "estimation"). **1.** A BELIEF. Usually a belief based on personally developed views. That which one thinks about something, but not necessarily implying a definite judgment. **2.** Judgment. Often a judgment formed by an expert. **3.** A statement (**a**) backed by rational arguments, and (**b**) either presented with some doubt as to its truth or (**c**) presented with the realization that its truth could be doubted. **4.** A belief (idea, statement) which lacks supporting evidence. **5.** Used as the translation for Greek words such as *DOXA,* which imply knowledge that is uncertain, changing, bordering on the illusory.

opposites (metaphysics) (L., *oppositus,* past participle of *opponere,* "to set or place against," "to oppose," from *ob,* "against," and *ponere,* "to place"). Refers to the fundamental opposing forces in the universe operating to cause change such as attraction/repulsion; motion/rest; potential/actual; being/nonbeing; mind/matter; love/hate; good/evil; light/darkness; hot/cold; wet/dry; fire/water. Opposites imply a difference of kind, a diametrically opposed quality, and an interaction or antagonism. *Opposite* is sometimes loosely used as a synonym for *contradictory* and for *contrary.*

optimism (L., *optimus,* "the best"). **1.** A disposition to see things from the most promising and hopeful perspective. ("Every cloud has a silver lining," whereas the pessimist would say "Every silver lining has a cloud.") **2.** Everything is ordered for the best. (An extreme form: This is the BEST OF ALL POSSIBLE WORLDS.) **3.** The world as it stands is not the best possible world but it possesses much good and so will its future. **4.** The present world is good and it will be even better in the future. **5.** Humans are able to control evil in themselves and in society. Opposite to PESSIMISM. Compare with MELIORISM. See PERFECTABILITY OF MAN.

order (L., *ordo,* "row," "series," "course," "array," "rank," "class," "degree." Related to *ordiri,* "to begin"). **1.** A formal or regular arrangement of anything (in contrast to SYSTEM, which implies a definite, methodological or logical plan or order). **2.** A class, type, or level. **3.** The position or rank of a thing in a hierarchy or a series. **4.** Command (as in a legal or moral order).

ordinary language philosophy. The view that by analyzing ordinary language (its meanings, implications, forms, and functions) and showing how its general philosophic outlook and basic presuppositions reveal a truth about reality, we can better understand the nature of and hence resolve the problems of philosophy. Principal tenets: **1.** The language used in everyday conversation (ordinary language) is adequate for philosophical use. **2.** Such a language presupposes a structure or view of reality that is correct. **3.** Any departure from ordinary language creates needless philosophical and metaphysical perplexities (puzzles, nonsense). **4.** The solutions to the problems of philosophy are to be found in not misusing ordinary language words and their meanings.

There is very little in the way of a typical or common set of beliefs among ordinary language philosophers. Some are determinists, some are not. Some are believers in God, some are not. Some are behaviorists, some are not. Some are scientifically oriented, some are not. But in general, ordinary language philosophers are in agreement that philosophical perplexities cannot be resolved by the formal procedures of symbolic logic. Ordinary language is the key to their solution. Ordinary language is not artificial (formal), nor is it a calculus. It presupposes insights into the structure of reality and everyday experience that cannot be gained by the use of artificial systems. Formal systems are also inapplicable to ethical and psychological problems. John L. Austin, Ludwig Wittgenstein, Gilbert Ryle, John Wisdom are names that have been associated with ordinary language philosophy. In most cases it is difficult to draw a sharp distinction between ordinary language philosophy and linguistic philosophy or linguistic analysis. See ANALYSIS, LINGUISTIC; ANALYTIC PHILOSOPHY.

organicism. 1. Any theory that explains the universe on the basis of an analogy to a living organism. **2.** Any theory that explains the universe as the function of a whole causing and coordinating the activities of the parts. Compare with ANIMISM; HOLISM; VITALISM. Opposite to MECHANISM.

organic unity. See UNITY, ORGANIC; UNITY, ORGANIC (ARISTOTLE).

organismic explanation. Any explanation which regards the properties of a whole **(a)** as being distinct from the properties of the individual parts (or groupings of parts) and **(b)** as being as necessary to explain something as an analysis of the interaction of the parts is necessary to its explanation.

Wholes are considered not merely as the quantitative sums of their parts but as qualitatively different from their sums. Compare with entries under EXPLANATION.

organon (Gk., "organ," "instrument," "tool for making or doing something"). Plato used this word to refer to "an organ of sense." *Organon* is the title given to the logical works of Aristotle, implying that logic is a "tool" to be used for acquiring philosophic knowledge (for "doing" philosophy) and is not to be regarded as an end in itself. Francis Bacon titled a book *Novum Organum,* referring to his new method or tool of empirical investigation that was to supersede Aristotle's. See LOGIC (ARISTOTLE).

orthodox (Gk., *orthodoxos,* from *orthos,* "right," "straight," and *doxa,* "opinion," "belief"). **1.** Refers to true or correct belief (opinion, doctrine, creed, idea) as opposed to *heretical* or *heterodox* belief. The doctrine decreed by an institution or group as the true one and the one to be followed. **2.** Approved belief. **3.** Conventional or traditional belief.

orthos logos. See LOGOS ORTHOS.

ostensive (L., *ostendere,* "to show," "to stretch out before," from *ob,* "to," and *tendere,* "to stretch"). Showing by pointing to, or exhibiting.

ostensive definition. See DEFINITION, TYPES OF (**13**).

ought. Implies that (**a**) something should be done that is not being done and/or (**b**) something should not be done which is being done. An expression of OBLIGATION, DUTY, or constraint.

ousia (Gk.). "ESSENCE," "the inner essential nature of a thing," "the true being of a thing."

P

pacifism (L., *pacificare,* "to make to be at peace," from *pax,* "peace," and *facere,* "to make"). Some basic beliefs of pacifism: **1.** In general, opposition to the use of personal violence in attempting to achieve individual and social aims. **2.** Opposition to militarism, military ideals, and war as a means of accomplishing goals or settling disputes. **3.** Encouragement of cooperative, supportive relationships among individuals without the type of competition that destroys such relationships. **4.** Encouragement of arbitration, diplomacy, appeal to humaneness as means of settling international and political disputes.

pain (Gk., *poinē,* "penalty"). Bodily suffering and/or mental anguish. Regarded as a polar concept to PLEASURE. Attainment of pleasure and avoidance of pain are considered the primary human motivating forces. Pain is regarded as a negative and negating element in human experience and conduct.

panentheism. See GOD CONCEPTS.

panlogism (Gk., *pan,* "all," and *logos,* "the study of," "reason," "the rational"). **1.** The theory that the universe is the expression of the LOGOS (the Eternal Universal Reason or Mind). **2.** The *Logos* pervades all things and all activity in the universe.

panpsychism. See GOD CONCEPTS.

panpsychism (metaphysics) (Gk., *pan,* "all," and *psychē,* "soul," "spirit," "mind"). Everything in the universe possesses (**a**) consciousness (mental life, mind, soul, spirit) or (**b**) a level of consciousness. All things in exis-

tence have inner lives of feeling, willing, thinking, conating. See HYLO-
ZOISM; MIND-STUFF THEORY OF MIND.

pantheism. See GOD CONCEPTS.

paradigm (Gk., *paradeigma,* from *para,* "beside," and *dekynai,* "to show,"
meaning "model," "exemplar," "archetype," "ideal"). **1.** A way of looking at something. **2.** In science, a model, pattern, or ideal theory from
which perspective phenomena are explained. **3.** An ideal situation or ex-
emplification, as in *"A paradigm case of this disease. . . ."*

paradox (Gk., *paradoxon,* from *para,* "contrary to," and *doxa,* "opinion").
1. A statement (tenet, belief, concept, notion) which is contrary to accepted opinion, or opposed to what is regarded as common sense, but
which may be true. **2.** A statement which on the surface appears absurd
or even self-contradictory, but which **(a)** is true or **(b)** may be true. **3.** An
apparent dichotomy (or self-contradiction) which when overcome denies
something that is regarded as true. **4.** A situation where two statements
that are incongruent (contrary, exclusive of each other) both appear to be
true, and both must be accepted in action. **5.** A statement which when regarded as true leads to its being false, and which when regarded as false
leads to its truth (or leads to a truth).

paradox, Epimenides'. Epimenides was a Cretan, who declared that all Cre-
tans without exception were liars. Was Epimenides telling the truth?

paradox, hedonistic. See HEDONISTIC PARADOX.

paradox, liar. Often called the *Megarian Paradox* after the school of Me-
gara of which Eubulides of Miletus, Euclid's successor, who invented the
paradox, was a member. Also referred to as *Eubulides' paradox.* The
paradox may be stated in a number of ways: **1.** A person says "I am lying." Is what that person says true or false? (The statement seems to be
true if what the person said is false, and false if what the person said is
true.) **2.** A person says "What I am now saying is false." (This statement
appears to be false only if true, and true only if false.) **3.** A person says
"If I am lying, is what I have just stated false?" (It would be false if what
the person said were true, and true if what the person said were false.)

paradox, logical. In general, a logical paradox is composed of two contrary,
or contradictory, statements, both of which seem to have good supporting
arguments. Compare with ANTINOMY. A logical paradox results when
two acceptable lines of argument lead to conclusions that seem contrary
or contradictory. Logical paradoxes may be a consequence of: **1.** a misap-
plication of the rules of logic; **2.** a violation of the rules of logic which
cannot be clearly expressed (or is not clearly seen); or **3.** the inapplicabil-
ity of the rules of a logic to the situation. In **3** some reformulation of the
logic is necessary either **(a)** to avoid the paradox or **(b)** to resolve it.

paradox of God's omnipotence. Some of the traditionally stated "paradoxes"
that have to do with God's omnipotence: If God is all-powerful: **1.** Can

He create a squared circle? **2.** Can He undo the past? **3.** Can He create a rock big enough so that He cannot move it? **4.** Can He invent problems that He cannot solve? **5.** Can He annihilate Himself and never come back to life? **6.** Can He deny His essence? See EVIL, THEOLOGICAL PROBLEM OF; OMNIPOTENT.

paradox of God's omniscience. If God is all-knowing (and all-powerful) how is this compatible (**a**) with human freedom of will and (**b**) with God's own freedom of will, since presumably such complete foreknowledge entails that an all-powerful God has created things to occur exactly in the way that He knows—and wants—them to occur? See OMNISCIENT.

paradox of self-reference. A paradox that arises from statements such as: "All generalizations are false." (Since this is a generalization it must be false, and if false, true, but if true, false.) "No knowledge is possible" (yet claiming this is knowledge). "There are no absolutes." (Is this an absolute?) "Everything is uncertain"; "Nothing-at-all exists"; "I do not exist."

paradox of tragedy. See TRAGEDY, AESTHETIC PARADOX OF.

paradox of the ugly. See UGLY, PARADOX OF THE.

paradoxes, Socratic. See SOCRATIC PARADOXES.

paradoxes, Zeno's. See ZENO'S PARADOXES.

paralogism (Gk., *paralogismos,* from *para,* "beside," and *logizesthai,* "to reason"). **1.** Any reasoning that is false in form. **2.** Any error or fallacy in reasoning. **3.** Fallacious syllogistic reasoning.

paranormal. Literally "beyond the normal," used as a synonym for "extrasensory" or "parapsychological." See PARAPSYCHOLOGY.

parapsychology (Gk., *para,* "beside," "alongside of," "against," and *psychē,* "mind," "soul," "spirit," "understanding," and *logos,* "the study of"). The study of psychological phenomena that deal with PARANORMAL or extrasensory powers (ESP) and events. Classified under this are phenomena such as: CLAIRVOYANCE, levitation, mind reading, occult or spiritual presences, PRECOGNITION, PRESCIENCE, EXTRASPECTION, psychokinesis, TELEPATHY.

parsimony, principle of. Also referred to as the *principle of simplicity.* Refers to the prescription to (**a**) simplify explanation (see OCKHAM'S RAZOR), and/or (**b**) economize effort toward a goal.

participation (Plato). See MIMĒSIS.

particular (L., *particularis,* from *pars, partis,* "a part"). **1.** An INDIVIDUAL member of a class in contrast to the characteristics that describe the members of that class. **2.** "Some" in contradistinction to "all." **3.** In metaphysics, any individual existing unity interrelating with other unities. A unit.

particulars, egocentric. Generally synonymous with indexical signs. See SIGN, INDEXICAL.

passion. 1. An excessive, intense, or overpowering impulse or emotion such as rage, sexual lust, anger, jealousy. **2.** The overpowering emotion **(a)** which is the result of such things as antipathy or inordinate desires, and **(b)** which controls or rules behavior.

Passion is associated in classical philosophy with the irrational, with the tendency toward illicit, irascible, uncontrolled behavior, with the sinful, with lack of discipline and self-direction. In Plato, for example, one has no freedom of the will when a slave to passion. Being mastered by passion makes one less than human.

passive intellect/reason, the. See REASON, ACTIVE/PASSIVE (ARISTOTLE).

past. 1. Time gone by. All events that have happened. (All present events and future events will become members of the class "past" at some time. Therefore this class is not a fixed class, but an ever-growing class.) **2.** Something at a former time. **3.** Something that has elapsed (gone by).

pathetic (Gk., *pathētikos,* from *pathētos,* "subject to suffering," from *pathein,* "to suffer"). **1.** Having to do with feelings or emotions, or **2.** that which results from feelings or emotions.

In classical philosophy, *pathetic* (sometimes *pathetical*) referred to those things that affected or stimulated the *tender emotions* such as pity, grief, compassion, sorrow.

pathetic fallacy. Incorrectly projecting (attributing) human emotions, feelings, intentions, thoughts, traits upon events or objects which do not possess the capacity for such qualities. See ANIMISM; METAPHOR.

pathos (Gk., *pathos,* "a suffering," "a passion," "anything that befalls one," "an incident," "an accident," "what one has suffered," "misfortune," "calamity," "EMOTION," "FEELING" or *pathein, paschein,* "to suffer"). **1.** That which excites emotions. **2.** The name for emotions, usually specifically for the tender emotions. See PATHETIC. **3.** Suffering. The undergoing of distress, grief, or anguish.

In English usage, pathos is contrasted with *ĒTHOS,* in the sense that pathos is a private, individual, personal experience, whereas ethos refers to the feelings in the context of a community. Pathos in Greek also meant "pain," "suffering," as found in the adage *pathei mathos:* "Suffering teaches." See SYMPATHY.

per accidens (L., "by accident," "accidental," "nonessential," "by limitation." The Latin *per* means "through," "throughout," "by," "for" and is used in English as a prefix in words such as perchance, perforce, perform. The Latin *accidens* is the present participle of *accidere,* "to happen"). **1.** Referring to a mode of existence that is not essential to the nature of a thing, to a thing's being what it is (and what it should be according to its nature). **2.** Referring to a characteristic of a thing acquired by happenstance—without intention and without resulting from its inner nature. **3.** Referring to activities or properties of a thing that are not required for its recognition or identification. Compare with *PER SE.*

peras (Gk., "limit," "form," "end," "shape," "boundary"). The Pythagoreans and Plato used the word to refer to that principle (law, power) that forms (shapes, patterns, structures) the infinite or the nonlimited (the APEIRON). They also used *peras* in a moral sense, as that principle that controls (limits) behavior in a rational, ordered way, avoiding disharmony and excesses.

perception (L., *perceptio,* from *percipere,* "to receive," "to take"). **1.** The bringing of things into awareness by the use of our senses and especially thereby being able to name them and/or identify them as objects in the external world. In general, perception is regarded as an interpreting and synthesizing of sensations. **2.** An object of perception is any item present to consciousness, including sense data, an image, an illusion, a vision, an idea, a concept. **3.** An immediate intuitive cognition or evaluation of an idea (or situation) or the ability to have such cognition or evaluation. 3 is related to the concept of insight. Perception is usually regarded as the organization and interpretation of bare sense data. Compare with SENSATION. See CONSCIOUSNESS; EXPERIENCE.

perception, confused (Leibniz). 1. The subconscious or unconscious perceptions that are not clearly apprehended by the intellect but which nevertheless affect the tendencies of thought and emotion. **2.** Those ideas that are not fully (clearly and distinctly) understood in all their implications to the rational mind. See MONADS (LEIBNIZ).

perception, representative theory of. 1. Objects are independent of (separate from) the ideas we have of them from perception. **2.** Our ideas of objects "represent," "copy," "correspond to," give us a "map" or "diagram" of the external world of objects. **3.** These objects cause our ideas of them by physically stimulating our sense organs. **4.** The mind processes these stimuli in the act of perception to form our ideas.

perception, sense. See SENSE PERCEPTION.

perception, temporal. 1. Perception in which the awareness of time is present and often predominates. **2.** The belief in the direct perception of time much as we have a direct perception of colors.

perception, theories of. 1. The *causal theory:* Perception is of and is caused by externally existing objects stimulating our sense organs. **2.** The *creative, constructive,* or *generative theory:* Perceptions are caused by the mind and exist only insofar as the mind is having them. **3.** The *selective theory:* Perceptions are those complexes of sensa that the mind consciously or unconsciously selects and puts into an order (cognition).

percepts (L., *percipere,* "to take," "to receive"). The data of perception. That which appears (or exists) in an act of perception. Contrasted with CONCEPTS (ideas, beliefs, notions, opinions) that refer to abstractions (universals, classes, generalizations). Percepts refer to particulars (individual objects, images, sensations), to concrete items in experience. When not used as a synonym for SENSE DATA, percepts are usually regarded as the mind's first step in organizing undifferentiated sense data.

perfect (L., *perfectus,* past participle of *perficere,* "to perform," "to finish," from *per,* "through," "by," "for," and *facere,* "to make," "to do"). **1.** Complete. Possessing the essence and/or all the properties that belong to the nature of something. **2.** Pure. Without qualification, as in **1** but without any properties accruing to it that are accidental or incidental. **3.** Faultless. Having no potential for defects and having no defects.

perfectibility of man. The belief that the human being **1.** is capable of further development and will develop further his moral and social sensitivities and behavior; **2.** can eventually actualize all of his moral and social potentialities; and **3.** (sometimes) that this process is a continuous onward and upward evolutionary and social process. Compare with OPTIMISM.

perfection (classical). The state of complete fulfillment of a thing whereby all of the potentialities inherent in its nature or essence have been actualized to the utmost for its good.

perfectionism (ethics). 1. Perfection (**a**) of our moral character or (**b**) of all moral character is the highest good to be aimed at in life as opposed to such ethical ends as pleasure, utilitarianism, duty. **2.** Perfection is the highest virtue of humanity and all other virtues necessarily follow from it.

performative act. 1. That act which in fact follows from what is said, and/or **2.** that act done as part of what is being said.

performative (performatory) language. See LANGUAGE, PERFORMATIVE.

perlocutionary expression/act (perlocution). 1. An act that has a specific effect upon feelings, thoughts, or behavior. Examples: frightening someone, inciting someone to anger. **2.** What we do (to ourselves and/or to others) when we say things, when we use language.

In general, a perlocutionary act is the act successfully performed by means of the illocutionary act (such as communication of an image or meaning or evoking a response in someone). Compare with ILLOCUTIONARY EXPRESSION/ACT (ILLOCUTION); LOCUTIONARY EXPRESSION/ACT (LOCUTION).

per se (L., "through itself," "by itself," "intrinsically," "innately"). **1.** In general, *per se* refers to the essential and indispensable properties that a thing possesses; to its nature. Contrasted with *PER ACCIDENS.* **2.** If a thing exists *per se* relatively, it can be called a substance (substantial, possessing an essence, an individual entity or unity). **3.** When applied to God (or Substance, Ultimate Being, the Universe), *per se* refers to our conceiving this God without having to refer Him to any other concept from which His concept is derived. God is that being who exists *per se* in a complete, totally independent way. God as Pure Being is *per se* in an absolute sense. See *A SE;* ASEITY. Nothing except God has the characteristic of being unaffected by anything else. All other things can be said to be *per se* only relatively. See PERSEITY.

per se esse (L., "to exist by its own being, in and for itself out of its own inherent necessity"). When predicated of God it means eternally existing by His own being, in and for Himself out of His own inherent necessity and inseparably connected with all things as their source and sustainer.

perseity (L., *per se,* "by itself," "intrinsically," "innately"). The state in which a thing is "by itself," acting out of the conditions of its own true inner nature, but (as opposed to ASEITY) always in contrast with or in conjunction with something else. Anything in a state of perseity may be regarded as a substance, and the degree to which it fully manifests its essential inner nature, to that extent it possesses purity of perseity. No matter how perfect a state of perseity is reached, it falls short of aseity (which is reserved for God) since it cannot attain complete independence from God as the efficient cause of its nature and activity.

per se subsistere. Latin, "to subsist by itself, of its own nature, and to require no other thing for its continued existence."

person (L., *persona,* "a mask used by actors," "part," "role," "person," "personage"). **1.** That to which we can ascribe both (**a**) mental characteristics and (**b**) bodily characteristics. **2.** The unity of bodily and mental actions in activity. **3.** The bodily form, or outward appearance, of a human being. **4.** The real, true self of a human being.

personal identity. 1. Sameness of self (consciousness, mind). The awareness of being the same conscious unity at different times and places. **2.** The identification of a persistent or enduring unity of activity (personality, individuality, character) throughout change of activity or behavior.

Among other things, personal identity implies: (**a**) the existence of a memory; (**b**) bodily activities; (**c**) the ability to identify oneself (one's "sameness"); (**d**) the ability never to fail to know something that has happened or is happening to one. Compare with entries under EGO; SELF.

personalism. A philosophy having the following basic beliefs: **1.** The characteristics possessed by the "person" and "personality" are the keys with which the universe and all things in it can be understood. **2.** The whole of existence is an expression of a universal Personal Consciousness and can be analyzed in terms of the forms of human personality. **3.** Reality is a system of persons (selves, personalities, egos). **4.** "Persons" are irreducible elements of all existence and cannot be explained by anything else. **5.** "Person" and "personality" are the highest levels attainable in the universe and are to be esteemed as being the highest values attainable in the universe.

Personalism has taken many forms in the history of philosophy, such as absolutistic, idealistic, realistic, theistic, critical, teleological, pantheistic, panpsychistic, phenomenological, monadistic, monistic. Personalism is almost indistinguishable from most forms of IDEALISM. See ANIMISM.

personalism, realistic. See REALISM, PERSONAL.

personality. 1. Individuality. The distinguishing traits of a person that stand out in one's awareness of him. **2.** The recurrent basic and general mental and behavioral patterns exhibited by a person. **3.** The sum total of the mental and behavioral actions ascribed to a person.

personification. 1. Attributing personal qualities or form to external reality, in particular to the inanimate world. See ANIMISM. **2.** A way of thinking such as in mythology, children's fiction, etc., in which abstract ideas or inanimate objects are endowed with personal (or personality) traits. **3.** The depicting of a person or creature as representing a force, or abstract quality, or thing. See HYPOSTATIZATION; REIFICATION/REISM. Example: The goddess *Moira* was the personification of the concept of fate. **4.** Being the embodiment of some characteristic, as in "He was the personification of greed."

perspective (L., *perspicere,* "to look through," from *per,* "through," and *specere,* "to look"). **1.** The point of view from which something is seen. **2.** The basic presuppositions consciously or unconsciously assumed by which a conclusion is reached or an analysis made. **3.** Delineation of that which is possible or significant in the process of organizing and resolving a problem.

pessimism (L., *pessimus,* "worst," superlative of *pejor,* "worse"). **1.** The tendency to take the worst, or least hopeful, view of things. Opposite to OPTIMISM. **2.** Viewing things from the emotions of sorrow, pity, gloom, despondency, hopelessness, meaninglessness, absurdity, pain, death, and believing that they are the basic and inescapable ingredients of life.

pessimism (metaphysics). **1.** The view that all things are ordered for, or tend toward the worst. Opposite to BEST, PRINCIPLE OF THE. **2.** The world is essentially evil and will remain so in spite of human effort. Opposite to MELIORISM. **3.** This is the worst of all possible worlds. Opposite to BEST OF ALL POSSIBLE WORLDS, THE.

pessimism (Schopenhauer). **1.** We ought not to take joy in being alive but ought rather to bemoan that fact. Nonexistence is preferable to existence. Life is something that ought not to be. **2.** If the individual had a choice, he would have declined life, had he first understood its hopelessness. **3.** All states in life end up as frustrated, unhappy, illusory, or painful. **4.** Life is fraught with suffering, disappointment, uncertainty, disillusionment, helplessness, despair, and death. **5.** The world is the worst possible: that than which nothing worse can be created or conceived. **6.** The world is the expression of a blind, irrational Will. Everything possesses the will to live and the necessary consequence is an existence of suffering. **7.** Individuals can overcome the world and their suffering by such means as philosophic contemplation, transcendence through the aesthetic experience, and compassion.

petitio principii. Sometimes simply *petito.* Also *circular reasoning* (L., "begging of the question"). The informal fallacy of already assuming in an argument what is to be proved as a conclusion. See CIRCULARITY; FAL-

LACY, TYPES OF INFORMAL (**13**); VICIOUS CIRCLE ARGUMENT. Sometimes used to refer generally to deductive arguments since their conclusions are implicitly or explicitly included in their premises.

phantasia (Gk., "imagination," "the faculty or power by which an object is given or appears, *phanetai,* to the mind"). Used in Plato to mean "a mere image," "a fantasy," "an unreality."

phantasma (Gk., "that object presented to the mind," "sensation," "sense representation," "an appearance," "phantasm"). Used to mean an apparent likeness, a semblance of the original upon which it is modeled and (sometimes) from which it emanates as a film. Occasionally it is used to mean a vision or dream. See entries under *EIDOLA.*

phenomenalism. Some of the principal tenets of phenomenalism: **1.** Only phenomena (SENSE DATA) can be known as they appear to our consciousness. **2.** We cannot know the ultimate nature of a reality in itself. **3.** What we know is dependent upon the activity of consciousness. The reality of an external, physical object is based on its being perceived by someone. **4.** Knowledge is limited to what can be perceived (observed) in consciousness about the external world and what can be perceived by introspection about our mental activities and states. **5.** Reality is the totality of all possible conscious experiences. **6.** MATTER is the permanent possibility of sensation. Material objects are sequences or groups of actual or possible sensa. The physical world cannot be said to exist apart from the actual or possible sensa. The physical world cannot be said to exist apart from the actual or possible sense data of some perceiver. **7.** Physical (material) objects are logical constructions based on perception (sense data). The meanings of statements about physical objects can be fully analyzed in terms of, can be fully reduced to, statements about patterns of sense data (phenomena). See KNOWLEDGE (MILL).

phenomenology (Husserl). Edmund Husserl conceived phenomenology as a descriptive, introspective analysis in depth of all forms of consciousness and immediate experiences: religious, moral, aesthetic, conceptual, sensuous. The true focus of philosophy should be the exploration of the life-world *(Lebenswelt)* or the subjective, inner life *(Erlebnisse),* emphasizing the intentional character of consciousness, and without assuming the conceptual presuppositions of the empirical sciences. Philosophy is not, and cannot be, a factual science. Philosophy has its own unique methods and findings, which are essentially different from those of the natural sciences and from those of the formal systems of logic and mathematics. Phenomenology studies and describes the intrinsic traits of phenomena as they reveal themselves to consciousness. The aspect of Husserl's phenomenology which seeks to unearth the essential, interrelated set of laws of human consciousness is called *transcendental phenomenology.* See BRACKETING (HUSSERL).

phenomenon (Gk., *phainomenon,* from *phainesthai,* "to appear," and *phain-*

ein, "to show," "to appear"). **1.** Object of perception. That which is perceived. **2.** That as it appears to our consciousness. **3.** Object of sense experience. That as it appears to our senses. **4.** Any observable fact or event. The plural is phenomena. Contrasted with NOUMENON.

philia (Gk., "friendly love," "attraction," "personal affection," "fondness," "appealing," "affinity toward"). Contrasted with ERŌS, which refers to sexual love, and AGAPE, which refers to moral or spiritual love and, in Christianity, the love of God by humans and the love of humans by God. The term *philia* was used to refer to the force of attraction/love in nature as opposed to *neikos,* the force of repulsion/hate, both forces being a necessary cause for all change in nature.

philosopher, the. Eulogistic term referring to Aristotle used by the medievalists from the early thirteenth century when his works were being translated into Latin from Arabic and Greek sources; used especially in veneration by Thomas Aquinas.

philosopher-king (Plato). The concept of a supreme, completely rational and righteous ruler(s) of a utopia as envisaged in Plato's *Republic.*

philosophes. French term applied to the eighteenth-century French philosophers, including Condorcet, Condillac, Rousseau, Diderot, Voltaire.

philosophy (Gk., *philosophia,* from *philos,* "love," or *philia,* "friendship," "affection," "affinity for," "attraction toward," and *sophos,* "a sage," "a wise one," or *sophia,* "wisdom," "knowledge," "skill," "practical wisdom or experience," "intelligence"). Philosophy has as many meanings as philosophers engaging in it. Some basic definitions: **1.** The speculative attempt to present a systematic and complete view of all reality. **2.** The attempt to describe the ultimate and real nature of reality. **3.** The attempt to determine the limits and scope of our knowledge: its source, nature, validity, and value. **4.** The critical inquiry into the presuppositions and claims made by the various fields of knowledge. **5.** The discipline which tries to help you "see" what you say and to say what you "see." Pythagoras was the first to call himself a *philosophos:* a philosopher. *Sophia* meant for him the knowledge of the underlying reasons or causes for things as they appear to us, knowing the reasons why a thing is what it is. This entails an esoteric knowledge of mathematical forms that constitutes true reality as opposed to knowledge of everyday appearances.

philosophy, first. See FIRST PHILOSOPHY.

philosophy, Gestalt. See GESTALT PHILOSOPHY.

philosophy, ordinary language. See ORDINARY LANGUAGE PHILOSOPHY.

philosophy, political. See POLITICAL PHILOSOPHY.

philosophy, speculative. See SPECULATIVE PHILOSOPHY.

philosophy, synoptic. See SYNOPTIC PHILOSOPHY.

philosophy, synthetic. See SYNTHETIC PHILOSOPHY.

phronēsis (Gk., "prudence," "practical wisdom," "thoughtfulness," "a minding or intending to do something"). **1.** Knowing how and when to act in the appropriate (proper, acceptable, mannerly, rational) manner relative to the given circumstances. **2.** Knowing (**a**) the right goals to seek, and (**b**) the proper and most efficient ways of achieving them. **3.** The wisdom that comes from experiencing and learning from life. Compare with entries under *SOPHIA*.

phronēsis (Aristotle). **1.** Knowledge wisely applied to everyday living. Practical wisdom. **2.** That faculty (power, ability, capacity) in humans which (**a**) enables them to discover what the correct (proper, right) action is in a given situation and (**b**) makes human desires conform to reason (or allows reason to control such desires). *Phronēsis* entails knowledge of the goods (ends, goals) of rational human conduct and knowledge of the means and their proper application in achieving those desirable rational goods. See *DIANOIA*.

physical (Gk., *physicos,* "natural," *physis,* "nature," *phyein,* "to produce," "to grow," "to become"). Referring to: **1.** Anything that is a part of nature or the universe. **2.** Any material thing. **3.** That which (**a**) can be analyzed as existing in time and space, (**b**) is believed to be externally real, and (**c**) is potentially publicly verifiable.

A physical thing is regarded as a three-dimensional object (entity, being, existent, etc.) that can move (or change), or can be moved, or has movement. A *physical event* is regarded as a change (process, movement, alteration, activity) in or upon a physical thing (or among physical things). *Physical causation* is the causal relation existing between or among physical events. See entries under *MATTER*.

physical object. See *MATERIAL OBJECT*.

physicalism. The theory that the language of any science is (should be) translatable into a language containing terms and concepts that refer only to empirically observable and testable characteristics of events.

physicalism (mind/body). The theory that mental events (states, processes) are identical with brain events. Sensations, for example, are one and the same as specific neurological and bodily changes occurring in an individual. See *MIND/BODY, IDENTITY THEORY OF*.

physis (Gk.). A word whose use has had a long history with varied meanings. It is related to the Greek word *phyein,* "to grow," "to bring forth," "to produce." **1.** In general *physis* means Nature, or whatever exists outside of humankind. **2.** Specifically, when applied to humans it means the "nature" of a human (the natural qualities, powers, condition of a person); and when applied to things it means "a natural object," "the constituents of a physical entity." Usually contrasted with *NOMOS*. A further metaphysical use for *physis* in Greek philosophy was to refer to the ultimate reality or realities of things as opposed to their appearances; to refer to the real, essential "nature" of reality, or the true "nature" of things.

Four other common meanings for the word *physis:* (**a**) the origin (source, beginning, foundation) of a thing; (b) the physical constitution and structure of a thing; (c) the stuff (substance, substratum, composition) out of which things are made, or used to make things; (d) the natural kind (genera, species, class, type) of a thing, its classification.

physis (**Aristotle**). Some meanings: **1.** NATURE. All that which occurs in the natural order of things, in contrast to *TECHNĒ*, which encompasses all that which is created by humans. (But even *technē* is ultimately a subcategory of *physis*.) **2.** The inner impulse possessed by things that is the cause of their development (change, processes, activities). **3.** That essence or form of a thing that is in a process of becoming, of making a thing into something other than what it was. **4.** The study of anything that changes in any of the varieties of change. See CHANGE (ARISTOTLE). Compare with *NOMOS*.

physis (**Plato**). Plato often used the word *physis* to refer (a) to the intrinsic and essential realities of things: their natures, powers, inherent qualities, and (b) to the realm of the Perfect and Eternal Ideas. The emphasis in this use was upon the "true" perspective upon nature and reality as opposed to an illusory or inadequate one.

physis (**Stoics**). The word was used by the STOICS to express their pantheistic and panpsychistic tendencies. *Physis* meant (a) all of nature, but (b) a nature that is a living rational organism, (c) imbued with a universal Mind (see *LOGOS*) and (d) of which humans and all things were a necessary part. In effect *physis* was identical with God viewed as the whole of nature itself, or as the active, guiding, rational force in nature. The principal characteristics of *physis* for the Stoics were: rationality, necessity (fate), and goodness. It is *physis* which gives the individual knowledge of what is good, rational, and to be accepted in life. (The Stoics divided philosophy into three areas: logic, ethics, and physics. This restricted use of the word *physis* referred to the study of natural phenomena.)

pity (L., *pietas,* "piety," "kindness," "pity"). **1.** A feeling of compassion for the suffering of another or of others. **2.** A feeling of grief. **3.** A feeling of mercy. **4.** A feeling of sorrow or commiseration.

Pity in one or more of the above senses has served as a motivating force for ethical conduct. See EMPATHY; KATHARSIS (ARISTOTLE); PASSION; PATHOS; SYMPATHY.

Platonism. The philosophy of Plato and/or the philosophy of those who have based their approach on that of Plato. The following are some of its general beliefs: **1.** This world as it appears to our senses is not the real world. There are two realms: (a) the real realm of Perfect Unchanging Eternal Ideas (forms) known only by our intellect, and (b) the illusory, or the less real, realm of concrete, individual, changing objects known by our senses and existing as imperfect copies of the Perfect Ideas. The real world is nonspatial and nontemporal. The actual world is spatial and temporal. **2.** Abstract entities such as universals, souls, forms, essences, exist in the real world independently of our conception of them, and they are more real than sensible objects. **3.** Humans, through the use of their reason, can control their base emotions and their irrational nature and thereby develop morally and spiritually. Humans do evil because they lack knowledge of the good. **4.** Philosophic knowledge of the true, good, and beautiful is essential to the development of righteousness and the proper guidance of oneself and of others. Philosophic knowledge can be attained by the rigorous application of reason through a process of dialectic. **5.** Humans possess a soul and it is immortal. **6.** There is a spirituality and a rationality that pervades all the universe. See BEAUTY; BECOMING; BEING; BEST, PRINCIPLE OF THE.

pleasure. 1. State or feeling of delight, joy. **2.** Gratification. **3.** That feeling which results from the satisfaction of a drive, desire, need. **4.** That feeling of enjoyment resulting from activity. **5.** That feeling which is a consequence of the exercise and fulfilling of an act of will. Contrasted with PAIN.

pleasure principle. See UTILITY, PRINCIPLE OF.

plenitude, principle of (metaphysics). A perfect universe is **(a)** one that is as full of as many diverse existences as is possible, and **(b)** one in which given an infinite amount of time all the possible combinations of existence that can be expressed will be expressed.

plenitude, principle of (methodology). Explanation of any kind should take into consideration the plethora of qualities found in existence and not reduce them either **(a)** to one form of explanation or **(b)** to the simplest theory. Contrasted with OCKHAM'S RAZOR; PARSIMONY, THE PRINCIPLE OF.

plenum (L., *plenus,* "full," "fullness"). **1.** An occupied space. **2.** All space, every part of which is filled with matter. Space without void or emptiness. (Opposite to empty space, or vacuum.) *Plenum* is often used to refer to Parmenides' one, eternal, indivisible, unmoving, immovable, unchanging Reality.

pluralism (L., *pluralis,* from *plus, pluris,* "more," "more than one"). Pluralism is characterized by beliefs such as the following: **1.** There are more than one and more than two kinds of fundamental realities. Contrasted with DUALISM; MONISM. **2.** There are many separate, irreducible, and independent levels of things in the universe. **3.** The universe is basically indeterminate in form; it has no basic harmonious unity or continuity, no fundamental rational and coherent order.

pluralism, ethical. See ETHICS, PLURALISTIC.

plurality of causes. See CAUSES, THE PRINCIPLE OF THE PLURALITY OF.

pneuma **(Stoics).** In Stoic philosophy *pneuma* meant "spirit," "soul," "the agency of life and rationality," and was used somewhat interchangeably with *LOGOS.* All things possess a *pneuma.* These *pneumata* are incorporeal (immaterial) forces that enter and leave objects. Some STOICS regarded them as very fine material entities such as they believed were contained in fire. There is an overall universal *pneuma* that is the cause of the eternal cyclical pattern of all things and the cause of their return into the material substratum, from which they are again organized into definite objects. This creative force brings matter together into patterns and sustains for a time the unity and continued existence of objects.

poiēsis (Gk., "poetry," "the art of poetry"). The term referred to anything made either by poets or craftspeople, or to the activity of making something.

poiēsis/poietikos (Aristotle). Aristotle classified knowledge into three general groups: **1.** THEŌRIA, abstract or cognitive knowing; **2.** PRAXIS, practical knowledge that comes by doing, from activity or development of a manual skill; and **3.** *poiēsis* or *poetikos,* knowledge that is involved in making, producing, or creating something. See KNOWLEDGE (ARISTOTLE).

poietikos (Gk., "capable of making something," "one who is creative or productive"). The term was applied to both craftspeople and poets.

polar concepts. See POLARITIES.

polarities (Gk., *polos,* "a pivot," "a pole," "an axis," "a hinge"). **1.** The extremes in a range of degrees. **2.** OPPOSITES or contraries. **3.** Ideas that contrast in almost every respect, such as good/evil, love/hate, right/wrong, moral/immoral, just/unjust, beautiful/ugly, light/dark, odd/even, hot/cold.

When one member of a polarity is thought to exist, ontological status is usually also affirmed for its contrasting member. Examples: Light cannot exist without the existence of darkness. Love cannot exist without hate existing. If good did not exist in reality, then there would be no evil.

political philosophy. That area of philosophy that studies the characteristics and problems of people as, in Aristotle's phrase, political animals. Some of the issues it focuses upon: **1.** The origin, nature, purpose, and importance of government (states, ruling bodies) in human development. **2.** The classification of governments that have existed and their philosophies. **3.** The structure of utopias and their possible attainment. **4.** The relationship between the individual and government, obedience and freedom, control, suppression, censorship, and the power of government. **5.** The area of freedom from governing bodies. **6.** The extent to which one can, or should, disobey the law. **7.** The rights and protection of minorities. **8.** The right of nations to wage war. **9.** The analysis of value concepts such as justice, equality, freedom, liberty, rights, possession and use of property.

politics (Gk., *politikos,* "of, for, or pertaining to citizens," *politēs,* "a citizen," "a member of a city or state," *polis,* "a city or state" "one's country, city, or state," "a body of citizens," *politeia,* "citizenship," "the rights of a citizen"). **1.** That which has to do with governing. **2.** Managing, directing, and enforcing the affairs of public policy and decisions or of political parties. **3.** That field of study which deals with civil-social problems and develops approaches to their solution.

politics (Aristotle). Aristotle wrote a treatise titled *Politeia,* which title has been translated as *Politics.* Politics is for Aristotle a brand of practical knowledge. See *PRAXIS.* Politics is that part of ethics which deals with people in group activity. Humans are animals of the *polis* (the city-state). The natural tendency of humans is to form into groups, to act within groups, and to act as groups. The purpose (end, goal) of politics is the same as that of ethics, and the same as that of human life in general: to attain *EUDAIMONIA,* the vital well-being (happiness) of the individual.

polla (Gk., "many," "very many," "much," "too much") Used in many senses. The two principal senses in philosophy: **1.** to contrast with *HEN* ("one," "oneness"), and **2.** to refer in the expression *hoi polloi,* to "the many," "the commonality of the people," what "the majority" think.

polydaemonism. See SPIRITISM.

polytheism. See GOD CONCEPTS.

polytypic concept. A concept which if any of its major characteristics is claimed to be logically necessary, it is then possible to present a case that does not have that characteristic, but nevertheless would be accepted as an example of the concept. Examples: species, life, animal, insect, human, house. Most of our definitions and concepts have this polytypic character. Our understanding of words is generally based on whether they have a number of characteristics presented in their definition, not on their having all these characteristics. See DEFINITION; FAMILY RESEMBLANCE (WITTGENSTEIN).

positivism (Comte). Some of its main tenets: **1.** *The Law of Three Stages.* The history of thought can be seen as an unavoidable evolution composed of three main stages: (a) the *theological* stage, during which anthropomorphic and animistic explanations of reality in terms of wills (egos, spirits, souls) possessing drives, desires, needs predominate; (b) the *metaphysical* stage, during which the "wills" of the first stage are depersonalized, made into abstractions, and reified as entities such as "forces," "causes," "essences"; and (c) the *positive* stage, in which the highest form of knowledge is reached by describing relationships among phenomena in such terms as succession, resemblance, coexistence. The positive stage is characterized in its explanation by the use of mathematics, logic, observation, experimentation, control. Each of these stages of mental development has corresponding social, economic, cultural correlates. The theological stage is essentially authoritarian and militaristic. The metaphysical stage is basically legal and ecclesiastical. The positive stage is one characterized by technological and industrial activity. As these stages change so do the features of their correlates. **2.** Progress, the fulfillment of the evolutionary cycle of the Three Stages, is inevitable. **3.** The sciences are one unified whole, but in differing stages of development. They are also related in a hierarchical order of dependency; for example, astronomy must develop before physics can become a field in its own right; biology must reach a given point of sophistication before chemistry can begin its development. **4.** Reality can be understood by means of basic concepts such as organic unity, order, progression, succession, resemblance, relation, utility, reality, movement, direction. **5.** The highest form of religion in its evolution is the religion of universal humanity or reason (devoid of references to God).

positivism, logical. Sometimes simply *positivism*. Sometimes referred to as *logical empiricism* (see EMPIRICISM, LOGICAL), *scientific empiricism, scientific positivism*. Some of the tenets of logical positivism: **1.** The acceptance of the verifiability principle (see VERIFIABILITY, PRINCIPLE OF), which is a criterion for determining that a statement has cognitive meaning. The cognitive meaning of a statement (as opposed to its emotive or other levels of meaning) is dependent upon its being verified. A statement is meaningful if-and-only-if it is, at least in principle, empirically verifiable. Some rock-bottom sense experience (positive knowledge) must be reached before a statement can have cognitive meaning. **2.** All statements in mathematics and logic are analytic (tautologies) and true by definition. They are necessarily true statements useful in organizing cognitively meaningful statements. Their concepts are not verified (discovered by examining reality) but are definitional conventions applied to reality. **3.** Scientific method is the only source of correct knowledge about reality. (There have been attempts to construct a unified system of all the sciences under one logico-mathematical-experiential methodology.) **4.** Philosophy is the analysis and clarification of meaning with the use of logic and scientific method. (Some logical positivists attempt to eliminate all philosophies that are not constructed as the logico-mathematical sciences are.) **5.** Language is in essence a CALCULUS. With formalization it can be handled as a calculus (**a**) in solving philosophical problems (or showing which of them are pseudo-problems), and (**b**) in clarifying the foundations of science. Logical positivists and empiricists have made attempts to construct artificial, formally perfect languages for philosophy in order to gain efficiency, precision, and completeness of the physical sciences. **6.** Metaphysical statements are meaningless. They are not empirically verifiable and they are not fruitful tautologies. There is no possible way to determine their truth (or their falsity) by appeal to experience. No possible experience could ever support metaphysical statements such as "The Nothing itself nothings" (*"Das Nichts selbst nichtet"*—Martin Heidegger), "The Absolute is beyond Time," "God is Perfect," "Pure Being has no characteristics." Metaphysical questions are pseudo-questions. Metaphysics is to be relegated to nonsensical utterances. **7.** In an extreme version of positivism, statements about the existence of the external world, and of external minds independent of our own minds, are considered meaningless because there are no empirical ways of verifying them. **8.** The acceptance of an emotive theory in axiology. Values do not exist independently of the human ability to place values. Values are not objects in the world. They cannot be found by experimentation, testing, or experiencing them as we experience or verify the existence of objects. Values are not absolute. Values are statements, but not empirical statements. "Killing is evil," "Abortion is wrong," "Thou shalt not steal," "That sculpture is beautiful," are statements that have no empirical or descriptive content at all. They do not reflect, or refer as a standard, to a transcendent perfect realm (such as Plato's archetypes). Nor is their source a supernatural God. Statements of that sort express our attitudes, preferences, feelings, convictions, conditioning *about* such activities as killing, abortion, stealing, beauty. They do not directly communicate facts or information or cognitive knowledge. They indicate such things as our approval, disapproval, acceptance, nonacceptance, affinity or nonaffinity for certain things. Some of the names associated with logical positivism: Herbert Fiegl, Philipp Frank, Moritz Schlick, Rudolph Carnap, A. J. Ayer. See MEANING, VERIFIABILITY THEORY OF.

possible/possibility (L., *possibilis,* from *posse,* "to be able"). **1.** Capable of existing (occurring, being, happening). **2.** Capable of becoming. Capable of coming into existence. Having the POTENTIAL to exist. **3.** That which usually happens, but does not *have* to happen. **4.** That which might happen. Not contrary to what could happen, or to what might happen, or to what has happened, or to what is happening. **5.** That which will happen given enough time. **6.** Free (at liberty) to happen or not to happen. **7.** True insofar as our knowledge indicates. **8.** Thinkable. **9.** Not a self-contradiction. **10.** Anything that is not self-contradictory and not (empirically or logically) necessary. Anything that is not impossible. Contrasted with ACTUALITY; CERTAIN. Compare with NECESSARY.

post hoc, ergo propter hoc. See FALLACY, TYPES OF INFORMAL **(21)**.

post res (L., "after reality," "after things"). Used by medieval philosophers in the context of NOMINALISM, whereby universals were regarded as existing only as abstract names after the fact of experiencing things and were not prior to, and not a causal agent for, the existence of material objects. See *ANTE RES; IN RES.*

postulate (L., *postulatum,* "request," from *postulare,* "to demand"). **1.** A statement (**a**) needed as an assumption and/or (**b**) asserted (**c**) without proof and/or (**d**) as self-evident, usually in the context of a formal system of logic or mathematics. **2.** A statement (**a**) accepted as true without itself having a logical proof given for it and (**b**) used to derive other statements that form a coherent system of logical or logico-empirical analysis. **3.** An assumption, presupposition, or hypothesis (essential preliminary assertion or condition) granted or posited so that a study (inquiry, investigation) may be carried out in a systematic way.

Related to concepts such as ASSUMPTION, AXIOM, primitives of a system.

postulates of practical reason, the (Kant). Also *the moral postulates*. The unprovable but necessary and practical presuppositions (ground) for morality: **1.** the existence of a God; **2.** immortality; **3.** free will. See ETHICS (KANT).

postulates of pure reason, the (Kant). Also *the postulates of thought*. See CATEGORIES OF THE UNDERSTANDING, THE (KANT).

potency (L., *potentia,* from *potens,* "potent," *potis,* "able," and *esse,* "to be"). **1.** The quality of possessing power. **2.** The ability to exercise power, to act. **3.** The capability (capacity) to become something of a definite sort. Opposite to ACTUALITY.

potency, active. The innate capacity and tendency of a thing to become or to do something specific to its nature. Example: a rosebud becoming a flower. Contrasted with POTENCY, PASSIVE.

potency, passive. The capability of a thing to become or to do something that is not specific to its nature as a necessary, innate capacity or tendency. Example: using a rosebud to make perfume. Contrasted with POTENCY, ACTIVE.

potency, pure. That which has not in any way manifested any actual form in existence and which therefore cannot be identified—does not possess a "whatness" (see QUIDDITY) about it but only a "thatness." See MATTER, PRIME.

potential/potentiality. 1. Latent. **2.** Existing as a possibility. **3.** Existing as a necessary possibility, one that must and will express itself. **4.** POTENCY. **5.** Power. **6.** Ability. That which is possible and can be done by something. **7.** The innate CAPACITY (and tendency) of a thing to actualize its inherent nature (form, essence).

potential/potentiality (Aristotle). For Aristotle: **1.** A potential can be actualized only by something already actualized which acts as a cause in the potential's actualization. **2.** Also, potential exists in some way to be actualized and in this sense has a level of being that is itself actual, that is actually present for example as an inherent capacity or form. See PRIME MOVER (ARISTOTLE); UNMOVED MOVER (ARISTOTLE).

***pour soi* (Sartre).** (Fr., "for itself," "for oneself"). A phrase used by Sartre to refer to that type of personal existence in which one acts as an aware, pure subject initiating free choices and responsibly assuming the consequences of actions for oneself and others in a process of self-direction of one's life. These qualities of *être* (being) *pour soi* belong only to humans as individuals. Sartre contrasts *pour soi* with *EN SOI*. Opposite to inauthentic existence, ALIENATION, ESTRANGEMENT. See EXISTENTIALISM; BAD FAITH (Sartre).

power (L., *posse, potesse,* "to be able"). **1.** The ability to act, or to make something. **2.** The ability to respond and/or resist. **3.** The FORCE (ENER-

GY), effort, strength exerted in **1** and **2**. See *DYNAMIS*.

power (Aristotle). The three general categories of power: **1.** that which is the agent or cause of change in something; **2.** that capability (CAPACITY: POTENTIAL) in things enabling them to act and/or to do things; and **3.** that ability or tendency of a thing to remain itself, to retain its substantial form in spite of efforts to change it.

practical reason. See REASON, PRACTICAL (ARISTOTLE).

praedicabilia (L., "those things which can be attributed to any subject whatever"). *Praedicabilia* refers to the CATEGORIES or MODES by which anything can be classified, defined, or understood. Usually the list contains five such classes: **1.** GENUS, **2.** SPECIES, **3.** *DIFFERENTIA*, **4.** QUALITY (attribute, characteristic, property), and **5.** ACCIDENT. The English *praedicables* is sometimes used rather than the Latin.

praedicamenta (L., "those things which can be attributed [predicated of] a thing"). Understood by medieval philosophers to be identical with ten of Aristotle's categories: **1.** substance, **2.** quantity, **3.** quality, **4.** time, **5.** place, **6.** relation, **7.** position (state, condition), **8.** activity, **9.** passivity, **10.** possession. See CATEGORIES (ARISTOTLE).

pragmatic fallacy. See FALLACY, TYPES OF INFORMAL, **(40)**.

pragmatic theory of truth. See TRUTH, PRAGMATIC THEORY OF.

pragmatics. A branch of SEMIOTICS. The study of what we *do* to and with symbols apart from their meanings. Pragmatics deals not with what symbols mean or designate or how they are related to other symbols, but with how those who invent symbols, and/or those who interpret symbols are related to, are affected by, and use those symbols.

pragmatism (Gk., *pragma,* "a thing done," "an act," "work," "a thing of consequence," from *prassein,* "to do"). Some of the main views in pragmatism: **1.** Knowledge is derived from experience, experimental methods, and practical efforts. Pragmatism is critical of metaphysical speculation in arriving at truth. **2.** Knowledge must be used to solve the problems of everyday, practical affairs; to help us adapt to our environment. Thinking must relate to practice and action. **3.** Ideas must be referred to their consequences (results, uses) for their truth and meaning. Ideas are guides to positive action and to the creative reconstruction of experience in confronting and adjusting to new experiences. **4.** Truth is that which has practical value in our experience of life. It serves as an instrument, or means, **(a)** in the attainment of our goals and **(b)** in our ability to predict and arrange the future for our use. **5.** Truth is changing, tentative, and asymptotic. **6.** The meaning of an idea (theory, concept, belief) is the same as **(a)** the practical uses to which that idea may be put and **(b)** the practical consequences stemming from it. Compare with CONVENTIONALISM; INSTRUMENTALISM; OPERATIONALISM.

praxis (Gk., "doing," "an activity," "an action or act," "practical ability or manual skill"). Usually refers to practical human conduct, including

ethical and political activity. Contrasted with *POIĒSIS/POIETIKOS* (ARIS-
TOTLE); *THEORIA*. See KNOWLEDGE (ARISTOTLE); VIRTUES, DIANOETIC
(ARISTOTLE).

Marx used *praxis* to refer to the synthesis of theory and practice.

precept (L., *praeceptum,* from *praecipere,* "to take beforehand, "to teach,"
from *prae,* "before," and *capere,* "to take"). **1.** That which is given and
intended as a rule (maxim, principle) of action or conduct, especially
moral or religious conduct. **2.** That which is accepted as a regulative or
working principle in the organization and direction of conduct.

precognition (L., *praecognitio,* from *praecognoscere,* "to foreknow," from
prae, "before," and *cognoscere,* "to know"). **1.** Strong version: Foreknowledge. Knowing what is to occur before it happens. **2.** Weak version:
Foresight. Foreseeing what is going to occur, or might occur. From the
point of view of paranormal phenomena, precognition is thought to have
a "nonsensory" and noninferential source. See PARAPSYCHOLOGY; PRE-
DICTION; PRESCIENCE.

preconscious. That aspect of the mind *prior,* or *ante,* to consciousness,
which can be brought to consciousness by such acts as attention, concentration, stimulation. Example: I may not be presently conscious of my
teacher's name but when asked, I become conscious of it; it was in a preconscious "state." Preconscious is contrasted with subconscious and unconscious. Compare with ANOETIC.

predestination (theology) (L., *praedestinatus,* past participle of *praedestin-
are,* "to predestine," from *prae,* "before," and *destinare,* "to decree beforehand"). Also *foreordination, preordination.* The doctrine that **(a)** all
events that have happened, are happening, and will happen have been
predetermined to happen (and are being caused to happen) by God and
(b) that whether one's soul is to go to heaven or hell has already been decreed by the will of God. See FATE; FATALISM.

predeterminism. 1. The theory that every event has a cause which is necessitated to be that cause at the exact time it is that cause and at no other
time, in accordance with the designs of some operating principle (God,
natural necessity, eternal forms). **2.** All things in the universe are "governed" by, or operate in accordance with, fixed causal laws that compel
things to happen the way they do happen without exception and according to a necessitated sequence in time. See FATALISM.

Most predeterminists hold that if humans were omniscient they would
be able to perceive the necessitated scheme and interconnections of all
events in the universe and thereby be able to predict what would happen,
and what has happened, at any point in eternity.

predicament (L., *praedicamentum,* from *prae,* "before," and *dicere,* "to
say," "to declare"). **1.** A state (condition, situation, problem) that is unpleasant, unfortunate, especially with reference to good/bad, right/
wrong, proper/improper. **2.** A problem which cannot be avoided and for

which there is no solution. Example: The fear of death is a human predicament. It may be handled with courage or intelligence, fear or irrationality, but it cannot be eliminated. Compare with DILEMMA.

predicament, egocentric. See EGOCENTRIC PREDICAMENT.

predicate (L., *praedicatus,* past participle of *praedicare,* "to proclaim," from *prae,* "before," and *dicere,* "to say," "to speak"). **1.** To assert or affirm something about something else. **2.** That which is affirmed or denied of a subject. Example: Grass is green. Snow is not green. Green is the predicate affirmed of (is predicated of) grass and denied of snow. In a categorical statement (proposition), the predicate appears as the term after the copula. See ATTRIBUTE; QUALITY.

predicate, simple. A property such as "red" **1.** that is not reducible to any other property, **2.** that cannot be further analyzed, and **3.** that must be defined, or can only be known, ostensively by pointing.

prediction (L., *praedictus,* past participle of *praedicere,* "to predict," from *prae,* "before," and *dicere,* "to say," "to tell," "to declare"). **1.** Foretelling. Declaration that something will happen before it happens, as in prophecy, augury, divination, precognition. **2.** Inferential knowledge asserted prior to an event about something that actually comes about and/or is expected to come about, made on the basis of regularities found in past experiences.

preestablished harmony (Leibniz). Mind and body do not interact. God has established a noncausal perfect harmony of activity between them analogous to the noncausal harmony of activity existing between two clocks whose ticking is synchronized perfectly. God has foreknowledge of all the possible harmonious parallel relationships that could exist between mind and body. He chooses to bring into existence all those possible minds whose ideas fit perfectly with the activities of human bodies, each expressing in a proper sequence the representation of the other. See MIND/ BODY RELATIONSHIPS, THEORIES OF (**4**); MONADS (LEIBNIZ).

prehension (L., *prehensus,* from *prehendere,* "to grasp," "to seize"). **1.** Mental grasp. Mental APPREHENSION. **2.** The process of perception (thought or feeling) whereby one takes something into one's level of attention and relates accordingly.

prehension span. The maximum number of things that the mind can grasp at any given moment of attending.

premise. Also *premiss* (L., *praemissus,* past participle of *praemittere,* "to send before," from *prae,* "before," and *mittere,* "to send"). **1.** A statement which is in fact true or which is assumed to be true, employed (usually together with at least one other such statement) to argue toward a conclusion. **2.** In traditional categorical logic, one of the two statements which in a syllogism follow the standard categorical form from which a conclusion is reached. **3.** Any statement which serves as a, or the, basis for an argument or inference.

preordination. See PREDESTINATION (THEOLOGY).

prescience (L., *praesciens,* present participle of *praescire,* "to foreknow," from *prae,* "before," and *scire,* "to know"). **1.** Foreknowledge. **2.** Foresight. Knowledge of what will happen. Generally used in the context of an immediate, noninferential knowledge. See PARAPSYCHOLOGY.

prescriptivism (L., *prescribere,* "to write (order) beforehand," from *prae,* "before," and *scribere,* "to write"). **1.** In ethics and religion, the view that moral rules of action are commanded and necessitated by an authority that is their only source of justification. Example: "Thou shall not kill," prescribed by the authority of God. Contrast with ETHICS, DESCRIPTIVISM IN. **2.** In science, when a law is given a "prescriptive" status, it becomes a reified principle that *makes* things happen the way they do; things must act in accordance with its decree. Thus the prescriptive, as opposed to the descriptive, interpretation of natural law would maintain that the "law" of falling bodies necessities bodies to fall as they do and no other way, and bodies must so conform; otherwise they "violate" the law. Compare with entries under LAW, NATURAL.

present, the (L., *praesens,* "that is before one," present participle of *praeesse,* "to be before," from *prae,* "before," and *esse,* "to be"). That immediate, instantaneous, momentary, and transient part of time (or durationless instant) at which any given experience takes place. Any given point in consciousness that can be declared a NOW. Existing not as a past or a future.

Present time is often thought of on the analogy of a point on a line taking place immediately or instantaneously at the moment that the point is recognized. Metaphorically it is often thought of as the "cutting" or "knife" or "boundary" that invisibly separates the past from the future.

present, the timeless. The grammatical use of a verb such as "is" in the present tense without intending any reference to the present as distinct from the future or the past. The tenseless use of verbs whereby they do not relate to any specific time period, but may be said to relate to any and all time periods. Example: If *A* is larger than *B,* and *B* is larger than *C,* then *A* is larger than *C.*

presentment/presentational immediacy (L., *praesentatio,* "a showing or appearance of something"). That which is directly perceived in consciousness from any source such as sensation, reason, memory, imagination, alone or in combination. Often used interchangeably with DATUM.

presuppose. 1. To require something antecedently if something else is to be what it is. Examples: For something to be a rock presupposes that it is hard. To hit a ball presupposes that there is someone who can hit it. **2.** To assume that something is logically or definitionally dependent. Examples: A cause presupposes an effect. Being a husband presupposes the existence of a woman.

presupposition (L., *prae,* "before," and *sub,* "under," and *ponere,* "to put").

1. An implicit or explicit ASSUMPTION made in the act of viewing something or in the process of inference. **2.** That which must be assumed in order to arrive at a desired conclusion. **3.** Conjecture. That which can be reasonably assumed on examination of the circumstances or evidence.

preternatural. Also *praeternatural* (L., prefix *praeter,* "past," "by," "beyond," "more than," and *natura,* "nature"). That which is beyond and/or different (irregular, abnormal) from what is natural (ordinary, explicable) but which is not supernatural and/or miraculous.

prevarication (L., *praevaricatus,* past participle of *praevaricari,* "to walk crookedly," from *prae,* "before," and *varicare,* "to straddle," "to bend"). **1.** Deviation from the truth or fact. **2.** Evasive tactics in an argument. **3.** Committing an equivocation in discourse for the purpose of misleading. **4.** A quibble or logical shuffle in order (**a**) to avoid the truth or reality of a situation, and/or (**b**) to avoid the impending or stated conclusion of a good argument. See EQUIVOCATION; SOPHISM.

prima facie (L., "at first view," "so far as appears on the surface," "on the first appearance," from *primus,* "first," and *facies,* "appearance").

prima facie **duties (Ross).** Duties (**a**) which are regarded as morally self-evident, (**b**) which tend to be absolute duties, and (**c**) which are to be regarded as absolute duties if no other PRIMA FACIE duty conflicts with them. A modified version of Kant's notion of absolute or unconditional duties: those moral actions one must always, without exception, perform. See ETHICS (KANT).

William David Ross is the leading exponent of *prima facie* duties. A list of such duties: **1.** The duty which arises because of *my* previous acts: (**a**) the duty of *fidelity* to promises made and (**b**) the duty of *reparation* for wrongful acts. **2.** The duty which arises out of the previous acts of *others,* such as gratitude. **3.** The duty of *beneficence,* of promoting the greatest amount of good. **4.** The duty of *nonmaleficence,* of refraining from harming other people. **5.** The duty of *justice,* the equitable distribution to others of goods. **6.** The duty of *self-improvement* in respect to intelligence, abilities, virtue, compassion.

primary and secondary substance. See SUBSTANCE, PRIMARY AND SECONDARY (ARISTOTLE).

primary qualities. See entries under QUALITIES, PRIMARY/SECONDARY.

prime matter. See MATTER, PRIME.

prime mover. **1.** In the sense of "First" mover: That self-moving Being (God) that gave the initial impetus to put the universe in motion. (Before this event no motion existed in the universe.) The beginning cause of all activity. Compare with UNMOVED MOVER. **2.** In the sense of a "sustainer" of motion: That Being (God) which at any given moment is the cause of and which maintains all motion in the universe, and without which there would be no motion in the universe. The ground of all activity. (This second meaning of Prime Mover can maintain that motion in the universe has existed infinitely, that is, coinfinitely with God.) See COSMOLOGICAL ARGUMENT FOR GOD'S EXISTENCE; FIRST CAUSE.

prime mover (Aristotle). 1. That Being (God) which moves the world by serving as an inspiration to the activity of its Form in structuring matter. **2.** The perfect and unchanging ultimate goal (end, purpose, reality) of the world which itself does not move but which is the occasion of love and affinity toward it by self-moving, intelligent agents in the world which attempt to actualize it. See UNMOVED MOVER, THE (ARISTOTLE).

principle (L., *principium,* "beginning," "foundation," from *primus,* "first," and *capere,* "to take"). **1.** The source or origin of something. **2.** The ultimate cause of something. **3.** A faculty or original endowment. In these first three senses, a principle is usually thought of as (**a**) innate, (**b**) immanent, and (**c**) found as an agent in a number of things. **4.** The rule or ground for a person's action. **5.** A general statement (law, rule, or truth) which serves as a basis for explaining phenomena. In **4** and **5**, the words *rule* and *law* are often used in place of the word *principle.*

principle, regulative. A principle used to guide our conduct or inquiry. It may be regarded as ideal only, as actually true, or as unprovable, nevertheless having practical and/or theoretical success. Examples: In science, some have considered the causal principle as only a regulative principle in scientific inquiry. In ethics, the CATEGORICAL IMPERATIVE has been considered a regulative principle for practical living.

principle of causation. See CAUSAL PRINCIPLE, THE.

principle of difference in identity. See DIFFERENCE IN IDENTITY, PRINCIPLE OF.

principle of excluded middle. See LAWS OF THOUGHT, THE THREE.

principle of identity. See LAWS OF THOUGHT, THE THREE.

principle of identity in difference. See IDENTITY IN DIFFERENCE, PRINCIPLE OF.

principle of indifference. See INDIFFERENCE, PRINCIPLE OF (PROBABILITY THEORY).

principle of individuation. See INDIVIDUATION (METAPHYSICS).

principle of induction. See INDUCTION, PRINCIPLE OF (METAPHYSICS).

principle of noncontradiction. See LAWS OF THOUGHT, THE THREE.

principle of nonsufficient reason. See REASON, PRINCIPLE OF NONSUFFICIENT.

principle of parsimony/simplicity/economy. See OCKHAM'S RAZOR.

principle of sufficient reason. See REASON, PRINCIPLE OF SUFFICIENT.

principle of uncertainty. See UNCERTAINTY, HEISENBERG'S PRINCIPLE OF.

principle of uniformity of nature. See UNIFORMITY OF NATURE, PRINCIPLE OF.

principle of universal causation. See CAUSAL PRINCIPLE, THE.

principle of universality. See UNIVERSALITY, PRINCIPLE OF (MORALITY).

principle of utility. See UTILITY, PRINCIPLE OF.

prior (L., *prior,* "former," "previous"). **1.** Antecedent. Preceding in the order of time. **2.** Preceding in order of (**a**) knowledge, (**b**) classification, (**c**) hierarchy (rank, order), (**d**) source (origin), (**e**) cause, or (**f**) privilege. Opposite to *posterior.* See A POSTERIORI; A PRIORI.

privacy, epistemic. Also *private knowledge.* **1.** The content of consciousness that is inaccessible to anyone except the person having it. See EGOCENTRIC PREDICAMENT. **2.** That knowledge a person hàs, such as of his pains, pleasures, feelings, emotions, that cannot be known by others, cannot be made available to public knowledge, and cannot be directly verified by public knowledge. Opposite to PUBLICITY, EPISTEMIC. See PRIVILEGED ACCESS.

privation (L., *privatio,* "privation," from *privare,* "to deprive"). **1.** Negation. **2.** State of lack. The absence of.

privation (Aristotle). **1.** A lack of form where it can be (or should be) present. **2.** A lack of some attribute which a thing (**a**) usually possesses, (**b**) is capable of possessing, and (**c**) ought to possess.

privative term/word/name. A term denoting negation (lack, absence of).

privileged access. Refers to the brute fact that a person has direct and immediate knowledge of the contents of his consciousness (as opposed to the inferential knowledge based on overt behavior that others have of his consciousness).

probabilism. 1. The theory that certainty about reality is utterly unattainable since reality is not a completely rational system. Probable knowledge of things and of human conduct is the only kind of knowledge we can have. A rational person is one who, faced with the lack of certainty, is directed by probabilities. See entries under SKEPTICISM. **2.** Empirical science must assign probability values to hypotheses (theories) and in this way show their degree of confirmation or disconfirmation. Compare with IMPROBABILISM.

probability. 1. A determination of the rational expectation for the occurrence of an event. **2.** Chance. **3.** A theory or calculus of chance such as the measurement of the likelihood of the occurrence of a particular event by determining the rate of its frequency. **4.** Possibility. See EXPLANATION, SCIENTIFIC.

probability, classical theory of. The ratio of the occurrence of an event to all the other possible alternatives. Example: Two dice can be thrown in thirty-six possible combinations (assuming that it is equally probable for each to occur). Eleven of these include at least one six. The probability of getting at least one six is $^{11}/_{36}$.

probability, relative frequency theory of. Sometimes the *actuarial theory of probability.* Determines the rate of frequency at which something will occur, expressed as empirical statistical statements of the ratio of the number of times a thing happens to the number of times it *can* happen. Examples: (**a**) The probability that a given person will be bald is calculated as the number of bald persons divided by the total number of persons (bald and with hair). **(b)** In determining the chances that a given individual X will die in the next twenty years, personal knowledge about him, such as age, sex, occupation, years of marriage, number of children, is obtained. The probability of his survival to any given age is estimated on the basis of a class of persons that comes close to having characteristics such as those possessed by X. The characteristics of this class and their actual relationship to longevity is derived from statistical analyses and applied relative to X.

probability, subjective. 1. The determination of **(a)** the degree to which one believes something or **(b)** the intensity of one's inclination to believe something (as opposed to not believing it). Example: Calculating **(a)** or **(b)** in terms of the odds or bets a believer would be willing to take about the possible occurrence or truth of something. **2.** The expression in an utterance (as opposed to a determination or description) of **(1)**.

probable (L., *probabilis,* from *probare,* "to try," "to prove"). **1.** Likely to be the case. That which is supported by good grounds (arguments, observation, inference) which incline one to believe but leave room for some doubt. **2.** Likely to happen. That which is not demonstrably certain to occur, but which has some evidence in its favor for occurring. **3.** That area of knowledge between complete disbelief and complete CERTAINTY. **4.** A close approximation to what is the case or is believed to be the case.

problem of evil, the. See EVIL, THE THEOLOGICAL PROBLEM OF.

problem of induction. See INDUCTION, PROBLEM OF.

problematic/problematical. 1. Doubtful. **2.** Uncertain. **3.** Possible. **4.** Probable.

process, dialectical. See LOGIC, DIALECTICAL.

process philosophy. Alfred North Whitehead was the leading exponent of process philosophy, a theory that emphasizes the creative and novel advance of nature. Some of its tenets: **1.** Nature is a continuously changing but progressing series of events. **2.** The fundamental ground of reality is not substance in which properties inhere, but process: directional and unified change. **3.** There are no durationless instants except as abstract concepts. **4.** Language and its concepts cannot without creating paradoxes express **(a)** the continuous (no instants, no discrete units) nature of processes (change, becoming) or **(b)** the identity (individuality, unity, wholeness) of events in process. See CONCRETENESS, THE FALLACY OF MISPLACED; CONCRETION; CONCRETION, THE PRINCIPLE OF (WHITEHEAD); INGRESSION; SIMPLE LOCATION, FALLACY OF.

projectionism (epistemology). The theory that sensations exist as external qualities independently of consciousness. Sensations are had as the subjective content of consciousness and also are externally focused upon (projected) by such acts as localizing, positioning, distancing.

prolegomenon (Gk., from *prolegein,* "to say beforehand," "to foretell," "to state publicly"). A preliminary statement serving as a preface or as a general introduction to something that is to follow. The plural is *prolegomena*.

prolēpsis (Gk., "conception," from *prolambanein,* "to receive or take beforehand," "to anticipate an event, action, or truth"). An innate, preconceived idea that comes to consciousness without deliberate rational effort considered as (**a**) potentially present in all rational beings but expressed only by some, or as (**b**) universally expressed by all rational beings. Sometimes a *prolēpsis* is regarded as derived not from an innate source but from the sense experiences common to all humans.

proof (L., *probare,* "to try," "to approve," "to prove," and *probus,* "proper," "good"). **1.** Demonstration. A process which establishes (provides firm evidence or complete JUSTIFICATION for) a truth or a fact. **2.** In logic, the series of arguments based on the rules of INFERENCE of that logic that are used to derive the conclusion from the premises. Compare with EXPLANATION.

proof, transcendental (Kant). Proof that shows that what is proved is a necessary condition for all possible human experience and hence applicable to all phenomena; without it experience would be impossible and phenomena of a certain kind could not be known. See KNOWLEDGE (KANT).

propensity (L., *propensio,* "inclination," "disposition," "proneness"). **1.** A natural innate tendency, inclination, disposition, bent, or bias. **2.** Same as **1** but as a mental set which also includes desires, urges, appetition, cravings. **3.** The tendency or predisposition of conscious states to interrelate or to be associated due to conditioning or to the nature of our mental operations.

proper (L., *proprius,* "proper," "one's own"). **1.** Correct. Conforming to usage, convention, or conduct. **2.** Belonging to a thing's natural constitution or essence. **3.** Befitting one's nature, endowments, or inclinations. **4.** Designating one individual only as in "proper" noun. See SENSIBLES, PROPER (ARISTOTLE).

property. That which is PROPER to a thing. The attribute or quality (characteristic, feature, etc.) which a thing is said to possess. Usually a property is something that can be possessed by other members of the class in which it is found and also by members of other classes.

proposition (L., *propositio,* "proposition," from *pro,* "before," and *ponere, positum,* "to lay down," "to put," "to place"). **1.** A SENTENCE or STATEMENT which asserts or denies something (**a**) that has two possible truth values, true or false, has two possible relations to fact, truth or falsity; or (**b**) that can be, at least in theory, verified or confirmed as true. **2.** The meanings that statements have; that which statements "propose" or express. In this sense, a distinction is made between sentences and propositions (statements). Example: "Adam loves Jane" and "Jane is loved by Adam" are two different sentences but they express the same proposition (statement). See SENTENCE/STATEMENT DISTINCTION. For a more complete listing see entries under SENTENCE and STATEMENT.

proprium (L., "property," "proper to a thing"). **1.** That quality which is unique to a class but which is not essential to its identification or definition. Example: The ability to be humorous is a quality that only the class "human" can have but it is not essential that a human have that quality to be known as human or to be defined as human. **2.** Also used to refer to "essence," or "that which is properly and indispensably a part (property) of the nature of a thing."

prosyllogism. That syllogism whose conclusion has become a premise of another syllogism in an argument.

Protagorean relativism. See RELATIVISM, PROTAGOREAN.

protocols (Gk., *prōtokollon,* which referred to the first leaf glued to the rolls of papyrus and documents, from *prōtos,* "first," and *kolla,* "glue"). The basic, irreducible content of immediate experience on the basis of which empirical statements are formulated. See GIVEN, THE.

psi. Often used as a synonym for *extrasensory powers, phenomena, or perception.* See ESP. From the transliteration of the Greek letter ψ (psi), used as an abbreviation for parapsychological or PARANORMAL functions or phenomena. See PARAPSYCHOLOGY.

psychē (Gk., "soul," "mind," "breath," "breath of life," "spirit," "life"). *Psychē* was used originally to refer to the state of being alive; then to the principle of life (a breath, an invisible vapor, a spirit, a soul in things that causes life); then to the source of consciousness and also of conscience; then to the WORLD SOUL.

psychological atomism. See ATOMISTIC PSYCHOLOGY.

psychological behaviorism. See BEHAVIORISM.

psychological egoism. See EGOISM, PSYCHOLOGICAL.

psychological hedonism. See HEDONISM, PSYCHOLOGICAL.

psychologism. 1. The nonpejorative meaning: **(a)** All philosophical concepts and problems can be reduced to some form of psychological analysis. **(b)** All the fields of philosophy can be explained on the basis of psychological principles, and fields such as ethics can be seen to be nothing more than applied psychology. **(c)** The essential characteristics of psychological analysis are: (1) introspection and (2) observation. **2.** The pejorative meaning: Psychologism is the mistake of assuming that philosophical concepts and problems can be reduced to and resolved by psychological analysis. The failure to distinguish between the psychological treatment of the origin of our knowledge in an activity of thinking and the nonpsychological structure, quality, and veracity of the content of that knowledge.

psychology, association. See ASSOCIATIONISM.

psychology, atomistic. See ATOMISTIC PSYCHOLOGY.

psychology, behavioristic. See BEHAVIORISM.

psychology, faculty. See FACULTY PSYCHOLOGY.

psychology, functional. See FUNCTIONAL PSYCHOLOGY.

publicity, epistemic. Also *public knowledge* (L., *publicus,* "public." *Epistemic* comes from the Greek *epistēme,* "knowledge"). **1.** Knowledge that (a) is communicated and (b) shared and (c) made accessible to others. **2.** Knowledge as in **1** but in addition tested or verified by a number of people. **3.** Knowledge such as about the size or shape of objects, that can be directly known by many people or inferred by many people. Opposite to PRIVACY, EPISTEMIC.

punishment. The infliction upon a person of pain, suffering, loss, deprivation, penalty, for a crime or fault which has been committed intentionally and in disobedience, usually as a violation of a law.

punishment, rehabilitative theory of. Some of the main views: **1.** The purpose of punishment is to change, to remold, the behavior of the offender. **2.** Punishment for the sake of punishment, or for revenge, is evil and unjust. The only occasion for the infliction of punishment is when it will benefit the person being punished.

punishment, retributive theory of. Sometimes *retaliative theory of punishment.* Commonly understood as "an eye for an eye, and a tooth for a tooth," or as "the punishment must fit the crime." Some of the main tenets: **1.** The purpose of punishment is revenge and/or to extract from the offender something equal to the wrong he has committed. **2.** This is done not necessarily to rehabilitate the offender but to correct an inequity or moral imbalance that the offense has created. **3.** Injustice consists in permitting someone to injure others without being injured proportionately in return. **4.** Punishment is a deterrent.

punishment, utilitarian theory of. Some of the main views: **1.** The purpose of punishment is to assist in producing good: the greatest good of the greatest number. **2.** Punishment is intrinsically evil but can be justified by the good results it produces. If punishment does not produce good consequences, it should not be administered.

pure act. Sometimes *pure actuality.* **1.** The completely actualized being, God, in whom there can never be any POTENCY. **2.** That state or process in which everything is actualized, without in any way being dependent upon something else for its ACTUALIZATION and activity.

pure experience. 1. The immediately given mental states such as sensations, feelings, images prior to (or devoid of) interpretation, judgment, conceptualization, and structuring. **2.** Those mental states such as sensations, feelings, images that remain when purged of interpretation, judgment, conceptualization, and structuring. Compare with EXPERIENCE.

purgation (L., *purgare,* "to purge," "to purify," "to cleanse," from *purus,* "pure," and *agere,* "to make," "to do"). **1.** The act of purifying, cleansing, or exculpating (a) emotions, (b) guilt, or (c) moral defilement or sin. **2.** The state of being cleansed of such things listed in (**1**). See KATHARSIS.

purism. The insistence upon purity (nicety, singleness of taste, etc.) in things, for example in the use of words, or in the strict adherence to the letter of the law or to a sacred text.

Puritan ethic. Some of the views associated with the Puritan ethic: **1.** The highest human values to be got out of life are through hard physical work that has definite practical results for oneself and the community in which one lives. **2.** Living is a dedication to work, which produces, and is pervaded by, moral values such as industriousness, discipline, honesty, moderation, temperance, devotion, humility before God, frugality, thrift, simplicity, acceptance of toil, hardship, and pain, self-sufficiency, dedication to family life and to others in developing a sense of community, and awareness of the purpose and presence of God, from whom these values stem and for whom these values are expressed.

purpose (L., *pro*, "before," and *ponere*, "to place"). **1.** INTENTION. **2.** Design. **3.** That which one sets before oneself as an object (result, END, aim, plan) to be reached or attained. See TELEOLOGY.

putative (L., *putare*, "to reckon" "to suppose"). **1.** Supposed. **2.** Deemed or reputed to be the case. **3.** Disputable. Used in phrases such as "putative entities," "putative truth."

Pyrrhonism. Pyrrhonism generally connotes extreme SKEPTICISM. Refers to the doctrines of the Greek philosopher Pyrrho and his followers. Some of its main tenets: **1.** One must suspend judgment *(EPOCHĒ)* about the true nature of reality since all one can know are one's sensations and they are relative and inconsistent. **2.** Arguments can be given for any position one wishes to defend. **3.** One must accept the fact that one's knowledge is limited and be content not to inquire into more than can be known or comprehended. **4.** One must strive for *ATARAXIA*, an imperturbability of mind and body, an indifference *(APATHEIA)* stemming from the acceptance of whatever happens. **5.** The highest values in life are calmness, independence, and self-sufficiency.

Pythagoreanism. Refers to the doctrines of the Greek philosopher Pythagoras, and his followers, and to the general philosophic approach associated with Pythagoras' philosophy. Some of the basic beliefs associated with Pythagoreanism: **1.** The universe is an eternal rational unity: a ONE. **2.** It functions according to mathematical principles. **3.** Reality cannot be known by means of our senses but must be comprehended by seeing the universe as a rational, harmonious patterning of geometric forms, ratios, and numbers. **4.** The fundamental principles of the universe are limiting/unlimiting, order/disorder, odd/even, good/bad. **5.** The immaterial soul of the human being is a fragment of the WORLD SOUL. **6.** The soul is imprisoned (entombed) in the body and seeks to unite itself fully again with the World Soul. **7.** Souls transmigrate at death from one body to another body. **8.** Souls exist in all living things. **9.** Animals and beans must not be eaten. **10.** Moderation (see *MĒ AGAN*) in all things is a virtue. **11.** Knowledge of oneself (see *GNŌTHI SE AUTON*) is essential to righteous behavior.

Q

Q.E.D. Acronym for the Latin *quod erat demonstrandum,* "that which was to be demonstrated," sometimes used immediately before (or after) the conclusion much as we use the word *therefore*.

qua (L., "as," "as far as," "insofar as").

qualia (L., "quality," "property," "nature," "state," "kind," "condition"). Sometimes used as a synonym for SENSA. Often *SENSE QUALIA. Qualia* is the Latin plural but is used in English with either a singular or plural meaning. *Quale* or *qualis* is the Latin singular and refers to "of what kind or property" a thing is or has.

qualities, primary/secondary. 1. Primary qualities are (**a**) those qualities such as motion, rest, size (extension), shape (figure), solidity (impenetrability), number, structure, (**b**) which are believed to be inherent characteristics of matter in itself and not to depend for their existence on consciousness. **2.** Secondary qualities are those (**a**) sensed qualities such as of color, smell, taste, sound, heat, cold, (**b**) which are believed to be caused in us by the primary qualities inherent in matter and (**c**) which depend for their existence on the operations of the mind. Primary qualities exist in reality independently of an observer. Secondary qualities exist only as content in consciousness. This distinction has in general been made since the time of Leucippus and Democritus (see ATOMISM, GREEK), and was commonly accepted during the rise of modern science by thinkers such as Galileo, Boyle, Newton. The distinction in philosophy is mainly associated with Locke. See *NOMOS.*

qualities, tertiary (L., *tertiarus,* "containing a third part," and *qualis,* "the constitution of a thing"). Sometimes *tertiary values*. **1.** Qualities added by the mind to the primary and secondary qualities, constituting thus a third quality. Those qualities (or values) produced by the presence of a mind capable of appreciation, interest, selectivity, judgment, concentration; such as goodness, truth, beauty. **2.** Those interpretive and evaluating responses and reactions of consciousness (to the primary and secondary qualities) that are regarded as essential to human experience and to reality as are the primary and secondary qualities.

quality (L., *qualitas,* from *qualis,* "how constituted," "as a thing is"). **1.** That characteristic (**a**) which is possessed by a thing and (**b**) by which the thing is recognizable. For example, sweetness is a quality of honey. **2.** That content of consciousness usually associated with external objects produced by physical stimuli. For example, sweetness is not a quality of honey but a quality of consciousness produced by physical processes.

PROPERTY, ATTRIBUTE, CHARACTERISTIC are a few of the words used as synonyms for quality. In many respects, quality may be regarded as having the most general meaning. A *property* is often thought of as a special or particular quality. An *attribute* is often used in the context of an inherent, essential, or necessary quality. A *characteristic* usually refers to a distinctive (distinguishing) quality or property or to a typical quality or property.

quality (Kant). See CATEGORIES OF LOGIC, THE (KANT); CATEGORIES OF THE UNDERSTANDING, THE (KANT).

quality (logic). In traditional categorical logic, quality refers to whether a categorical statement is affirmative or negative.

quality, accidental. A nonessential, incidental, or fortuitous quality. See ACCIDENTAL ATTRIBUTE.

quality, emergent. See EMERGENT, AN.

quantification, suppressed. A form of ambiguity where in ordinary conversation we do not know whether the word or sentence refers to all members of a class or only to some. Example: "Children are naughty." It is unclear whether "All children are naughty" or "Some children are naughty" is meant. See entries under AMBIGUITY.

quantifier (logic). A word (symbol, sign) that indicates "all," "some," or "no."

quantifier shift fallacy. The fallacy of confusing universal and particular (existential) quantities in an argument or inference. Example: Inferring the statement "All those who don't mind taking exams are good students" from the statement "All good students don't mind taking exams." See entries under FALLACY.

quantity (Kant). See CATEGORIES OF LOGIC, THE (KANT); CATEGORIES OF THE UNDERSTANDING, THE (KANT).

quantity (logic). In traditional categorical logic, quantity refers to whether a categorical statement is universal or particular.

quiddity (L., *quidditas,* "the whatness of a thing," from *quid,* "what"). **1.** The essence ("whatness") of a thing; that which answers the question *"Quid est?"* ("What is it?") and therefore serves as the essential distinguishing characteristic in its definition. **2.** Often used in ordinary English to mean a trivial nicety or a quibble.

quintessence (L., "the fifth essence," from *quinta,* "fifth," and *essentia,* "essence"). **1.** Used by the Scholastics to name the eternal and immutable celestial objects in Aristotle's superlunary world. In Aristotelianism the purest and highest essence found anywhere is possessed by celestial bodies, which were regarded as a fifth element following the traditional four: earth, air, fire, water. See ELEMENTS, THE FOUR. **2.** Also used by the Scholastics to refer to the highest and most nearly perfect essence or power possessed by a natural body. **3.** Used in English to mean the finest or the most nearly perfect example of something.

R

random. 1. Aimless. Without a definite direction, order, purpose, system, method, aim. **2.** Happening by CHANCE or haphazardly. Related words: casual, fortuitous, accidental, spontaneous.

ratio (L., "reason," from *reri, ratus,* "to reckon," "to think"). Used in a general philosophic sense to refer to the human ability to discriminate, to identify, and to relate things.

    In medieval philosophy, *ratio* (reason) was usually distinguished from *intellectus* (intelligence). *Ratio* leads one to practical action and to a commonsense view of the world and exists prior to the development or activity of human intelligence. *Intellectus* is the foundation for theorizing, speculating, abstracting, inferring, and contemplating. See entries under INTELLECTUS.

ratiocination (L., *ratiocinatus,* past participle of *ratiocinari,* from *ratio,* "reason"). **1.** Reasoning. The mental process of logical or exact thinking. **2.** Proof. The specific logical demonstration of the reasoning leading to a conclusion.

rational (L., *rationalis,* "rational," from *ratio,* "reason"). **1.** Containing, or possessing REASON or characterized by reason. **2.** Capable of functioning rationally or participating in rational inquiry. **3.** Capable of being understood. **4.** In conformity with reason. Intelligible. Sensible. Reasonable. **5.** Adhering to qualities of thought such as consistency, coherence, simplicity, abstractness, completeness, order, logical structure.

rational self-interest. Also *enlightened self-interest.* See EGOISM, ALTRUISTIC; EGOISM, ETHICAL.

rationale (L., *rationale,* neuter form of *rationalis,* "rational"). **1.** An explanation of the basic principles used in the support of an idea, hypothesis, opinion, theory, etc., or **2.** the basic principles themselves.

rationalism. In general, the philosophic approach which emphasizes reason as the primary source of knowledge, prior or superior to, and independent of, sense perceptions. Some main tenets: **1.** By the process of abstract reasoning (thinking) we can arrive at fundamental, undeniable truths **(a)** about what exists and about its structure, and **(b)** about the universe in general. **2.** Reality is knowable—or some truths about reality are knowable—independently of observation, experience, and the use of empirical methods. **3.** The mind is capable of knowing some truths about reality that are prior to any experience (but which are not analytic truths). These truths are innate ideas and isomorphically conform with reality. **4.** Reason is the principal origin of knowledge, and science is basically a rationally conceived deductive system only indirectly connected with sense experience. **5.** Truth is not tested by sense-verification procedures, but by such criteria as logical consistency. See TRUTH, COHERENCE THEORY OF. **6.** There is a rational (deductive, logicomathematical, inferential) method that can be applied to any subject matter whatsoever and that can provide us with adequate explanations. **7.** Absolute certainty about things is the ideal of knowledge and is attainable to some extent by finite minds. Absolute certainty (and necessity) is the essential characteristic both of reality and of all true knowledge. **8.** Only those necessary and self-evident truths derived from reason alone can be known as true, real, and certain; all else is subject to falsification, illusion, and uncertainty. **9.** The universe (reality) follows the laws and rationality (form) of logic. The universe is a rationally (logically) designed system whose order conforms to logic. **10.** Once this logic is mastered, all things in the universe can be seen to be deducible from its principles or laws. Contrasted with schools of thought such as EMPIRICISM; POSITIVISM, LOGICAL; INTUITIONISM; revelationism.

Rationalists, Continental (European). Notably René Descartes, Benedict Baruch Spinoza, and Gottfried Wilhelm Leibniz.

rationalize. 1. The positive sense: to make rational or to endow something with reason or reasonableness. **2.** The pejorative sense; to present what one wants to appear as a good rational justification for a belief or action that in truth **(a)** has no good justification, and/or **(b)** has another more plausible but embarrassing justification. The reasons given in a rationalization are usually untruthful inventions that are more acceptable to one's ego than the truth. See ETHICS; CASUISTIC.

rationes seminales/causales (L., "seminal reasons" or "causal reasons"). Refers to the physical powers (tendencies or "seeds") potentially present in matter. Material things are analogous to seeds. Seeds contain within themselves the potential (the potency) to become the fully matured plant.

So material things are in a latent state, ready to receive the right conditions for their full development. The Latin equivalent of *LOGOS SPERMATIKOS*.

real (L., *realis,* "real," from *res,* "a thing"). **1.** Actually existing apart from our perception. True. Having substantive or objective existence. Opposite to fictitious, false, erroneous, imaginary, illusory, unreal, seeming, apparent, appearance, phantasm, fantasy, artificial. **2.** Existing inherently in the thing itself, for example as an ESSENCE or as a structure, and not as we see it in appearance. **3.** Actuality. An actual situation. That which is now occurring, not a past, future, or theoretical occurrence. Opposite to IDEAL, HYPOTHETICAL, POTENTIAL, POSSIBLE. Related to positive, actual, authentic, verifiable, veritable, genuine, factual, external.

real definition. See DEFINITION, TYPES OF (**5** and **16**).

real dispute. See VERBAL DISPUTE.

realism. 1. The attempt to see things as they are without idealization, speculation, or idolization. **2.** The dedication to facts regardless of how unpleasant they may be.

Realism can be interested in how things *ought* to be, but only after an honest and objective assessment of how things *are* in fact. See also UNIVERSALS (REALISM).

realism, Aristotelian. The theory that universals (essences, abstractions, general terms) **1.** exist only within objects in the external world (as opposed to a world or realm of ideas); **2.** exist independently of our perception of them; **3.** our intellect abstracts them from our sense perceptions of the objects in which they inhere; and **4.** this resulting abstraction is the foundation for our knowledge of reality. See UNIVERSALS (ARISTOTLE).

realism, commonsense. 1. The attempt to provide a justification for the (realistic) beliefs of the ordinary (common) person which are derived from his everyday experiences of the world around him. **2.** The view that the external world is as it appears to us. Often referred to as *direct realism* or *natural realism.* Both meanings are associated with Thomas Reid's Scottish School of commonsense philosophy.

realism, epistemological. 1. The theory that universals (essences, abstract concepts, general terms, relations) exist in reality independently of our consciousness—or of any consciousness. Universals exist in the external world even when not perceived. Opposite to NOMINALISM. For most realists, these externally objectively existing universals have more reality than the concrete, particular objects in which they are seen, or from which they are abstracted. **2.** The theory that that which is known *about* a thing exists (in essential respects the same way) *in* the thing known, and would exist without the knower. Compare with CONCEPTUALISM.

realism, naive. The belief that the world is as we perceive it. There is no distinction between what the world appears to be like (appearance) and what the world is really like (reality). Sense data impart correct (accurate, true) information about things. See MONISM, EPISTEMOLOGICAL. Often used in a pejorative sense.

realism, personal. The theory that personality (**a**) is the real ground for the sustenance of all existing things, (**b**) is present as an active presence in all things, and (**c**) can be known directly in an intuitive apprehension or identification with things in nature. See PERSONALISM.

realism, Platonic. Universals (forms, essences, ideas, abstractions, general terms) such as "humanity," "redness," "circularity," "beauty" **1.** exist in the external world (or in a realm of perfect forms) independently of our perception of them; **2.** are unchanging and eternal; **3.** have a greater reality than our sense perceptions or than external material objects; **4.** are the causal agents (or the models for) the existence of particular objects (are the reasons why objects are as they are rather than being some other way); and **5.** are the means by which reason recognizes contrasts, and identifies things and thereby gains knowledge. See UNIVERSALS (PLATO).

reality. 1. That which is. Opposite to APPEARANCE. **2.** Everything that is. The sum total of all that exists. The UNIVERSE. **3.** All that which exists apart from CONSCIOUSNESS.

reality, objective and formal. Objective reality is the external reality to which our language and perceptions refer and is contrasted with formal reality, which refers to the modes of thought employed in understanding reality and/or to the logical interrelationships of ideas as ideas. See OBJECTIVE EXISTENCE (REALITY).

reason. 1. The intellect. The capacity to abstract, comprehend, relate, reflect, notice similarities and differences, etc. **2.** The ability to infer.

Reason when thought of as a FACULTY is contrasted with the faculty of the will, the faculty of appetition, the faculty of sentience, the faculty of intuition, etc., and is usually believed to be a characteristic of humans and not of lower animals. Reason is regarded as distinct from FAITH, REVELATION, INTUITION, EMOTION, FEELING, sentiments, sensations, perceptions, experience. See INTELLECT; UNDERSTANDING.

reason (Kant). 1. Reason is one of two intellectual faculties. Understanding is the other. See UNDERSTANDING (KANT). Understanding innately possesses *A PRIORI* ideas by which it structures experience (or reality). These ideas cannot be derived from our experience, nor are they found in pure experience. See KNOWLEDGE, SYNTHETIC *A PRIORI* (KANT). **2.** Reason in contrast to understanding is an active principle driven by an impossible demand to transcend the limitations of all human experience and arrive at a comprehension of an absolutely unconditional and all-inclusive reality. **3.** Reason must be content (**a**) to be the overseer of what is possible and what is impossible for the understanding to know, and (**b**) to examine and apply all the possible ways by which experience can be structured and made empirical.

reason, active/passive (Aristotle). Also active/passive intellect. The active reason enables the passive reason to acquire the sensible form or image *(PHANTASMA)* of the object being sensed or perceived. The active reason must make the phantasm explicit to awareness by means of abstracting it from sense experience. See *NOUS PATHETIKOS* (ARISTOTELIANISM); UNIVERSALS (ARISTOTLE); VIRTUES, DIANOETIC (ARISTOTLE).

reason, insufficient. See INDIFFERENCE, PRINCIPLE OF (PROBABILITY THEORY).

reason, postulates of practical (Kant). See POSTULATES OF PRACTICAL REASON, THE (KANT).

reason, practical (Aristotle). 1. The faculty with which we perceive (a) what means are available to us in order to achieve a goal, (b) which among these means are the most efficient and/or the most appropriate, and (c) how to employ these means in actual conduct. **2.** Deliberation (reasoning, thinking) about (a) what we will do and (b) what we will not do, that results in a decision (choice, action, resolution). See KNOWLEDGE (ARISTOTLE); *PRAXIS.*

reason, practical (Kant). 1. Reason that originates knowledge about moral conduct (and is also the source of religious feelings and intuitions). **2.** Reason that reflects on the possibilities provided us by freedom of the will. Contrast with REASON, THEORETICAL (KANT); REASON, PURE (KANT).

reason, principle of nonsufficient. The chances (probability) of two things happening can be regarded as being the same if there are no good (sufficient) reasons for saying that they are not the same, that one will happen rather than the other. See INDIFFERENCE, PRINCIPLE OF (PROBABILITY THEORY).

reason, principle of sufficient. 1. All things (objects, events, changes, causes) are (a) related to each other in a necessary relationship (by necessity); (b) require each other in that relationship; (c) cannot be other than what they are; and (d) there is a reason for all this. **2.** All things are what they are because that is the best rational way for them to be. **3.** All things occur for a reason and (a) would not occur unless that reason existed and (b) would be different if their reason for being were different. See *AITIA.*

reason, principle of sufficient (Leibniz). Leibniz held to three principles: The *Principle of the Best* or of *Perfection* (see BEST OF ALL POSSIBLE WORLDS, THE [LEIBNIZ]), which he applied to all actuality as opposed to possibility; the *Principle of Noncontradiction,* which he regarded as the foundation of all necessary truths (the truths of logic or reason); and the *Principle of Sufficient Reason,* the basis of all contingent events in the universe, of all matters of fact.

The Principle of Sufficient Reason asserts that nothing happens in the universe without a reason for its happening that way rather than another way. There is a reason why an object is that object and not another. (Humans are not able to comprehend all such sufficient reasons for the occurrence of events, but if they knew all things sufficiently they could give a reason why things are as they are and not otherwise, why the universe is the way it is rather than its being some other kind of universe.)

The main arguments for the Principle of Sufficient Reason: Since no two things can ever be identical (see IDENTITY OF INDISCERNIBLES, PRINCIPLE OF [LEIBNIZ]), there must be a reason for this, and that reason must exist in (and have been put into) the very being of things. For Leibniz, the sufficient reason for things and for the universe exists (must exist) outside the infinite series of contingent events. The ultimate sufficient reason subsists in a necessary substance, or MONAD (God), the source of all the (rational) activity of the universe and of its necessitation.

reason, pure (Kant). Reason functioning on its own without relationships with other faculties of consciousness such as will or appetition. Contrast with REASON, PRACTICAL (KANT); REASON, THEORETICAL (KANT).

reason, theoretical (Aristotle). Sometimes *contemplation*. **1.** Reasoning or thinking in order to arrive at knowledge (**a**) of what is the case, (**b**) of what inevitably or necessarily must be the case, and (**c**) of what possibly may be the case (*if* certain conditions occur). This activity results in a conclusion (statement, knowledge, action) of some sort. **2.** The faculty with which **1** is done. See KNOWLEDGE (ARISTOTLE).

reason, theoretical (Kant). Reason that constructs intellectual knowledge, such as scientific knowledge. Contrast with REASON, PRACTICAL (KANT); REASON, PURE (KANT.)

reason, universal. See *LOGOS*.

reasoning. 1. The process of inferring conclusions from statements. **2.** The application of logic and/or abstract thought patterns in the solution of problems or the act of planning. **3.** The ability to know some things without recourse directly to sense perceptions or immediate experience.

Reasoning is one kind of thinking (or state of consciousness) that can be contrasted with others, such as daydreaming, dreaming, imagining, remembering, intuiting, imaging, perceiving, sensing, doubting, suppressing, inhibiting, controlling, selecting, deceiving. It is possible that some element or form of reasoning can be involved in any of these. Reasoning can be used for a variety of purposes: to deceive, to argue, to debate, to doubt, to persuade, to express, to explain, to apologize, to rationalize, etc. It seems that any form of conscious activity can be affected and structured by the reasoning process.

reasoning, analogical. See ANALOGICAL REASONING.

reasoning, discursive. The process of proceeding from premises to a conclusion.

reasons. 1. Statements used in support of a conclusion, or an idea, or a fact. That rational JUSTIFICATION which makes something intelligible. **2.** Statements made to explain purposive actions, or goal-oriented activity.

3. Sometimes used as a synonym for "causes" (see CAUSE), as in the statement "The reasons for the rain are . . . " but "reasons" may be distinguished from "causes" in two principal ways: **(a)** The time at which reasons are offered is not necessarily synchronous with the actually operating cause. Reasons can be provided before, after, or during the operation of the cause. **(b)** Reasons are explanatory and are not physically or causally relevant to the occurrence of a causal series.

receptivity (L., *recipere*, "to take back," from *re*, "again," and *capere*, "to take," "to seize"). **1.** In general, the passive process of COGNITION, ranging anywhere from sense experience to abstract thought. Usually contrasted with creativity, physical activity, intentional actions. **2.** Specifically, receiving sensations (impressions, ideas, images) in the act of knowing **(a)** as opposed to forming those sensations into concepts and/or **(b)** as opposed to formulating abstract concepts.

reciprocity (ethics). The giving in return of equal good (rights, benefits) for the good received.

recognition (L., *recognitio*, from *re*, "again," and *cognitio*, "knowledge," and from *recognoscere*, "to know once again"). **1.** The acknowledgment of the knowledge and/or identity of something. **2.** The acknowledgment that something known and/or identified has been part of one's previous awareness.

recollection (L., *recollectus*, "recollect," past participle of *recolligere*, "to collect," from *re*, "again," *col*, the assimilated form of *com*, "with," and *legere*, "to gather"). **1.** Remembrance. The ability to remember, to use one's memory or to recall something. **2.** That which is remembered.

Recollection is often used interchangeably with remembrance, REMINISCENCE, or MEMORY. *Recollection* implies a deliberate conscious effort to remember or to recall something to consciousness. *Remembrance* often connotes the condition of being kept in consciousness. *Reminiscence,* used more in the plural, now suggests a retrospective recall of items in our consciousness about the past and usually ones that have some significance or sentimental attachments. *Memory* is a general term for anything brought to consciousness about the past and is believed by common sense to be a mental reproduction of past experiences. See *ANAMNĒSIS.*

recta ratio (L., "right or correct reason," referring to the Law [Necessity] of Nature). The Latin equivalent of *LOGOS ORTHOS.* See entries under LAW, NATURAL.

recurrence, eternal. Also *eternal return* or *eternal reemergence.* **1.** The belief that all events in the universe **(a)** have occurred an infinite number of times in the past in their exact details and order, and **(b)** will so occur again an infinite number of times in the future. **2.** The repetition of general cyclic patterns in the universe: the seasons; day and night; birth and death; plant growth and decay; order out of chaos. **3.** The unending emergence of an ordered universe out of a state of chaos into which the ordered universe continually dissolves to reemerge. See CONFLAGRATION (STOICS); STOICS, THE.

recursive (L., *recurrere,* "to run back," from *re,* "again," and *currere,* "to run"). Referring to a procedure that can be continued without end unless something is specified to terminate it.

recursive definition. See DEFINITION, TYPES OF (17).

reductio ad absurdum (L., "reduction to absurdity" or "reducing to absurdity"). A method of arguing in which a statement is established as true because its falsity leads to absurd, unacceptable, or contradictory conclusions. In formal deductive reasoning, the procedure is as follows: (a) Negate the conclusion of the argument. (b) Add this negated conclusion to the premises (which are accepted as true). (c) Deduce a contradiction from these premises which include the negated conclusion. (d) If such a contradiction can be derived, then the initial argument is valid, the original conclusion logically follows from the original premises. We have in effect shown that the negation of the conclusion leads to something that is necessarily false or absurd. See DIALECTIC (ZENO).

reductio ad absurdum, **principle of.** That which implies its own denial is always false.

reductio ad impossibile (L., "the reduction to an impossibility" or "reducing to the impossible"). Refers to the method of arguing for the truth of a statement by proving that its negation (or nonacceptance) leads to impossible statements and unacceptable consequences.

reductionism/reductivism. 1. In the philosophy of science, the belief that all fields of knowledge can be reduced to one type of methodology, or to one science, which encompasses principles applicable to all phenomena. (Physics has been considered as that basic science to which all other sciences can be reduced and of which they are extensions.) **2.** In metaphysics, the belief that all things can be reduced to one kind of thing (substance, process, matter, God, form, idea) that is ultimate, necessary, and the most real.

reductive fallacy. Also the *"nothing but" fallacy.* Sometimes referred to as the *naturalistic fallacy.* **1.** Erroneously believing (a) that a complex whole is nothing but, or identical with, its parts or causes, and/or (b) that a complex whole can be entirely explained in terms of the description of its parts or causes. Example: Mental states are caused by neural processes. Neural processes can exist without the occurrence of mental states. Therefore mental states are nothing but neural processes. **2.** The error of explaining a phenomenon and regarding its explanation as being real rather than the phenomenon being explained. Compare with the *genetic fallacy* in FALLACY, TYPES OF INFORMAL (39).

reductive materialism. See MATERIALISM, REDUCTIVE.

reductive mechanism. See MECHANISM.

reference (L., *re,* "again," and *ferre,* "to bear"). **1.** The relation to something. **2.** REFERENT. That which is referred to. **3.** Designation. That which is indicated or signified by a word.

reference, transsubjective. Also *objective reference, transcendental reference.* The reference of an idea to some independently existing external object.

referent. That to which something refers.

reflect (L., *reflectere,* "to bend back," from *re,* "again," and *flectere,* "to bend"). **1.** To consider. To think seriously about. Ponder. **2.** To contemplate or think about. **3.** To concentrate one's thoughts back upon a problem or idea.

reflection (Locke). Used interchangeably with most meanings of INTROSPECTION. Reflection is the source of our awareness of our existence and mental states and activities such as perceiving, reasoning, thinking, believing, willing, hearing, touching, seeing. Reflection coupled with sensation provides us with the complex ideas such as of active tendencies, powers, identity, unity, solidity, extension, pleasure, pain, substance, infinity, cause and effect, etc. See IDEAS OF REFLECTION (LOCKE); and other entries under IDEAS with reference to Locke.

reflexive (L., *reflectere,* "to bend back"). **1.** Referring to that which is, or can be directed (reflected) back to the subject or to a thing. **2.** Referring to any expression whose meaning can be applied to any of its terms.

refutation (L., *refutare,* "to refute," "to repel"). A denial. Usually a formal disproof of an argument or statement showing its falsity or error. Sometimes, showing that some assertion has not been supported correctly or proved true. See COUNTEREXAMPLE, METHOD OF.

regulative principle. See PRINCIPLE, REGULATIVE.

rehabilitative theory of punishment. See PUNISHMENT, REHABILITATIVE THEORY OF.

reification/reism (L., *res,* "a thing"). Sometimes *concretism.* The fallacy of taking abstractions and regarding them as actually existing entities that are causally efficacious and ontologically prior and superior to their referents. Example: Taking the noun *good* to refer to an actually existing entity (much as the word *table* refers to an actual individual entity) that exists objectively as a cause for good things or that exists as an ideal standard in another realm to be imitated. Often used interchangeably with HYPOSTATIZATION. See CONCRETENESS, FALLACY OF MISPLACED (WHITEHEAD).

reincarnation (L., *re,* "again," and *incarnere,* "to incarnate," from *in,* "in," and *caro,* "flesh"). Literally, to again become flesh. Synonymous with METEMPSYCHOSIS and TRANSMIGRATION.

relation (L., *relatio,* "relation"). **1.** Connection. **2.** Qualities predicable of two or more things taken together. **3.** An ordering of two or more things.

relation (Kant). See CATEGORIES OF LOGIC, THE (KANT); CATEGORIES OF THE UNDERSTANDING, THE (KANT).

relations, doctrine of internal. 1. The theory that (**a**) a thing is what it is because its relations with other things (and especially the whole of which it is a part) are what they are. (No thing, or no part of a thing, would be what it is unless its relations to other things were exactly what they are.); (**b**) A thing is what it is because its relations with other things (and especially the whole of which it is a part) are not different from what they are and have been. (No thing, or no part of a thing, would be what it is if its relations to other things were different from what they in fact are and have been.) **2.** The view that all events in the universe are causally related to all other events. To know the truth of any event in the universe, one must know all the causes operating on it, hence all that is happening in the universe. **3.** All relations are inherent in the nature (essence) of the things being related.

relations, external. Things are related externally if the relationship expressed about them is not essential to, or does not directly affect, their natures (or our understanding of the terms involved). Example: "The car is near the house." Contrasted with RELATIONS, INTERNAL.

relations, internal. Things are related internally if the relationship expressed about them is essential to, or directly affects, their natures (or our understanding of the terms involved). Example: "Human beings are rational animals." Contrasted with RELATIONS, EXTERNAL.

relativism (value theory). The theory that values: **1.** differ from society to society, person to person, **2.** are conditioned by the peculiarities of the society in which they arise, **3.** are not universally applicable at all times or in all places, **4.** are correct or incorrect, desirable or undesirable only relative to whether or not they conform to a common norm or to common acceptance. Opposite to ABSOLUTISM. See SUBJECTIVISM (VALUE THEORY). Contrast with OBJECTIVISM (VALUE THEORY).

relativism, Protagorean. A theory about the relativity of knowledge and the RELATIVITY OF SENSE PERCEPTION. Often referred to as the *homo mensura* (man is the measure) theory based on a saying attributed to Protagoras the Sophist: "Man is the measure of all things; of things that are that they are, and of things that are not that they are not." Some of the beliefs in Protagorean relativism: **1.** What is perceived is as it is perceived by the perceiver. **2.** What is perceived is true to the perceiver. **3.** Truth is identical to what is perceived and relative to the physical condition of the perceiver. **4.** Given different organs of sense, what is perceived will be different and what is regarded as true will be different. **5.** Truth does not exist independently of a perceiver and his assertion that something is true. **6.** It is erroneous to say that one person is right (has the truth) and another person is wrong (does not have the truth) about sense perception. **7.** Whenever truth is not related to perception and people agree about it, then it can be seen to be based upon a common agreement or consent to call that thing true and not upon any descriptive state of affairs. Examples of some of the above points: X says "The wind is cold." Y says "The wind is warm." Neither statement is incorrect. Neither X nor Y is uttering false statements. Both statements are true relative to how X and Y perceive (feel) the wind. No method or standard exists which transcends those perceptions and which can be used to determine which statement is true and which is false. See APPEARANCE/REALITY; SOPHISTS.

relativity of sense perception. The relativity of sense perception is supported by arguments such as the following (which are also used to support the distinction between APPEARANCE/REALITY): **1.** The same thing sometimes appears differently to the same person. A raincoat appears black in the classroom. The same raincoat appears purple in the moonlight on a rainy night. **2.** The same thing sometimes appears differently to different persons. The raincoat appears black to me but yellow to my neighbor who is color blind. **3.** Sensed qualities such as color, odor, heat are not qualities which inhere in the objects we are perceiving, but are qualities (appearances) relative to the structures of our sense organs. What we sense or is produced in us is thus contrasted with what is really "out there" in reality such as atoms in motion, empty space. See QUALITIES, PRIMARY/SECONDARY. **4.** What we perceive cannot be what a thing is like at the moment we are perceiving it since it takes time for perception to occur and the reality of the thing has in the meantime changed. Example: The sun as we *perceive* it now is not the sun as it *is* now, but is merely an appearance of what it was eight minutes ago, or more accurately, an appearance caused by an unknown (and unknowable) reality that existed eight minutes ago. See RELATIVISM, PROTAGOREAN.

relatum **of a relation.** The term to which a relation goes. In the statement "Jane is the wife of Ralph," "Ralph" is the *relatum*.

relevancy. 1. The relationship that exists among **(a)** terms (ideas, concepts, words) such that they can be related to each other to form meaningful statements (or further meaningful ideas, concepts, words) and/or **(b)** terms that are classified as members within the same class of meanings. **2.** In inductive logic, the degree (probability) of reasonable expectation that one thing will be, or is, empirically (or causally) related with another thing.

religion, philosophy of. The central questions studied in the philosophy of religion: **1.** The definitions of religion. **2.** The varieties of God concepts. **3.** The definitions of God and his characteristics. **4.** The arguments for God's existence; their variety and validity. **5.** The meanings and the interrelationship of faith, reason, revelation, dogma. **6.** The nature, value, and validity of mysticism and the religious experience. **7.** The meaning and use of religious language. **8.** The existence of immortality. **9.** The source and sanction of morality in religious thought. **10.** The relationship between church and state, philosophy and religion, science and religion. **11.** Is there a divine cosmic purpose?

religion, types of definitions of. The definitions of religions vary between two poles: total reference to supernaturalism (religion is the belief in and worship of a divine transcendent reality that creates and controls all things without deviation from its will) and total reference to humanistic ideals (religion is any attempt to construct ideals and values toward which one can enthusiastically strive and with which one can regulate one's conduct).

religious experience. The characterization of the religious experience takes a variety of forms from **1.** the view that the experience is of an object, that one directly confronts a divine being (see MYSTICISM) to **2.** the view that the religious experience refers not to an object but to a *quality* of experience, to a consummatory or peak experience in which one feels actualized or in which one becomes ecstatically aware of one's highest ideals and aspirations. See MYSTICAL EXPERIENCE.

reminiscence (L., *reminisci,* "to recollect"). **1.** Remembrance. The act of recalling experiences. **2.** RECOLLECTION. That which is remembered. **3.** ANAMNĒSIS.

reminiscence (recollection/remembrance), Plato's doctrine of. See ANAMNĒSIS (2).

reportive definition. See DEFINITION, TYPES OF (9).

representation (L., *repraesentare,* "to represent," from *re,* "again," and *praeesse,* "to be before"). A likeness of. A picture, copy, or model of.

representative perception, theory of. See PERCEPTION, REPRESENTATIVE THEORY OF.

representative theory of meaning. See MEANING, REPRESENTATIVE THEORY OF.

res cogitans (L., "a thinking thing," "a thinking being," "a thinking self"). A phrase principally used by Descartes to signify "thinking substance" in contradistinction to RES EXTENSA which signified "extended (material) substance." This thinking substance for Descartes referred to both the individual mind or thinking self and to that spiritual thing or soul that served as the underlying pervading ground for all individual minds or thinking selves. See ENS.

resemblance, family. See FAMILY RESEMBLANCE.

res extensa (L., "an extended thing," "a material thing," "material being"). A phrase principally used by Descartes to signify "material (physical) substance" in contradistinction to RES COGITANS, which signified "thinking substance." This material substance for Descartes referred to the underlying ground for all material (mechanical) change in the universe and possessed no characteristics of mind or life.

residues, method of. See METHODS, MILL'S INDUCTIVE.

responsibility. The concept of responsibility is grounded on notions such as the following: **1.** OBLIGATION. There are actions that a rational being must and can perform. **2.** Liability. One's neglect of these actions is punishable. **3.** One's observance of these actions is subject to reward (honor, praise).

All three notions are based on the view (**a**) that human motives are causes of behavior; (**b**) that they can be conditioned (controlled, affected, modified) by such things as reward and punishment; and (possibly) (**c**) such motives must and should be conditioned. Related to the concepts of *answerability, accountability,* and *self-control.*

retributive justice. See JUSTICE, RETRIBUTIVE.

retributive theory of punishment. See PUNISHMENT, RETRIBUTIVE THEORY OF.

retrospection (L., *retrospicere,* "to look back," from *retro,* "back," and *specere,* "to look"). **1.** The ability to reflect, or the act of reflecting (looking back) on things past and/or on past items or operations of consciousness. **2.** The remembering of past mental states and functions in an attempt to describe them. An act of INTROSPECTION but not of what are regarded as presently occurring mental events. See EXTRASPECTION; REFLECTION.

return, eternal. See RECURRENCE, ETERNAL.

rhetoric (Gk., *hretorikē,* "rhetoric," "the art of oratory," from *hrētōr,* "orator," "rhetorician," "public speaker," "pleader"). **1.** The art of expressive, persuasive speech and argumentation. **2.** The art of using eloquent (elegant) language to impress as well as to persuade. See *SOPHISTĒS.*

right. 1. That which one has due to him. **2.** That upon which one has a just demand. **3.** That to which one has a proper claim. **4.** The privilege (freedom or power) given to one, sanctioned and safeguarded by what is regarded as an authoritative source such as God, a king, law, a social group, custom, tradition, conscience.

right, moral. The right to perform certain activities (**a**) because they conform to the accepted standards or ideas of a community (or of a law, or of God, or of conscience), or (**b**) because they will not harm, coerce, restrain, or infringe upon the interests of others, or (**c**) because there are good rational arguments in support of the value of such activities.

right, political. The power (right) to perform certain activities in a politically organized society such as to run for office, vote, petition, lobby, communicate with and criticize public officials, speak out and not be censured, express and defend one's beliefs, protect one's property.

right reason. See *LOGOS ORTHOS.*

rights, civil. Those rights granted to citizens of a community by the power of its legal and legislative authorities.

rights, human. Those rights (claims, needs, ideals) to be achieved by individuals and/or provided by society such as a good education, decent housing, healthcare, a secure job, an adequate standard of living, freedom from interference in the pursuit of goals, freedom from oppression, equality of opportunity.

rights, inalienable. Rights which are natural, innate, incapable of being denied. Their source and inviolability are considered beyond civil, political, legal, or other forms of rights, and universally possessed by all humans. Example: the right to protect one's life or property.

rights, legal. 1. The power (right) to use the legal system for things such as (**a**) defense against charges, (**b**) claims against others, (**c**) protection against others, (**d**) the change and/or correction of laws. **2.** The right to equality of treatment under law with respect to (**1**).

rights, natural. Freedoms (privileges, prerogatives, powers, claims) possessed innately (see RIGHTS, INALIENABLE) and/or assumed by the very fact of being a human being. Contrasted with RIGHTS, CIVIL. Lists of natural rights usually include life, liberty, equality, the pursuit of happiness, ownership of property, the right to work, equality of opportunity, equality of treatment under law.

It is generally held that both natural rights and civil rights constitute the foundation of social justice. It is sometimes held that natural rights and inalienable rights are really forms of civil rights. In either case governments are the principal means of protecting and maintaining any system of rights.

romanticism. An expression of a romantic temperament, or the product of that temperament, in the history of art and of philosophy (and in other fields). Some of the qualities and characteristics associated with romanticism: **1.** A stress on immediate sensation and the intense feelings aroused by nature and by events in it. **2.** A tendency to personify nature (Mother Earth, World Spirit) and to identify emotionally with its processes and forces. **3.** An emphasis on the uniqueness, the importance and ultimate sacredness of the individual and his powers. **4.** A distaste for the orderly, rational, intellectual, and moderate. A lust for spontaneity, disorder, variety, unpredictability, uncertainty, rebellion, the wild, the fanciful, the extravagant, the strange, the atypical, the novel, the eccentric. Compare with DIONYSIAN SPIRIT. **5.** A drive for freedom: freedom from restraint as an individual and as an artist, freedom of the artist to treat his subject matter as openly, honestly, and candidly as he wishes, freedom to rebel from anything an artist regards as a suffocating hold of the past. Contrasted with CLASSICISM.

rule, semantical. A METALINGUISTIC rule that says something about the meaning of symbols (words, expressions) used in an object language.

S

same and other, problem of the. See IDENTITY, PROBLEM OF.

sameness. 1. IDENTITY. 2. Similarity. 3. Uniformity of kind.

sanction (L., *sanctio,* from *sancire,* "to make sacred," "to fix unalterably").
1. That which obligates and hence motivates someone to act or not to act
in accordance with a precept or rule. 2. A binding force (influence, power) which induces conformity to or observance of such things as a law, a
moral command, a custom, a mode of behavior. A "sanction" may refer
to, or be given by, an authority, peer or social pressure, institutions, God,
conscience, a sense of duty.

satire (L., *satira,* from *satura,* "a dish filled with a variety of fruit," "a
medley," from *saturatus,* "sated," or from *satis,* "enough"). Some form
of artistic expression that ridicules in a cutting way what is considered to
be abuse, vice, foolishness. See SOCRATIC IRONY.

scepticism. See entries under SKEPTICISM.

schema (Gk., *schema,* "form," "shape," "figure," "outline," "plan"). The
plural is schemata. 1. In traditional categorical logic, the figure of a syllogism. 2. In metaphysics, the application upon our experiences of the
forms (categories, intuitions, innate ideas, etc.) by which things are understood. 3. In epistemology, the application of concepts according to
rules in order to organize and/or formulate the content of our experience.

schism (Gk., *schisma,* "a division of opinion," from *schizein,* "to split," "to
cleave," "to separate"). 1. A division of belief within a group or institution that leads to factions and possible separation. 2. The actual separation (secession) of a faction.

Scholasticism (Gk., *scholastikos,* "enjoying leisure," "devoting one's leisure time to learning," "a scholar," from *scholazein,* "to have leisure or time to do a thing," or "to keep a school," "to devote oneself to studies").

Scholasticism is used historically **1.** to refer to the entire medieval Christian movement in Western philosophy, beginning as early as the fifth century with St. Augustine and lasting until the mid-seventeenth century, or **2.** to refer to medieval Christian philosophy between A.D. 1000, about the time of St. Anselm, and about A.D. 1300, shortly after St. Thomas Aquinas. (Some other important figures of the period: Peter Abelard, Peter Lombard, Bernard of Clairvaux, John of Salisbury, Alexander of Hales, St. Bonaventure, Albertus Magnus, Duns Scotus, William of Ockham. During this time there was a resurgence of interest in logical and rational inquiry, stemming from new translations of Greek texts, especially those of Plato and Aristotle, that were being introduced through Arabic sources.)

Scholasticism was characterized by **(a)** an intense interest in logical and linguistic analysis, in order to **(b)** create a systematic presentation and defense of Christian belief based on **(c)** the Bible as the revealed word of God; **(d)** The Church's authoritative interpretation and extension of the Bible; and **(e)** the accepted knowledge of past Christian writers. Some of the principal trends in Scholasticism were (1) to reconstruct Greek thought so that it was consistent with, and supported, Christian faith; (2) to subordinate philosophy to faith (and faith to revelation as seen and interpreted by the Church); (3) to use reason and the deductive techniques of logic to systematize and defend the Christian faith.

science, philosophy of. Some of the main areas of concentration in the philosophy of science: **1.** The study of **(a)** the concepts, presuppositions, and methodology of science; **(b)** their conceptual and linguistic analysis; **(c)** their extension and reconstruction for more consistent and precise application in obtaining knowledge. **2.** The study and justification of the reasoning processes used in science and its symbolic structure. **3.** The study of how the various sciences are interrelated, similar, or different and the degree to which they exemplify a PARADIGM of scientific method. **4.** The study of the consequences of scientific knowledge for such matters as: our perception of reality; our understanding of the processes of reality or the universe; the relationship of logic and mathematics to reality; the status of theoretical entities; our sources of knowledge and their validity; the nature of humanity, its values and place in the processes around it. All the above studies entail discussions of concepts such as: explanation, verification, confirmation, probability, control, experimentation, prediction, measurement, facts, evidence, classification, models, hypotheses, theories, laws, deduction, induction, causation, definitional systems (axioms, theorems, postulates), artificial languages. See METHOD, SCIENTIFIC.

scientific empiricism. See EMPIRICISM; POSITIVISM, LOGICAL.

scientific explanation. See EXPLANATION, SCIENTIFIC.

scientific method. See METHOD, SCIENTIFIC.

scientism. 1. Strong version: Science is the *only* method for obtaining knowledge. **2.** Weak version: Science is the only method we presently have that is a reliable source of knowledge.

The pejorative connotation of scientism: the unwarranted idolization of science as the sole authority of truth and source of knowledge.

secondary qualities. See entries under QUALITIES, PRIMARY/SECONDARY.

secular (L., *saeculum,* "a race," "the world," "an age"). Temporal, earthly, or worldly. Contrasted with sacred, spiritual, religious, holy.

self. 1. Same. Identical. **2.** The identity of anything regarded abstractly. **3.** An individual considered as an entity or as an identical person. **4.** An agent acting of its own nature. **5.** That which is the object of an action. **6.** The unity (ego, subject, memory, mind, "I," awareness, consciousness knower) that endures throughout change and is aware of its unity, its endurance, and the change. **7.** The entire sequence of mental events of which one can be aware at any given moment. See entries under EGO. Compare with PERSONAL IDENTITY.

self-alienation. 1. That state of awareness in which the "self" becomes foreign, or strange to itself, with the accompanying feelings of knowing the actions (and their results) of the "self" objectively, as one knows an object produced by an artist. **2.** The act of keeping one's self or mental states at an emotional distance. See ALIENATION; ESTRANGEMENT. That self-alienation which is not total has as its counterpart moments of DEALIENATION in which an affinity for social engagement and individual commitment are felt.

self-consciousness (self-awareness). 1. The experience of the items and activities of one's CONSCIOUSNESS such as sensations, images, thoughts, feelings, emotions, desires. **2.** The AWARENESS that one has consciousness or is conscious. (The consciousness that one has awareness or is aware.) **3.** The ability to treat one's consciousness as an object of knowledge. **4.** The ability of a subject (consciousness) to become an object to itself, or to become objective about itself. **5.** The ability to see oneself as others might.

self-contradiction. See CONTRADICTION, SELF-.

self-determination. Referring to the belief that a human being is able to cause or control his choices in opposition to external and internal forces compelling him to do otherwise. See entries under FREE WILL.

self-evident. Obvious (evident) without needing proof. Sometimes *A PRIORI.*

self-existence. Also *self-sufficient existence.* An existence needing nothing else for its existence but upon which other things depend for their existence. See NECESSARY EXISTENCE.

self-identity. 1. The way in which one imagines, characterizes, or views oneself. **2.** That self one believes oneself to be, and with which one identifies or is involved.

self-interest. See EGOISM, ETHICAL.

selfishness. 1. Refers to acting in order to procure one's own benefit (interest, satisfaction), and (usually) only one's own benefit and (usually) at the exclusion or expense of someone else's benefit. **2.** Showing a concern only for oneself. See entries under EGOISM.

self-realization theories. Also *self-actualization* or *eudaimonistic theories.* Theories that emphasize that the highest good of human beings is the development of their emotional and intellectual potentials. See EUDAIMONIA.

self-reference, paradoxes of. See PARADOXES OF SELF-REFERENCE.

self-transcendence. 1. The view that the self (or thought, consciousness, mind) involves an awareness of itself that goes beyond any of its immediate states, acts, or processes. **2.** The state of (**1**).

semantical rule. See RULE, SEMANTICAL.

semantics (Gk., *sēmantikos,* "significant," *sēmainein,* "to signify," *sēma,* "a sign," "a mark," "a token of identity." *Sēma* also meant a grave that had a sign to indicate something about the dead person). The study of the relationship of linguistic symbols to things other than themselves with reference (**a**) to what they mean (see INTENSION), and (**b**) to what they refer to. See EXTENSION. Compare with SYNTAX; PRAGMATICS.

semantics (linguistics). The study of: **1.** the meanings of symbols and how these meanings change, **2.** the variety of symbols (signs, gestures, words) and speech forms used to communicate meanings, **3.** the relationship of these symbols to each other, and **4.** their effect upon human behavior.

semantics, descriptive. The scientific study of, or the description of, natural languages. Often synonymous with *linguistics.*

semantics, formal. The analysis of such things as (**a**) the connections between a given theory and the logical calculus by which it is formulated, and (**b**) the relationships between the syntactical and semantical levels of logic.

semantics, problems of. Questions such as the following are asked in the study of semantics: **1.** What does "meaning" mean? **2.** What kinds of meaning are there? **3.** How is meaning communicated? **4.** What is a language? **5.** What is the relationship of language and meaning—how is meaning formed by language? **6.** What type of meaning is conveyed by proper names, singular terms, general terms, descriptions, definitions? **7.** What determines that two linguistic expressions have the same meaning? **8.** In what way does the context of a linguistic expression create and/or affect meaning? **9.** What is the distinction between literal meaning and figurative meaning? (How and what meaning is communicated by metaphor, simile, irony, analogy, etc.?) **10.** Under what conditions can we say that a meaning is ambiguous, vague, imprecise, inconsistent, etc.? See LANGUAGE, PHILOSOPHY OF.

semantics, pure. The analysis of formal or artificial languages.

semasiology (Gk., *sēmasia,* "signification," "meaning"). The study of (a) the meanings of words, (b) the development of these meanings, and (c) the senses in which words may be understood.

seminal reasons. See *LOGOS SPERMATIKOS; RATIONES SEMINALES/CAUSALES;* STOICS, THE.

semiosis (Gk., *sēmeion,* "a sign," "a signal to act," "a mark of proof"). Semiosis refers to both (a) the process of functioning as a symbol (sign, linguistic expression, speech form) and (b) that state of understanding (behavior, response) which the symbol produces.

semiotics. 1. The study of (a) the nature and kinds of signs, (b) what they mean, (c) how they are used, and (d) how they produce the intended effect, or communicate the intended meaning. 2. Sometimes the term *semiotics* refers to the analysis of the language used in scientific method.

sempiternal (L., *sempiternus,* from *semper,* "always"). Always ETERNAL. Everlasting.

sensa (plural; the singular is *sensum).* 1. The private content (data, items) of our immediate consciousness or awareness such as smells, colors, shapes, sounds, tactile qualities. 2. The private, immediate, and directly GIVEN content of our perceptions. That upon which our perceptions are based and out of which they are formed. 3. The private, immediate, and directly given object of our sensing or of our sensation. Sensa are usually distinguished from external physical objects; they are conceived as numerically distinct from physical objects. Physical (material) objects such as tables, chairs, animals, plants are regarded as externally real, locatable in space and time, publicly observable at the same time by more than one perceiver and existing in the same publicly defined space. Physical objects persist independently of sensa associated with them, and persist during the process of changing sensa. See *QUALIA.*

Material objects (see OBJECTS, MATERIAL) are often thought to be known (perceived) indirectly by inference from something more immediate and direct, such as sensa. We feel a certainty about having, or being presented with, sensa, but we do not feel that same certainty about perceiving material objects.

Sensa may or may not be considered to be caused by external sources. They may or may not be considered to resemble the physical objects that cause them or that they are associated with. Sensa are generally regarded as transitory, lasting only during the time in which they are sensed. They are not usually considered as efficacious; they cannot produce effects upon other things, nor can they act on them in any way. Sensa are indubitable, incorrigible, and certain. The word *sensa* is often used with a connotation closely akin to "image." The singular form is sensum. Often used interchangeably with SENSE DATA.

sensation (L., *sensatus,* "gifted with sense [or intellect]," from *sensus,* "sense," "feeling," "perception"). 1. The immediate and direct mental product of neural activity that results from the activation of sense organs by external stimuli and/or internal brain stimuli. **2.** The CONSCIOUSNESS (awareness, experience) itself of items such as sounds, colors, smells, etc., produced by the senses. See SENSES, THE FIVE. **3.** The simplest, specific items of consciousness produced by our senses, such as a high C, green, a chocolate taste.

A sensation is regarded as private and a spontaneous ultimate content or object of consciousness. It is often distinguished from PERCEPTION, which involves judgment, inference, interpretation, bias, preconceptualization, and is thus subject to error; sensation is regarded as incorrigible, a "rock-bottom" given, a "raw sensum" or "brute fact." For many, sensation connotes more of a relationship with FEELING (but not with EMOTION) and perception more of a relationship with cognition.

Sensation is often used synonymously with *sense impression, sense datum, sensum, sensibilium.*

sensationalism (epistemology). Sometimes *radical empiricism* (see EMPIRICISM, RADICAL). Some of the main views of sensationalism: **1.** Perception is the association of sensations (sensa, sense data). **2.** All knowledge has its source in sensations. **3.** All knowledge can be reduced to sensations; all empirical (hence meaningful) statements can be analyzed into statements that have as their content the interrelationship of sensations. **4.** Knowledge can be verified (confirmed, validated) only with reference to sensations.

sense, internal. The innate ability of the mind (consciousness, self) to introspect—to become aware of its inner states and activities.

sense, internal and external (Kant). Internal sense is the *A PRIORI* awareness (intuition, knowledge) of TIME or the form of time. External sense is the *a priori* awareness of spatial attributes or the form of SPACE. See KNOWLEDGE (Kant).

sense, manifold of. See MANIFOLD, SENSORY (Kant).

sense, moral. See MORAL SENSE.

sense data. 1. The specific, immediate, incorrigible, and irreducible qualities or content of sensations. **2.** That which is given to us directly and immediately such as color, shapes, smells, without identification of them as specific material objects such as a green ball, an onion, etc. Sense data are usually thought to be devoid of judgment, interpretation, bias, preconception. The singular is *sense datum.* Often used interchangeably with SENSA.

sense perception. An unanalyzable mental state, or act, that is related to, and dependent upon, the functions of sensory organs.

sense perception, relativity of. See RELATIVITY OF SENSE PERCEPTION.

sense *qualia*. 1. The qualities of sensations considered in abstraction, such as whiteness, sourness. **2.** The qualities sensed in association with specific objects such as a white rose, a sour grape. See *QUALIA; SENSIBILE.*

senses, the five. The common classification: sight (visual), hearing (auditory), touch (tactile), taste (gustatory), smell (olfactory).

sensibile (L., "a sensible," "that which can be perceived by a sense"). "That which impresses a sense, an object of sense. Words often used as synonyms: *sensum,* sense datum, sense *quale* (or *qualis).* The plural form is *sensibilia.* See QUALIA.

sensibility (Kant). The power (ability, faculty) by means of which we have sensations. This power is passive or receptive, as opposed to reason or understanding which is active and structuring. See INTUITION (KANT.)

sensibles, common (Aristotle). Qualities of objects that are (can be) grasped by different senses. Examples: motion, rest, shape, size, number. Contrasted with proper sensibles.

sensibles, proper (Aristotle). Qualities of objects that are grasped by only one sense; if that sense functions it cannot but perceive that quality (sensible) unique to it. Examples: taste, smell, color, sound. Contrasted by Aristotle with common sensibles. According to Aristotle our senses are not in error about the fact that they have sensibles unique to them: Vision is unique to our sense of sight; sound to our sense of hearing; touch to our sense of touch; etc.

sentence (L., *sententia,* from *sentire,* "to think," "to feel," "to perceive"). A grouping of words (symbols, signs) according to a SYNTAX, expressing an idea or thought, and used for a variety of purposes such as declaring, asserting, pleading, requesting, commanding, interrogating, persuading, etc. Often used interchangeably with "statement" and sometimes with "proposition," but see SENTENCE/STATEMENT DISTINCTION.

sentence, categorical. A sentence that has a subject-verb-predicate form and that affirms or denies a property or membership in a class.

sentence connectives. 1. The words used to connect or relate sentences or statements such as "and" in "Bill is a bachelor *and* Oakland is north of Santa Barbara." **2.** The symbols used in logic to connect sentences or statements.

sentence/statement distinction. The distinction between a SENTENCE and a STATEMENT is based on points such as the following: **1.** *Different sentences may make the same statement.* Examples: **(a)** "Beth loves Jon" and "Jon is loved by Beth" are two different sentences, but both make the same statement. **(b)** *"Sebestyen hazament ennui"* is a sentence and its translation, "Sebastian has gone home to eat," is a sentence. They may be regarded as two sentences that make the same statement, that have the same meaning. **(c)** The declarative sentence "All reasonable persons believe in the existence of free will" and the rhetorical question "How can any reasonable person deny the existence of free will?" are different sentences but they say the same thing—make the same statement. **2.** *The same sentence may be used to make different statements.* Examples: **(a)** The sentence "He has black hair" is a true statement when applied to

Adam but that same sentence when applied to John is a false statement. **(b)** The sentence "The grass is green" is a sentence that makes a true statement about the grass on Marian's lawn during June but it makes a false statement about that same grass during August. Therefore a sentence is called a true or false sentence whenever the statement it makes is a true or false statement. See PROPOSITION.

sentience (L., *sentiens,* from *sentire,* "to feel"). Elementary incipient (inchoate or just beginning) consciousness at the level of sensuousness or primal sensations. Animals are presumed to be sentient creatures.

sentiment (L., *sentire,* "to feel"). **1.** Feeling. Emotion. **2.** Sensibility toward something. **3.** A mental attitude (judgment, thought) permeated with and/or predisposed by a feeling or an emotion such as in the phrases "the moral sentiment of sympathy," "the religious sentiment of compassion." In Hume, sentiment and SYMPATHY served as the ground of all moral action.

set. Any collection regarded as a whole (totality) of individual things (members) that can be clearly distinguished in some way. See CLASS; *GENUS.*

sign (L., *signum,* "sign"). **1.** Anything that stands for something else. **2.** Anything that represents (stands for, signifies, indicates) an object (or a relation or an activity) to someone who understands it or responds to it. Examples: "Clouds of certain kinds are signs of snow." See SIGN, NATURAL. "The mark $>$ is a sign for the relation "greater than." "The mark ∞ is a sign for the concept of infinity." "A written musical note is a sign for a certain tone to be played." "The ringing of the doorbell is a sign that someone is at the door." "The cat's hair standing on end is a sign to that dog not to attack."

sign, conventional. A sign devised and/or stipulated to mean a specific thing, such as a gesture meaning "go away," or a buzzing sound meaning the end of a round, or a color meaning to stop. X is a conventional sign of Y when human beings designate it as such. A word signifies, or is a sign of, a meaning or of a thing. Conventional signs are conventional in the sense that human beings could have used a different sign to indicate or stand for that same meaning or thing. Compare with SIGN, NATURAL.

sign, iconic. 1. Sometimes *representational sign.* A sign that resembles, or has an apparent resemblance to, that which it signifies. The word *curve* on a road sign does not resemble that which it signifies, but a curve drawn on the road sign as a line curving in a direction similar to the one that the road takes does "resemble" that which it signifies and is classified as an iconic sign. (That one thing resembles another does not make them signs of each other.) **2.** A sign that signifies an attribute (characteristic, property, quality) by exhibiting it. See ICON.

sign, indexical. A sign whose meaning is dependent upon, and relative to, the characteristics of the user (speaker) and the context in which these characteristics and signs are found. Despite the fact that the reference changes from one context to another, indexical signs (for example, "now," "I") continue to mean the same thing. Indexical signs are not verbally descriptive but disclose their referents in as direct a way as possible. Some words that are regarded as indexical signs (sometimes referred to as demonstratives): this, that, he, she, you, I, them, now, then, here, there. Gestures such as pointing, nodding of the head toward something, raising of the eyebrows to indicate a referent, etc., are also regarded as indexical signs. Often referred to as *egocentric particulars*.

sign, indicative. See *ENDEIKTIKON*.

sign, natural. Implied in saying that X is a natural sign of Y is their factual (causal) association together in a number of instances which allows one to anticipate or predict, or infer, that Y will be followed by X. X is a natural sign of Y when a certain relation is assigned between X and Y: clouds of a certain sort are a "sign" of snow; smoke is a "sign" of fire; fever is a "sign" of illness. The relationship is not one which has been created by human convention (see SIGN, CONVENTIONAL), nor is there necessarily a resemblance between X and Y (see SIGN, ICONIC). The relationship is a description of a nonlinguistic, natural, or causal order which can be observed and from which observations we have constructed the notion that X is a (natural) sign of Y.

signal (L., *signale,* from *signum,* "sign"). **1.** A sign (**a**) used to give notice of something, such as of a danger, and/or (**b**) used to give notice to something, such as a cough giving notice to the husband not to be so indiscreet. **2.** A previously agreed upon sign used to initiate action.

signification (L., *significare,* from *signum,* "sign," and *ficare,* "to make"). **1.** The meaning of something. **2.** The act of giving meaning to something. **3.** Making a meaning known by the use of symbols, signs, gestures, etc. See CONNOTATION.

simple location, fallacy of. The phrase was coined by Whitehead to refer to what he regarded as fallacious: the belief that reality consists of bits of matter isolated from each other at given locations in space and time. See PROCESS PHILOSOPHY.

simple predicate. See PREDICATE, SIMPLE.

simpliciter (L., "simply," "absolutely," "without qualifications").

simpliciter (**God**). Not subject in any way to differentiation, classification, or analysis. In medieval philosophy ultimately applicable only to God. God does not exist as a "this," or a "that." God is *simpliciter* and not *compositum*.

simplicity, principle of. See OCKHAM'S RAZOR.

sine qua non (L., "without which not"). Referring to the indispensable and necessary characteristic an idea or thing must possess to be what it is.

skeptic (Gk., *skeptikos,* "thoughtful," "reflective," "curious," from *skeptesthai,* "to consider," "to examine," "to look carefully about"). **1.** One who suspends judgment about something because of doubt and/or because he is waiting for more or better evidence. See EPOCHĒ; AGNOSTIC. **2.** One whose attitude is critical and usually destructively so. Compare with CYNICISM; PESSIMISM. **3.** One whose attitude is critical and inquiring. **4.** A disbeliever. One who has doubt about or does not believe in a doctrine. **5.** One who believes in SKEPTICISM or uses it as a philosophic method.

skepticism. 1. A state of doubting. **2.** A state of suspension of judgment. **3.** A state of unbelief or nonbelief. Skepticism ranges from complete, total disbelief in everything, to a tentative doubt in a process of reaching certainty.

skepticism (Carneades). The main points in the skepticism of the Greek philosopher Carneades were: **1.** Knowledge of what is correct information about reality, and what is incorrect information, is impossible. All we can ever have are images (representations, copies, PHANTASIA) of an external world, but we are never sure which images are accurate and which are inaccurate, since the human mental set contributes to the interpretation and understanding of those images. **2.** Truth does not exist; only degrees of probability exist. **3.** Probability is the only guide to life. The individual does not need the certainty of truth in order to act and to understand. (If one waited for the certainty of truth before acting or understanding, one would be able neither to act nor to understand.) The individual must—and in reality does—act and understand only on the basis of what is probable. **4.** Some beliefs can be rated as more probable than other beliefs. (This rating is subjective and relative to the individual and depends on the context in which the individual finds himself. **5.** The highest degree of probability of a belief is related to its intensity and immediacy in our experience, and to its relationship to other intense and immediate experiences. The lowest degree of probability of a belief is related to its not having any ground in our experience. **6.** The more probable we feel a belief is, the greater should be our *tendency* to accept it, but we should never allow this tendency to be so overwhelming that it forces us to acquiesce or to assent. Life is a continual and never-ending quest.

skepticism (Cratylus). No knowledge can be had of reality. One cannot say anything about anything. The communication of knowledge or of anything at all is impossible because all things are in perpetual change. The language used to communicate changes in the process of communication; the speaker is in a process of change; the meanings and ideas change even as one is thinking and uttering them; the recipient of the communication is in change; the total environment is in continual change without anything ever remaining the same. Cratylus concluded that one cannot say anything about anything and that one should not try. He refused to talk since talking appeared to him senseless, meaningless, a waste of effort. He merely wiggled his finger to indicate that he was fleetingly responding to stimuli. See CHANGE (CRATYLUS).

skepticism (Descartes). Descartes' skepticism, sometimes called *provisional* or *methodological skepticism,* consists of doubting all things until something is reached that cannot be doubted. Descartes' skepticism is based on two fundamental questions: **1.** What do I in fact know clearly and distinctly that is so absolutely certain as to be beyond any doubt whatever? **2.** What further knowledge is it possible to derive from this certainty? (Descartes was never really skeptical about there being such an indubitable truth and he was not skeptical about there being a definite procedure for attaining a complete deductive knowledge based upon this indubitable truth. Descartes believed it is possible to rise above skeptical doubt and find knowledge that is absolute, certain, necessary, and self-evident, which serves as the ground for all other knowledge and for knowledge of all reality.) For the sake of argument, Descartes doubts the existence of everything. He denies the existence of the external world, external minds, God, etc. Perhaps everything is a dream. Perhaps a powerful, malicious daimon is deceiving him. But there is one fundamental thing that cannot be doubted: that he exists to be deceived; that he exists to be having a dream; that he exists in the very act of denying. One can doubt even that one is doubting, but one must exist to be doing the doubting. See COGITO ERGO SUM. Thus by means of a provisional and methodical skepticism one can clearly and distinctly grasp an indubitable truth. According to Descartes all true ideas must be known this clearly and distinctly, and ideas that are thus known are true. Among these ideas are: the existence of an external world and of other minds; the existence of God and his characteristics; that God can never be a deceiver (it can be clearly and distinctly perceived that God is not liable to any errors or defects since if He were He would not be God, and deception necessarily follows from a defect); that God supports the principle that all ideas which are clearly and distinctly perceived are true (since God is completely benevolent He would not lead us into error). See IDEAS, CLEAR AND DISTINCT (DESCARTES).

skepticism (Gorgias). The Greek philosopher Gorgias propounded an extreme form of skepticism sometimes referred to as NIHILISM, which denied the possibility of knowledge and doubted whether anything existed at all. The main argument: No thing can be said to exist. (The stronger nihilistic version: Nothing exists.) If anything did exist, we would not be able to know it, and if we were able to know it we would not be able to communicate it.

skepticism (Hume). The main points in Hume's skepticism: **1.** The individual cannot ever obtain knowledge about any subject matter beyond the relationships of his ideas. The only knowledge an individual can have is of what he can directly experience (observe, perceive, have an impression of). **2.** No knowledge can be had of anything existing behind our impressions such as that of substance or God. Any knowledge claimed to be of something beyond our sense impressions is the consequence of speculative reasoning from immediate sense impressions to their supposed source or cause. **3.** No good rational justification can ever be given for believing anything that is not an immediate sense impression. Anything that can be imagined or conceived is possible; therefore there can never be any definite evidence (**a**) to refute anything (since anything is possible), or (**b**) to assert anything (to assert that either something *is* the case or *must be* the case). **4.** No factual truths about the external world or about reality can ever be arrived at by either induction or deduction. Inductive reasoning rests on an unjustifiable assumption that natural events will occur in the future as they have occurred in the past, that the future will be similar to the past. No possible experience can ever indicate that similar past (or present) connections between natural events will apply to future events. Such connections are based on psychological states such as habit, custom, convention, expectation, hope. Deductive reasoning deals with the necessary connections among statements; it can never show us that such necessity exists in the external world. Nothing in our experience indicates a necessary connection, a necessary tie or bond between impressions or between a cause and its effect. It is impossible to know that any particular state of affairs is necessarily connected with another state of affairs. Such necessity does not exist. **5.** Thus no empirical or rational justification can ever be given for such things as the belief in substance, the belief in the existence of an external world, the belief in the existence of a God, the belief in the existence of a self. These beliefs can have only psychological defenses and explanations based on things such as custom, habit, convention, constancy, and coherence among our impressions and their ideas, the principles of the association of our ideas. See CAUSE AND EFFECT RELATIONSHIP (HUME); KNOWLEDGE (HUME); SKEPTICISM, MITIGATED (HUME).

skepticism (Kant). Kant's skepticism represents a middle point between extreme skepticism and complete dogmatism. Kant was skeptical about speculative metaphysical claims to knowledge of true reality, reality as it is in itself. See *DING AN SICH, DAS;* ILLUSION, TRANSCENDENTAL (KANT). Yet there is a specific kind of knowledge that is both universal and necessary. Such knowledge has to do with the conditions any experiencing process must satisfy before it can be recognizable as experience. These conditions are the conditions for all possible experiences.

The main points in Kant's skepticism: **1.** Knowledge is initiated in an experience (in the process of experiencing) but (**a**) knowledge cannot be reduced to experience and (**b**) knowledge does not come directly from (pure) experience. Knowledge comes from the structuring of experience that is involved in the process of experiencing. **2.** Space and time are the necessary intuitions (structurings, forms) of all possible experiences. No experience is possible without its being imbued with, or structured by, the

intuitions of space and time. **3.** The categories (see entries under CATE-
GORIES [KANT]) are the necessary and universal conditions for having
any knowledge at all about what we are experiencing. **4.** Space and time
and the categories (including the logical forms for making inferences and
judgments) are the modes in which what comes from the world around us
must be shaped if experience is to exist at all. The world cannot be experienced except in these modes. **5.** By transcendental analysis we can reveal the universal, necessary, and innate conditions that are impressed
upon all experiencing and upon all knowledge. (But we can never know
whether or not reality-in-itself or things-in-themselves are in space and
time, or operate according to these categories of our understanding.) **6.**
The knowledge derived from transcendental analysis does not and cannot
give us a further knowledge (**a**) about any realm that transcends our actual or possible experiences (such as of a supernatural realm, or of a self-
identity that is the source of our perceptions and knowledge, or of a reality distinct from the phenomenal world), or (**b**) about any specific content
to experience. **7.** Speculative metaphysical knowledge that goes beyond
the limits of all possible experiencing cannot be had because there is no
method (**a**) for determining *if* and *how* the conditions for our possible experiencing are applicable and (**b**) for determining what conditions are and
what are not applicable. See KNOWLEDGE (KANT).

skepticism (Locke). Some of the main points in Locke's skepticism: **1.** The
external world (as distinct from substance) exists and can be known only
to a limited extent. **2.** We can never know the essence of substance. Substance is "a something we know not what." **3.** Knowledge of the external
world may be thought of as somewhere between the truly existing but unknowable reality of substance and the ideas by which we understand
things. **4.** We can have a clearly formed idea of things such as God, matter, personal identity, spirit, but we cannot know the essence of any of
them. (Though we can know *that* they exist.) **5.** Knowledge cannot be extended further than our sensations and the reasoning powers applied to
them. **6.** A great deal about the universe will always be unknown because
of the limitations of human knowing. See KNOWLEDGE (LOCKE).

skepticism (Sextus Empiricus). The version of skepticism held by the Greek
philosopher Sextus Empiricus is characterized by the following views: **1.**
We should suspend judgment (see *EPOCHĒ*) about whether knowledge is
possible or impossible. **2.** No belief can be said to be probable or improb-
able, more probable or less probable. **3.** One should not attach oneself to
or accept any belief. **4.** No belief and no disbelief can ever be proved correct or false. (No method for proving or disproving any belief can ever
exist.) **5.** Believing and disbelieving should be avoided because they bring
with them emotional and mental turmoil, and the aim of life should be
ATARAXIA, serenity of mind and spirit.

skepticism, mitigated (Hume). Beliefs have neither rational nor empirical justification; nevertheless there are some that we are bound to accept in the everyday course of affairs, such as the existence of the external world, the existence of other minds, the existence of a self, the existence possibly of some general intelligence pervading the universe.

skepticism, mitigated or limited ("mitigate" comes from L., *mitigatus,* the past participle of *mitigare,* "to make mild," "to soften," from *mitis,* "mild," and *agere,* "to do"). The denial of, or the suspension of, judgment about (**a**) certain means for attaining knowledge such as speculation, revelation, intuition, faith, sense perception, or reason, and/or (**b**) certain kinds of knowledge (for example, of a self, of other selves, of an external world, of a supernatural world). Usually any knowledge that is accepted is not granted certainty, but only a high degree of probability or possibility. Mitigated or limited skepticism is opposed to claims to unique and esoteric knowledge.

skepticism, Platonic. No knowledge is possible by means of sense perception (but knowledge and ultimate truth can be reached by the use of reason).

skepticism, Socratic. A general form of skepticism found in Socrates' remark "All I know is that I know nothing." In an important sense Socratic skepticism is a provisional and voluntary suspension of all knowledge in order to reach knowledge or certainty with the use of a definite method from, so to speak, "a clean slate." See SOCRATIC IRONY; SOCRATIC METHOD.

skepticism, solipsistic. The theory that one can know (**a**) that one exists and (**b**) that one is having certain ideas. All else is subject to denial or to suspension of judgment.

slave morality (Nietzsche). The name given by Nietzsche to any system of thought (**a**) that controls and convinces the oppressed, suppressed (defeated, downtrodden) that they are in actuality better off and superior to those who are oppressing them; (**b**) that creates fear of change and creative assertion; and (**c**) that idolizes passivity, duty, control of emotions, acceptance of authority and tradition. See SUPERMAN; TRANSVALUATION OF VALUES (NIETZSCHE).

social contract theory (Hobbes). Natural existence without a social contract means a state of war of one against all, and all against all; no one would have property, rights, or claims. One must submit oneself to a contract for self-preservation and protection (guaranteed by a being, or other source of military and legal power, to which allegiance and financial support is given).

social Darwinism. See DARWINISM, SOCIAL.

Socrates' *daimōn.* (The Greek word *daimōn* is also transliterated as *daemon.*) Socrates used the word *daimōn* (and *daimonion*) to refer to an inner voice pictured as a genie or spirit sitting on the lobe of his ear, that warned him about, or forbade, certain actions. See CONSCIENCE; *DAIMŌN.*

Socratic irony. Refers to: **1.** Socrates' habit of pretending humility and ignorance, and by a series of questions and answers, leading his listeners to knowledge—knowledge that could only be prodded by someone with a great deal of skill and wisdom. **2.** Socrates' declaration that the oracle at Delphi saying that he was the wisest of human beings must have meant that he was the wisest because he knew that he knew nothing. **3.** Socrates' assumed willingness to learn by means of questioning others since he said he did not possess knowledge, and in the process exposing their errors and lack of knowledge.

Socratic irony connotes a paradoxical mixture of humbleness on the one hand and arrogance on the other. It refers basically to declaring one's ignorance about a topic on which one in reality is extremely knowledgeable.

Socratic method. The method of instruction whereby a series of questions and answers are asked and given, eliciting (**a**) points of view, meanings, attitudes, concessions, opinions, moral feelings, etc., that eventually establish, or lead to a sense of, a general truth or ideal, and (**b**) unrealized knowledge (as Socrates elicits a theorem in geometry from the ignorant slave boy in the *Meno*) that one does not know one possesses. Socrates regarded himself as a midwife (*maieutria*) using this method to assist in the birth of ideas—ideas already formed and carried (impregnated) in the mind and the nature of human beings. See MAIEUTIC.

Some of the main features in Socrates' distinctive use of this method: **1.** A highly critical and analytic discussion leading to an intense self-examination on the meanings and implications of one's ideas and on the ground for one's beliefs, usually in a conversation (dialogue) with another person who is part of a group. (Members of the group ask and answer questions and may occasionally take the leading parts.) **2.** It is wrong to accept beliefs merely on the ground that they are accepted by one's group, are handed down by tradition, or are part of a body of knowledge. The only foundation of knowledge is that which can withstand the scrutiny of rational inquiry. **3.** The leader (Socrates) serves as the gadfly. With Socrates' probing examination of another person's beliefs it becomes evident (**a**) that the meanings of the concepts being discussed (such as piety, justice, beauty, virtue, good, or courage) are unclear, confused, and untrue; (**b**) that these meanings have no rational justification or consistency; and (**c**) that the beliefs and conduct based on them lead to irrational thought and to irrational behavior. **4.** The main person in the conversation (discussion, dialogue) claims expert knowledge of the subject matter to be discussed. Socrates asks questions, initially short and simple, to which he prefers short and simple answers. These answers present a series of interrelated statements from which Socrates draws absurdities, inconsistencies, and conclusions that are in opposition to the original confident assertions and that serve to indicate the conceit of the person who has dogmatically asserted dogmatic knowledge of the topic being discussed. (It appears that the result, if not the aim, of Socratic dialectic is not only to show that the person cannot rationally justify his knowledge claims, but that he really does not know what he is talking about, that he does not know truth, that he is, if he will only stop to admit it, intellectually conceited and overly confident about something he thinks he knows but really does not.) **5.** Once the embarrassment is resolved about not having a real grasp of the concepts being discussed—once humility is established—then the serious task is undertaken of beginning to philosophically construct an adequate and acceptable rational foundation for the concept by means of asking and answering a series of questions, and by means of denying and assenting to ideas as they are presented, until better knowledge is reached. **6.** The principal controlling pattern of this process of question/answer, denial/acceptance to points as they are brought up is that the knowledge obtained must conform to the general categories (forms, values) of good, beauty and truth—none of which for Socrates could ever exist alone. **7.** Thus Socratic method or dialectic is a continuing quest for truth by constant critical analysis, interrogation, self-examination and further analysis, questioning, and self-examination. The concern is to uncover truth no matter how hurtful it might appear to us in the beginning. Socratic method is the persistent tendency to follow a rational argument through to its conclusion regardless of what that conclusion is. Of course, the Socratic assumption is that if that conclusion were completely rational it would conform to the good, beautiful, and true, since the good, beautiful, and true are truly rational. See DIALECTIC (SOCRATES); SKEPTICISM, SOCRATIC.

Socratic paradoxes. Some: **1.** No one does evil of one's own free will. **2.** If one knew the good, one would not hesitate to do it. **3.** One commits evil only from ignorance of what the good is. (Evil is caused by ignorance.)

These are regarded as paradoxical statements because it is presumed to be obvious (**a**) that one does, and can do, evil, of one's own free will; (**b**) that one often does know the good yet does evil; and (**c**) that one can commit evil not out of ignorance but in full knowledge that what he is doing is evil.

Socratic quest, the. 1. To find the ESSENCES (universals, ideal forms) that make things what they are and according to which they must (should) behave, and **2.** to organize the individual's conduct in accordance with these essences that are necessary and rational, and operate everywhere for the best. **3.** To examine life and know oneself. See *GNŌTHI SE AUTON*.

Socratic skepticism. See SKEPTICISM, SOCRATIC.

Socratic theory of definition. 1. An ideal definition gives us the ESSENCE (that without which a thing would not be what it is) of that to which a word refers. See DEFINITION, TYPES OF (5) and (16). **2.** This essence will be seen to be single and simple. **3.** It will answer the question "What is the central and essential element which makes that thing what it is?" **4.** In answering this question we will come to know (**a**) that which actually makes all courageous things courageous (beautiful things beautiful, good things good, or true things true, etc.), and (**b**) that in terms of which we recognize and are able to name a courageous thing courageous (a beautiful thing beautiful, etc.). **5.** With this knowledge as a standard, we can then rationally, methodically become courageous (or become beautiful, good, or truthful, etc.). See DIALECTIC (SOCRATES).

solipsism, epistemological. (L., *solus,* "alone," "single," "sole," and *ipse,* "self"). **1.** The theory that one's consciousness (self, mind) cannot know anything other than its own content. See EGOCENTRIC PREDICAMENT. **2.** One's consciousness alone is the underlying justification for, and cause of, any knowledge of the existence or nonexistence of anything at all. Contrasted with OBJECTIVISM (EPISTEMOLOGY).

solipsism, metaphysical. Literally, "I myself only exist." The theory that no reality exists other than one's self. The self (mind, consciousness) constitutes the totality of existence. All things are creations of one's consciousness at the moment one is conscious of them. "Other" things do not have any independent existence; they are states of, and are reducible to, one's consciousness.

sophia (**Aristotle**). Sophia, translated as "theoretical wisdom," was regarded by Aristotle as the highest intellectual virtue, thus the highest of all the virtues. Aristotle distinguished *sophia* from PHRONĒSIS, "practical wisdom." See VIRTUES, DIANOETIC (ARISTOTLE).

A human is capable of *sophia* because there is in his nature something unique and divine; humans come close to the intellectual activities of God. The highest function possible for God and for humans is thinking, reasoning, using intelligence. The highest form of thinking is about objects (first principles of all things) which are eternal, unchanging, necessary, and certain—those objects which cannot be other than what they are. The study of FIRST PHILOSOPHY gives us *sophia*.

sophism (Gk., *sophisma,* "a skillful act," "a clever device," "a sly trick," "a captious argument," "a quibble," "a FALLACY"). A specious and subtle argument, usually presented as a formal argument, that is intended to deceive and/or mislead. See PREVARICATION.

sophistēs (Gk., "a master of one's craft or art," "one adept at doing (or teaching) something." Used synonymously with the Greek word *phronimos,* "one who is clever in matters of life," and with *sophos,* "a wise man"). In Athens, *"sophistēs"* was used specifically to refer to a *Sophist* (a professor, a teacher) who taught grammar, RHETORIC, political affairs, logic, law, mathematics, literary and linguistic analysis. At first the Sophists were held in high respect. For a variety of reasons they fell into ill repute and the word Sophist came to mean "a cheat" or "a quibbler" (or both). See SOPHISTS.

sophistic. 1. Used to refer to an argument (**a**) that is fallaciously subtle and clever and **(b)** that is intended to deceive and/or mislead. **2.** Sometimes used synonymously with ERISTIC. Aristotle distinguished between sophistic and eristic arguments on the basis that sophistic arguments are engaged in for a fee and eristic arguments merely for the victory.

sophistry. 1. Showy and intentionally fallacious reasoning in order to deceive, to mislead, to persuade, or to defend a point regardless of its value or truth. **2.** Disputation for the sake of disputation. **3.** The techniques, teachings, and practices of the SOPHISTS, especially as they engaged in **1** and **2**.

Sophists. Itinerant professors (teachers, philosophers) of Ancient Greece who lived during the fourth and fifth centuries B.C. Among the most important names: Protagoras of Abdera (c. 481 to c. 411 B.C.), Gorgias of Leontini (c. 485 to c. 380 B.C.), Prodicus of Ceos (probably born before 460 B.C.; death date unknown but probably after 399 B.C.), Hippias of Elis (probably born before 460 B.C.; death date unknown), Antiphon of Athens (c. 480 to 411 B.C.), Thrasymachus of Chalcedon (dates unknown but alive during the time of Socrates), Callicles (dates unknown but alive during the time of Socrates).

The Sophists (see *SOPHISTĒS)* are said to have taught for a fee (which in the opinion of Socrates was an evil thing to do, since if anyone had something good and true to teach people he should feel it his duty to communicate it without pay). They taught a variety of subjects: grammar, rhetoric, the art of persuasion, the art of defending oneself in court, political affairs, moral conduct, logic, legal principles, mathematics, natural sciences, literary criticism, linguistic analysis. They taught whatever one wanted to learn. They generally seemed to be interested in teaching the art *(TECHNĒ)* of how to improve oneself and succeed in life.

The Sophists fell into ill repute in the eyes of other philosophers. They were regarded as eloquent but captious and fallacious reasoners, as adroit at specious reasoning, as logic choppers, as appealing to and taking advantage of popular trends and wishes for their own monetary gain, as telling people what they wanted to hear, as teachers of persuasion and verbal manipulation of others, as being interested not in the attainment of truth but in how to refute an argument merely for the sake of refuting it, and in how to defend any argument whatever, as teaching that victory in argumentation at whatever cost, outwitting opponents, is the sole aim of disputation no matter how bad the argument, as being able to make the worse appear the better and the better appear the worse.

Some of the main ideas of the Sophists: **1.** The *relativity of sense perception.* The individual is the measure of all things. Things are as one says they are and sees them as being. See RELATIVISM, PROTAGOREAN. **2.** The *relativity of knowledge.* Knowledge and truth are relative to the social, cultural, and unique personal predispositions of the individual. There is no absolute truth. **3.** The *denial of knowledge of any ultimate* *reality behind our sensations.* The natural world can only be known in terms of those sensations that appear to our consciousness. There is no reality such as a WORLD SOUL or universal mind behind the phenomena as they appear to and are interpreted by our sensations and perceptions. **4.** EMPIRICISM. All knowledge is ultimately based on our direct and immediate experiences as they occur to us in consciousness. **5.** Laws are the product of humans living in society. Laws are made by those who have power in order to keep the weak in control, or laws are made by the weak in order to keep the strong from asserting themselves and taking over. **6.** The state of society is a progressive state from a state of primitive nature out of which humans came and in which it was a battle of each with everyone else. **7.** Morality is a product of humans. Wherever humans group together, especially to act in a concerted way, rules of conduct emerge to regulate behavior. Morality not only originates in human activities and institutions, it is also sanctioned and maintained by them. God has nothing to do with morality. **8.** If humans could do evil and get away with it without being punished they would do so. Humans do good only because they are afraid of the repercussions of doing otherwise. **9.** The basic motivating force in humans is egoism (self-interest, selfishness). **10.** Humans are not born innately virtuous. If humans are virtuous they have become that way through social and intellectual conditioning. **11.** Virtue can be taught. Virtuous conduct is something that can be developed. **12.** Respect of others must not be based on heritage, tradition, privileged status, class, or birth, but on what excellences an individual has perfected. **13.** There is a distinction between *NOMOS,* those things that are true and necessary and are given or devised by convention (law, society, our own perceptions), and *PHYSIS,* those things that are true and necessary and are given by nature.

sophocracy (Gk., *sophos,* "wise," and *kratein,* "to rule"). A state governed by wise individuals and/or by wisdom.

sophos (Gk., originally meaning "one who is skilled in any handicraft or art," or "one who has expertise or excellence of skill"). It was also applied to "one who is clever in matters of common life, who is prudent, shrewd, cunning, wise," and to "one who is skilled in profound learning and knowledge." *Sophos* was used to mean "a sage," "a seer," "a prophet," "a wise one who encompasses all of the ideal virtues and who commands utter respect." (Sometimes used interchangeably with *SOPHISTĒS.*)

sōphrosynē (Gk., "soundness of mind," "moderation," "discretion," "self-control," "temperance"). Used in Greek philosophy in a variety of meanings. **1.** The state of harmony or serenity reached when rational faculties control one's desires and emotions. *Sōphrosynē* is not to be thought of only as a state but also as the power (ability) to achieve such a state. **2.** The state of contentment felt when the mean between pleasures and pains is attained. **3.** The ability to know and choose the good and to rec-

ognize and avoid evil. **4.** Temperance. One of the four virtues. See VIR-
TUES, CARDINAL.

soul. The following characteristics, or combinations of them, have been ascribed to the soul: **1.** Eternality. **2.** An immaterial or spiritual entity (substance, being, agent). **3.** Something separable and entirely different from
the body and matter which persists throughout the changes of the body.
4. The activating cause of life and consciousness (although in CREATION-
ISM it is held that God creates the soul as He does matter at an instant in
eternal time). **5.** Immortality. **6.** The ability to enter the body at birth
and leave the body at death (and in some cases during life). **7.** The ability
to transmigrate or reincarnate (see METEMPSYCHOSIS), or to pass on to
heaven or hell, or into *nirvana*. **8.** Inexplicability. The soul is not in any
way subject to a materialistic or mechanistic explanation, not even in
terms of very fine material particles believed in by the Greek atomists
(see ATOMISM, GREEK) and by the STOICS. Compare with entries under
EGO and SPIRIT.

soul (Plato). The soul is a disembodied spiritual being that: **1.** can exist independently of matter and all things (except God), **2.** is (or is the source of)
the real person, self, or consciousness, **3.** moves itself (is self-moving), **4.**
is the cause of the motion of matter which cannot move itself, **5.** is eternal (ungenerated by anything else), **6.** is simple, **7.** is self-sufficient, **8.** is
incorruptible, and **9.** is the source of all the best and good.

One's body and all matter are corporeal (material) composites. The
soul is not a composite. The soul has no parts. (The soul is simple and irreducible to any other elements.) The soul is not corporeal. It is incorporeal (immaterial). The soul is entombed in (imprisoned by or attached
to) a body. The incorruptible soul does its best to fight against the cor-
rupting influence of the body. See FACULTIES OF THE SOUL (PLATO); MO-
TION (PLATO).

soul, concept of the (Aristotle). The following is one of several accounts that
can be given of Aristotle's concept of the soul: The soul is the FORM, or
functioning excellence, of a particular living body. The soul is the capacity of the organism to act in certain ways. The soul is to the body as vision
is to the eye. The soul is inseparable from the body physically (functionally) as well as logically. It is inconsistent to say that the act of seeing can
exist without the functioning of an eye, or that the functioning of an eye
can exist without the act of seeing. So it is inconsistent to say that certain
functions (soul) of the body can exist without a living organism, or that a
living organism can exist without certain functions (soul).

soul, functions of the (Aristotle). The main functions (or activities) of the
soul: **1.** The *nutritive* or *vegetative*, having to do with growth, nourishment, and survival. (Plant life has only this level of soul). **2.** The *sensate*
(sensitive, perceptive), having to do with receiving and reacting to sensations and feeling. (All animal life has this level as well as the previous

level of soul.) **3.** The *Volitional.* Self-motion (and self-direction in the higher animals) and the power of causing motion. **4.** The *rational* or *intellectual*, related especially to the ability to reason and use symbols, and which is the essential characteristic only of humans. These functions are related in a hierarchy of emerging qualities, each level incorporating qualities of the previous level. Living organisms can be classified according to the number of faculties they possess (and this is related to the degree of complexity possessed by the organism).

soul, rational and nonrational parts of the (Aristotle). The soul, according to Aristotle, has a rational part and a nonrational part (which may be thought of as including all the parts of the soul that are not rational). The rational part is itself divided into two parts: **(a)** The *completely rational* which deals with eternal objects and pure theory (see FIRST PHILOSOPHY [ARISTOTLE]) and **(b)** the *not so completely rational* which deals with the mundane affairs of everyday living and bodily needs such as our appetites, cravings, and desires. See REASON, PRACTICAL (ARISTOTLE). Insofar as these appetites and desires are controlled by reason (or insofar as they conform in their own way to reason) then they are classified as rational. Insofar as they do not, then they are irrational. Moral virtue (see VIRTUES, MORAL [ARISTOTLE]) is the rational control of our desires and appetites (or the conformity of our desires and appetites to reason). Moral virtue involves a choice as to the way the desire or appetite is to be handled—by means of reason or not.

soul/body dualism. See DUALISM, DESCARTES' SOUL/BODY; MIND, TYPES OF THEORIES OF.

sound (logic). A deductive argument which is formally valid and whose premises are all (empirically) true, hence its conclusion must be true as well, is said to be sound. Example:

> Premise 1: All animals are mortal.
> Premise 2: All dogs are animals.
>
> ---
>
> Conclusion: Therefore, all dogs are mortal.

space (L., *spatium*, "space"). **1.** That which can be characterized by a dimension. **2.** Linear distance. **3.** Time distance. Interval. Duration. **4.** Extension. That which has area or volume as determined by the three dimensions length, width, and height. **5.** Boundary. That area in which something exists (moves, changes). **6.** Receptacle. That in which all things are found. **7.** A void. Empty or devoid of something. **8.** The void, nothingness.

space (Aristotle). For Aristotle the principal meaning of space must be sought in the concept of *place* thought of as that absolute location (in a place or at a place in the cosmic space) of a thing (or the boundary of a figure). Things tend to seek their natural places in the universe. Their not being in their natural places is one source of motion.

space (atomists). The Greek atomists (see ATOMISM, GREEK) regarded space as a void (pure empty space) that existed between atoms and in which atoms moved. No motion would be possible without this empty space. All things in the universe are composed of atoms and empty space.

space (Descartes). Space and MATTER (material substance) are one and the same thing. Anything that occupies space is extended and that extension *is* space. Space is the volume physical things take up. There is no VOID or empty space.

space (Kant). Kant did not regard space as indentical with matter, or as a receptacle, or as a void, or as absolute, or as the relationship of external real objects. Kant attempted to present a consistent subjectivistic view of space. The mind organizes and orders pure (nonspatial) experience by means of the intuition of space, by means of the subjective projection of the concept of space upon pure experience. See SENSE, INTERNAL AND EXTERNAL (KANT); SPACE/TIME (KANT).

space (Leibniz). Space has two aspects: the objective or ontological and the subjective or psychological. In both, external space is not real. Only the MONADS are real: **1.** Space is the relationships of the internal properties of monads. **2.** Space is that which makes many diverse perceptions cohere among themselves (or is that sense of coherence). See SPACE/TIME (LEIBNIZ).

space (Plato.) Space is a receptacle that (**a**) contains or receives the (basically mathematical) activity of matter, and (**b**) restrains that activity by providing the structures and limits in which that activity can take place.

space, absolute (Newton). Newton held a metaphysical view of space (and time) as being absolute and unchanging: **1.** Motion (movement) can be explained by reference to this framework of absolute and unchanging space (and time). **2.** There is no need to refer motion to other motions. **3.** The three-dimensionality of space is an intrinsic, essential, and necessary attribute of space (and space of reality). **4.** Space is separable from time. **5.** These truths about space are contingent truths.

space-time. 1. a structure consisting of, or **2.** a four-dimensional analysis in terms of, three perpendicular and linear dimensions (length, width, and height) and a fourth of an interval or duration (time).

space/time (Kant). According to Kant: **1.** We do not derive our ideas of space and time by abstracting them from experience. **2.** We do not derive our ideas of space and time from experience of succession, precedence, simultaneity, concurrence, coexistence, proximity, etc. These experiences themselves presuppose our having the ideas of space and time. **3.** Space and time are *A PRIORI* intuitions. They are pure, intuitive, nonconceptual ideas. **4.** Knowledge of space and time is (**a**) clearly, immediately, intuitively possessed; (**b**) not framed or given by concepts; (**c**) all experiences presuppose this intuition and depend upon it for a form. **5.** Space and time are "pure" intuitions in the sense that their essence is known *prior* to experience and is not an outcome *of* experience. **6.** Space and time are the *form* of experience—the form which all experience takes—and are *not* the *content* of experience. **7.** Space and time structure experience (sensation) in the very act of its being experienced (sensed) and known. **8.** Space and time apply to anything we know through our experience (senses). **9.** Time applies to anything we experience as an inner flow of consciousness (and since consciousness cannot be consciousness unless it is a flow, then time is constantly an aspect of consciousness). See SPACE (KANT).

space/time (Leibniz). Leibniz' theory of space/time has two aspects, the objective or ontological and the subjective or epistemological: **1.** Space and time are not absolute and are not independently real as entities but are the order (relationship) of succession and coexistence in which real entities (the MONADS) are related to the coexistence of things. Time is relative to the cosuccession of things. **2.** Space and time are systems of relations abstracted by the mind from particular contingent experiences (and at that not clearly perceived). In this sense space and time are logical constructs expressing relations based on experience and are not substances, or real entities. See SPACE (LEIBNIZ).

space-time continuum. Some of the main concepts: **1.** All physical (material) things are part of a four-dimensional framework. See SPACE-TIME. **2.** Nothing can exist or be conceived to exist except in a space-time continuum. **3.** Any location and description of a thing must be given in terms of the four space-time coordinates. **4.** The universe, and any object within it, can be interpreted as changeless (immutable, motionless) only insofar as it is said to exist in space (three dimensions) without being related to time. **5.** All things are in a space-time continuum and space cannot be separated from time (except in abstraction). All things are in a state of process. **6.** Changing events regarded in abstraction from the time dimension are the source of our concept of physical "objects" that exist substantially and that endure without change. **7.** The space-time continuum which is the universe can be analyzed as a very general structure determined by the configurations and relationships of four-dimensional events represented by such concepts as mathematical points in four-dimensional geometric patternings (for example, by using non-Euclidian geometries such as the elliptic geometry of G.F.B. Riemann in which space is regarded as positively curved [curving] as in a sphere, or the hyperbolic geometry of N. L. Lobachevsky in which space is regarded as negatively curved [curving] as in a saddleback). **8.** Specific events within this space-time continuum can be analyzed in the same way. For example, gravity is to be thought of as a characteristic of space-time configurations ("fields") or relationships rather than as a property of matter. The same can be done with concepts such as force, mass, power, etc.

species (L., *species,* "an outward appearance," "a kind," "a type," "a shape," "a form," "an idea," "a sort"). **1.** The subclass of a large class (GENUS) **2.** One of the subclasses into which a class may be divided.

speculative philosophy. 1. In the nonpejorative sense: philosophy which constructs a synthesis of knowledge from many fields (the sciences, the arts, religion, ethics, social sciences) and theorizes (reflects) about such things as its significance to humankind, and about what it indicates about reality as a whole. **2.** In the pejorative sense: philosophy which constructs idle thoughts about idle subjects.

speech acts. Any of the variety of things done and affected in the act of speaking such as describing, informing, commanding, persuading, altering another's opinion, expressing feelings, etc. See PERFORMATIVE ACT.

speech situation. The name given to the following set of conditions: **1.** A speaker makes an utterance using symbols (or signs) in order to communicate. **2.** That utterance is understood, interpreted, and judged by the one to whom it has intentionally been addressed. **3.** A behavioral response of some sort (such as an answer or an action) is generated in the receiver of the utterance. **4.** (**a**) Some information (a meaning, a fact, a reference to an object, etc.) has been conveyed and/or (**b**) some change has been initiated. See entries under LANGUAGE.

spirit (L., *spiritus,* "spirit, breath," from *spirare,* "to breathe," "to blow"). **1.** The breath of life. The cause of life conceived as a fine vapor or air that animates the organism. In human beings it has sometimes been conceived as mediating between body and soul. It has also often been viewed as a gift of God (or the gods) and/or even as part of the very breath of God. **2.** The SOUL. That immaterial agent in humans which causes consciousness (including willing) and the life functions such as growth, appetition, feeling. (In some views, the cause also of CONSCIENCE.) **3.** The WORLD SOUL. **4.** A disembodied soul such as a ghost. This disembodiment may take several forms: (**a**) a soul without a body inhabiting an unseen world such as Hades, Heaven, Hell; (**b**) a soul without a body but appearing to the living in the likeness of a body; (**c**) a soul without the physical body to which it was attached during life but attached to its spiritual body such as at one's resurrection after death.

Spirit is regarded as having characteristics similar to soul such as immateriality, intangibility, (sometimes) eternality, (sometimes) immortality.

spiritism. The belief (**a**) in the existence of spirits affecting the real world and/or humanity and (**b**) that human beings can by specific means such as propitiation, ritual, initiations, etc. come into contact with spirits in order to (**c**) receive their powers, alter their activity, or communicate with them.

The acts, service, or works produced by a spirit are called *spiriting.* The belief in and worship of many spirits is often called *polydaimonism.*

These spirits may take a variety of forms from disembodied nature spirits, to manes, to deities. In most instances spiritism is used interchangeably with SPIRITUALISM.

spiritual. 1. Immaterial. Incorporeal. Consisting of SPIRIT. **2.** Referring to the higher faculties (mental, intellectual, aesthetic, religious) and values of the mind. **3.** Referring to nonmaterial human values such as beauty, goodness, love, truth, compassion, honesty, holiness. **4.** Referring to moral, religious, and aesthetic feelings and emotions. Contrast with CARNAL.

spiritualism (metaphysics). 1. The view that the underlying, ultimate reality (or foundation of reality) is spirit or a WORLD SOUL which (a) *is* the universe or pervades the universe at all its levels of activity; (b) is the cause of its activity, order, and direction; and (c) stands as the only completed and rational explanation for the existence of the universe. See *LOGOS; PNEUMA; NOUS.* **2.** The view that only the Absolute Spirit exists (and its consequent finite spirits such as humans), and all else is a product of the Absolute Spirit.

state (L., *status,* "a position," "a standing"). **1.** Condition. The mode or state of being of something. **2.** The level, rank, standing of something, especially in a hierarchical order. **3.** Quality of living and/or position in life. **4.** A situation (a) viewed in terms of its actual relationships to other things and/or (b) viewed from the point of view of its potential relationships to other things.

state, disposition. Sometimes *dispositional state.* **1.** A state of mind such as a mood, want, emotion, inclination that tends to lead to certain kinds of behavior whenever certain conditions are present. Examples: **(a)** "I am frustrated" discloses a state of mind in which if an annoyance occurs then some expression of irritability will follow. That state of frustration predisposes one to certain kinds of behavior. **(b)** "He is a charitable person" indicates that under specific situations he will tend to act with compassion, help, tolerance, sacrifice. **2.** A physical state such as malleability, solubility, rigidity, fluidity that describes (a) what the object can be made to do—or does—under given conditions and/or (b) what behavior it tends to engage in. Example of **a**: "Buttermilk is nutritious" implies a "disposition" toward a specific activity—what buttermilk will do—if certain conditions are satisfied. Example of **b**: "Helium expands" suggests a "disposition" to behave in a certain way unless prevented. All disposition states may be classified as occurrent states (see STATE, OCCURRENT) but not all occurrent states can be classified as disposition states. See DISPOSITION.

state, occurrent. A state of consciousness at any given moment such as a feeling. Examples: "I feel morose," "I feel excited." Contrasted with STATE, DISPOSITION.

state of nature. See NATURE, STATE OF.

statement. Any sentence or group of sentences used to assert or deny something. Often used interchangeably with *sentence* and *proposition.* To "make a statement" is to write or utter a sentence or sentences so that something true or false is said. See SENTENCE/STATEMENT DISTINCTION.

statement, analytic. 1. A statement that is true by definition—true due to the meanings assigned to the words in the statement—and needs no verification in experience to be true. Example: "A triangle is a three-sided figure." "Matter occupies space and exists in time." "A thing cannot be both true and false at the same time and in the same respect." **2.** A statement that contains the meaning of the predicate in the meaning of the subject. Example: the subject of the statement "All bachelors are unmarried males" is "bachelors" and the predicate is "unmarried males." (The copula is the verb "are" connecting the subject and predicate.) The predicate is merely repeating what is already understood as the meaning of the subject. By definition, it could never be the case that a bachelor is married. (If he were married we would not call him a bachelor.) Thus the meanings of the words themselves make the statement true—true under any and all sets of conditions (even if there were no unmarried males), at any place or time in the universe (on Mars, at the edge of our galaxy, or in any galaxy).

Analytic statements have the following characteristics: **(a)** If they are denied, a self-contradiction ensues. (If I deny that bachelors are unmarried males, yet still accept the meaning of "bachelor," I then contradict myself.) **(b)** They need no verification in experience. (I do not need to find an actual bachelor to know the truth of the statement. It would still be true if there were no bachelors.) **(c)** They cannot be empirically disproved. (I cannot go out in the world and find a bachelor who is married.) **(d)** They are true by definition, true by their linguistic and logical structures, and thus do not as such provide information about the real world (although they can be applied to the real world). The information they provide us is contained in their linguistic meanings and logical form. They help us construct and clarify concepts but they do not necessarily point to specific referents beyond themselves. Contrast with STATEMENT, SYNTHETIC.

statement, logically impossible. See IMPOSSIBLE, LOGICALLY.

statement, logically independent. 1. A statement that does not logically follow from another statement. **2.** A statement that cannot be derived by the rules of inference of a logical system. **3.** A statement whose truth or falsity has no effect on the truth or falsity of another.

statement, metalinguistic. See METALANGUAGE.

statement, synthetic. Sometimes *synthetic proposition* or *sentence.* An empirical statement that describes a state of affairs. A statement which is informative, whose predicate adds something not definitionally contained in the subject. For example, the subject of the statement "The table is red" is "table" and the predicate is "red." (The verb "is" is the copula connecting the subject and predicate.) The predicate states something more than what is contained in the meaning of "table." The content of the predicate is not definitionally (not linguistically or logically) derived or derivable from the meaning of the subject. To discover whether or not it is true that the table is red one must go beyond the statement itself and find an existing state of affairs which will indicate the truth or falsity of the statement. Unlike analytic statements (see STATEMENT, ANALYTIC), synthetic statements are not true under any and all sets of conditions, nor are they true at any place or time in the universe, but depend for their truth (or falsity) upon specific conditions, places, and times in the universe.

Synthetic statements have characteristics such as: **1.** If you deny their truth, you are not involved in contradiction. (If I deny that the table is red, and say that it is gray, I am not involved in a contradiction for it could very well be true that it is gray rather than red, or it could be true that it is gray in appearance to me since I am color-blind, but red in appearance to other people.) **2.** Synthetic statements, at least in principle, can be falsified (or verified). (Theoretically there must be conditions under which their falsity would be accepted, otherwise they would not be classified under the heading of synthetic statements. They would be true by their linguistic and logical form.) **3.** Synthetic statements are informative. They tell us about the world and refer to things in the world.

statement/sentence distinction. See SENTENCE/STATEMENT DISTINCTION.

stoa (Gk., "a roofed colonnade or a portico"). The STOICS may have received their name from this word because it is thought that they taught and gathered at such a portico in Athens.

Stoics, the. A school of philosophy founded in Athens around 305 B.C. by Zeno of Citium, a city in Cyprus. Zeno and his disciples were called Stoics probably because Zeno lectured at a *STOA*. The Stoic philosophy lasted as an influential system of belief for over five hundred years during the Hellenistic, Roman, and Christian periods. It drew its inspiration primarily from two sources: Socrates and Heracleitus. The main Stoic philosophers: Zeno of Citium (c. 336 to c. 264 B.C.), Cleanthes of Assos (c. 331 to c. 232 B.C.), Chrysippus of Soli (c. 280 to c. 206 B.C.), Posidonius (c. 135 to 51 B.C.), Cicero (106 to 43 B.C.), Seneca (c. 4 B.C. to c. A.D. 65), Epictetus (c. A.D. 50 to c. 138), Marcus Aurelius (c. A.D. 121 to c. 180).

Some of Stoicism's leading beliefs: **1.** The universe is a rational whole. The universe is pervaded by the *LOGOS*. **2.** Knowledge of the functioning of the universe as a whole (as a MACROCOSM) provides us with knowledge and of how each individual thing (the MICROCOSM) must behave. **3.** Everyone must follow the rational will of the universe and live in conformity with the divine laws of nature, just as everyone must follow and live in conformity with the laws of one's country. **4.** Everyone must accept with equanimity his rightful place in the scheme of things and fulfill the nec-

.essary purposes of that place. **5.** Duty (see KATHĒKON) is doing the most rational thing possible in accordance with the rational necessity fated by the World Soul. **6.** All virtues are forms of knowledge. See VIRTUES (STOICS). No one can be virtuous without knowledge. **7.** The cardinal virtues of reason, courage, justice, and self-discipline are ends in themselves. Virtuous living is the only good and the ultimate aim of life. **8.** The study of philosophy leads one to the virtuous life. **9.** Concomitant with the attainment of the virtuous life is the attainment (**a**) of KATHĒKON, (**b**) of APATHEIA, and (**c**) of AUTARKEIA. **10.** Apatheia is the psychological state of insensitivity or indifference to pleasures and pains, emotions and passions, joys and grief, anxieties and mental elation. Apatheia is a state of tranquility of mind and body—a psychic detachment from mental and physical disturbances. **11.** Autarkeia is a state of self-sufficiency—a state of nondependence upon anyone else for survival and the satisfaction of physical and emotional needs. **12.** All people are related as common, co-operating, rational members fulfilling the design of the World Reason (LOGOS or PNEUMA). **13.** Everyone possesses a part of the eternal World Reason. **14.** Morality is a rational system transcending nationality, race, and class differences. **15.** All things are predestined. **16.** All things recur eternally. See ADIAPHORA; CONFLAGRATION (STOICS); LOGOS ORTHOS; LOGOS SPERMATIKOS; PHYSIS (STOICS); RECURRENCE, ETERNAL.

struggle for existence. See NATURAL SELECTION (DARWIN).

stuff, neutral. A nonmental and nonphysical substance usually regarded as unknown and unknowable, considered by some philosophers to be the underlying ground for the existence of both mental and physical events.

subject (L., *subjectus*, "lying under," "subjected," from *subjicere*, "to throw or place under," from *sub*, "under," and *jacere*, "to throw"). **1.** That of which something (a quality, relation, characteristic, attribute, property) may be affirmed (or denied). **2.** That in which something may be said to inhere. Used in a metaphysical sense, it is interchangeable with words such as SUBSTANCE, SUBSTRATUM, ground, BEING, the REAL, REALITY, the ABSOLUTE. **3.** The thinking agent. That being which supports or is the cause of mental functions and events. **4.** The MIND. **5.** The EGO.

subjective. 1. Referring to that which is derived from the mind (the consciousness, the ego, the self, our perceptions, our personal judgments) and not from external, objective sources. **2.** That which exists in consciousness but has no external, objective reference or possible confirmation. **3.** That which is relative to the knower's own individual experiences (sensations, perceptions, personal reactions, history, idiosyncrasies).

Subjective is contrasted with OBJECTIVE and with public (see PUBLICITY). It is also used to refer to the experiencing modes and processes of the experiencer (subject) in contrast to the things (objects) in the real world that he is experiencing. Subjective is often used pejoratively to connote privately arrived at judgments based on emotional or prejudiced grounds without the support of some objective, logical analysis.

subjectivism (epistemology). 1. The theory that all knowledge **(a)** has its source and validity in the knower's subjective mental states, and **(b)** knowledge of anything objective or externally real is hypothesized or based upon inference from these subjective mental states. **2.** Everything that is known is **(a)** a product selectively structured and created by the knower, and **(b)** it cannot be said that there is an externally real world to which it corresponds.

subjectivism (ethics). See ETHICS, SUBJECTIVISM IN.

subjectivism (value theory). The theory, especially in aesthetics and ethics, that **(a)** values are entirely dependent upon and relative to the modes of human experiencing; **(b)** values are reflections of the feelings, attitudes, and responses of the individual, and have no independent objective or external reality or source; and **(c)** objects or activities are valuable or good insofar as they produce desired or desirable pleasurable states of consciousness, feelings, subjective experiences. Opposite to OBJECTIVISM (VALUE THEORY). Compare with RELATIVISM (VALUE THEORY).

sublimation (L., *sublimatus,* from past participle of *sublimare,* "to elevate," from *sublimis,* "high"). **1.** The transference of a suppressed desire to a new object. **2.** Substituting another object and/or activity for one aimed at by an instinct, impulse, feeling, drive, desire. Example: channeling the sex drive toward artistic expression.

sublime, the (L., *sublimis,* "high," "lifted up," "exalted"). The feeling or experience of (or that object which produces a feeling of) **(a)** grandeur, nobility, majesty, elevated beauty, amazement, awfulness, horror, terror, impending doom, the terrible, that is **(b)** mingled with pleasure and awe, and **(c)** that captivates and completely involves the mind.

The sublime can include feelings (emotions) of pain, danger, power, emptiness, obscurity, privation, loneliness, vastness, the infinite, God, the universe. When these emotions stand out by themselves as only ugly, threatening, and undesirable, they cannot be labeled "sublime." The sublime is associated with the beautiful, with the fascinating, with the appealing, with that which is exhilarating and which attracts.

sublime, the (Kant). 1. The feeling stemming from the power and greatness of our reason. Though our imagination staggers at the vast complexity of the universe, our finite reason produces ideas that reach out to grasp the intricacy, the totality, and the infinity of things. **2.** The feeling stemming from our awareness of a moral sense and destiny. We recognize our weaknesses as finite selves, yet we can also recognize our duty to each other, and we can strive to transcend our mortal condition and become aware of our worth as moral creatures. **3.** The feeling stemming from being confronted with a terrifying power that can utterly destroy us at any moment, yet at the same time having a sense of safety and being aware of a pleasurable attraction to that power.

subliminal (L., *sub,* "under," and *limen,* "threshold"). Sometimes synonymous with subnoetic and ANOETIC. Existing below the threshold of consciousness; not yet strong enough to be recognized by consciousness.

subset. Any given set such that all its members are members of another given set.

subsistent (L., *subsistere,* "to stand still," "to stay," "to remain alive," from *sub,* "under," and *sistere,* "to stand"). **1.** Having being or existence. **2.** Characterizing that thing (entity, object, being, existence) which does not exist in time or space but which is nevertheless real such as a relation, number, universal, value, ideal, spirit, soul, god. Subsistents in the last three senses are usually thought of as eternal and immaterial and in many cases also as nonmental.

subsistent forms. Those forms that are not in any way corporeal (material). They are free from all matter and from the necessity to relate to matter in order to act and to exist. Each subsistent form is its own species. They can have no individuation or particularization. Example: angels. Contrasted with SUBSTANTIAL FORMS.

sub specie aeternitas (L., "under the view or aspect of eternity"). The phrase is used to signify the attempt to see all things at once in one thought without any past or future as a species of eternity—as God might grasp them. The term is commonly associated with Spinoza.

substance (L., *substantia,* from *substare,* "to be under," "to be present," "to be firm," "to support"). **1.** That which is the underlying ground (support, substratum) of all phenomena. **2.** That upon which everything else depends for its existence and (usually) which itself does not depend for its existence on anything else. **3.** That which is real. Real existence as opposed to appearance or illusion. That which exists in and of itself. **4.** That without which a thing would not exist, would not be what it is. **5.** That in which properties inhere. That which possesses properties but which itself is not a property. **6.** That which endures throughout the changes of its properties. **7.** The real ESSENCE of a thing. That without which a thing could not be what it is and would be something else. **8.** The primary and the most important aspect of a thing. The essential nature of a thing in terms of which a thing is recognized and defined and without which it could not exist as that thing. **9.** MATTER. The material of a thing. **10.** BODY. The body of a thing.

substance (Aristotle). 1. The definition of anything always involves reference to a substance. **2.** A definition of the substance of a thing is present in any definition of a thing. **3.** Knowledge of substance is always prior to our knowledge of a particular thing. We must know *what* a thing is (its "whatness") before we can know its categories such as quantity, quality, position, etc. See CATEGORIES (ARISTOTLE) and further entries for Aristotle under SUBSTANCE.

substance (Descartes). There are three kinds of substances in Descartes' philosophy: **1.** *God substance:* the infinite, uncreated Being that depends upon nothing other than itself in order to exist. The completely perfect Necessary Existence upon which all things depend for their creation and continued existence. It is eternal, spiritual, immaterial, immutable, indivisible, not spatial, not temporal, omnipresent, omnipotent, omnibenevolent, creator of the universe, creator of all the other kinds of substances, and its essence is innately known to us. **2.** *Created finite spiritual substance* such as the immaterial soul of each individual. The essence of human spiritual substance is to think and have thoughts. It is not extended, hence it is intangible, invisible, nonspatial, and nontemporal. It occupies and uses material bodies but is not confined to bodies, since it may enter heaven bodiless. By the pineal gland at the base of the brain, it interacts with bodies to produce consciousness, mind, ideas, willing, imagination, etc. **3.** *Created finite material substance* such as bodies, material objects, matter, the universe. The essence of physical, bodily substance is extension. It occupies space, exists in time, is tangible, visible, locatable, changing, divisible, has shape and can be moved from place to place.

The following are some of the assumptions involved in Descartes' concept of substance: (**a**) Substance is that which can be conceived alone by itself without needing something else in terms of which it is known, and without depending on something else for its existence. (This would in effect leave only one true substance—God substance.) (**b**) Each substance has a distinct essence which it never loses. If it did lose it, it could no longer exist, it could no longer function, and it would no longer be known or knowable. (The essence of spiritual substance is thinking; the essence of material substance is extension.) The other properties possessed by substances are called modes of these essences, or essential attributes. For example, all the properties of spiritual substance such as imagining, doubting, willing, are modes (expressions, exemplifications, manifestations) of its essence—thinking. (**c**) Substances interact. (**d**) They oppose each other. (**e**) They logically and ontologically exclude each other. (They can be conceived and can exist without each other.) (**f**) Substances must exist; otherwise attributes (properties, qualities, etc.) would not have anything in which they inhered (the attribute *thinking* would not be an attribute of anything). Both the concept of thinking and that of extension would be meaningless. It is contradictory to say that thinking occurs but there is nothing that is doing the thinking. It is contradictory to say that a spatial dimension exists but there is nothing that is extended or that has that dimension. See KNOWLEDGE (DESCARTES).

substance (Kant). 1. The word *substance* does not, and cannot, refer to something independent of our consciousness. (If it did, it would have no possible meaning.) **2.** The qualities such as unity in variety, endurance, permanence, persistence that we attribute to "substance" are modes of our perceiving, structuring, and understanding the phenomena of experience. See CATEGORIES OF THE UNDERSTANDING, THE (KANT).

substance (Locke). 1. The word *substance* refers to an unknown, and unknowable, something which is the underlying base for the appearance of all natural phenomena. Substance is "something we know not what" that would be left if all the properties or qualities of a thing were taken away. **2.** Our idea of there being a substance is derived from, and composed of **(a)** our complex ideas of the powers (forces, tendencies) that things have to affect each other and to affect us and **(b)** the associations of qualities that happen together in time and space and which we group together. We cannot conceive of these powers or qualities as subsisting by themselves; therefore we assume the existence of a substance which is their cause and in which they inhere. Substance is their "supposed but unknown support." See QUALITIES, PRIMARY/SECONDARY (LOCKE).

substance (logical positivism). Metaphysical concepts such as substance and attributes (qualities, properties, etc.) can be reduced to statements about language. The difference between substance and attribute is the linguistic difference between noun (substance) and adjective (attribute). Substance is not an entity-thing but a "thing-word." Attribute is not a quality-thing but a "quality-word." Words such as *good, beauty, badness, ugliness,* are not actually existing entities. They have been so regarded because as "thing-words" they have been hypostatized or reified. See HYPOSTATIZATION; REIFICATION/REISM.

substance (Plato). Plato presents a variety of meanings for substance. Three principal ones: **1.** That which **(a)** is the primary cause of the existence of things, **(b)** maintains their continuing order, thereby sustaining their intelligibility, and **(c)** makes things intelligible to us. Compare with DE-MIURGE. **2.** The universal form or idea that is present in each class of things. See IDEAS (PLATO). **3.** *OUSIA.* The essential being or nature of things which differentiates them from other things and makes them what they are.

substance (Spinoza). 1. God (the Universe) and substance are one and the same thing. **2.** Substance is one, infinite, eternal, absolutely independent and self-sustaining. **3.** Substance is that which exists in and of itself, needing nothing else in order to exist. **4.** Substance is that upon which all things depend for their existence but which depends upon nothing other than itself for its own existence. **5.** Substance is that which is conceived without the assistance of any further concepts to make it intelligible.

Substance (God, the Universe) has infinite *attributes,* two of which we know: mind (thought) and matter (extension). The principal MODES of mind are intelligence and volition. The principal modes of matter are change (motion) and stasis (rest). These two attributes are infinite from the *NATURA NATURANS;* from *NATURA NATURATA* they are finite.

substance, primary and secondary (Aristotle). Sometimes translated as First and Second substance. Primary substance refers to particular, concrete, individual things such as an individual human, or that particular horse, or that specific house (things that are designated by nouns and serve as the subjects of sentences). A primary substance exists only as a subject and never as a predicate. (It conveys a "thisness" and "thatness" about it, as opposed to secondary substance, which conveys a "whatness" about it.) Primary substances are individual existents which exist in a relatively nondependent ontological and logical relationship to other things. Their existence does not entirely depend on something else and understanding of them is not derived from the knowledge of some prior concept.

Whereas primary substance refers, for example, to the individual man "Socrates," secondary substance refers to that which can be predicated of a primary substance (and by which a primary substance is identified). For example, "man" can be predicated of "Socrates," as in the sentence "Socrates is a man." A secondary substance exists because of something else. Secondary substances are those things within which the primary substances are included as species and genera. For example, the individual man "Socrates" is included in the species "human" and the genus for this species is "animal." Thus the species "human" and the genus "animal" are said to be secondary substances. The genera and species to which individual things belong are secondary in the sense that (a) they would not exist and (b) they would not be recognized without the existence of the primary substance to which they are applied (and in which they inhere).

Primary substance has to do with particulars ("this"), and secondary substance has to do with universals (with the differing "kinds" of things, the "whatness" of things). Whereas qualities such as redness, roundness, softness, can be had in degrees substances cannot. For example, Adam is the particular, concrete, individual thing *that* he is because of *what* he is; Adam's body has taken on the form of "human" (as opposed to, say, "horse") which form is the cause of his having the characteristics of the human that he is.

The more actual concrete properties secondary substance can be seen to have, the more substantial or real it is. A species is more truly a substance than its genus, and the individual member of that species is even closer to a true substance. Example: The actual dog Charlie is more substantial than its species (domesticated canine) and more substantial than its genus *Canidae* (which includes dogs, foxes, jackals, and wolves).

As primary substance, the single, concrete thing (object, unit, whole) possesses attributes from all the categories. The same attributes applicable to the primary substance are also applicable to every genus and species. In this sense, genus and species can be considered as subjects, as substances in their own right. The substance of any one member of the genus or species is not a different substance from the substance of any other member of the genus or species. For example, in the statement

"Socrates is a human," the substance of "human" is the substance of Socrates and not a transcendent or independent substance. "Human" stands for an entity. This entity (human) is the subject (in this case Socrates) of which it is predicated.

Using Aristotle's metaphysical writings, one can interpret secondary substance as that form (essence, idea, universal) which causes primary substance to be what it is and which maintains its continued existence.

substance as a category (Aristotle). The category which alone of all the categories (**a**) has no opposite or contrary to which it can be contrasted; (**b**) has none of the qualities of the other categories; (**c**) includes within it reference to all the other categories; (**d**) is prior in existence and in our knowledge to the other categories; (**e**) is independent of them (but they are not independent of substance); and (**f**) whose meaning is not obtained by specific reference to the other categories. See CATEGORIES (ARISTOTLE).

substance as a particular subject (Aristotle). Any subject (noun) of a sentence which cannot be predicated of another subject and which is not included in another individual thing can be termed a substance.

substance as substratum (Aristotle). 1. That to which qualities attach. That in which qualities inhere. **2.** That which endures (persists, subsists) as itself throughout its changing qualities and in which 1 takes place. **3.** That which can possess or receive contrary qualities. Since substance in this sense has no opposite, and change is from opposite to opposite, substance itself does not undergo change, does not either as matter or form come into existence or pass out of existence. What does come into existence is a particular, concrete object which is a combination of form and matter: a "this-such-of-a-kind." Both matter and form are already in potential existence before the existence of the particular, concrete "this-such-of-a-kind." The origin of this particular involves the development of both matter and form from a potential existence to an actual existence.

Substance as substratum or substrate is not in itself a particular thing and therefore must be distinguished from Aristotle's other meanings of substance. Substance as a substratum lacks characteristics such as separability, specific unity, particularization, a "thisness" or "thatness." That substratum which has a "thisness" or particularity about it and thereby can be recognized as having assignable properties, is then "a substance" of some sort. See GENESIS (ARISTOTLE).

substance as a universal term (Aristotle). Any subject (noun) of a sentence which cannot be included as part of an individual thing but which can be used to predicate something of it, can be termed a substance. Thus any universal can be regarded as a substance. See UNIVERSALS (ARISTOTLE).

substance theory of the mind. See MIND, TYPES OF THEORIES OF.

substantia (L., "that of which a thing consists," "a being," "an essence," "material," "contents"). A post-Augustinian Latin word sometimes used as a replacement and synonym for the English "substance." The word *substantia* was probably created out of the literal meaning of the Greek word *HYPOSTASIS*, "standing under." The adjective form is *substantialis*.

substantial (L., *substantialis*, "of or belonging to the essence of something or to substance," "essential"). **1.** Material. **2.** Of or pertaining to SUB-STANCE. **3.** REAL.

substantial forms. Forms which imbue themselves into matter, thereby giving it a particular being. Examples: vegetative souls, animal or sensating souls. Substantial forms are not material. Substantial forms need to enter matter in order to manifest themselves and reveal their potential, whereas SUBSISTENT FORMS do not. In all members of the same species or class the substantial forms are all of the same kind, and it is in terms of the class to which they belong that they are identified and known.

substantialism. The belief that constant, unchanging realities or substances underlie all changing phenomena.

substitutivity, Leibniz's principle of. Stated in Latin: *Eadem sunt, quae sibi mutuo substitui possunt, salva veritate,* which may be translated as: "Those things which can (at any time) be mutually substituted one for the other, without changing their truth, are identical."

substratum (substrate) (L., *substratum*, "a spreading or laying under," from past participle of *substernere*, "to strew under," from *sub*, "under," and *sternere*, "to strew," "to stretch out"). **1.** That (a) which underlies, maintains, causes, or supports a thing and (b) in which the qualities of the thing inhere. **2.** That permanent, unchanging subject, structure, or cause of phenomena and its properties. **3.** That (a) which remains identical as the selfsame thing despite the changes of its properties and (b) which remains when all the properties are taken away from the object. **4.** The ground of all being. See entries under SUBSTANCE.

subsumption (L., *sub*, "under," and *sumere*, "to take," "to put"). **1.** The act of subsuming or the state of being subsumed under something else. **2.** In logic, the act or the state of including (a) the species under its genus and the individual under the species, or (b) the particular instance under a generalization, rule, or law.

sufficient reason, principle of. See REASON, PRINCIPLE OF SUFFICIENT; REASON, PRINCIPLE OF SUFFICIENT (LEIBNIZ).

sui generis (L., "of its own kind," "alone of its kind," or "unique"). When regarded in an absolute sense it refers to the universe or to God.

summum bonum (L., "the highest good," "the ultimate good," "the supreme good," "the final good"). **1.** That ultimate final goal (aim, end, purpose, value) of human life for the sake of which everything else is done. **2.** That which is (or should be) desired or valued as the most cherished and most sought after experience or object. The following are some things that have been regarded as the *summum bonum* of life: pleasure, happiness, the greatest happiness of the greatest number, virtue, self-actualization, fulfillment of duty or conscience or the voice of God, perfection, self-mastery, contemplation, a good will, love of humankind, love of God, ecstasy, beatitude, salvation, power, money. **3.** In metaphysics and theology, the highest value or good in a hierarchy of values or goods that cannot be subordinated to any other. (The other values (**a**) are listed in a subordinate and descending order of preference and/or (**b**) are seen to be ontologically related to that highest good which is their source, inspiration, cause. All goods in the case of **b** derive their value from the power of the *summum bonum* to impart value to the other dependent goods.)

summum genus. See GENUS, SUMMUM.

superman. The term usually translating and associated with Nietzsche's ÜBERMENSCH or "Overman." That level of humanity far superior to the present one toward which we must aspire and which is the aim of evolution. See SLAVE MORALITY (NIETZSCHE).

supernatural, the (L., *super,* "over," "above," "beyond," and *naturalis, natura,* "nature"). A realm of being which: **1.** is superior in power and reality to the universe, **2.** exists beyond the universe, **3.** transcends the powers and laws of the universe, **4.** is in some manner and to some degree in control of the universe, **5.** (usually) is able to suspend the laws of the universe in order to produce miracles, and **6.** (usually) is thought to create the universe out of nothing. Compare with PRETERNATURAL.

supernaturalism. Sometimes *supranaturalism.* **1.** The belief in a realm of existence over and above the material realm of existence. **2.** The belief that there are powers (forces, agencies, energies) beyond the universe which affect the course of events in the universe. **3.** The belief in a transcendent God: a God who exists in another realm and as a totally different existent from the universe. Opposite to MATERIALISM; NATURALISM.

supposition (L., *suppositio,* "a placing under," "a substitution," from *supponere,* "to put or set under," from *sub,* "under," and *ponere,* "to put," "to place"). The act of positing, supposing, assuming something tentatively or hypothetically without its being given in experience, for the sake of the development of an argument which may lead to something capable of being experienced.

supranaturalism. See SUPERNATURALISM.

suspension of disbelief. Sometimes *suspension of belief.* The interruption of a disbelieving attitude so that one may imaginatively and perhaps sympathetically enter into the perspective of another system of thought (a religion, a philosophy, a play, a ritual) in order to see the interconnections of and experience the feelings of that system.

suspension of judgment. See EPOCHĒ.

syllogism. Any valid deductive argument having two premises and a conclusion. The premises are so related to the conclusion that they imply it; the conclusion must follow.

syllogism, categorical (Gk., *syllogismos,* "a reckoning all together," "a reasoning," "a syllogism," from *syn,* "with," "together," and *logizesthai,* "to reckon"). **1.** A valid deductive argument (**a**) expressed in categorical statements, (**b**) composed of two premises (a major and a minor premise) and a conclusion, (**c**) containing three and only three terms, of which (**d**) one is found only in the premises and once only in each premise and (**e**) the other two are found once each in the conclusion and once each in each premise, and (**f**) the premises of which taken together necessarily imply the conclusion. Example:

Major Premise: All humans are mortal.
Minor Premise: Adam is a human.

Conclusion: Therefore, Adam is mortal.

2. A valid deductive inference (**a**) stated in categorical statements (**b**) in which a conclusion connecting two terms (a major term which is the predicate of the conclusion, and a minor term which is the subject of the conclusion) is (**c**), deduced from two premises that connect those two terms to a third term (the middle term).

symbol (Gk., *symbolon,* "a sign by which one knows or infers a thing," "an outward sign representing a hidden meaning or an abstract idea," from *symballein,* "to put together," "to compare," from *syn,* "with," and *ballein,* "to throw"). **1.** Something (usually a visible sign) that stands for an idea or object. **2.** That (a word, a mark, a gesture) which is used to represent something else (a meaning, a quality, an abstraction, an idea, an object). **3.** That which is given meaning by means of common agreement and/or by convention or custom. (This may range anywhere from a flashing light that means an emergency, to a gesture that means boredom, or to a musical notation that means a high *C*.)

The meaning of "symbol" is often limited to a conventional sign (see SIGN, CONVENTIONAL): something constructed by society or by individuals and given a more or less standard meaning that members of that society agree upon or share. This restricted sense of "symbol" is contrasted with a natural sign. See SIGN, NATURAL.

sympathy (Gk., *sympatheia,* "fellow feeling," "sympathy," from *syn,* "with," and *pathos,* "suffering," "passion," "emotion," "feeling"). **1.** Feeling something believed to be that which another person (or living creature) is also feeling. **2.** Having feelings that correspond to or duplicate those that another person (or creature) is experiencing. **3.** Partaking of, sharing, or participating in the feelings of others. **4.** Fellow feeling toward another person or toward others, especially in sorrow, grief, affliction, TRAGEDY. **5.** The feeling of sorrow for the suffering of another creature or creatures and/or of another person or persons. **6.** The conscious or nonconscious shared feelings, inclinations, or emotions of people that induce further common feelings, conformity, harmony, or mutual understanding. **7.** The formal or informal expression of any of the above feelings.

Sometimes used loosely as a synonym for EMPATHY. Sometimes called or included in SYNAESTHESIA. Related words: PATHOS; PITY; commiseration (which implies a profound pity, sorrow, or grief about another person's suffering); compassion (which is a deeply felt tenderness for another person or living creature, especially in reference to severe or inevitable distress, misfortune, pain, anguish, or suffering).

sympathy (ethics). 1. (a) The feeling of unity and emotional involvement with and resemblance to fellow humans whereby **(b)** one has a desire to live in harmony with and cooperate with them. (This may be extended to all living things and/or creatures.) **2.** The tendency in human nature to identify with the feelings of humanity in general and of individual persons, in order to promote such things as harmony, cooperation, respect, love, order, and peace in society. In Hume, sympathy and SENTIMENT were the foundations of morality.

synaesthesia. Also *synaesthesis* (Gk., *syn,* "with," and *aesthēsis,* "sensation"). **1.** Concomitant sensation. The experience of one kind of sensation but apprehended as another sensation, as when a sound is felt to have a characteristic color. **2.** EMPATHY and SYMPATHY.

syncretism (Gk., *syngkrasis,* "a blending," "a tempering," "a mixing together," "uniting"). The bringing together of, or the attempt to bring together, conflicting ideologies into a unity of thought and/or into a cooperating, harmonious social relationship.

synoptic philosophy. The attempt to envision in an abstract way an all-inclusive world view and to see the relationships of all things with one another in accordance with basic principles of change and activity. See entries under METAPHYSICS.

syntactics. The study of the grammatical structures into which the symbols (words) of a language can be put in order to convey meaning. Synonymous with most meanings of SYNTAX.

syntax (Gk., *syntaxis,* "a putting together," "an order," "an arrangement," "an organization," "a structure," "a grammatical construction"). **1.** The grammatical structure of sentences. **2.** The grammatical construction of sentences. **3.** The proper structuring (arranging, constructing) of words into sentences according to grammatical rules and to usage. **4.** The study of **(a)** the structural or grammatical relationships among symbols and **(b)** the ways in which these symbols can be arranged in order to communicate meaning.

Syntax focuses mainly on the grammatical interrelationships of the structures of a language and their systematic organization, in comparison with SEMANTICS, which deals with the meaning level of language and its components.

synthesis (Gk., *synthesis,* "a putting together," "a composition," "a combination," from *syn*, "with," and *tithenai*, "to place"). **1.** The bringing together of separate ideas or differing ideologies into a whole. **2.** The result of **1. 3.** The combining of things (ideas, concepts, qualities) into more complex wholes from simpler things. **4.** The result of **3. 5.** The third phase in the dialectical process of thesis, antithesis, synthesis. See DIALECTIC (HEGEL).

synthetic (Gk., *synthetikos*, "one skilled in putting together," "one who constructs or structures"). Referring to a statement (sentence, proposition, judgment) which asserts something about the real world (and not about how words are used or about the meaning of words). "Synthetic" is contrasted with analytic, tautological, definitional, *A PRIORI*, certain, necessary, APODEICTIC, and used interchangeably with contingent, empirical, probable, *A POSTERIORI*, descriptive.

synthetic philosophy. 1. In general, the attempt to combine all the fields of knowledge into a coherent, consistent unity. **2.** Specifically, the philosophy of Herbert Spencer, which attempted to combine all the sciences into a connected whole.

system (Gk., *systēma*, "a whole compounded of parts," "a system," "a composition," from *syn*, "with," and *istanai*, "to place"). **1.** An assemblage of things unified into a consistent whole by a regular interrelationship (interaction, interdependence, interconnection) of its parts. **2.** An assemblage of things (objects, ideas, rules, axioms, etc.) arranged in a coherent order (of subordination, or of inference, or of generality, etc.) according to some rational or intelligible principle (or plan, or scheme, or method). **3.** The principle or method of operation by which **1** and **2** are achieved and/or explained (as in the phrases "the system of logic," "the system of physical laws," "the system of classification"). See ORDER.

T

table of categories. See CATEGORIES OF THE UNDERSTANDING, THE (KANT).

table of judgments, logical (Kant). See CATEGORIES OF LOGIC, THE (KANT).

tables of investigation, the three (Bacon). Francis Bacon propounded a procedure for scientific research that he named Tables (or Rules) of Investigation (or Presentation). They are: **1.** *The Table of Affirmation* or *The Rule of Presence:* Enumerate and examine all the varied positive examples of the phenomena under investigation that have the same characteristics. Bacon cited as an example the study of heat. All the variety of instances having heat present in them must be listed and studied—the sun, light, fire, friction, the human body. **2.** *The Table of Negation* or *The Rule of Counterexample:* Cite all the negative cases in which, for example, heat is not present but where one might think it should be, as in things such as the skin of dead persons, some reflections of light. **3.** *The Table of Comparison* or *The Rule of Differing Degrees:* Examine and compare the differences among phenomena in order to find any correlations that exist among their differences. See BACONIAN METHOD.

tabula rasa **(Locke)** (L., "a smoothed or blank tablet"). Locke used this phrase as a simile to partly describe his concept of the mind. Some of the main points: **1.** The mind before birth (or a specific experience) is like a blank tablet (or slate or piece of white paper). **2.** By means of stimuli from the external world, sensations (simple ideas) are imprinted upon that tablet. **3.** Such an activity is the source and the ground of all knowledge and thinking. **4.** There are no innate ideas or principles. **5.** The mind is a passive entity: a receptacle that is able to receive stimuli, sensations, ideas, knowledge, but not able to create them on its own.

taste. Personal preference.

tautology (Gk., *tautologia,* "tautology," from *tauto,* "the selfsame," and *logos,* "word," "meaning"). **1.** The repetition of the same meaning but using different words. Example: "audible to the ear." **2.** Restating the same idea but in different words. Example: "That bachelor is unmarried." **3.** In categorical logic, expressing a quality or meaning in the predicate which is already contained implicitly or explicitly in the subject. Examples: "All women are human." "All bachelors are unmarried males." "All colored objects are colored." "All causes have effects." "All subjects have predicates." **4.** Any statement which is necessarily true because of its meaning. Examples: "All black horses are black." "Bachelors are unmarried males." "Every effect has a cause." "If she is a mother, then she is a parent." "That which is green is colored." "Every cube has twelve edges." "Today is tomorrow's yesterday, and today is yesterday's tomorrow." "If today is Saturday, then tomorrow is Sunday." **5.** Any compound sentence (statement) that is necessarily true because of its logical form. Examples: "If all X's are Y's, then no X's are non-Y's."

The following points apply to tautologies: (**a**) Their truth cannot be, need not be, and is not established by referring them to sense experience or empirical testing. Their truth is known merely by understanding the meanings of the statements and/or their logical form (and also by logically inferring their truth from statements so understood); (**b**) they are always necessarily true under all conditions, true by definition. If they are denied, a self-contradiction ensues. (**c**) They cannot be falsified by experience. The rules of inference in logic and mathematics are tautologies. See *A PRIORI;* STATEMENT, ANALYTIC. Contrasted with CONTINGENT (LOGIC).

techne (Gk., "art," "skill," "craft," "cunning of hand," "technique," "a trade," "handiwork," "a system or method of making or doing something"). Found in English words such as technic, technical, technicality, technician, technique, technology, technological, technosophy. **1.** The very general meaning of *techne,* especially as found in Aristotle, refers to anything deliberately created by humans in contrast to anything not humanly created. (The latter is a product of *PHYSIS,* or nature.) This sense of *techne* includes houses, shoes, paintings, songs, vases, toys, bombs, and excludes things found in nature such as lakes, mountains, people, stars. **2.** A less general meaning of *techne* refers to "a handiwork," "a craft," "a technique," "a skill." This includes any skill (**a**) in *making* things (sculpture, clothes, shoes, poems, vases), (**b**) in *doing* things (teaching, healing, managing, diplomacy), (**c**) in *acting* (reciting poetry, dramatizing an event on stage), (**d**) *dancing,* and (**e**) *singing.* **3.** Specifically, *techne* refers to the knowledge of *how* to do or make things (as opposed to *why* things are the way they are); *how* to achieve a desired end or how to produce something. **4.** *Techne* also refers to the rational, professional knowledge of the *rules of procedure* involved in making or doing things. The Greeks included a variety of sciences and arts under the heading of *technē*, such as all of the crafts which we regard as the fine arts, the industrial-vocational arts, the applied sciences (technology), the medical arts and medical sciences. In the class of *technē* which we call fine arts, Plato had three general categories: (**a**) the *musical arts* (songs, dances, instrumental performances, and combinations of these); (**b**) the *visual arts* (sculpture, architecture, painting, pottery making, mosaics) and (**c**) the *literary arts* (lyric, epic, and dramatic poetry; drama; the dialogue). See entries under POIĒSIS.

For the Greeks an aesthetic response or attitude is possible both to *technē* in any sense of that term (fine art, useful art, productive art, action) and to *physis* (nature) in any of its aspects. We can have an aesthetic relationship as much to a sunset or to a piece of driftwood as we can to a sculpture. Compare with FINE ARTS.

teleological animism. See ANIMISM, TELEOLOGICAL.

teleological argument for the existence of God. The teleological argument for God's existence has a variety of forms. The following are a few: **1.** Order (purpose, design, pattern) exists in the universe. Order cannot exist without an orderer. Therefore, God exists as the source of that order. **2.** Things move toward goals; they struggle to complete themselves. God exists as the intelligent being that (**a**) impels things toward their goals, (**b**) sets up the goals, and (**c**) designs the means by which these goals are to be attained. **3.** The universe as a whole has a purpose toward which it is struggling. God exists as the creator and the sustainer of that purpose. See DESIGN, ARGUMENT FROM.

teleological causation. See CAUSES, ARISTOTLE'S FOUR.

teleological ethics. See ETHICS, TELEOLOGICAL.

teleological explanation. See EXPLANATION, TELEOLOGICAL.

teleology (Gk., *telos,* "end," "purpose," "completed state," and *logos,* "the study of," "the rational principles of"). The study of phenomena exhibiting order, design, purposes, ends, goals, tendencies, aims, direction, and how they are achieved in a process of development. See EXPLANATION, TELEOLOGICAL. Contrast with DYSTELEOLOGICAL.

telepathy (Gk., *tēle,* "far," "far off," "at a distance," and *pathos,* "emotion," "feeling," "passion," "suffering"). **1.** The communication of information (ideas, feelings) from one person to another without the use of the five senses, and without any physical contact or known physical means of transferring that information **2.** The ability to obtain information as in **1.** **3.** Mental states and processes of one person directly affecting the bodily and/or the mental states and processes of another person whether known to that other person or not. Telepathy is characterized as being nonsensory, noninferential, immediate, and a direct transfer of information. See CLAIRVOYANCE; EXTRASPECTION; PARAPSYCHOLOGY.

telos (Gk., "the completion or fulfillment of something," "the completed stage of an activity," "the end," "the result," "purpose," "goal," "aim," "that final point toward the achievement of which a process is directed").

temperament (L., *temperamentum,* "a mixing in due proportion," "temperament"). The general bodily or mental character or predisposition of the personality. Temperaments were classified as sanguine, phlegmatic, bilious (or choleric), melancholic, etc.

temporal (L., *temporalis,* from *tempus,* "time"). 1. Characterized by or referring to time. 2. Temporary. Limited by, or in, time 3. Transitory (as opposed to eternal). 4. Materiality. Material time. 5. Secular. Earthly. That which has to do with this life or world as opposed to the supernatural, heavenly, sacred, or eternal world. 6. Pertaining to that which is political, civil, earthly, common (as in *temporal power* versus *clerical power*).

term (L., *terminis,* "a boundary," "a limit," "an end"). 1. Any word or phrase that can be applied to something. 2. Any word or phrase that has a meaning, as in, "Please define your terms." 3. Any of the things being related in a statement. Example: In the statement "Adam loves karate," Adam and karate are the terms being related by the relationship "loves." 4. Any member of a function, series, or sum, as in "the terms of this sequence," "the terms of this binomial equation."

term (categorical logic). The SUBJECT or PREDICATE of a categorical statement. Example: In the categorical statement "Adam is strong," "Adam" is the subject term and "strong" is the predicate term.

term, distributed. A term is distributed whenever it is preceded explicitly or implicitly by a universal quantifier; whenever it refers to all the items it can mean; whenever it refers to all of its EXTENSION; whenever what it says is applicable to every instance of it. Otherwise it is an *undistributed term.* See DISTRIBUTIVELY.

term, empty. See EXTENSION, EMPTY.

term, privative. See PRIVATIVE TERM/WORD/NAME.

tertiary qualities. See QUALITIES, TERTIARY.

Tertullian's dictum. See *CREDO QUIA ABSURDUM EST.*

testability principle. See CONFIRMATION, PRINCIPLE OF; VERIFIABILITY, PRINCIPLE OF.

thanatism (Gk., *thanatos,* "death"). The belief in the complete cessation and annihilation of consciousness (the soul, the mind, the self, the ego) at death. Opposite to ATHANATISM.

thanatology (Gk., *thanatos,* "death," and *logos,* "the study of"). The study of death and dying in all its aspects.

theism (Gk., *theos,* "divine," "God"). 1. Belief in divine things, gods, or a God. Opposite to ATHEISM. 2. Belief in one God (monotheism) transcending but yet in some way IMMANENT in the universe. Contrasted with DEISM. Other characteristics usually associated with this monotheistic Deity of theism: God is personal, the creator, the sustainer of existence, omnipotent, omnibenevolent, omniscient, supreme in power, reality, and value, the source and sanction of all values, and accessible to human communication. See GOD CONCEPTS.

theodicy (Gk., *theos,* "God," and *dikē,* "justice," "right"). **1.** The discipline that attempts to justify the ways of God to humanity. **2.** The attempt to vindicate the goodness and justice of God in ordaining or allowing moral and natural evil and human suffering. **3.** The attempt to make God's omnipotence and omnibenevolence compatible with the existence of evil. **4.** The attempt to defend the belief that this is the best of all possible worlds.

theology (Gk., *theologia,* from *theos,* "God," and *legein,* "to speak," or from *logos,* "the study of"). **1.** The study of the relation of the divine (or ideal, or eternally unchanging) world to the physical world. **2.** The study of the nature, being, and will of God (or the gods). **3.** The doctrines or beliefs about God (or gods) of particular religious groups or of individual thinkers. **4.** Any coherently organized body of doctrine concerning the nature of God and His relationship with humans and the universe. **5.** The systematic attempt to present, interpret, and justify in a consistent and meaningful way the belief in gods and/or God. See FIRST PHILOSOPHY (ARISTOTLE).

theology, negative. Sometimes *via negativa.* **1.** Theology based on the belief that God's being so vastly exceeds our human finite being that none of His characteristics can be known in any real or full sense. None of the attributes of God reveals His true nature. We can know "that" God is (*quod sit*) but not "what" He is (*quid sit*) in Himself. **2.** Theology which holds that we can only know what God is by knowing what He is not.

theorem (Gk., *theōrēma,* "a theory," "a sight," "a view," "a rule," "a principle"). **1.** That which is regarded and established as a principle (rule, law, necessary truth). **2.** That formula in a logical calculus for which there is a proof and which is used to deduce other statements.

theoretical. 1. Depending upon, or confined to, speculation and/or theory. Opposite to actual, real, applied. **2.** Not practical. Having no applicability. **3.** Obscure and/or abstract. **4.** Having to do with issues concerning generalities and/or general principles about things rather than about what exactly is to be done or should be done.

theoretical construct. See CONSTRUCT, THEORETICAL.

theoretical reason (Kant). See REASON, THEORETICAL (KANT).

theōria (Gk., "a looking at," "viewing," "beholding," "rational contemplation," "knowing"). Used by Plato to mean "contemplation" or "the intuitive grasp of the intelligible eternal Forms." Used by Aristotle to refer to abstract, intellectual knowledge and contrasted with *PRAXIS* and *POIĒSIS.* See *DIANOIA; POIĒSIS/POIETIKOS* (ARISTOTLE).

theories of perception. See PERCEPTION, THEORIES OF.

theory. (Gk., *theōria,* "a beholding," "a looking at," "viewing"). **1.** An apprehension of things in their universal and ideal relationships to one another. Opposite to practice and/or to factual existence. **2.** An abstract or general principle within a body of knowledge that presents a clear and systematic view of some of its subject matter, as in a "theory" of art or the atomic "theory." **3.** A general, abstract, and idealized principle or model used to explain phenomena, as in the "theory" of natural selection. **4.** A hypothesis, supposition, or construct assumed to be true and on the basis of which phenomena can be predicted and/or explained and from which further empirical knowledge can be deduced.

theory, scientific. The distinctions among concepts such as THEORY, LAW, and HYPOTHESIS are not finely drawn. These are a few things that can be said about scientific theory: **1.** A theory contains many terms that are not directly observable. (Direct experience does not give us a "meson," a "neutrino," a "photon," etc.) A theory is based on indirect evidence and is assumed for pragmatic reasons as being useful in systematizing, simplifying, and explaining phenomena. **2.** There is no direct and definite empirical procedure for identifying and verifying the terms and models of a theory. (Experimental tests may be conducted that seem indirectly to indicate the existence of the concepts and referents of the theory, such as traces on photographic film indicating the existence of radiation, etc.) **3.** The terms in a theory are not defined as precisely as the terms found in scientific laws. **4.** A theory depends upon the confirmation or verification of laws for its usefulness, logical support, and acceptance. **5.** A theory is a part of a system of interrelated concepts that imply the existence of phenomena that can be described by laws. Some laws may be deduced from theories. **6.** Theories are used to support or explain a law. (Usually laws are not thought of as dependent upon the theories that are sometimes used to explain them. Theories may change, or contrasting theories may be used to support, explain, or describe a law.) **7.** A theory is often more abstract, less concrete, than a law. **8.** A theory often has the capability of predicting phenomena, extrapolating to new phenomena, and suggesting further applications, and is considered as valuable or correct to the extent to which it can do these things. **9.** A theory can apply to new experimental observations without itself undergoing many conceptual alterations. **10.** Theories are often not formalized, and one of the main aims of science is to construct more formalized systems of theories.

theory of types. See TYPES, THEORY OF.

thesis (metaphysics). See MATERIALISM, DIALECTICAL (MARX-ENGELS).

thing-in-itself, the. See *DING AN SICH, DAS.*

thinking. 1. A mental activity whereby a person uses concepts acquired in the process of learning and directs them toward some goal and/or object. **2.** Any of the mental activities of which we are conscious, such as reflecting, inferring, remembering, introspecting, retrospecting, doubting, willing, feeling, understanding, apprehending, perceiving, meditating, imagining, pondering, etc.

thinking, black-and-white. See BLACK-AND-WHITE THINKING.

this. An indexical sign (see SIGN, INDEXICAL) such as "not," "that," "I," "here" that (**a**) attempts to disclose the meaning of its referent directly (usually ostensively) by such maneuvers as pointing, (**b**) on its own contains no descriptive dimensions until amplified further, (**c**) when applied has in each case a different referent, and (**d**) attempts to select or discriminate features of reality thereby focusing attention upon specific items in our consciousness.

thought, a. That of which we are conscious (ideas, willing, imagining, understanding, perceiving, sensing, feeling) at any given moment.

thought, the three laws of. See LAWS OF THOUGHT, THE THREE.

time. 1. That in which events are distinguishable in terms of the relations of before and after, beginning and end. (Sometimes this is thought of as a *nonspatial medium* [*realm, order*] in which things change and events take place.) **2.** That which is distinguished by the relationships of before and after, beginning and end, and which is inseparable from change. **3.** The measurable aspect of duration (instants, intervals)—a particular point, moment, period, portion, or part of duration or of what endures. **4.** The irreversible succession of instants (events, segments, points, intervals, durations) conceived of as a linear progression or only as a directional line. **5.** A measure of change, or change itself observed, as in the positional change of the sun or the hands of a clock, or the qualitative change of the color of an object or sharpness of a sound or sight. Such changes are often used as a reference for comparison to other changes; for example the cycle of the moon is called a month, and is used as a measure of time to compare to the cycle of light and darkness which we call a day.

time (Kant). 1. The intuited infinite continuum (of all present and possible experience) and **2.** the immediately given innate *a priori* form by which the given is experienced as a flow. See SENSE, INTERNAL AND EXTERNAL (KANT); SPACE (KANT); SPACE/TIME (KANT).

time (Plato). Time is "the moving image of perfect eternity." By this Plato meant that time is an imperfect imitation of the timeless unchanging realm of perfect ideal forms. Change, succession, and hence time are merely the results of the mind's inability to grasp things all at once (*SUB SPECIE AETERNITAS*) in their entirety. Time is a product peculiar to the mind and dependent on its functions.

time, absolute (Newton). Some of the basic points in Newton's concept of absolute time: **1.** Absolute time is independent of natural (physical) events and is prior in existence to natural events. **2.** Absolute time is mathematical time, a homogeneous mathematical order. **3.** Its essential nature is to flow uniformly without regard and without relation to any external thing.

4. Absolute time is eternal. It flowed before the creation of the universe.
5. Absolute time is directional. It has an absolute direction and movement.

Newton's concept of absolute time was opposed to the concept of relative time, which held that time and space were sets of relations among objects and were never independent of objects and of change.

time, subjective. 1. Positive meaning: Time is the sense of a now, or a present, which implies also a sense of a past and a future. Subjective time is usually regarded as a continuous but heterogeneous flow of an irreversible series of successive states which cannot be sharply divided. Subjective time is not a passive but an active sense of a process directed into a future, or being taken into a future. It is something experienced intuitively, immediately, concretely as an ongoing activity. Subjective time as immediately felt is not quantified (but it can be quantified). **2.** Negative meaning: Time is unreal and only a product of the operations of our consciousness and/or imagination. Time as something existing independently of consciousness is an illusion. What we regard as the "past" is merely a part of a memory-state. The "future" is merely an expectation in consciousness at any given moment of its operation.

timeless. 1. Not in time. **2.** That which cannot be described in terms of tenses, or time.

timeless present. See PRESENT, THE TIMELESS.

timocracy (timarchy). (Gk., *timē,* "esteem," "honor," "dignity," "worship," and *kratein,* "to control," "to rule," "to govern"). **1.** Plato: A state in which the love of honor, glory, esteem is the highest ideal and the ruling principle of government. **2.** Aristotle: A state in which honors are distributed according to the evaluation of property held. **3.** A state ruled by leaders of honor, worth, competence, and esteem as opposed to class, heredity, power, privilege.

timology (Gk., *timē,* "honor," "worth," "valuation," "esteem," and *logos,* "the study of"). **1.** The study of value or what makes a thing valued. See AXIOLOGY. **2.** The belief that values are intrinsically worthwhile without regard to external justifications. Opposite to RELATIVISM.

token. 1. A particular and individual sign such as a word, an utterance, a gesture. **2.** The instance or replica of a written or spoken word.

Contrasted with TYPE, which is an instance of a particular kind of token. Example: In the statement "The color was not the one I wanted," there are eight instances (tokens) of words and two instances (tokens) of the type "the." The former may be called word-tokens and the latter word-types (or type-tokens). See AMBIGUITY, TYPE-TOKEN; TYPE/TOKEN DISTINCTION.

tragedy (Aristotle) (Gk., *tragōdia,* "tragedy." The original meaning was "goat song." It stems from early times when either a goat was given as a prize for the best lyric tragedy, dance, or song, or the actors clothed themselves in goat skins). The main elements of tragedy are: **(a)** a work of dramatic art (as opposed to narrative art), **(b)** that depicts serious action, character, and thought, **(c)** structured with a beginning, middle, and end that is a complete story in itself, **(d)** of appropriate length, not too long, yet not too short, **(e)** with a plot, **(f)** in which a great person of noble stature is seen inexorably to fall from a state of happiness to a state of undeserved suffering or misery, **(g)** all presented in an artistic setting of fine language, diction, song, and spectacle, and **(h)** that is an interconnected whole which produces feelings such as awe and relief and the purgation of the emotions of pity and fear. See KATHARSIS (ARISTOTLE). Compare with COMEDY (ARISTOTLE).

tragedy, aesthetic paradox of. Tragedy, like other works of art, provides us with aesthetic beauty and pleasure. But tragedy depicts happenings that are not pleasurable to perceive, are painful, traumatic, and in some cases border on the ugly. Compare with UGLY, THE PARADOX OF THE.

transcendence (Sartre). Refers to one's relation to, or purposive direction into, the future in accordance with ideas, emotions, hopes, preparations, goals.

transcendence of the ego. See EGO, TRANSCENDENTAL (KANT).

transcendent (L., *transcendere,* from *trans,* "across," "over," "beyond," and *scandere,* "to climb"). **1.** Superior, supreme, surpassing, exalted, of superlative quality. **2.** Beyond what is given to our experience. **3.** Referring to that which is forever beyond the grasp of ordinary experience and scientific explanation. **4.** Independent and separate.

transcendental analytic (Kant). Refers to Kant's attempt to analyze all *A PRIORI* knowledge in terms of the concepts found in the ideal and pure cognition of the understanding. See CATEGORIES OF LOGIC, THE (KANT); CATEGORIES OF THE UNDERSTANDING, THE (KANT).

transcendental deduction. See DEDUCTION, TRANSCENDENTAL (KANT).

transcendental dialectic (Kant). See DIALECTIC, TRANSCENDENTAL (KANT).

transcendental ego of apperception. See APPERCEPTION, TRANSCENDENTAL.

transcendental idealism. See IDEALISM, TRANSCENDENTAL (KANT).

transcendental illusion. See ILLUSION, TRANSCENDENTAL (KANT).

transcendental knowledge (Kant). See KNOWLEDGE, TRANSCENDENTAL (KANT).

transcendental logic. See CATEGORIES OF LOGIC, THE (KANT).

transcendental philosophy (Kant). 1. In general, the name given to the philosophy of Kant. **2.** Specifically, the *A PRIORI* analysis of pure reason that Kant proposed, which would present and analyze the basic concepts of pure reason and trace out all its implicit concepts and assumptions.

transcendental table of the pure concepts of the understanding. See CATEGORIES OF THE UNDERSTANDING, THE (KANT).

transcendental proof (Kant). See PROOF, TRANSCENDENTAL (KANT).

transcendentalia/transcendentia (L., "transcendentals"). A term used in medieval philosophy to refer to any idea (concept, notion) that applies to all existence of whatever kind. The list includes: *res* (Thing), *ens* (Being), *aliquid* (Something), *unum* (One, Unity, Whole), *verum* (True), *bonum* (Good, Perfect). These ideas were believed to go beyond (transcend) Aristotle's categories (see CATEGORIES [ARISTOTLE]) because it was believed they could not be subsumed under them.

transcendentalism. 1. The belief in the superiority of the intuitive or spiritual over the empirical and scientific. Holds that there is an ideal, spiritual reality beyond the space-time world of our experience that can be grasped and with which all things are infused. Associated especially with Ralph Waldo Emerson and his followers, who have been called transcendentalists. (The name was erroneously applied to them because of an incorrectly supposed relationship to Kant's philosophy—see TRANSCENDENTAL PHILOSOPHY [KANT].) **2.** That in philosophy which goes beyond (transcends) empiricism or what is experienced in order to ascertain the *A PRIORI* fundamental principles or structuring processes of all knowledge.

transmigration. Also REINCARNATION, METEMPSYCHOSIS (L., *transmigrare*, from *trans*, "across," and *migrare*, "to migrate"). The passage at death of a spirit or soul into another body.

transsubjective reference. See REFERENCE, TRANSSUBJECTIVE.

transvaluation of values (Nietzsche). Sometimes *reevaluation of values.* The phrase used by Nietzsche to indicate that humans must revolt against and transcend the customary values and narrow-mindedness of society. See SLAVE MORALITY (NIETZSCHE).

triad (Gk., *tria*, "three"). A relation or group of three.

triad, inconsistent. See ANTILOGISM.

trichotomy/trichotomizing (Gk., *tricha*, "threefold," "in three parts," and *temnein*, "to cut"). The division of things into three basic parts that are regarded as fundamentally and/or irreducibly different. Examples: "A human is composed of body, mind, and soul." "Three realities exist: the realm of God, the realm of spirits, and the realm of nature."

truth. The quality of being true or correct according to some ground or test for establishing the reality of a statement (propositon, idea, thought, belief, opinion). There are a number of such grounds or tests for justifying truth: the approximation, conformity, or correspondence to facts; the COHERENCE among ideas; the pragmatic usefulness of ideas; EXPERIENCE; FAITH; AUTHORITY; INTUITION; self-evidency; revelation; tradition. "Truth" assumes that what it applies to does depict fact or reality and appeals for support to all of these methods or a mixture of these methods. Not all statements can be labeled by the word *truth* (or by the word *falsity*). Examples: *proposals* (they are accepted or rejected, not true or false); *resolutions* (they are followed or violated); *promises* (they are kept or not kept); *suggestions* (they are heeded or go unheeded); *commands* (they are obeyed or disobeyed).

truth, coherence theory of. The view that a statement (proposition, idea, thought, belief, opinion) is true if it can be put logically, consistently, systematically into a coherent body of knowledge whose every member entails and is entailed by every other member. The truth of the whole body of knowledge is relative to the degree to which it is a complete picture of absolute reality. Some further views of the coherence theory of truth: **1.** One cannot establish a correspondence between an idea and something that is not an idea (such as a fact, or an objective referent); only logical relationships among ideas can be established. **2.** A statement (idea, concept, etc.) is true if it is logically consistent with other statements accepted as true. **3.** Knowledge is a system of logically (conceptually) interrelated truths (statements, ideas) and a (partial) truth is any member of that system. (Individual truths are only partly true with respect to other truths in the system.) **4.** The collection of all the coherent truths constitutes the truth (admittedly unattainable). **5.** The ABSOLUTE is the all-inclusive truth from which all other truths derive their being, and from which they may be logically deduced. **6.** All phenomena in the universe are connected by logical necessity and flow necessarily from the Absolute. The coherence theory of truth is associated with the rationalistic and/or idealistic metaphysics of philosophers such as Leibniz, Spinoza, Hegel, Bradley, where mathematics (geometries in particular) are taken as the model for truth. Contrasted with TRUTH, CORRESPONDENCE THEORY OF.

truth, correspondence theory of. The view that a statement (proposition, idea, thought, belief, opinion) is true if what it refers to (corresponds to) exists. That to which it truly corresponds is called a fact. The process of finding such a correspondence or conformity is called VERIFICATION or CONFIRMATION. Example: The statement "Tina is sitting on my desk" is true if it corresponds to the observed fact of her sitting on my desk. The statement otherwise is false. Contrasted with TRUTH, COHERENCE THEORY OF.

truth, performative theory of. Calling something "true" is merely performing an act of concession (assent, acceptance, agreement) with what has been stated. "Truth" is not a quality or property of anything but is a SPEECH ACT (a performative act); it has nothing to do with the true or false description of a state of affairs. Sometimes referred to as the *ditto theory.* See LANGUAGE, PERFORMATIVE; PERFORMATIVE ACT.

truth, pragmatic theory of. A statement (proposition, idea, thought, belief, opinion) is true if it "works" or has practical results such as control, predictive value, or if it stimulates creative inquiry, resolves problems in science and everyday life, makes us happy.

truth, relativity of (Sophists). Whatever seems to be true, or is declared to be true by someone, is true for him and since it is true for him, it then *is* true. See RELATIVISM, PROTAGOREAN.

truth frequency. See PROBABILITY.

truths of fact (Leibniz). Statements (propositions, assertions) that are not necessarily true since they may be denied without contradiction; they just happen to be true of something about this particular real world or might happen to be true of something about a particular possible world. Statements that are not true of all objects in the universe but only about some.

truths of reason (Leibniz). Statements (propositions, meanings, ideas, concepts) that are true everywhere and in all possible worlds. They are not true only by definition, but apply descriptively to the real, external world. No amount of power, not even God's, can change these factual truths about reality, since they are the very formal structures (limitations) in which events must take place. Truths of reason cannot be denied without contradiction. The prime example of a truth of reason for Leibniz was the Law of Noncontradiction: A thing cannot be both *A* and not *A*. The other principal ones: the law of identity, the law of excluded middle, and the law of sufficient reason. See LAWS OF THOUGHT, THE THREE; REASON, PRINCIPLE OF SUFFICIENT (LEIBNIZ).

tychē **(Aristotle)** (Gk., "luck," "fortunate coincidence"). That which occurs unexpectedly, was not necessitated to happen, but which serves a purpose or can be taken advantage of to achieve some desired goal. An event unintended yet which fulfills a plan or wish one might have had. Example: You happen to meet a friend at the marketplace; you ask him to pay you the five dollars he borrowed a few weeks ago; it was *tychē* (luck) that you bumped into him; it was *tychē* that he had money on him to pay you back; you use the money to buy a ticket to the latest tragedy; you had not intended to go because you didn't have enough money; that lucky occurrence (*tychē*) of meeting your friend and getting your money back makes possible your seeing the tragedy which you had wanted to see but couldn't afford; the final *tychē* was that it was the last day for the tragedy's showing. Aristotle distinguished an "accident" or a "spontaneous event" (*automaton*) from *tychē* in that accidents are unexpected, out-of-the-ordinary events which do not and cannot serve any possible intention or goal.

tychē **(Plato).** CHANCE. One of the three causes for events in the universe. The other two are: nature (*PHYSIS*) and human purposiveness (*TECHNĒ*).

tychism (Gk., *tychē*, "luck," "chance," "fortunate happening or coincidence"). **1.** The view that chance is objectively real and is one of the conditions for the occurrence of events in the universe **2.** The belief that much if not all of evolution happens according to chance variations and events.

type. 1. A class of things all of whose members can be regarded as members of the same class—the same type of thing. **2.** An instance of a particular kind of TOKEN (word, utterance, gesture). Example: In the statement "The color was not the one I wanted" there are eight words (word-*tokens*) and one word-*type*, namely "the," found twice. The word-type

may be regarded as one word but as two word-tokens. See TYPE/TOKEN
DISTINCTION.

types, theory of. Developed by Russell and Whitehead. The basic concepts
are: (**a**) predicate (or class) and (**b**) predicate of a predicate. A predicate
applies to individual things (instances). A predicate of a predicate applies
to predicates of individual things but cannot be said to apply to the individual things themselves that possess the predicate. Predicates can be
analyzed on different levels. Example: The property "red" in the statement "The apple is red" is a first-order type. The property "red" in the
statement "Red is a property of apples" is a second-order type.

type-token amgibuity. See AMBIGUITY, TYPE-TOKEN.

type/token distinction. The distinction between a TYPE and a TOKEN distinguishes between two senses of referring to something. Example: If I ask
"How many words are there in the sentence 'The color was not the one I
wanted' "? I may be given a reply that there are eight words or a reply
that there are seven words. In a sense both answers are correct. There are
eight different words regarded as tokens, but only seven different words
regarded as types, since two of the eight words (tokens) ("the" and
"the") are of the same type. See AMBIGUITY, TYPE-TOKEN; TOKEN.

U

ugly, paradox of the. The ugly, whether found in works of art or in ordinary experience, is supposed to be distasteful and unappealing yet under certain circumstances, the ugly has an appealing aesthetic fascination and pleasure associated with it. See TRAGEDY, AESTHETIC PARADOX OF.

uncaused cause. A cause that has no cause. A cause that causes things to happen but which itself has no cause to cause it to cause things to happen. Applied to an eternal God or to an eternal universe and to human free will. See FIRST CAUSE; PRIME MOVER; UNMOVED MOVER, THE.

uncertainty, Heisenberg's principle of. For subatomic particles, both the exact position and the exact momentum (motion, velocity) cannot be known at the same time. If the position is known, then a determination of its motion will be uncertain; when the motion of the subatomic particle is known, the determination of its position will be uncertain. (A corollary of this principle is that the process of investigating subatomic phenomena affects what is being investigated and therefore the phenomena as observed do not depict true reality.) Heisenberg and others have used this principle to defend the concepts of (a) uncaused events and (b) free will. In these respects it is referred to as the *Principle of Indeterminancy or Indeterminance*. See INDETERMINISM (ETHICS); INDETERMINISM (METAPHYSICS).

understanding. 1. The ability to have knowledge and thereby to comprehend, to discern, to judge, to interpret, or to explain. See COMPREHENSION. 2. REASON. The FACULTY of knowing. In "faculty" conceptions of the mind, the understanding is regarded as a faculty of the mind by which reality is grasped and adjusted to. In CARTESIANISM, for example, it is the purpose of the faculty of the understanding to present reality to us clearly and distinctly. Occasionally it falls short of this aim and presents it obscurely, confusedly, and sometimes falsely as in the case of hallucinations, mirages, illusions, deceptions.

Understanding is usually contrasted with the WILL. See INTELLECT.

understanding (Kant). That aspect of thinking which deals (a) with concepts, judgments, and principles and (b) with the categories in terms of which pure sensation is synthesized and thereby brought into our unity of consciousness. See CATEGORIES OF THE UNDERSTANDING, THE (KANT); REASON (KANT).

understanding, pure concepts of the (Kant). See CATEGORIES OF THE UNDERSTANDING (KANT).

understanding and the will. See entries under WILL AND THE UNDERSTANDING.

undetermined. Refers to the inability of assigning (a) truth values to a statement, or (b) causes to an event.

unextended. Without spatial dimension.

unhappiness (Mill). Identical (a) with pain and (b) with the privation of pleasure. Contrast with HAPPINESS (MILL).

uniformitarianism, physical. The belief that (a) the universe exhibits the same order (laws) throughout and (b) what exists now is the product of physical activity taking place over an extremely long period of time.

uniformity of nature, principle of the. 1. The theory that what has happened once will happen again provided the circumstances for its happening are similar, and it will happen as often as those same circumstances recur. **2.** The theory that events occur in repeated patterns throughout the universe. This is based on the assumption that since events have been seen and can be seen to occur in repeated patterns and in a general regularity, all events will continue to occur in such repeated patterns. See INDUCTION, PRINCIPLE OF (METAPHYSICS). **3.** The theory that nature is uniform throughout: Given a set of conditions X followed by a set of conditions Y, upon repetition of the same set of conditions X, the same set of conditions Y that followed X will occur. Compare with CAUSAL UNIFORMITY, THE PRINCIPLE OF.

unity, functional. See FUNCTIONAL UNITY.

unity, organic. The unity of a whole whereby the functions of the parts are interrelated with the functions of other parts within the whole. The human body is usually given as a typical example of an organic unity: The workings of the lungs depend upon the workings of the heart, the blood vessels, the brain, the kidneys, and other organs, and the workings of each of these organs to some extent is interrelated with the workings of the lungs. See FUNCTIONAL UNITY.

unity, organic (Aristotle). A unity such that its parts are integrated to fulfill a primary activity; all parts serve as means to the accomplishment of ends and ultimately *an end*. No part of an organic unity acts independently or in isolation from any other part. Any change occurring to a part makes a difference to the functions of the other parts and to the whole. In a truly perfect organic unity, everything that is necessary for the performance of its function would be there, and anything that was not necessary for the performance of its function would not be there.

unity, principle of organic. The intrinsic value of a unity is not equal to the sum total of the intrinsic values of its parts.

unity in variety and variety in unity, principle of (metaphysics). Variety exists in nature; yet a recognizable form or unity can be discerned. Example: A large variety of trees exists, but there is unity of structure and function within that variety. Varieties exist even within these unities, which varieties themselves have a unity. Example: Avocado trees are a unity among the variety of trees, but among this unity of avocados is a variety of avocado trees, etc. See IDENTITY, PROBLEM OF.

universal (L., *universalis*, "universal," "belonging to all of a group"). **1.** That which pertains to the whole or to all of a class either COLLECTIVELY or DISTRIBUTIVELY. **2.** General. A general statement, or generalization about a large number of things, as opposed to a statement about only a few of them. **3.** Unlimited. All-encompassing or all-reaching. **4.** Total. Entire.

universal (epistemology). 1. A general concept common to a number of things. A feature (characteristic, quality, property) that particular things share, or have in common, with other particular things. **2.** That which is predicable of many individual things and by which we then classify them into a class. Examples: "Female" (or "femaleness") is predicable of Simone, Anne, Lori, Barbara, Diana; hence it may be regarded as a universal. "Red" (or "redness") is common to a number of things such as "red" apple, "red" table, "red" lips; hence it may be regarded as a universal. Universals are usually common nouns or adjectives, and are contrasted with proper nouns which are regarded as individuals and not as universals. **3.** An abstract or general word (term, idea, class, concept) such as beauty, goodness, truth, redness, justice, equality which indicates something common that is repeated in a number of things or names and thereby can be recognized, identified, named, and classified according to kinds, classes, genera/species, properties, unities, wholes.

universal (logic). 1. Affirmation or denial of the whole of a class. Opposite to PARTICULAR. **2.** Any of the five most general relations in the traditional logic of classification: GENUS, SPECIES, *DIFFERENTIA*, PROPERTY, and ACCIDENT.

universal, absolute concrete. See ABSOLUTE, THE (HEGEL).

universal causation, the principle of. See CAUSAL PRINCIPLE, THE.

universal reason. See *LOGOS*.

universalia ante res (L., "universals before reality," or "universals independent of things," or "universals as existing apart from particulars"). Applied to the Platonic view of universals. See UNIVERSALS (PLATO).

universalia in rebus (L., "universals in reality," or "universals in things," or "universals as existing within particulars." Sometimes *universalis in re,* using the singular ablative *re*). Applied to the Aristotelian view of universals. See UNIVERSALS (ARISTOTLE).

universalia post res (L., "universals after reality," or "universals derived from particulars." Sometimes *universalia post rem,* with the singular accusative *rem*). Applied to NOMINALISM and CONCEPTUALISM.

universality, principle of (morality). The principle that what is considered right (good, correct) for one individual must also be considered right for any other individual in the same situation. Example: Saying that Richard ought not to steal in a given situation implies that Lauri and any other individual in a similar situation ought not to steal.

universalizability, principle of (ethics). 1. The theory that a moral principle or judgment must apply universally in the same way under the same circumstances to all individuals; otherwise it cannot be regarded as a moral principle or judgment. **2.** The theory that moral principles must be such that they can be practiced by anyone at any time without immoral consequences.

universals (Aristotle). The main points in Aristotle's theory of universals: **1.** Universals exist independently of the mind. **2.** Universals do not exist independently of the things in which they are recognized. **3.** Universals are externally real but are not separable from their particulars except in abstraction as concepts. They are real entities existing *in* particulars. **4.** A universal exists as that feature of a particular which is common to or shared by other particulars. A universal is a property predicated of an individual thing which individual thing is one among many about which this property may be predicated. **5.** The mind becomes aware of universals by a process of abstracting the concept of this common property from the particulars in experience, from the concrete things which contain this common property. Apprehension of a universal is the same as the formation of a concept. Aristotle calls this *intuitive induction.* **6.** A general outline of intuitive induction: Sense perception and experiencing lead to memory. Memory serves as a means of recognizing what is common in any present experience and identifying it with something in past experience. By being fixed in the mind and abstracted in thought, what is common becomes a concept recognized as a universal. See REALISM, ARISTOTELIAN; REASON, ACTIVE/PASSIVE (ARISTOTLE).

universals (conceptualism). 1. Universals are concepts (thoughts, ideas) that are constructed by the mind after experiencing particulars and recognizing the common quality they share. **2.** Universals exist as concepts put into an abstract language after our experience of particular things. We can never have knowledge of universals prior to an experience that has been conceptualized. **3.** Universals as concepts predicate something that correctly describes reality. See CONCEPTUALISM.

universals (nominalism). Universals are not objects or entities. They exist neither *in* particulars nor in another realm. Universals exist only as general words or names such as "man," "manness," "red," "redness," "cow," "cowness," that have linguistic functions, and that can be applied in conventional usage to things. There is no correspondence possible between the universal "red" or "redness" and a particular red thing. See NOMINALISM.

universals (Plato). The main points in Plato's theory of universals: **1.** Universals exist independently of minds. **2.** Universals as ideal, perfect entities exist in another unchanging realm (see FORMS, PLATO'S THEORY OF IDEAL) that is separate from this world and the particular things within it. **3.** Universals as ideal entities are never perfectly exemplified (copied, imitated, participated in) by things in this world; nevertheless vague emulations of them can be seen by the intellect in the world of sense experience. **4.** Universals are apprehended in a process of ANAMNĒSIS, a "recollection," "reminiscence," "recovery" of knowledge which was with us from a previous existence. With the proper stimuli our ordinary sense experiences revive this latent innate knowledge. **5.** Knowledge of all universals is prior to experience, and experience is formed, shaped, and structured by this knowledge. See REALISM, PLATONIC.

universals (realism). Universals exist in reality independently of our awareness of them. Platonic realism holds that universals are separate entities distinct from the particular things in which they may be found. Aristotelian realism holds that universals are externally real concepts that are not separable from the particulars in which they are found.

universe, a. Any distinct field or system of reality or thought conceived as complete and closed usually for the purpose of analysis, as in "universe of discourse." Compare with CLASS.

universe, the (L., *universus,* "universal," from *unus,* "one," and *vertere,* "to turn," thus "turned or combined into one"). Everything that is, was, and will be. The totality of existence in all its forms; the whole of space and time and all that is subsumed under them. See COSMOS.

universe of discourse. Sometimes referred to as *the* or *a realm of discourse.* The area of things being talked about (communicated, discussed, presented, reasoned about, etc.) whether explicitly stated or tacitly implied.

univocal. 1. A statement which is neither equivocal (see EQUIVOCATION) nor ambiguous. **2.** The application of a term to things with exactly the same meaning. Example: "I am applying the word *good* in a univocal sense to both God and humans."

unknowable, the. See AGNOSTICISM.

unlimited, the. See *APEIRON.*

unmoved mover, the (Aristotle). Sometimes referred to as the prime mover. See PRIME MOVER (ARISTOTLE). **1.** Two main interpretations can be given of Aristotle's Unmoved Mover: (a) The Unmoved Mover is a perfect, unchanging ideal, transcendent to nature or the universe. (b) The outermost heaven is the first source of motion for the universe; it causes or initiates the motion of the universe by its own self-originating motion. The motion of the heavens is an eternal, cyclical (circular) and perfect motion. 2. Ignoring for the most part the distinction between the two interpretations, the following are the principal points in Aristotle's view of an Unmoved Mover, most of which can be applied to either interpretation. The unmoved mover is (a) eternal, (b) self-moving (although there are portions of Aristotle's writings that imply that the Unmoved Mover is an unchanging, nonmoving ideal that moves the universe by just being there as a beloved object moves the lover), (c) self-sufficient, nondependent on anything else for its existence or for its nature, (d) one, a unity, (e) a substance—the Primary Substance that is the source of all other things, (f) completely actualized—no latency or potentiality is part of its essence, (g) immaterial, (h) good, (i) unchanging, (j) immutable (cannot be changed), and (k) Divine Thought or Mind. 3. For Aristotle, there can be an infinite regress of material movements but only in a special sense. Material motion is not a brute fact, not an ultimate in the nature of things. Material motion needs a causal explanation. Motion in the universe is not self-activating but needs accounting for. Matter is not self-activating. Aristotle believed that organisms have self-motion but that this self-motion requires a motion, or a cause outside itself, to initiate its self-movement. All material motion has its source in an Eternal Mover that is itself Unmoved. 4. The Unmoved Mover did not cause movement in any physical way such as by physical contact or physical action. Ordinarily, that which is moved is acted upon or reacts with that which does the moving. The Unmoved Mover is not an actively engaged principle of order, planning, purposing, directing, affecting the material universe as was Plato's DEMIURGE. The Unmoved Mover moves things as an ideal moves or motivates a human being: by being the perfect object of desire or aspiration. The Unmoved Mover does not make motion, does not impart motion, does not sustain or maintain motion; it *elicits* motion. 6. The Unmoved Mover moves things without itself being moved. It itself is not moved by anything else. (Where the Unmoved Mover is regarded as Pure Self-motion as in 1b, it passes its motion on to all other things but its own motion is not passed on to it from any other source.) 7. The Unmoved Mover is Pure Actuality without any potential for change, without any matter. It must exist solely as actuality because it actualizes all the potential motions in the universe. The Unmoved Mover is not actualized by anything else. It is self-actualized just as it is self-activated. Everything else is actualized by it. The Unmoved Mover is not in any way in a state of potential. Matter is always in some degree of potential for change and motion. 8. As Pure Actuality the Unmoved Mover is substantial and a Primary Substance, since it is able to move all other kinds of substances and is their ultimate source. **9.** The Unmoved Mover is immaterial, noncorporeal. It is spatially unextended. **10.** The Unmoved Mover is eternal. Material motion, physical change is eternal and therefore that actualized existence which is its cause must also be eternal. **11.** As the object of desire for all things the Unmoved Mover is good. **12.** The Unmoved Mover is unchanging and immutable, as is Pure Thought. **13.** The Unmoved Mover is an Eternal, Divine Mind or Thought and is the object of its own thinking and activity. Aristotle's famous passage from the *Metaphysics:* "Thought thinks itself as object in virtue of its participation in that which is being thought." See entries under SUBSTANCE referring to Aristotle.

use/mention distinction. The *use* of a linguistic expression (a term, word, symbol, etc.) refers to its occurrence in language in order to speak or communicate about something to which the expression refers or which it means. The *mention* of a linguistic expression (which can be indicated by using quotation marks around its written form) has to do with communicating something *about* the linguistic expression itself and it therefore has a metalinguistic reference. Example: In the statement "'Virginia is strong' is a sentence with sixteen letters," reference is not being made to something beyond the sentence but *to the sentence itself;* mention is being made *of the sentence itself.*

utilitarian theory of punishment. See PUNISHMENT, UTILITARIAN THEORY OF.

utilitarianism. Sometimes referred to as the *greatest happiness theory*. Utilitarianism as a systematic ethical theory was first propounded by Jeremy Bentham (see HEDONISTIC CALCULUS [BENTHAM]) and his student John Stuart Mill. Its main tenets are: **1.** One should so act as to promote the greatest happiness (pleasure) of the greatest number of people. **2.** Pleasure is the only intrinsic good and pain is the only intrinsic evil. **3.** An act is morally right (**a**) if it brings about a greater balance of good over evil than any other action that could have been taken, or (**b**) if it produces as much good in the world as or no less good in the world than would any other act possible under the circumstances. **4.** In general, the moral worth of an act is judged according to the goodness and badness of its consequences.

utilitarianism, act. Two central ideas of act utilitarianism: **1.** The moral worth of an act is judged according to the good (pleasant) or bad (unpleasant) consequences that are produced by each individual act judged in itself. **2.** At any given moment act in such a way so that your act will promote the greatest good of the greatest number.

utilitarianism, rule. 1. The moral worth of an act is judged according to the good (pleasant) or bad (unpleasant) consequences that ensue from following a general moral rule of conduct such as "Never lie," "Never steal," "Never murder." **2.** Act in accordance to that moral rule that brings more good (pleasurable) consequences than would another rule, or than would no rule at all. **3.** Obey those moral rules which produce the greatest happiness of the greatest number of people.

utility, principle of. Sometimes referred to as the *pleasure principle.* **1.** The doctrine which holds (**a**) that pleasure and the absence of pain are in fact desired by all human beings, and (**b**) that each person seeks his own pleasure. **2.** The doctrine that one ought to do that which brings about the greatest happiness (pleasure) to the greatest number of people, or to the community as a whole.

The "proof" for the principle of utility is founded on what is believed to be the undeniable, universal, empirical observation that everyone in fact desires pleasure and since this is the case then it has to be admitted that pleasure is desirable and of paramount worth. UTILITARIANISM is based on the principle of utility in the following way: It is a fact that pleasure is desired and hence desirable. Every individual should strive to produce as much pleasure as possible for the greatest number of people (based on the implied assumption that in procuring the greatest amount of pleasure for the greatest number one thereby procures pleasure, or the greatest amount of pleasure, for oneself).

utility calculus. See HEDONISTIC CALCULUS (BENTHAM).

utopia (Gk., *ou,* "not," and *topos,* "place," hence literally, "a land of no place," "a never-never land," or from *eu,* "well," "good," and *topos,* "place," hence literally "a good or perfect place"). **1.** An ideal or perfect society. Plato's *Republic* and *Laws,* in describing the perfect or ideal state, present utopias. The word was first used, however, by Sir Thomas More in his book describing an imaginary island that had an ideal political, economic, religious, legal, and social structure. Others, since More's time, who have written utopias: Tommaso Campanella, *The City of the Sun* (1612), Francis Bacon, *New Atlantis* (1627), Morelly, *Code de la Nature* (1755), Étienne Cabet, *Voyage en Icaria* (1888), Edward Bellamy, *Looking Backward* (1888), William Morris, *News from Nowhere* (1890), H. G. Wells, *A Modern Utopia* (1905).

Three distinct attitudes can be taken toward utopias: (**a**) that they are visionary and ideal, but they can be approximated if not fully achieved in reality; (**b**) that they are visionary and ideal, and they cannot be approximated in reality, although they may serve as standards for evaluation of existing societies; and (**c**) that they are totally unrealistic visionary and idealistic schemes with no value whatever. See UTOPIAN. Contrast with DYSTOPIA.

2. The pejorative sense of utopia: a naive description of an unrealizable and impractical ideal state.

utopian. 1. In the positive sense, *utopian* refers to (**a**) a perfect or ideal society or to features of a perfect or ideal society, or (**b**) to one who is a visionary or an idealist about a perfect society. **2.** In a negative sense, *utopian* refers to an impractical, chimerical scheme of social regeneration that involves imaginary and unattainable perfections.

V

vague/vagueness. Not definite. Not clearly defined or expressed, such as a "vague" word, concept, idea, or statement. A word may be said to be vague or to exhibit vagueness under any of the following conditions: **1.** When no agreement can be reached whether the word or its contradictory applies to a given situation especially even when more factual information is obtained. Example: The word *bald* is vague in those contexts in which a decision cannot be reached as to whether or not to apply the word to a specific person. No rules are specified as to how many hairs a person must have on his head not to be called "bald." More factual information as to the exact number of hairs on the person's head will not resolve the vagueness, since vagueness has to do with the imprecision and indefiniteness of the meaning of the word itself. When vague words are made more nearly exact they lose the import of their ordinary language usage. **2.** When a word has borderline cases in its application and no determination can be made as to whether or not in that instance it should, or can, be applied. Examples: "bald," "hairy," "crowded," "happy," "race." **3.** When the denotation of a word is not precisely known or ascertainable from its meaning or common usage and there is no definite way of delimiting or determining its application. Examples: "elderly," "young," "stiff," "difficult."

Vagueness is distinct from AMBIGUITY. In ambiguity, the two or more meanings a word has may be quite precise and definite. Ambiguity is not a problem of meaning but a problem of which meaning is being used in a given context. In general vagueness applies to both concepts and words,

309

ambiguity mostly to words. Vagueness is also to be distinguished from generality. General statements need not be vague, and vagueness need not be associated with general words or terms. Vagueness is sometimes thought to be associated with the subjective meanings attached to a word and the unwillingness to admit an application for it. What one might call "warm" another might prefer to call "hot." But this is of secondary significance to a definition of vagueness.

valid (L., *validus,* "strong," from *valere,* "to be strong"). **1.** Justified. Supported. **2.** Not defective but correct. **3.** Founded on truth or fact.

In general, a set of concepts or beliefs is said to be valid in the above three senses whenever it is coherent within itself, consistent with known and significant evidence, and fits in with other accepted concepts or beliefs. Contrast with INVALID.

valid (logic). A deductive argument is valid whenever its conclusion necessarily follows from the premises; *if* the premises of the argument are true, then its conclusion cannot be false; the conclusion too must be true.

valid inference. See INFERENCE.

value (L., *valere,* "to be worth," "to be strong"). **1.** Worth. The quality of a thing which makes it desirable, desired, useful, or an object of interest. **2.** Of excellence. That which is esteemed, prized, or regarded highly, or as a good. The opposite of a positive value is "disvalue" (sometimes "dysvalue") or "negative value." Good would be a value and its opposite, evil, would be a "negative value," or a "disvalue."

value, instrumental. Sometimes *pragmatic value.* **1.** The value a thing has in producing desired consequences or results. **2.** A value put on something that is used as a means of acquiring something that is desired or desirable. Instrumental values need not be of intrinsic value, but may be neutral or even intrinsically of disvalue.

value, intrinsic. See GOOD, INTRINSIC.

value, theory of. See AXIOLOGY.

value, utilitarian. **1.** The value a thing has in being useful for the accomplishment of some purpose. **2.** The value a thing has in promoting the greatest good of the greatest number.

values, objectivity theory of. **1.** The theory that values such as good, right, truth, beauty exist in the real world and can be found as real subsisting entities, qualities, or relations much in the same fashion as we can find objects, qualities, or relations such as tables, red, bigger than. **2.** The view that values are objective in the sense that they can be supported by careful and consistent rational argumentation as being the best under the circumstances.

values, relativity of. The belief (a) that values are relative to social and personal preferences (attitudes, likes, dislikes, feelings, tastes, predispositions, etc.) conditioned by one's environment, culture, and genetic make-up; (b) that values differ (radically in many cases) from culture to culture; (c) that judgments such as right/wrong, good/bad, correct/incorrect, cannot be (and should not be) applied to them; and (**d**) that there are not, and cannot be, any universal, absolute, and objective values applicable to all people at all times.

values, subjectivity of. The view that values such as good, right, truth, beauty do not exist in the real objective world but are personal feelings, attitudes, and interpretations of reality.

variable (logic). 1. Any one of a class without the specification of any particular instance of that class. Example: *p* may stand for any statement, such as "Henry is a male." **2.** The symbol symbolizing **1**. **3.** A symbol used as a substitute for statements, predicates, terms, objects, meanings.

variations, methods of concomitant. See METHODS, MILL'S INDUCTIVE.

variety in unity. Refers to the qualitatively diverse or disparate parts of a whole, yet all of which contribute in their unique ways to the total unification or integration of the whole.

The lack of variety in unity is said to lead to such things as monotony and boredom. Continued repetition leads to lack of attention and interest. The lack of unity in variety leads to chaos and confusion. Compare with UNITY IN VARIETY AND VARIETY IN UNITY, PRINCIPLE OF (METAPHYSICS).

verbal (L. *verbum,* "a word"). **1.** That which has to do with words. **2.** Used in a pejorative sense: That which has to do only with words rather than with the issues or ideas that are involved. In ordinary language sometimes referred to as *verbalism.* See VERBAL DISPUTE. **3.** That which is expressed in written or spoken words. **4.** In ordinary usage verbal often refers to that which is expressed only orally and not written, as in "a verbal agreement." **5.** Sometimes used in ordinary language as a synonym for "literal" or "word-for-word," as in "the verbal translation of the Greek phrase."

verbal dispute. Sometimes *definitional dispute, semantical dispute,* or *verbal problem.* A dispute caused by the meanings of the words or concepts being applied. Contrasted with a *real dispute,* which is a disagreement regarding the facts or real issues of a situation. Example: the verbal dispute engendered by the question "If a tree fell in the forest and no consciousness existed to perceive its falling, would its falling produce a sound?" No real dispute exists about the facts of the situation. Any dispute refers to the meaning of the word *sound.* The answer to the question can be yes in terms of one meaning of the word *sound* (defined as the presence of physical vibrations whether or not humans are present) and no in terms of another meaning of the word *sound* (defined as the auditory sensation produced in a human). In order to resolve a verbal dispute, agreement has to be reached about the meanings of words to be used and not about the facts to which the words are to be applied.

veridical (L., *verdicus,* from *verus,* "true," and *dicere,* "to tell," "to say," "to speak"). **1.** Truthful. **2.** Characterized by truth. **3.** Truth-indicating or truth-telling, as in "a veridical experience."

Nonveridical experiences include hallucinations, illusions, delusions, mirages. Such experiences are not used, and cannot be used, as sources of true statements about reality.

verifiability, principle of. Sometimes *verifiability principle, verification principle,* or *principle of verification.* **1.** Strong version: A statement is meaningful if-and-only-if it is empirically verified. Compare CONFIRMATION, PRINCIPLE OF. **2.** Weak version: A statement is meaningful if-and-only-if it is at least in principle empirically verifiable. Identified with logical positivism and logical empiricism. See MEANING, VERIFIABILITY THEORY OF; POSITIVISM, LOGICAL.

verifiability theory of meaning. See MEANING, VERIFIABILITY THEORY OF.

verification (L., *verificare,* from *versus,* "true," and *facere,* "to make"). **1.** The process of determining the truth of a statement by empirical methods. **2.** The scientific testing of a statement to ascertain its truth. **3.** CONFIRMATION of a statement.

verity (L., *veritas,* "truth," "reality," "the true nature of something," from *verus,* "true," "real," "genuine," "actual"). **1.** That which is true or real. **2.** The quality of being true or real. **3.** The conformity of a statement with fact, a truth or reality.

Eternal verities are truths (ideas) that are true, have been true forever in the past, and will remain true everlastingly. Usually they are known *A PRIORI.*

vicious circle argument. Sometimes *PETITIO PRINCIPII,* or *vicious circle proof* (L., *circulus in probando*). A fallacious and/or inane method of arguing. An argument or proof which uses a statement (or a series of statements) S^1 to justify another statement S^2 which in turn is used to prove S^3, etc., until a last member in the series of logically connected statements is used to provide evidence for the initial statement S^1 and thereby the entire series is then believed to have been completely proved.

vicious circle principle (Russell). The main principle in Russell's theory of types originally presented in his *Principia Mathematica:* Whatever involves all the members of a collection of things must not be considered as a member of that collection. Examples: "All generalizations are false": that generalization about all other generalizations is not to be included as a member of those other generalizations but is to be considered a higher type, or order, of generalization. "All red things are red": the class of all red things includes all red objects but cannot itself be considered as being red (as being a red thing or as a red class). It is a fallacy to generalize about the type of all of whatever it is that we say are the types we are generalizing about. Thus no whole or totality can contain members that are defined in terms of itself. See TYPES, THEORY OF.

virtues (Stoics). The principal or cardinal virtues in Stoicism are: reason, courage, justice, and self-discipline.

1. Reason, or intelligence, consists of (a) knowing what is good (the best, the correct, the proper, the most rational under the circumstances) and **(b)** knowing how to attain the good and/or avoid evil. **2.** Courage consists of **(a)** knowing what to fear and what not to fear and **(b)** being able to control one's fear in the presence of a crisis. **3.** Justice is **(a)** knowing how to be righteous, knowing how to give to others what is rightly due to them as individual human persons and members of a universal brotherhood and **(b)** knowing how to get from them in return what is rightly due to oneself. **4.** Self-discipline (which incorporates both the notions of self-sufficiency and self-control) is **(a)** knowing what desires or drives to give in to and what to resist and **(b)** knowing one's reality without deception and illusion.

For the Stoics the virtuous life is the only good but is unattainable without knowledge. The end of the virtuous life is the ideal of complete self-sufficiency and self-mastery of the individual living according to the harmonies of one's inner rational nature and the corresponding universal rational necessity existing in the cosmos.

virtues, cardinal (L., *cardinalis,* from *cardo,* "hinge," "that upon which a thing depends or turns," and *virtus,* "strength, courage," from *vir,* "man"). The highest ideals or forms of conduct in a given culture. All others are of secondary importance to them and are derived from them and/or depend upon them for their existence. Greek culture stressed four basic (cardinal) virtues: WISDOM or PRUDENCE, COURAGE, JUSTICE, and moderation or temperance (see *SŌPHROSYNĒ*). Christian teaching added the virtues of FAITH, hope, and charity or love.

virtues, dianoetic (Aristotle). Also *intellectual virtues* (Gk., *dianoētikos,* from *dia,* "through," and *noein,* "to resolve in the mind"). **1.** The intellectual (rationally thought-out) virtues or values. **2.** In Aristotle the phrase *aretai dianoētikai* refers to the values inherent in the awareness (and acceptance) of the rational principles which guide moral conduct. This is contrasted with the moral virtues (see VIRTUES, MORAL [ARISTOTLE]) which have to do with the everyday reasoned control of our sensitive and appetitive life. According to Aristotle, the rational part of the soul has two parts: **(a)** that which contemplates the unchangeable, universal, eternal principle of things; **(b)** that which contemplates objects which are subject to change. The *ARETĒ* (functioning excellence) of the first is the intellectual virtue of *SOPHIA,* abstract wisdom (theoretical intelligence) and the *aretē* of the second is *PHRONĒSIS,* practical wisdom (prudence, thoughtfulness, ability, and intention to do the right thing.) See *DIANOIA.*

virtues, moral (Aristotle). Those functioning excellences (*aretai*) of human conduct that are controlled by the rational part of humans. See *ARETĒ.* Some of the main points in Aristotle's ethical philosophy: **1.** Moral virtues are achieved by means of a consistent practice that creates a habit of action. **2.** The principal ingredient in this process is the following of the mean between extremes. See MEAN, THE (ARISTOTLE). Extremes are to be regarded as vices. For example, the moral virtue of courage is the mean between two extremes: that of foolhardiness (rashness, stupidity) and that of cowardice (being overwhelmed by fear). **3.** An action is not in itself a virtuous action merely because it follows the mean. An action is a morally virtuous action because it conforms with, or is controlled by, reason. Insofar as that action conforms with or is controlled by reason, it will automatically involve a mean between extremes.

vital force. Sometimes *vital impetus, vital principle.* A form of energy, regarded as unique and distinct from others (such as mechanical, chemical, molecular), that is manifested in living phenomena and is the cause of life. Usually regarded as nonphysical. See *ÉLAN VITAL.*

vitalism. In general, vitalism is the belief that the activities of living organisms are due to a VITAL FORCE or vital principle that is different from other physical forces in the universe. Other names that have been used for this living force or principle: DEMIURGE; *ÉLAN VITAL;* ENTELECHY; *NOUS* (PLATO); *PSYCHĒ* (ARISTOTLE). Vitalism has many things in common with HOLISM and organismic biology. All three contend that there is an ultimate, radical, and real dichotomy between living (organic) and nonliving (inorganic) phenomena. Some of the main beliefs of vitalism: **1.** The functions of a living thing are manifestations of a force (entity, substance, energy, impulse, impetus, *élan vital,* agent) that is within it. **2.** Usually this force is regarded as being nonphysical, invisible, intangible, and as exemplified in the activities of living things; examples are striving to attain a goal, replication, self-regulation, self-repair, consciousness. Such behavior, according to vitalists, cannot be explained in a purely mechanistic or materialistic way. **3.** Living things cannot be reduced to a complex of inorganic substances. **4.** The vital force gives to living things special characteristics that are not found in nonliving things. **5.** Most vitalists regard the force as possessing a unity of its own that can exist independently of the physical bodies to which it gives life. See EVOLUTION, EMERGENT.

void (atomists). The atomists (see ATOMISM, GREEK) accepted the notion of a void, an empty space or vacuum, and called it a "not-being" (a "nothing") as opposed to "being" (the self-moving, eternal, material atoms). The void possesses no qualities whatever, no powers, no potentiality, no existence in any way. It is regarded as pure empty space, in which or at which there is absolutely nothing present. The void is the place atoms occupied before they moved to another place and the place that would be occupied by other atoms shortly. The atomists defended the void with arguments such as the following: Objects and the atoms of which they are composed could not move unless a void existed between the atoms. That a void exists in things is evidenced in that some objects can be compressed and some absorb liquids. In compression the atoms are pressed into the void existing between them. In absorption the atoms of a liquid enter into the empty interstices between the atoms of the object and occupy that void. Also it is in reference to a void that things can be distinguished, separated, and classified.

Philosophers including Parmenides, Aristotle, the Stoics, Descartes, Leibniz, Kant rejected the notion of a void.

volition (L., *volo,* "I will," *velle,* "to will"). **1.** The act of willing. **2.** The power of willing. **3.** The use of the faculty or power of will. Sometimes used synonymously with choice, determination, preference. See entries under WILL.

voluntarism (ethics). The belief that: **1.** The human will is the fundamental and ultimate ground in the making of moral decisions and in arriving at moral values. **2.** The will is superior to, and must govern the other criteria for, sources of moral worth such as conscience, the rational faculty, intuition, tradition, the feelings.

voluntarism (metaphysics). The belief that: **1.** The will is the primary and dominant factor in all human experience and in all the processes of the universe. **2.** The will thought of as a force (primarily as analogous to the human will) is the cause of change everywhere. **3.** This will (in most cases) is a nondirectional, nonpurposive, spontaneous, blind impulse, inescapably immanent in all things and the root cause of their behavior.

voluntary action. Some of the characteristics included in the concept of voluntary action: **1.** A voluntary action is one that is caused by an inner mental event such as willing (VOLITION), a drive, a desire, an interest, a motive, a demand to choose. **2.** It is not done because of external compulsion but due to an inner compulsion. (In general an INVOLUNTARY ACT is caused by some event external to the agent.) **3.** A voluntary action is done out of intent and deliberation, and hence is a self-determining act. See CHOOSING.

voluntary-involuntary actions. Actions that are caused by the agent himself by a self-determined inner COMPULSION to act (voluntary), but which are externally compelled (involuntary) against the true wishes of the agent, and contrary to what the agent would do on his own. Example: obeying a hijacker's commands.

vortex theory (Descartes). Descartes' vortex theory (or the theory of vortices) is shared by Cartesians and by Occasionalists. Many of these ideas had their source in Greek philosophy. The main points: **1.** Empty spaces or vacuums do not exist. A subtle matter (later called the "ether") fills the empty space erroneously supposed to exist, as in vacuums produced by pumps. See MATTER (DESCARTES). All space is occupied by something or other. No space can be unoccupied. Unoccupied space is a false appearance, an illusion, and a logical self-contradiction. **2.** The universe moves like a whirlpool (vortex) and the planets are like the objects carried by the movements of the whirl. **3.** By means of geometry and mathematical analysis (such as analytic geometry, which Descartes invented) explanations in accordance with the universe's whirl can be given for the coming into existence, the maintenance in existence, and the passing out of existence of all things in the universe. **4.** All action occurs by physical contact. Bodies are moved by other bodies by physical pressure, impact, and crowding. There is no such thing as action at a distance. **5.** The essence of matter is extension, to be inert (to be at rest), and to receive motion imparted to it by God. **6.** Matter of itself does not have the power to move. **7.** Matter of itself does not have the power to remain in motion (even when once set in motion). **8.** Matter of itself does not have the potential to move another body. **9.** God was the cause of all the motion in the universe at the moment of His creation of the material universe. **10.** The quantity of motion (and matter) in the universe remains the same as that quantity that God imparted at Creation. **11.** Had God not given matter (the universe) this motion, it would not of its own possess it, and matter (the universe) would be motionless. **12.** This motion is circular (vortical), geometrical, causally determined, and without final purposes of its own. See CARTESIANISM; OCCASIONALISM (MIND/BODY THEORY).

W

warranted assertibility. Sometimes *warranted assertion*. Refers to truth regarded as abstract knowledge secured by the strict use of the methods of logical and scientific inquiry whereby a state of affairs that is somewhat confused and unarticulated becomes ordered and unified in our experience. A phrase associated with the experimentalism and INSTRUMENTALISM of John Dewey.

ways, the five (Aquinas). See FIVE WAYS, THE (AQUINAS).

Weltanschauung (Ger., "a world view," "a comprehension of reality as a whole," "the overview of a cosmology," "one's all-inclusive conception or perspective of things and life"). Sometimes *Weltansicht*. Examples: the hippie *Weltanschauung*, the socialist *Weltanschauung*. See WORLD VIEW.

Weltschmerz (Ger., "world sorrow," "sentimental pessimism").

whatness. See QUIDDITY.

whole. 1. Total and complete. "Whole" refers to something that has parts and that has no parts lacking. "Total" implies that all the parts of a whole are present as an aggregate. **2.** A unity or system, as in "an organic whole." See *GESTALT*.

whole-part, principle of. The main points: **1.** The explanation of a whole is not complete when only its constituent parts have been explicated or analyzed. A full explanation must take into consideration the interrelationships on many levels of the parts integrally interacting with each other and producing functions or activities unexplainable in terms only of the enumeration of its parts. **2.** A whole in itself has properties (characteristics, qualities) that are distinct from any of the properties that can be found in its parts and/or that cannot be found in any of its parts. In this sense the whole is regarded as being "greater" than the totality of its parts. **3.** The parts of a whole are so interdependent that a change in any one of them will bring about a change **(a)** in all (or some) of the other parts and **(b)** in the properties or functions of the whole. Compare with HOLISTIC EXPLANATION.

wholism. See HOLISM.

will. The power to control and determine our actions in the context of our desires and intentions. See CHOOSING; VOLITION; and entries under VOLUNTARY.

will, autonomy of the (Kant). The condition of the (pure rational) will in which the will is guided (governed, directed, motivated) to choose unaffected by such things as consequences, results, ulterior ends, compulsion, fame, happiness, pleasure for oneself or for others, but affected only by an obligation to the rational and universal principles (laws, duties) of morality. Opposite to ENDS, HETERONOMY OF (KANT). See ETHICS (KANT).

will, faculty theory of the. The theory that the will is a FACULTY or a power of the mind that is able to cause itself to act in accordance with what has been chosen as the best.

will, free elective (Kant). The will is not affected by feeling or emotion at the time of its action. (Feeling later gives support to the free elective will.) See ETHICS (KANT).

will, the general. 1. Refers to an autonomous and sovereign personality (self, ego, will) regarded as possessed by society or the state that initiates and decides courses of action to be taken by its individual members or by a collection of them. Ideally, a conformity (harmony) should exist without coercion between the general will and the will of each individual (or the will of the collection of individuals, such as found in institutions). In this situation obeying the general will would in effect be obeying one's own will, and vice versa. **2.** The expression of the will of all. The unanimity of people about ethical, political, social, and economic values and goals. **3.** The general and objectively real public consensus that is (should be) the ground of political and ethical decision making, without which a society cannot properly function.

The general will is associated with the philosophy of Rousseau, who thought of it as the collective voice of the people to be respected and obeyed above all other authority.

will, the good (Kant). See ETHICS (KANT).

will and the understanding (Descartes). Will is the assenting or the dissenting to some choice, desire, or truth. The faculty of willing is related to the faculty of understanding in that the understanding enables one to perceive the alternatives from which one can choose but itself cannot accept or reject, affirm or deny a possible choice.

will and the understanding (Spinoza). Spinoza made no distinction between the understanding and the will. In his view, once the understanding has a clear and distinct idea it is then impossible for the will not to accept it. For Spinoza the perception of truth is identical with having knowledge of that perception and with accepting it.

will to believe (James). The central points: **1.** Belief in things for which there is no clear or conclusive evidence, or for which the evidence is not complete, is a human right and is necessary for intellectual and emotional adaptation to the exigencies of life. **2.** The will to believe in the absence of evidence is a reasonable and creative aspect of the mind, enabling decisions to be made and opening possibilities for discovery and commitment.

will to power (Nietzsche). The view that all human action is ultimately motivated by power and aims at control and/or superiority over others maintained and supported by power. The means and values used in this process are (should be) determined by the individual wishes and creative standards of the superman.

wisdom. 1. Prudent judgment as to how to use knowledge in the everyday affairs of life. **2.** The correct perception of the best ends in life, the best means to their attainment, and the practical intelligence in successfully applying those means. See VIRTUES, CARDINAL.

word. 1. A structuring of marks and/or sounds that retain their general form and the same or similar meanings at different times in the process of communication. **2.** An intelligible mark and/or an articulate sound that (**a**) symbolizes a meaning, (**b**) is regarded as an ultimate and independent unit of communication, and (**c**) is essential to the formation of a sentence. A word may have more than one meaning. A word may be syntactically classified in a number of ways such as noun, verb, adverb, adjective, preposition, conjunction, etc.

World Soul. Sometimes *World Mind, World Spirit*. The all-pervading immanent cause of order, life, and intelligence in all existing things, usually thought of on the analogy of the soul and its controlling and integrating influence on the body. The main argument for a World Soul is: The soul is the cause of order, life, and intelligence. Nothing that does not possess order, life, and intelligence can create something that has order, life, and intelligence, since like can only create like. Things in the universe possess order, life, and intelligence. Therefore, there must be a World Order, a World Life, a World Intelligence—in short, a World Soul—which is their source. See *LOGOS*.

world view. Sometimes referred to by the German *WELTANSHAUUNG*. **1.** The collection of beliefs (ideas, images, attitudes, values) that an individual or a group holds about things such as the universe, humankind, God, the future, etc. **2.** A comprehensive outlook about life and the universe from which one explains and/or structures relationships and activities.

A world view may be deliberately formulated or adopted, or it may be the result of an unconscious assimilation or conditioning process. It is the general perspective from which one sees and interprets the world.

Z

Zeitgeist (Ger., "the spirit of the time" or "the spirit of the age").

Zeno's paradoxes. Zeno of Elea, a disciple of Parmenides, attempted in a series of arguments to disprove positions contrary to Parmenides' philosophy that only the unchanging One exists and hence nothing in reality can move. Zeno's arguments proposed to show that the concepts of many (plurality), motion (change), and place (space) were inherently contradictory and led to absurdities, and therefore could not be used to explain the universe and its phenomena. The most famous of the paradoxes is the Achilles and the Tortoise Paradox, used to deny the existence of motion: If there is motion, then the slower (the tortoise) beginning first in a race will never be overtaken by the faster (Achilles). Achilles must reach the point to which the tortoise has already advanced. But during the time it takes Achilles to get to that point, the tortoise has advanced to another point. The tortoise may cover less ground; nevertheless he is still advancing since he is not at rest. The distances between Achilles and the tortoise are successively less but without limit (on the assumption of the principle of the infinite divisibility of magnitudes that there are an infinite number of points between any two points). The tortoise will always have a lead regardless of how close Achilles gets to the tortoise. Achilles, though he is the faster, will never overtake the tortoise. This is an absurd conclusion and therefore the statement "motion exists" from which it is derived is also absurd. See REDUCTIO AD ABSURDUM.

zetetic (Gk., *zētēsis,* "an inquiry," "an investigation," "a search for something," "a seeking for"). Referring to the inquisitive (inquiring) quality of (**a**) the investigator seeking truth, and/or (**b**) to the method of querying used by the investigator. Zetetic is usually used in the context of a common search for an unknown truth. See DIALECTIC.

Index of Philosophers